Inside the Amiga™

John Thomas Berry

Howard W. Sams & Co.
A Division of Macmillan, Inc.
4300 West 62nd Street, Indianapolis, IN 46268 USA

International Standard Book Number: 0-672-22468-2
Library of Congress Catalog Card Number: 86-62438
Acquisitions Editor: *James S Hill*
Editor: *Marie Butler-Knight*
Designer: *T. R. Emrick*
Illustrator: *Wm. D. Basham* and *Ralph E. Lund*
Cover Artist: *Celeste Design*
Compositor: *Shepherd Poorman Communication Corp.*
Printed in the United States of America

This book is dedicated to my mother, Dorothy Berry, not least for teaching me the importance of education, and to my father, Theron Berry, who taught me the importance of hard work.

John Thomas Berry

Contents

Preface

The Amiga is the first of a new wave of small computers. This machine combines the convenience of a personal computer with the kind of performance that has, until now, been found only on larger systems.

The Amiga is an easy machine to program, particularly in light of its power. However, its flexibility presents the software developer with a great many subsystems, details, and options.

In this book we will explore each of the major subsystems through concrete examples. Each example is meant to demonstrate a particular feature or detail of the machine and its operating environment. These example programs can then form the core of a library of functions to allow access to the Amiga's system services.

Some of the topics we will cover include:

- Access to the Amiga's three operating systems—Intuition, AmigaDOS, and the executive kernel—using the language C

- Creation and manipulation of windows, screens, gadgets, menus and other Intuition objects

- Multiprocessing under AmigaDOS, including ports and messages for communication between processes

- Amiga's powerful graphics capabilities for line drawing, area fill, polygon drawing, and text fonts

- Animation with hardware sprites

- Sound programming in both monaural and stereo, through the audio device

- Speech synthesis and the narrator device

- File management with AmigaDOS

The Amiga is an ideal environment for the programmer. Access to the system is through the C programming language, and all of our examples are in this language. Furthermore, the Amiga software environment is more like that of a large computer. Each subsystem of the machine is accessed not through a hardware-specific location but as a software object. Thus, we have the audio device, the narrator device, and the console device, to name just a few major ones. The examples in this book show how to handle this kind of programming.

Once the you finish this book, you will be in a position to write mature and exciting software for this multifaceted machine. No prior experience with system programming is necessary. Familiarity with the C language is assumed, but expertise is not required. In fact this book can serve as an excellent vehicle for perfecting knowledge of this most important programming language. However, first and foremost, this is a book about programming the exciting Amiga.

Acknowledgments

Let me take this opportunity to thank those who have helped me finish this enormous task: First to my wife Nancy and my daughter Rebecca an acknowledgment of their infinite patience and love; to Kim House, my favorite editor, and to Jim Stockford, my favorite taskmaster, for helping me keep the book on schedule; to Jerry Volpe for getting the project started; and finally, to the guys on the Well, for helping me to understand the Amiga and its many uses.

Introduction

Chapter 1

Overview of the System

Welcome to the world of the Amiga microcomputer. This system is easily the most sophisticated small computer in its price range. It offers:

- Superb graphics capability
- Quality audio circuitry with a software control system to support it
- A built-in speech synthesizer
- A multiprocessing operating system

In addition, two types of user interface are supplied:

- A windowing system whose focus is a mouse that can point at a display crowded with menus, gadgets, and other icons
- A more traditional terminal-like interface with system commands and I/O redirection

Furthermore, the terminal-like interface can exist in a window that shares the screen with other windows. The Amiga is a user's machine.

The Amiga is also a programmer's machine. Every effort has been made to facilitate access to what is an extremely complex system. This is possible through a software support system that is actually three interacting operating systems. Wherever possible, implementation details are separated out in a hierarchy of service routines, so that the software designer can go as deep into the machine architecture as is necessary to produce the desired result. Throughout the system, defaults are set up to take care of details that do not need to be dealt with intimately.

The multiprocessing capability of the Amiga puts it in a class beyond most small computers. One important thing that experienced programmers miss when they make the transition from large mainframe or minicomputers to small systems is the ability to run more than one task at a time. From a productivity standpoint, the advantage is obvious. You can do a compile in the background while editing another file. You can search a database at the same time as you create a document. You can even send a long output to the printer and perform other tasks while the printer is executing.

But beyond questions of productivity and convenience, multiprocessing affects the way you design applications. For example:

1. A database program might perform long searches as a coprocess with its interactive query language interpreter.
2. A text formatting program could process a file at the same time it accepts input from a user.

These simple examples help to illustrate the differences that programming under this kind of environment makes possible. You are not, however, forced to program in any particular way on the Amiga, especially when no effort has been expended to enforce a common interface. You do not even have to take advantage of the system's multiprocessing capabilities, but can write perfectly acceptable programs in the old-fashioned way—one application in memory at a time. Of course, even then you are using multiprocessing, because the system programs run in the background. Even the device drivers run in the background.

The Hardware Architecture

The hardware architecture of the Amiga is unique. Common among small computer systems is the traditional single central processing unit (CPU), which controls all activities of the machine. Input and output, memory management, and the disk drive interface—all must go through this single processor. The Amiga, in contrast, has a powerful CPU—the Motorola MC68000— but it also has a coordinated group of coprocessors and other support circuits to handle more specialized tasks. Not everything is handled by the main processor.

These specialized devices include:

- The *copper*, another general purpose processor that controls the graphics system
- Eight *sprite processors* that control the movement of these graphics objects in the display field
- The *blitter*, a device specialized to both move and combine data from one part of memory to the other

In addition to these processors, there are a number of support circuits that perform tasks in tandem with the main CPU.

- The audio system consists of four digital to analog converters that give the user maximum versatility in creating sounds.
- Thirty-two color registers are provided, each of which can be assigned any of 4096 possible colors.

The design philosophy of the Amiga has been to specialize the hardware wherever feasible, trusting that this will produce the most efficient design.

The organization of these support processors and circuits adds to their efficient operation. The Amiga is a bus-oriented system—in fact the bus is brought out of the system box in the form of an expansion plug on the side of the unit. Each coprocessor, each support circuit is on the bus. Most have independent access to the main memory through the bus—they are DMA (Direct Memory Access) driven. Furthermore, the system clock is arranged so that every other cycle is given to these specialized chips. The speed differential between the main CPU and the memory is such that, even accessing the bus only every other cycle, the CPU is running at full clock speed. Thus, true parallel operation occurs most of the time on the Amiga. It must be noted that during some blitter operations and other, similar mass movements, the coprocessor can steal the bus even from the CPU.

This DMA organization follows through to device drivers. The disk drive can transfer data directly between memory and a floppy diskette. There is no need to go first through memory. The input/output system is similarly arranged. This kind of organization is another feature found previously only on large computers. There are some restrictions on the DMA subsystem. The Amiga is capable of addressing up to eight megabytes of memory directly, but only the first 512 kilobytes are available to the specialized hardware.

The Software Architecture

The Amiga is really a software driven machine. There are no absolute memory locations or hardware addresses where certain key values are stored. System services are not accessed by changing memory locations. Since this is a multiprocessing system, we can never guarantee the absolute location of even key system software. Everything must be specified relative to the location of some key value in memory. Access to system routines is almost solely through software.

As mentioned earlier, the Amiga operating environment really consists of three cooperating but disparate operating systems:

1. The *executive kernel* is the most basic and the most minimal operating system supporting memory allocation, communication between processes and devices, low-level multitasking, and the primary input/output functions.

2. *AmigaDOS* is a traditional operating system, responsible for the file management system and high-level multiprocessing support.

3. *Intuition* is the icon-oriented, window-based system that is the primary interface for users.

Most executive kernel calls are beyond the scope of this book; however, the key functions will be discussed, particularly in the context of practical examples. A chapter is devoted to both AmigaDOS and Intuition.

The executive, as the lowest level, supports both of the other two components. The relationship between AmigaDOS and Intuition, however, is not as straightforward. This will be discussed again later in the book; a brief summary is all that can be given here. AmigaDOS is the next most basic operating system, supplying user-accessible services, particularly those related to the file system (e.g., directory displays and file manipulation commands). Intuition depends upon AmigaDOS to supply it with a file system; therefore, in this sense it is dependant upon AmigaDOS. However, there is not a clean hierarchy. Intuition also takes services directly from the executive, independent of any other subsystem. In practice, this complicated situation is not a problem for either the software developer or the user.

The programmer can easily move through all three levels of the operating system environment and use services from each one in an application; they are not mutually exclusive. This capability allows powerful software to be easily and quickly designed. If a particular system routine is not effective, it can be rewritten in terms of lower-level modules, without rewriting the entire application on a basic level. Machine level is accessed only when necessary and then only to the extent that is necessary.

Access to the System Software

The Amiga continues a modern trend in systems programming. Although assemblers are available for the MC68000 microprocessor and even for its configuration in the Amiga, the primary means of programming is through the high-level language C. There are many advantages to system programming in C. There is the great increase in productivity that always accompanies a move away from a machine specific programming language—each high-level statement represents more than one machine instruction. On the Amiga, using C helps the programmer deal more adequately with the inherent complexity of the machine. The level of hardware parallelism and the interacting coprocessor architecture almost require the abstraction offered by a compiled language such as C. Since the Amiga is a software dominated system, a means of accessing the system resources is needed. Each important object, whether hardware or software based, has an associated C structure data type associated with it. These structures are the programmer's hooks into the machine. In some cases, they allow very low-level access; one structure consists of hardware registers for the specialized chips. Much effort in each chapter will be spent describing these data objects.

The operating system services are accessed by C function calls. All three environments define their own sets of such functions optimized to their particular needs. For example:

- *OpenWindow( )* creates this Intuition object on the display field.
- *Date( )* returns values for the system clock maintained by AmigaDOS.
- *Wait( )* enables the executive kernel to suspend a task while waiting for a message at its port.

These are just examples. In the chapters that follow, we will be incorporating many such system functions in example programs.

You do not lose efficiency in using C. The operating system environment presupposes C as the support vehicle for systems programming. Most of the utility programs are written in this language, as well as a large number of existing applications. As C compilers become more sophisticated and more capable of optimizing their output, this situation can only improve.

The Organization of the Book

In this book, we hope to cover the principles and techniques that will allow the moderately skilled programmer to write large and mature applications taking advantage of the Amiga's powerful hardware and software. We cannot cover everything—that would create a truly encyclopedic work. We have tried to give the programmer insights into the Amiga's major subsystems and also a feeling for its design philosophy. After finishing the book, you should be in a position to deal with the Amiga and to discover even more of its secrets.

Each chapter in the book focuses on a particular subsystem. The basic objects and functions that define and manipulate that subsystem are explored.

Chapter 2 considers the programming environment offered under the three operating systems and discusses some of the peculiarities of using C on the Amiga.

Chapter 3 takes a long look at Intuition. It shows how to define windows and screens, and explores the notions of gadgets and menus.

Chapter 4 is devoted to multiprocessing under AmigaDOS, defining the notion of a process and explaining how to manipulate it under this operating system.

Chapter 5 explores the graphics capability of the Amiga, showing how to access the hardware support routines for such things as area fill and polygon drawing.

Chapter 6 concentrates on the hardware sprites. These are small graphics objects that can be moved independently of the rest of the Amiga graphics display system.

Chapter 7 gives access to the audio channels through the audio device. Programming in both monaural and stereo is covered and the flexibility of this device is revealed.

Chapter 8 teaches how to make the Amiga talk. Access to the two-part speech synthesizer is covered.

Chapter 9 returns to AmigaDOS to discuss the file management system.

Each chapter focuses on the essential set of structures and functions that will allow the programmer to use that subsystem to create useful designs.

It is assumed that the reader is familiar with the C programming language. No tutorial efforts are offered in this book, but example programs, for the most part, avoid the more obscure aspects of the syntax. This is not through any prejudice for or against a particular programming style. The example programs have one goal and that is to illustrate particular aspects of the Amiga. While the example programs tend to be simple and straightforward, there is no presumption or argument that production code need follow this rule.

The examples in the text are to be used as guides; each has been designed to represent a particular subsystem of the Amiga, usually a single feature. These programs should be studied and duplicated, but above all, they should serve as a springboard for more complex software. It is a truism that the only way to learn programming is to program, and it is doubly true on the Amiga. Each program should serve as the basis for a series of experiments, starting with code that is known to work and having as a goal some personal design. Often these programs can be easily merged to produce a more complex example.

The Amiga Programming Environment

Chapter 2

T he programming environment on the Amiga is designed to allow high-level access to the system resources. This access is accomplished primarily through the C programming language, using data objects defined within its syntax. This chapter will discuss how C is used to make these definitions and access the operating system. This discussion will serve as a general introduction to material which will be covered in greater detail in succeeding chapters. Use of the Lattice C compiler is assumed. The files and techniques peculiar to this implementation of the language are detailed.

Software Components

The Amiga is a complex computer with many interlocking hardware resources. The blitter, sound subsystem, and hardware sprites are just a few. This complexity is necessary to create a programming engine with the power to match the Amiga, but it also requires a correspondingly rich software environment to make the full power of these subsystems available to the user. The programmer must be able not only to get at the lowest levels of the machine, but also to coordinate the operation of many simultaneously operating parts.

Traditionally, access to the lowest levels of the computer have been via assembly language routines that access absolute hardware locations. The programmer must know the absolute physical address of each subsystem and how to activate and control it (Figure 2-1). Each has a unique set of values and its own commands, and each interacts with the other resources in numerous ways. The programmer must face the complexity of this situation.

The Amiga, in contrast, shields the programmer from this multifaceted task of hardware integration. Instead, a consistent and high-level interface is presented. As much as possible, each resource, whether hardware device or software subsystem, is accessed in a similar way. The same command set is used and similar kinds of data structures are created to pass values back and

**Figure 2-1. Traditional methods of accessing
hardware resources**

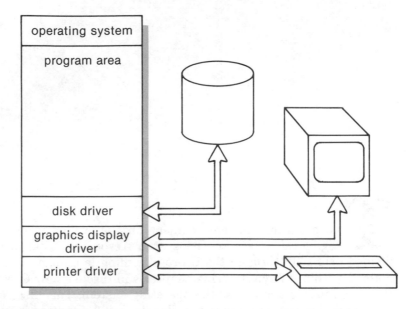

forth. Differences are represented by new interpretations of individual commands and by passing different values to an object. A write command to a
disk drive will put something on a disk, while the same write command to an
audio channel will result in the production of a sound (Figure 2-2). This
consistent interface increases flexibility in another dimension: redirecting
output from one device to the other is greatly simplified.

To create this shield, the Amiga has a multilayered operating system.
Each layer performs its own set of duties, presupposing the services of lower-
level functions and supplying the necessary objects for higher-level ones.
However, it must be emphasized that this is not a strong hierarchy, as is
commonly found in multitasking operating systems. The programmer is free
to utilize any level of the Amiga's software environment and even, with some
reasonable restrictions, to mix levels.

The three main components of the Amiga's operating system environment are:

1. The executive kernel
2. AmigaDOS
3. Intuition

These represent not only three different operating environments to the
software designer, but also different philosophies of design. Furthermore,
each has its strengths and weaknesses. Intuition is the primary operating
system for the Amiga. This is the one designed for the user of software. It is a
visual interface with windows and pop-down menus, all controlled by a

Figure 2-2. Commands will have different interpretation when applied to different devices

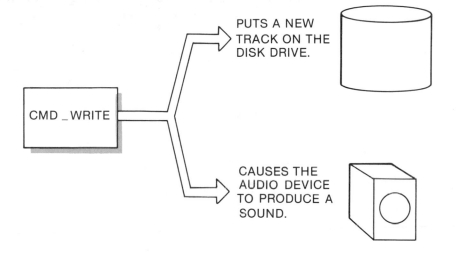

mouse. Its name describes the philosophy of its design: it is meant to be an intuitive command shell. A user should be able to access the Amiga through Intuition with only minimal outside instruction. For the programmer, Intuition is the most complex of the three operating systems to deal with.

AmigaDOS is a more traditional operating system. Organized around a command line interpreter that is reminiscent of the UNIX shell, this will seem more familiar to the experienced programmer. Two important subsystems are defined in this operating environment:

1. The file management system
2. The high-level multitasking system

Both of these topics need further elaboration and, in fact, a chapter is devoted to each. Suffice it to say here that things such as the directory and format for each kind of file are defined as a part of the AmigaDOS operating system. The notion of a process and the loading and unloading of software segments are integral parts of this DOS environment. Most software development is done in this familiar environment.

At the lowest level of the Amiga's software architecture is the executive kernel, the most basic operating system. In fact, the other two operating systems—Intuition and AmigaDOS—rest upon the executive kernel (Figure 2-3). The two primary duties of this subsystem are:

1. To provide a message sending system to support multitasking
2. To handle low-level, device-specific input and output

In many operating systems, this level would be unavailable to the programmer, but with the Amiga it is not only available, but access to it has been simplified. The executive kernel consists of a series of service functions that are easily called from any C program.

Figure 2-3. AmigaDOS and Intuition and their relationship to the executive kernel

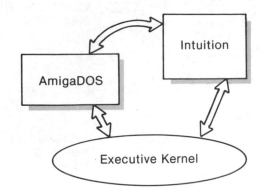

System Access

As with most modern computer systems, the Amiga is accessed through a high-level programming language, in this case the langugage C. C is an ideal programming vehicle particularly for small, complex systems. It has a small but powerful syntax that is ideal for the concise expression of complicated instructions. Most C compilers—including those available for the Amiga—produce reasonable if not optimal machine code.

No real compromise is made in abandoning the more traditional assembly language for the greater productivity of a high-level language. In the case of the Amiga, the software development environment is set up to presuppose programming in C. The gains made are great indeed. Since C readily and easily allows the linking of externally defined functions, any critical sections can still be rendered through an assembler and linked into a C program.

Each important subsystem of the computer has a corresponding object —usually a set of objects—defined in terms of a C structure data type. Some of these objects are shown below. A great part of what follows will be devoted to exploring these structures and seeing how they combine together to make the Amiga do its amazing feats.

Examples of structures used to represent operating system objects

```
struct IORequest {
    struct Message  io_Message;
    struct Device   *io_Device;
```

```
              struct Unit        *io_Unit;

              UWORD              io_Command;

              UBYTE              io_Flags;

              BYTE               io_Error;
          };

      struct IOStdReq  {

          struct Message     io_Message;

          struct Device      *io_Device;

          struct Unit        *io_Unit;

          UWORD              io_Command;

          UBYTE              io_Flags;

          BYTE               io_Error;

          ULONG              io_Actual,

                             io_Length;

          APTR               io_Data;

          ULONG              io_Offset;

      }
```

Using C

Figure 2-4 briefly reminds us of the functions performed by a C compiler. The most important function is to take ordinary text files containing C programming statements and to translate them into executable machine instructions. Subsidiary functions include error checking and the production of source listings. The C compiler on the Amiga works in conjunction with a linking editor or linker, ALINK, to produce the final loadable program modules. We presuppose the Lattice C compiler, as this was the first available for the Amiga. Different compilers may not conform to the same command sets and sequences. Producing a program on the Amiga is a three stage process:

1. Edit to produce a text source.
2. Compile to get an object file.
3. Link to an executable file.

Each one of these stages uses an independent program to accomplish its

Figure 2-4. Compiler as a production engine

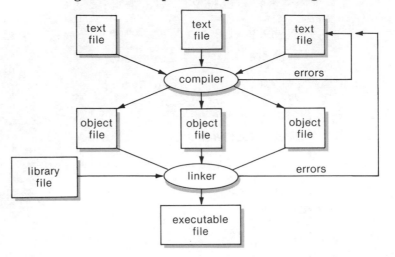

goal. The choice of a text editor is a personal decision with most programmers. A number are available for the Amiga. The compiler and the linker, however, are less open to choice; therefore, it seems appropriate to discuss their operation.

Lattice C

In this section specific implementation details will be discussed, so what follows immediately may not be applicable to other compilers. However, what follows in the rest of the book is the same for all versions of C.

The Lattice compiler is divided into two phases. Each phase can be invoked separately through its own command line:

1. *LC1* starts the first phase of the compile.
2. *LC2* begins the second phase.

In the first phase, a source file containing C statements is processed to produce an intermediate file. Among the tasks performed in this initial phase are:

*   Preprocessor command execution
*   Symbol table creation

The second phase takes the intermediate file produced earlier and creates an object file. The intermediate file is then removed from the disk. This object file contains a mixture of machine code and linkage information; it is not yet ready to execute.

Each stage of the compilation is invoked with a unique command line. For the first stage, the format is:

```
LC1  >listing_file  toggles  file_name
```

where

> **listing__file** names a disk file that will accept all messages including messages that would ordinarily be sent to the screen. This is an optional part of the command line and must be a fully qualified file. No default values are defined.
>
> **toggles** represents a list of compiler toggles that control the action of the compiler and can change some default values. This too is an optional part of the compiler command line.
>
> **file__name** indicates the source code file. Note it need not end in *.c* but if no extension is explicitly mentioned, this will be assumed.

The only requirement for starting a compile is that the source file name must be given, although optional arguments to the command line may help in the development process.

A complete list of the compiler toggles for the first phase of compilation is shown below. Among the more commonly used ones, we find:

> **-d** puts debugging hooks into the intermediate quad file. These can then be used later by an optional debugging program.
>
> **-dname** is equivalent to a *#define* statement in the source file. It can be used in conjunction with the *#ifdef* or *#ifndef* preprocessor statements.
>
> **-i** forces data elements to be aligned on long word (32-bit) boundaries. This alignment is important for compatibility with AmigaDOS structures.
>
> **-p** produces a file with the extension *.p*, that contains the source code along with the full expansion of the preprocessor statement. No executable file is produced.
>
> **-oo__name** gives the object file produced by the compiler a name different from the source file.

First pass compiler toggles

-b	this causes all static and external data references to go through a base register (A5 or A6).
-c<flags>	these control compatibility with earlier versions of the compiler. Flags may be concatenated with no white space between them
c	allows nested comments.
d	$ may be embedded in identifiers.
m	multiple character constants allowed.
s	generates only a single copy of identical string constants.

	u	forces character declarations to be unsigned.
	w	no warning for return statements not specifying a value.
-d		puts debugging information in the object file.
-d<name>		equivalent to #define <name>.
-d<name>=<value>		equivalent to #define <name> <value>
-i<name>		attaches <name> to any file in a #include statement except those already prefixed by a / ,\, or a period. Up to four such names may be specified in separate -i clauses.
-l		all data items except short and char will be long word aligned.
-n		truncates identifiers from 32 to 8 characters.
-o<name>		causes the quad file to be called <name>.
-p		causes a file with extention '.p' to be produced that contains the expansions of the preprocessor commands. No quad file is produced.
-u		automatic symbol definitions are cancelled.
-x		the storage class for externals is changed from external definition to external reference.

Compiler toggles are invoked just as they have been represented here, prefaced by a hyphen and surrounded by white space. For example, to compile a file named *src.c*, but create an object file named *obj*, and to make sure that all data is lined up on long word boundaries, the following command line would be used:

```
LC1  >df1:err_list -oobj   -l  src.c.
```

Note that we have given the full file name for the list file. The second phase of compilation has a similar command format:

```
LC2   toggles   file_name
```

Here **file__name** refers to a file with a *.q* extension, produced by the *LC1* phase of the compiler. A different set of toggles controls this stage.

-oo__name creates a different name for the object file produced by the compiler. It is similar to the toggle in the first phase.

-r makes all addressing relative to the program counter. This restricts the addressing range to 64K around this register, but is necessary to produce position independent code.

A complete listing of the second stage compiler toggles is shown below.

Second pass compiler toggles

```
-fn        specifies register A5 (n=5) or A6 (n=6) as the stack frame

           pointer.

-o<name>   change the name of the output file to <name>.

-r         causes the addressing to be PC relative;  this limits

           addressing range to 132k.  This is used for creating

           position independent code.
```

Invocation of this stage is similar to that of LC1.

```
LC2   -oobj   src
```

This command creates an object file *obj.o* from the intermediate file *src.q*. Note that there is no option for an error listing file in this second phase.

The compiler will report errors whenever it finds them. A successful compiler during the first phase will report nothing back to the screen. However, at the end of the second phase, the size of the resulting code will be displayed to the user in the form:

```
Module size  P=9999  D=9999  U=9999
```

where

P indicates the size of the executable code segment.

D is the size of the initialized data module.

U reports on the uninitialized data area.

All measurements are in bytes and are written in hexadecimal.

Lattice C contains a compiler driver or shell that will automatically invoke both phases of the compiler. It takes the general form:

```
LC   toggles   file_name1 file_name2...
```

Each file name must be separated from the others by white space.

The toggles list is created by a mixture of options from either phase as well as two toggles peculiar to this command line form. Only one argument is ambiguous: *-oo_name*. This ambiguity can be resolved by using *-qx* in place of *-o*. This form can also be used to change the default location for the quad file—it is automatically put in the RAM disk (RAM:). The *-v* command options make Lattice C verbose, displaying each line as it is executed.

Finally, Lattice C comes with an object modular disassemble, OMD, to help in debugging. This utility program provides a list of machine language instructions generated by a C program. It is invoked with the following command line:

```
OMD >list_file toggles object_name source_name.
```

where

> **list_file** specifies a target location for the file produced by OMD. The default is the screen.
>
> **toggles** represents commands to change the default setting of the program parameters:
>
> **object_name** is the file that is the source of all the attention.
>
> **source_name** specifies the source file from which the object file was produced.
>
> **-X9999** sets the maximum number of external items that can be dealt with by the utility. The default is 200.
>
> **-L9999** sets the maximum number of lines. Here the default is 100.

If the file was compiled with the *-d* option, a complete listing with both source and machine language is produced. Listing 2-1 shows a typical OMD output from a file that was compiled with the *-d* toggle. Listing 2-2 shows the OMD applied to the same file but compiled without the option.

Listing 2-1. Example listing compiled by the OMD disassembler. The file was compiled using the -d toggle.

```
LATTICE OBJECT MODULE DISASSEMBLER V2.00

Amiga Object File Loader V1.00
68000 Instruction Set

EXTERNAL DEFINITIONS

_main 0000-00    _sunit 0000-01    _sound 0000-02    _sound_data 0044-02

SECTION 00 "df1:demo" 0000011C BYTES


#include "exec/types.h"
#include "exec/memory.h"
#include "hardware/custom.h"
#include "hardware/dmabits.h"
#include "libraries/dos.h"
#include "devices/audio.h"


extern struct MsgPort *CreatePort();
struct IOAudio sound;

UBYTE sunit=0x0f,sound_data[128];

main()
```

Listing 2-1 cont.

```
{
0000 4E56FFFE                     LINK      A6,FFFE
0004 BFF9 00000000-XX             CMPA.L    __base,A7
000A 6406                         BCC       00000012
000C 4EF9 00000000-XX             JMP       __xcovf
 UBYTE i;

 if((sound.ioa_Request.io_Message.mn_ReplyPort=CreatePort("p3",0))==NULL)
0012 42A7                         CLR.L     -(A7)
0014 4879 00000001-01             PEA       01.00000001
001A 4EB9 00000000-XX             JSR       _CreatePort
0020 508F                         ADDQ.L    #8,A7
0022 23C0 0000000E-02             MOVE.L    D0,02.0000000E
0028 4A80                         TST.L     D0
002A 660A                         BNE       00000036
   exit(FALSE);
002C 42A7                         CLR.L     -(A7)
002E 4EB9 00000000-XX             JSR       _exit
0034 588F                         ADDQ.L    #4,A7


 sound.ioa_Request.io_Message.mn_Node.ln_Pri=10;
0036 13FC000A 00000009-02   MOVE.B      #0A,02.00000009
 sound.ioa_Data=&sunit;
003E 23FC 00000000-01   00000022-02 MOVE.L #01.00000000,02.00000022
 sound.ioa_Length=(ULONG)sizeof(sunit);
0048 7001                         MOVEQ     #01,D0
004A 23C0 00000026-02             MOVE.L    D0,02.00000026


 if((OpenDevice(AUDIONAME,0L,&sound,0L))!=NULL)  {
0050 7000                         MOVEQ     #00,D0
0052 2F00                         MOVE.L    D0,-(A7)
0054 4879 00000000-02             PEA       02.00000000
005A 2F00                         MOVE.L    D0,-(A7)
005C 4879 00000004-01             PEA       01.00000004
0062 4EB9 00000000-XX             JSR       _OpenDevice
0068 4FEF0010                     LEA       0010(A7),A7
006C 4A80                         TST.L     D0
006E 6718                         BEQ       00000088
   printf("Can't open Audio Device\n");
0070 4879 00000011-01             PEA       01.00000011
0076 4EB9 00000000-XX             JSR       _printf
007C 588F                         ADDQ.L    #4,A7
   exit(FALSE);
007E 42A7                         CLR.L     -(A7)
0080 4EB9 00000000-XX             JSR       _exit
0086 588F                         ADDQ.L    #4,A7
 }


 for(i=0;i<127;i++)
0088 422EFFFF                     CLR.B     FFFF(A6)
008C 102EFFFF                     MOVE.B    FFFF(A6),D0
0090 0C00007F                     CMPI.B    #7F,D0
0094 6416                         BCC       000000AC
```

Listing 2-1 cont.

```
     sound_data[i]=i;
0096 7200                               MOVEQ      #00,D1
0098 122EFFFF                           MOVE.B     FFFF(A6),D1
009C 2041                               MOVEA.L    D1,A0
009E D1FC 00000044-02                   ADDA.L     #02.00000044,A0
00A4 1080                               MOVE.B     D0,(A0)
00A6 522EFFFF                           ADDQ.B     #1,FFFF(A6)
00AA 60E0                               BRA        0000008C
     sound_data[127]=0;
00AC 4239 000000C3-02                   CLR.B      02.000000C3


     sound.ioa_Request.io_Command=CMD_WRITE;
00B2 33FC0003 0000001C-02               MOVE.W     #0003,02.0000001C
      sound.ioa_Request.io_Flags=ADIOF_PERVOL|IOF_QUICK;
00BA 13FC0011 0000001E-02               MOVE.B     #11,02.0000001E
     sound.ioa_Data=sound_data;
00C2 23FC 00000044-02  00000022-02 MOVE.L  #02.00000044,02.00000022
     sound.ioa_Cycles=100;
00CC 33FC0064 0000002E-02               MOVE.W     #0064,02.0000002E
      sound.ioa_Length=sizeof(sound_data);
00D4 23FC00000080 00000026-02           MOVE.L     #00000080,02.00000026
     sound.ioa_Period=508;
00DE 33FC01FC 0000002A-02               MOVE.W     #01FC,02.0000002A
     sound.ioa_Volume=64;
00E6 33FC0040 0000002C-02               MOVE.W     #0040,02.0000002C


  BeginIO(&sound);
00EE 4879 00000000-02                   PEA        02.00000000
00F4 4EB9 00000000-XX                   JSR        _BeginIO
00FA 588F                               ADDQ.L     #4,A7
  WaitIO(&sound);
00FC 4879 00000000-02                   PEA        02.00000000
0102 4EB9 00000000-XX                   JSR        _WaitIO
0108 588F                               ADDQ.L     #4,A7


  CloseDevice(&sound);
010A 4879 00000000-02                   PEA        02.00000000
0110 4EB9 00000000-XX                   JSR        _CloseDevice
0116 588F                               ADDQ.L     #4,A7
}

0118 4E5E                               UNLK       A6
011A 4E75                               RTS

SECTION 01 "df1:demo" 0000002C BYTES
0000 0F 70 33 00 61 75 64 69 6F 2E 64 65 76 69 63 65 .p3.audio.device
0010 00 43 61 6E 27 74 20 6F 70 65 6E 20 41 75 64 69 .Can't open Audi
0020 6F 20 44 65 76 69 63 65 0A 00 00 00 o Device....

SECTION 02 "df1:demo" 000000C4 BYTES
```

**Listing 2-2. Listing compiled by the OMD disassembler. The
file was compiled without using the -d toggle.**

```
LATTICE OBJECT MODULE DISASSEMBLER V2.00

Amiga Object File Loader V1.00
68000 Instruction Set

EXTERNAL DEFINITIONS

_main 0000-00    _sunit 0000-01    _sound 0000-02    _sound_data 0044-02

SECTION 00 "df1:demo" 0000011C BYTES
0000 4E56FFFE                        LINK      A6,FFFE
0004 BFF9 00000000-XX                CMPA.L    __base,A7
000A 6406                            BCC       00000012
000C 4EF9 00000000-XX                JMP       __xcovf
0012 42A7                            CLR.L     -(A7)
0014 4879 00000001-01                PEA       01.00000001
001A 4EB9 00000000-XX                JSR       _CreatePort
0020 508F                            ADDQ.L    #8,A7
0022 23C0 0000000E-02                MOVE.L    D0,02.0000000E
0028 4A80                            TST.L     D0
002A 660A                            BNE       00000036
002C 42A7                            CLR.L     -(A7)
002E 4EB9 00000000-XX                JSR       _exit
0034 588F                            ADDQ.L    #4,A7
0036 13FC000A 00000009-02            MOVE.B    #0A,02.00000009
003E 23FC 00000000-01  00000022-02 MOVE.L #01.00000000,02.00000022
0048 7001                            MOVEQ     #01,D0
004A 23C0 00000026-02                MOVE.L    D0,02.00000026
0050 7000                            MOVEQ     #00,D0
0052 2F00                            MOVE.L    D0,-(A7)
0054 4879 00000000-02                PEA       02.00000000
005A 2F00                            MOVE.L    D0,-(A7)
005C 4879 00000004-01                PEA       01.00000004
0062 4EB9 00000000-XX                JSR       _OpenDevice
0068 4FEF0010                        LEA       0010(A7),A7
006C 4A80                            TST.L     D0
006E 6718                            BEQ       00000088
0070 4879 00000011-01                PEA       01.00000011
0076 4EB9 00000000-XX                JSR       _printf
007C 588F                            ADDQ.L    #4,A7
007E 42A7                            CLR.L     -(A7)
0080 4EB9 00000000-XX                JSR       _exit
0086 588F                            ADDQ.L    #4,A7
0088 422EFFFF                        CLR.B     FFFF(A6)
008C 102EFFFF                        MOVE.B    FFFF(A6),D0
0090 0C00007F                        CMPI.B    #7F,D0
0094 6416                            BCC       000000AC
0096 7200                            MOVEQ     #00,D1
0098 122EFFFF                        MOVE.B    FFFF(A6),D1
009C 2041                            MOVEA.L   D1,A0
009E D1FC 00000044-02                ADDA.L    #02.00000044,A0
00A4 1080                            MOVE.B    D0,(A0)
00A6 522EFFFF                        ADDQ.B    #1,FFFF(A6)
```

Listing 2-2 cont.

```
OOAA 60EO                              BRA       0000008C
OOAC 4239 000000C3-02                  CLR.B     02.000000C3
OOB2 33FC0003 0000001C-02              MOVE.W    #0003,02.0000001C
OOBA 13FC0011 0000001E-02              MOVE.B    #11,02.0000001E
OOC2 23FC 00000044-02   00000022-02 MOVE.L #02.00000044,02.00000022
OOCC 33FC0064 0000002E-02              MOVE.W    #0064,02.0000002E
OOD4 23FC00000080 00000026-02          MOVE.L    #00000080,02.00000026
OODE 33FC01FC 0000002A-02              MOVE.W    #01FC,02.0000002A
OOE6 33FC0040 0000002C-02              MOVE.W    #0040,02.0000002C
OOEE 4879 00000000-02                  PEA       02.00000000
OOF4 4EB9 00000000-XX                  JSR       _BeginIO
OOFA 588F                              ADDQ.L    #4,A7
OOFC 4879 00000000-02                  PEA       02.00000000
0102 4EB9 00000000-XX                  JSR       _WaitIO
0108 588F                              ADDQ.L    #4,A7
010A 4879 00000000-02                  PEA       02.00000000
0110 4EB9 00000000-XX                  JSR       _CloseDevice
0116 588F                              ADDQ.L    #4,A7
0118 4E5E                              UNLK      A6
011A 4E75                              RTS
```

```
SECTION 01 "df1:demo" 0000002C BYTES
0000 OF 70 33 00 61 75 64 69 6F 2E 64 65 76 69 63 65 .p3.audio.device
0010 00 43 61 6E 27 74 20 6F 70 65 6E 20 41 75 64 69 .Can't open Audi
0020 6F 20 44 65 76 69 63 65 0A 00 00 00 o Device....

SECTION 02 "df1:demo" 000000C4 BYTES
```

The Linker

The two passes of the compiler produce an object code that is not yet ready to be loaded and run. It contains some directly executable machine code, but also references to functions and variables in other files and to library routines. All of these external references must be reconciled and the actual code loaded into the final executable program file. This final setup task is the job of ALINK, the Amiga's linker utility.

ALINK will accept several different kinds of files and will produce an executable object module. There are two basic file types that must be offered to ALINK as input:

1. **Primary binary input files.** These are the object files produced by the compiler. Any number can be combined to form a single executable program.

2. **Library files.** These, in contrast to the primary files, are precompiled functions. They may be part of a standard library or one created specifically by the user.

These are the basic files from which the executable module will be constructed.

ALINK is a two pass compiler. The first pass:

- Reads through the primary input files and the libraries recording the code segments
- Notes the external symbol information
- Creates the optional symbol map and cross reference table

The second pass is executed only if an executable file was explicitly specified. The default is not to produce this file.

During this final stage:

- The contents of the primary input files are copied to the output file.
- The necessary routines from the libraries are also copied.
- All external references are reconciled. An error will terminate the linking process at whatever stage it is discovered.

Two specific, non-fatal problems will cause the linker to issue a warning.

1. If, at the end of the first pass, a symbol is still undefined, a warning message will be displayed and the symbol will be set equal to zero.
2. If a symbol is defined more than once, a warning will be issued and only the first definition will be used. (If a library routine is redefined, no warning will be given, but only the first definition will be used.)

To invoke the editor, the following command line must be typed:

```
ALINK FROM in_files TO out_file WITH c_files VER m_name
LIBRARY l_files MAP m_file XREF x_file WIDTH 99
```

where

in_files is a list of object files. Each file must be separated by a comma or a plus sign.

out_file is the name of the executable file.

c_files is a file containing ALINK parameter values.

m_name is the destination for the messages generated by ALINK. Default is the display screen.

l_files is a list of library files. As with the input files, each one must be separated by a comma or a plus sign.

m_file is the destination of the symbol reference map.

x_file is the name of the cross reference table.

WIDTH 99 indicates the size of the output line for the map and the cross reference table.

Not all of these parameters are required to produce an executable file. Only the input files, the output file, and the libraries need be mentioned explicitly. The other parameters are available as aids to the user. Note that it is necessary to type the ALINK command line as one long line, although it will not entirely fit on a single display line. A carriage return indicates the end of the command.

The WITH parameter allows creation of a command file which can then be used to control the execution of ALINK. This file can contain any or all of the other parameters along with their values. A single parameter and its value are placed on each line which is then terminated with a semicolon. This command file would contain those parameters which are common to all compiles, perhaps the same libraries or the MAP or XREF options. Shown below are the contents of a typical file. Note that since ALINK ignores everything on the line after the semicolon, comments can be affixed to the file—another important programming aid.

Contents of a typical WITH file

```
LIBRARY  df0:lib/lc.lib+df0:lib/amiga.lib;  link both libraries.
MAP  df1:symbolmap.ref;  always put the map on the second disk.
XREF  df1:crossref.ref;  also the cross reference file.
WIDTH  3;                format is 3 symbols across.
```

The MAP parameter allows creation of a map of the executable module that will be produced by the linker. It is compiled during the first pass. This link map contains a listing for each segment of the output file consisting of:

- The file name that was the origin of the segment (truncated to eight characters)
- The segment reference number
- The type of the segment—data, code, etc.
- The size

In addition to this entry, a list of symbols in the segment, along with their values, is printed in ascending order. An example listing is shown in Listing 2-3. The MAP parameter is optional.

Listing 2-3. Listing compiled by the MAP option to ALINK.

```
0. CODE.   Memory Type PUBLIC Total Size 0001CC.
Hunkname: text

File: LIB:LStartUp.obj
Program Unit: No Name
Base: 000000  Size: 0001CC

Symbol                              Value

_XCEXIT                             0000013A
```

Listing 2-3 cont.

```
1. DATA.    Memory Type PUBLIC Total Size 00005C.
Hunkname: data

File: LIB:LStartUp.obj
Program Unit: No Name
Base: 000000  Size: 00005C
```

Symbol	Value
_NULL	00000000
__base	00000004
__mbase	00000008
__mnext	0000000C
__msize	00000010
__mstep	00000014
__tsize	00000018
__oserr	0000001C
__fperr	00000020
_console_dev	00000028
_SysBase	0000002C
_DOSBase	00000030
_LoadAddress	00000034
_WBenchMsg	00000038
__StackPtr	0000003C
__ProgramName	0000004C

```
2. CODE.    Memory Type PUBLIC Total Size 0001E8.

File: df1:strip.o
Program Unit: df1:strip
Base: 000000  Size: 0001E8
```

Symbol	Value
_main	00000000

```
3. DATA.    Memory Type PUBLIC Total Size 000034.

File: df1:strip.o
Program Unit: df1:strip
Base: 000000  Size: 000034


4. BSS.     Memory Type PUBLIC

File: df1:strip.o
Program Unit: df1:strip
Base: 000000  Size: 000000


5. CODE.    Memory Type PUBLIC Total Size 000000.
```

Listing 2-3 cont.

```
File: LIB:lc.lib
Program Unit: bufsiz
Base: 000000  Size: 000000


6. DATA.   Memory Type PUBLIC Total Size 000004.

File: LIB:lc.lib
Program Unit: bufsiz
Base: 000000  Size: 000004

Symbol                          Value

__bufsiz                        00000000


7. BSS.    Memory Type PUBLIC

File: LIB:lc.lib
Program Unit: bufsiz
Base: 000000  Size: 000000


8. CODE.   Memory Type PUBLIC Total Size 000000.

File: LIB:lc.lib
Program Unit: ctype
Base: 000000  Size: 000000


9. DATA.   Memory Type PUBLIC Total Size 000104.

File: LIB:lc.lib
Program Unit: ctype
Base: 000000  Size: 000104

Symbol                          Value

__ctype                         00000000


10. BSS.   Memory Type PUBLIC

 File: LIB:lc.lib
 Program Unit: ctype
 Base: 000000  Size: 000000


11. CODE.   Memory Type PUBLIC Total Size 000000.

 File: LIB:lc.lib
 Program Unit: error
 Base: 000000  Size: 000000
```

Listing 2-3 cont.

12. DATA.   Memory Type PUBLIC Total Size 000004.

  File: LIB:lc.lib
  Program Unit: error
  Base: 000000 Size: 000004

  Symbol   Value

  _errno   00000000

13. BSS.   Memory Type PUBLIC

  File: LIB:lc.lib
  Program Unit: error
  Base: 000000 Size: 000000

14. CODE.   Memory Type PUBLIC Total Size 000068.

  File: LIB:lc.lib
  Program Unit: exit
  Base: 000000 Size: 000068

  Symbol   Value

  _exit   00000000

15. DATA.   Memory Type PUBLIC Total Size 000000.

  File: LIB:lc.lib
  Program Unit: exit
  Base: 000000 Size: 000000

16. BSS.   Memory Type PUBLIC

  File: LIB:lc.lib
  Program Unit: exit
  Base: 000000 Size: 000000

17. CODE.   Memory Type PUBLIC Total Size 0000A0.

  File: LIB:lc.lib
  Program Unit: abort
  Base: 000000 Size: 0000A0

  Symbol   Value

  _Chk_Abort   00000000

Listing 2-3 cont.

---

18. DATA.   Memory Type PUBLIC Total Size 000004.

 File: LIB:lc.lib
 Program Unit: abort
 Base: 000000   Size: 000004

 Symbol   Value

 _Enable_Abort   00000000

19. BSS.   Memory Type PUBLIC

 File: LIB:lc.lib
 Program Unit: abort
 Base: 000000   Size: 000000

20. CODE.   Memory Type PUBLIC Total Size 000000.

 File: LIB:lc.lib
 Program Unit: fmode
 Base: 000000   Size: 000000

21. DATA.   Memory Type PUBLIC Total Size 000004.

 File: LIB:lc.lib
 Program Unit: fmode
 Base: 000000   Size: 000004

 Symbol   Value

 __fmode   00000000

22. BSS.   Memory Type PUBLIC

 File: LIB:lc.lib
 Program Unit: fmode
 Base: 000000   Size: 000000

23. CODE.   Memory Type PUBLIC Total Size 0002C8.

 File: LIB:lc.lib
 Program Unit: fopen
 Base: 000000   Size: 0002C8

 Symbol   Value

 _fopen   00000000

Listing 2-3 cont.

```
  _freopen                        00000052
  _fclose                         0000025A


24. DATA.    Memory Type PUBLIC Total Size 000000.

  File: LIB:lc.lib
  Program Unit: fopen
  Base: 000000  Size: 000000


25. BSS.     Memory Type PUBLIC

  File: LIB:lc.lib
  Program Unit: fopen
  Base: 000000  Size: 000000


26. CODE.    Memory Type PUBLIC Total Size 00014C.

  File: LIB:lc.lib
  Program Unit: fprintf
  Base: 000000  Size: 00014C

  Symbol                          Value

  _fprintf                        00000000


27. DATA.    Memory Type PUBLIC Total Size 000000.

  File: LIB:lc.lib
  Program Unit: fprintf
  Base: 000000  Size: 000000


28. BSS.     Memory Type PUBLIC

  File: LIB:lc.lib
  Program Unit: fprintf
  Base: 000000  Size: 000000


29. CODE.    Memory Type PUBLIC Total Size 0000F0.

  File: LIB:lc.lib
  Program Unit: fputs
  Base: 000000  Size: 0000F0

  Symbol                          Value

  _puts                           00000000
  _fputs                          00000096
```

Listing 2-3 cont.

---

30. DATA.   Memory Type PUBLIC Total Size 000000.

 File: LIB:lc.lib
 Program Unit: fputs
 Base: 000000 Size: 000000

31. BSS.   Memory Type PUBLIC

 File: LIB:lc.lib
 Program Unit: fputs
 Base: 000000 Size: 000000

32. CODE.   Memory Type PUBLIC Total Size 000000.

 File: LIB:lc.lib
 Program Unit: iomode
 Base: 000000 Size: 000000

33. DATA.   Memory Type PUBLIC Total Size 000004.

 File: LIB:lc.lib
 Program Unit: iomode
 Base: 000000 Size: 000004

 Symbol   Value

 __iomode   00000000

34. BSS.   Memory Type PUBLIC

 File: LIB:lc.lib
 Program Unit: iomode
 Base: 000000 Size: 000000

35. CODE.   Memory Type PUBLIC Total Size 000608.

 File: LIB:lc.lib
 Program Unit: IOS1
 Base: 000000 Size: 000608

 Symbol   Value

 _open   00000064
 _creat   000001F0
 _read   00000222
 _write   0000028A
 _lseek   0000030E
 _close   00000396

Listing 2-3 cont.

```
_unlink                     000003E6
_remove                     0000041A
_rename                     0000042A
_getch                      0000047E
_getche                     000004E0
_putch                      0000050E
_ungetch                    0000054E
_cgets                      0000056E
_cputs                      000005C4
```

36. DATA.   Memory Type PUBLIC Total Size 000010.

File: LIB:lc.lib
Program Unit: IOS1
Base: 000000   Size: 000010

37. BSS.   Memory Type PUBLIC

File: LIB:lc.lib
Program Unit: IOS1
Base: 000000   Size: 000000

38. CODE.   Memory Type PUBLIC Total Size 0003F0.

File: LIB:lc.lib
Program Unit: ios2
Base: 000000   Size: 0003F0

```
Symbol                      Value

__filbf                     00000000
__flsbf                     00000120
```

39. DATA.   Memory Type PUBLIC Total Size 000000.

File: LIB:lc.lib
Program Unit: ios2
Base: 000000   Size: 000000

40. BSS.   Memory Type PUBLIC

File: LIB:lc.lib
Program Unit: ios2
Base: 000000   Size: 000000

41. CODE.   Memory Type PUBLIC Total Size 00016C.

File: LIB:lc.lib

Listing 2-3 cont.

```
Program Unit: mem1
Base: 000000   Size: 00016C

Symbol                          Value

_lsbrk                          00000000
_sbrk                           00000060
_rbrk                           00000084
_MemCleanup                     000000B4


42. DATA.    Memory Type PUBLIC Total Size 000000.

   File: LIB:lc.lib
   Program Unit: mem1
   Base: 000000   Size: 000000


43. BSS.     Memory Type PUBLIC Total Size 00000C.

   File: LIB:lc.lib
   Program Unit: mem1
   Base: 000000   Size: 00000C


44. CODE.    Memory Type PUBLIC Total Size 000284.

   File: LIB:lc.lib
   Program Unit: mem2
   Base: 000000   Size: 000284

   Symbol                       Value

   _sizmem                      00000000
   _getmem                      00000010
   _getml                       00000026
   _rlsmem                      0000010A
   _rlsml                       00000124


45. DATA.    Memory Type PUBLIC Total Size 000000.

   File: LIB:lc.lib
   Program Unit: mem2
   Base: 000000   Size: 000000


46. BSS.     Memory Type PUBLIC

   File: LIB:lc.lib
   Program Unit: mem2
   Base: 000000   Size: 000000
```

Listing 2-3 cont.

---

47. CODE.   Memory Type PUBLIC Total Size 000088.

  File: LIB:lc.lib
  Program Unit: strcat
  Base: 000000 Size: 000088

  Symbol   Value

  _strcat   00000000
  _strncat   0000003A

48. DATA.   Memory Type PUBLIC Total Size 000000.

  File: LIB:lc.lib
  Program Unit: strcat
  Base: 000000 Size: 000000

49. BSS.   Memory Type PUBLIC

  File: LIB:lc.lib
  Program Unit: strcat
  Base: 000000 Size: 000000

50. CODE.   Memory Type PUBLIC Total Size 000024.

  File: LIB:lc.lib
  Program Unit: strlen
  Base: 000000 Size: 000024

  Symbol   Value

  _strlen   00000000

51. DATA.   Memory Type PUBLIC Total Size 000000.

  File: LIB:lc.lib
  Program Unit: strlen
  Base: 000000 Size: 000000

52. BSS.   Memory Type PUBLIC

  File: LIB:lc.lib
  Program Unit: strlen
  Base: 000000 Size: 000000

53. CODE.   Memory Type PUBLIC Total Size 000000.

  File: LIB:lc.lib

Listing 2-3 cont.

```
Program Unit: ufbs
Base: 000000   Size: 000000


54. DATA.    Memory Type PUBLIC Total Size 000004.

   File: LIB:lc.lib
   Program Unit: ufbs
   Base: 000000   Size: 000004

   Symbol                        Value

   __nufbs                       00000000


55. BSS.     Memory Type PUBLIC Total Size 000078.

   File: LIB:lc.lib
   Program Unit: ufbs
   Base: 000000   Size: 000078

   Symbol                        Value

   __ufbs                        00000000


56. CODE.    Memory Type PUBLIC Total Size 000068.

   File: LIB:lc.lib
   Program Unit: \lc\library\amiga\_exit
   Base: 000000   Size: 000068

   Symbol                        Value

   __exit                        00000000


57. DATA.    Memory Type PUBLIC Total Size 000000.

   File: LIB:lc.lib
   Program Unit: \lc\library\amiga\_exit
   Base: 000000   Size: 000000


58. BSS.     Memory Type PUBLIC

   File: LIB:lc.lib
   Program Unit: \lc\library\amiga\_exit
   Base: 000000   Size: 000000


59. CODE.    Memory Type PUBLIC Total Size 000000.

   File: LIB:lc.lib
```

Listing 2-3 cont.

```
Program Unit: _iob
Base: 000000  Size: 000000


60. DATA.   Memory Type PUBLIC Total Size 000000.

 File: LIB:lc.lib
 Program Unit: _iob
 Base: 000000  Size: 000000


61. BSS.    Memory Type PUBLIC Total Size 0001E0.

 File: LIB:lc.lib
 Program Unit: _iob
 Base: 000000  Size: 0001E0

 Symbol                        Value

 __iob                         00000000


62. CODE.   Memory Type PUBLIC Total Size 00087C.

 File: LIB:lc.lib
 Program Unit: _ptmt
 Base: 000000  Size: 00087C

 Symbol                        Value

 __pfmt                        00000000


63. DATA.   Memory Type PUBLIC Total Size 000014.

 File: LIB:lc.lib
 Program Unit: _pfmt
 Base: 000000  Size: 000014


64. BSS.    Memory Type PUBLIC

 File: LIB:lc.lib
 Program Unit: _pfmt
 Base: 000000  Size: 000000


65. CODE.   Memory Type PUBLIC Total Size 000000.

 File: LIB:lc.lib
 Program Unit: _pool
 Base: 000000  Size: 000000
```

Listing 2-3 cont.

---

66. DATA.   Memory Type PUBLIC Total Size 000010.

 File: LIB:lc.lib
 Program Unit: _pool
 Base: 000000 Size: 000010

 Symbol   Value

 __pool   00000000
 __melt   00000008

67. BSS.   Memory Type PUBLIC

 File: LIB:lc.lib
 Program Unit: _pool
 Base: 000000 Size: 000000

68. CODE.   Memory Type PUBLIC Total Size 000044.

 File: LIB:lc.lib
 Program Unit: \lc\library\68000\cxd33
 Base: 000000 Size: 000044

 Symbol   Value

 _CXD33   00000000

69. CODE.   Memory Type PUBLIC Total Size 000044.

 File: LIB:lc.lib
 Program Unit: \lc\library\68000\cxm33
 Base: 000000 Size: 000044

 Symbol   Value

 _CXM33   00000000

70. CODE.   Memory Type PUBLIC Total Size 000010.

 File: LIB:lc.lib
 Program Unit: cxferr
 Base: 000000 Size: 000010

 Symbol   Value

 _CXFERR   00000000

71. DATA.   Memory Type PUBLIC Total Size 000000.

Listing 2-3 cont.

```
File: LIB:lc.lib
Program Unit: cxferr
Base: 000000  Size: 000000


72. BSS.    Memory Type PUBLIC

File: LIB:lc.lib
Program Unit: cxferr
Base: 000000  Size: 000000


73. CODE.   Memory Type PUBLIC Total Size 0000D8.

File: LIB:lc.lib
Program Unit: \lc\library\68000\cxfxt5
Base: 000000  Size: 0000D8

Symbol                          Value

_CXFXT5                         00000000
_CXFNM5                         00000036


74. CODE.   Memory Type PUBLIC Total Size 000394.

File: LIB:lc.lib
Program Unit: \lc\library\68000\cxvfd
Base: 000000  Size: 000394

Symbol                          Value

_CXVFD                          00000000
_CXVDF                          000001BA


75. CODE.   Memory Type PUBLIC Total Size 000018.

File: LIB:lc.lib
Program Unit: No Name
Base: 000000  Size: 000018

Symbol                          Value

__xcovf                         00000000


76. CODE.   Memory Type PUBLIC Total Size 00026C.

File: LIB:lc.lib
Program Unit: _main
Base: 000000  Size: 00026C

Symbol                          Value
```

Listing 2-3 cont.

```
__main                              00000000


77. DATA.    Memory Type PUBLIC Total Size 000050.

 File: LIB:lc.lib
 Program Unit: _main
 Base: 000000  Size: 000050


78. BSS.     Memory Type PUBLIC Total Size 00008C.

 File: LIB:lc.lib
 Program Unit: _main
 Base: 000000  Size: 00008C

 Symbol                         Value

 _argc                          00000000
 _argv                          00000004


79. CODE.    Memory Type PUBLIC Total Size 000058.

 File: LIB:lc.lib
 Program Unit: cxovf
 Base: 000000  Size: 000058

 Symbol                         Value

 _cxovf                         00000000


80. DATA.    Memory Type PUBLIC Total Size 00006C.

 File: LIB:lc.lib
 Program Unit: cxovf
 Base: 000000  Size: 00006C

 Symbol                         Value

 _Text2                         00000000
 _BodyText                      0000002A
 _ResponseText                  00000044


81. BSS.     Memory Type PUBLIC Total Size 000004.

 File: LIB:lc.lib
 Program Unit: cxovf
 Base: 000000  Size: 000004

 Symbol                         Value
```

Listing 2-3 cont.

```
 _IntuitionBase                       00000000


82. CODE.   Memory Type PUBLIC Total Size 000000.
 Hunkname: _LVO

 File: LIB:amiga.lib
 Program Unit: No Name
 Base: 000000  Size: 000000

 Symbol                              Value

 _LVOExecute                         FFFFFF22*
 _LVOIsInteractive                   FFFFFF28*
 _LVOParentDir                       FFFFFF2E*
 _LVOWaitForChar                     FFFFFF34*
 _LVODelay                           FFFFFF3A*
 _LVODateStamp                       FFFFFF40*
 _LVOSetProtection                   FFFFFF46*
 _LVOSetComment                      FFFFFF4C*
 _LVODeviceProc                      FFFFFF52*
 _LVOQueuePacket                     FFFFFF58*
 _LVOGetPacket                       FFFFFF5E*
 _LVOUnLoadSeg                       FFFFFF64*
 _LVOLoadSeg                         FFFFFF6A*
 _LVOExit                            FFFFFF70*
 _LVOCreateProc                      FFFFFF76*
 _LVOIoErr                           FFFFFF7C*
 _LVOCurrentDir                      FFFFFF82*
 _LVOCreateDir                       FFFFFF88*
 _LVOInfo                            FFFFFF8E*
 _LVOExNext                          FFFFFF94*
 _LVOExamine                         FFFFFF9A*
 _LVODupLock                         FFFFFFA0*
 _LVOUnLock                          FFFFFFA6*
 _LVOLock                            FFFFFFAC*
 _LVORename                          FFFFFFB2*
 _LVODeleteFile                      FFFFFFB8*
 _LVOSeek                            FFFFFFBE*
 _LVOOutput                          FFFFFFC4*
 _LVOInput                           FFFFFFCA*
 _LVOWrite                           FFFFFFD0*
 _LVORead                            FFFFFFD6*
 _LVOClose                           FFFFFFDC*
 _LVOOpen                            FFFFFFE2*

 File: LIB:amiga.lib
 Program Unit: No Name
 Base: 000000  Size: 000000
 Symbol                              Value


 _LVOOpenLibrary                     FFFFFDD8*
```

Listing 2-3 cont.

```
_LVOVacate             FFFFFDDE*
_LVOProcure            FFFFFDE4*
_LVOTypeOfMem          FFFFFDEA*
_LVOGetCC              FFFFFDF0*
_LVORawDoFmt           FFFFFDF6*
_LVORawPutChar         FFFFFDFC*
_LVORawMayGetChar      FFFFFE02*
_LVORawIOInit          FFFFFE08*
_LVOOpenResource       FFFFFE0E*
_LVORemResource        FFFFFE14*
_LVOAddResource        FFFFFE1A*
_LVOAbortIO            FFFFFE20*
_LVOWaitIO             FFFFFE26*
_LVOCheckIO            FFFFFE2C*
_LVOSendIO             FFFFFE32*
_LVODoIO               FFFFFE38*
_LVOCloseDevice        FFFFFE3E*
_LVOOpenDevice         FFFFFE44*
_LVORemDevice          FFFFFE4A*
_LVOAddDevice          FFFFFE50*
_LVOSumLibrary         FFFFFE56*
_LVOSetFunction        FFFFFE5C*
_LVOCloseLibrary       FFFFFE62*
_LVOOldOpenLibrary     FFFFFE68*
_LVORemLibrary         FFFFFE6E*
_LVOAddLibrary         FFFFFE74*
_LVOFindPort           FFFFFE7A*
_LVOWaitPort           FFFFFE80*
_LVOReplyMsg           FFFFFE86*
_LVOGetMsg             FFFFFE8C*
_LVOPutMsg             FFFFFE92*
_LVORemPort            FFFFFE98*
_LVOAddPort            FFFFFE9E*
_LVOFreeTrap           FFFFFEA4*
_LVOAllocTrap          FFFFFEAA*
_LVOFreeSignal         FFFFFEB0*
_LVOAllocSignal        FFFFFEB6*
_LVOSignal             FFFFFEBC*
_LVOWait               FFFFFEC2*
_LVOSetExcept          FFFFFEC8*
_LVOSetSignal          FFFFFECE*
_LVOSetTaskPri         FFFFFED4*
_LVOFindTask           FFFFFEDA*
_LVORemTask            FFFFFEE0*
_LVOAddTask            FFFFFEE6*
_LVOFindName           FFFFFEEC*
_LVOEnqueue            FFFFFEF2*
_LVORemTail            FFFFFEF8*
_LVORemHead            FFFFFEFE*
_LVORemove             FFFFFF04*
_LVOAddTail            FFFFFF0A*
_LVOAddHead            FFFFFF10*
_LVOInsert             FFFFFF16*
_LVOFreeEntry          FFFFFF1C*
```

Listing 2-3 cont.

```
_LVOAllocEntry                    FFFFFF22*
_LVOAvailMem                      FFFFFF28*
_LVOFreeMem                       FFFFFF2E*
_LVOAllocAbs                      FFFFFF34*
_LVOAllocMem                      FFFFFF3A*
_LVODeallocate                    FFFFFF40*
_LVOAllocate                      FFFFFF46*
_LVOCause                         FFFFFF4C*
_LVORemIntServer                  FFFFFF52*
_LVOAddIntServer                  FFFFFF58*
_LVOSetIntVector                  FFFFFF5E*
_LVOUserState                     FFFFFF64*
_LVOSuperState                    FFFFFF6A*
_LVOSetSR                         FFFFFF70*
_LVOPermit                        FFFFFF76*
_LVOForbid                        FFFFFF7C*
_LVOEnable                        FFFFFF82*
_LVODisable                       FFFFFF88*
_LVODebug                         FFFFFF8E*
_LVOAlert                         FFFFFF94*
_LVOInitResident                  FFFFFF9A*
_LVOFindResident                  FFFFFFA0*
_LVOMakeFunctions                 FFFFFFA6*
_LVOMakeLibrary                   FFFFFFAC*
_LVOInitStruct                    FFFFFFR2*
_LVOInitCode                      FFFFFFB8*
_LVOException                     FFFFFFBE*
_LVODispatch                      FFFFFFC4*
_LVOSwitch                        FFFFFFCA*
_LVOReschedule                    FFFFFFD0*
_LVOSchedule                      FFFFFFD6*
_LVOExitIntr                      FFFFFFDC*
_LVOSupervisor                    FFFFFFE2*
```

```
83. CODE.   Memory Type PUBLIC Total Size 0000E4.
Hunkname: dos_lib

File: LIB:amiga.lib
Program Unit: No Name
Base: 000000  Size: 00001C

Symbol                            Value

_Open                             00000000

File: LIB:amiga.lib
Program Unit: No Name
Base: 00001C  Size: 000014

Symbol                            Value


_Close                            0000001C
```

Listing 2-3 cont.

```
File: LIB:amiga.lib
Program Unit: No Name
Base: 000030   Size: 00001C

Symbol                              Value


_Read                               00000030

File: LIB:amiga.lib
Program Unit: No Name
Base: 00004C   Size: 00001C

Symbol                              Value


_Write                              0000004C

File: LIB:amiga.lib
Program Unit: No Name
Base: 000068   Size: 000010

Symbol                              Value


_Input                              00000068

File: LIB:amiga.lib
Program Unit: No Name
Base: 000078   Size: 000010

Symbol                              Value


_Output                             00000078

File: LIB:amiga.lib
Program Unit: No Name
Base: 000088   Size: 00001C

Symbol                              Value


_Seek                               00000088

File: LIB:amiga.lib
Program Unit: No Name
Base: 0000A4   Size: 000014

Symbol                              Value


_DeleteFile                         000000A4
```

Listing 2-3 cont.

```
File: LIB:amiga.lib
Program Unit: No Name
Base: 0000B8  Size: 00001C
```

Symbol	Value
_Rename	000000B8

```
File: LIB:amiga.lib
Program Unit: No Name
Base: 0000D4  Size: 000010
```

Symbol	Value
_IoErr	000000D4

84. CODE.   Memory Type PUBLIC Total Size 000074.
Hunkname: exec_lib

```
File: LIB:amiga.lib
Program Unit: No Name
Base: 000000  Size: 000018
```

Symbol	Value
_AllocMem	00000000

```
File: LIB:amiga.lib
Program Unit: No Name
Base: 000018  Size: 000018
```

Symbol	Value
_FreeMem	00000018

```
File: LIB:amiga.lib
Program Unit: No Name
Base: 000030  Size: 000014
```

Symbol	Value
_FindTask	00000030

```
File: LIB:amiga.lib
Program Unit: No Name
Base: 000044  Size: 000018
```

Symbol	Value

Listing 2-3 cont.

```
_SetSignal                              00000044

File: LIB:amiga.lib
Program Unit: No Name
Base: 00005C   Size: 000018

Symbol                                  Value


_OpenLibrary                            0000005C


85. DATA.   Memory Type PUBLIC Total Size 000000.

File: LIB:amiga.lib
Program Unit: No Name
Base: 000000   Size: 000000

Symbol                                  Value

_AbsExecBase                            00000004*
_cartridge                              00F00000*
_bootrom                                00F80000*
_romstart                               00FC0000*
_romend                                 00FFFFFF*


86. CODE.   Memory Type PUBLIC Total Size 000034.
Hunkname: intuition_lib

File: LIB:amiga.lib
Program Unit: No Name
Base: 000000   Size: 000034

Symbol                                  Value

_AutoRequest                            00000000
```

XREF produces a cross-reference table containing a listing for each symbol in the file and a list of references for that symbol. Each reference consists of a code segment number and an offset value into that segment. This linker option uses the same header format as the MAP. This is illustrated in Listing 2-4.

The WIDTH parameter specifies the output format for the MAP and XREF tables. It indicates the number of symbols printed per line. The default is a single symbol per line.

Listing 2-4. Listing compiled by the XREF option to ALINK.

```
0. CODE.   Memory Type PUBLIC Total Size 0001CC.
Hunkname: text

File: LIB:LStartUp.obj
Program Unit: No Name
Base: 000000  Size: 0001CC
```

Symbol	Offset	Hunk	Offset	Hunk	Offset	Hunk
_XCEXIT	00000058	56				

```
1. DATA.   Memory Type PUBLIC Total Size 00005C.
Hunkname: data
File: LIB:LStartUp.obj
Program Unit: No Name
Base: 000000  Size: 00005C
```

Symbol	Offset	Hunk	Offset	Hunk	Offset	Hunk
_NULL						
__base	00000006	2				
__mbase	00000090	41				
__mnext	00000096	41				
__msize	0000008A	41				
__mstep	000000BC	44	000000CC	44		
__tsize						
__oserr	000001D0	35	00000276	35	000002FA	35
	0000036E	35	00000402	35	0000044A	35
__fperr	00000008	70				
_console_dev	0U000478	35	00000492	35	000004C8	35
	00000522	35	00000536	35	00000582	35
	00000598	35	000005D8	35	000005F6	35
_SysBase	00000004	84	0000001C	84	00000034	84
	00000048	84	00000060	84		
_DOSBase	0000000C	83	00000024	83	0000003C	83
	00000058	83	0000006C	83	0000007C	83
	00000094	83	000000AC	83	000000C4	83
	000000D8	83				
_LoadAddress						
_WBenchMsg	0000014A	76				
__StackPtr	00000002	75				
__ProgramName	00000018	79				

```
2. CODE.   Memory Type PUBLIC Total Size 0001E8.

File: df1:strip.o
Program Unit: df1:strip
Base: 000000  Size: 0001E8
```

Symbol	Offset	Hunk	Offset	Hunk	Offset	Hunk
_main	00000258	76				

```
3. DATA.   Memory Type PUBLIC Total Size 000034.
```

Listing 2-4 cont.

```
File: df1:strip.o
Program Unit: df1:strip
Base: 000000   Size: 000034


4. BSS.    Memory Type PUBLIC

File: df1:strip.o
Program Unit: df1:strip
Base: 000000   Size: 000000


5. CODE.   Memory Type PUBLIC Total Size 000000.

File: LIB:lc.lib
Program Unit: bufsiz
Base: 000000   Size: 000000


6. DATA.   Memory Type PUBLIC Total Size 000004.

File: LIB:lc.lib
Program Unit: bufsiz
Base: 000000   Size: 000004
```

Symbol	Offset	Hunk	Offset	Hunk	Offset	Hunk
__bufsiz	000003A2	38	000003D0	38		

```
7. BSS.    Memory Type PUBLIC

File: LIB:lc.lib
Program Unit: bufsiz
Base: 000000   Size: 000000


8. CODE.   Memory Type PUBLIC Total Size 000000.

File: LIB:lc.lib
Program Unit: ctype
Base: 000000   Size: 000000


9. DATA.   Memory Type PUBLIC Total Size 000104.

File: LIB:lc.lib
Program Unit: ctype
Base: 000000   Size: 000104
```

Symbol	Offset	Hunk	Offset	Hunk	Offset	Hunk
__ctype	00000104	2	0000004E	62	0000008E	62

Listing 2-4 cont.

```
                              000000DE   62   00000022   76   000000EA   76
```

10. BSS.   Memory Type PUBLIC

```
 File: LIB:lc.lib
 Program Unit: ctype
 Base: 000000  Size: 000000
```

11. CODE.   Memory Type PUBLIC Total Size 000000.

```
 File: LIB:lc.lib
 Program Unit: error
 Base: 000000  Size: 000000
```

12. DATA.   Memory Type PUBLIC Total Size 000004.

```
 File: LIB:lc.lib
 Program Unit: error
 Base: 000000  Size: 000004
```

Symbol	Offset	Hunk	Offset	Hunk	Offset	Hunk
_errno	00000040	35	000000A4	35	0000016E	35
	000001D8	35	0000024?	35	0000027E	35
	000002AA	35	00000302	35	00000332	35
	00000376	35	0000040A	35	00000452	35
	000003C0	38				

13. BSS.   Memory Type PUBLIC

```
 File: LIB:lc.lib
 Program Unit: error
 Base: 000000  Size: 000000
```

14. CODE.   Memory Type PUBLIC Total Size 000068.

```
 File: LIB:lc.lib
 Program Unit: exit
 Base: 000000  Size: 000068
```

Symbol	Offset	Hunk	Offset	Hunk	Offset	Hunk
_exit	00000030	2	00000070	2	000000B0	2
	00000014	75	000000A4	76	00000262	76
	00000050	79				

15. DATA.   Memory Type PUBLIC Total Size 000000.

Listing 2-4 cont.

```
File: LIB:lc.lib
Program Unit: exit
Base: 000000  Size: 000000


16. BSS.    Memory Type PUBLIC

 File: LIB:lc.lib
 Program Unit: exit
 Base: 000000  Size: 000000


17. CODE.   Memory Type PUBLIC Total Size 0000A0.

 File: LIB:lc.lib
 Program Unit: abort
 Base: 000000  Size: 0000A0

 Symbol                        Offset  Hunk  Offset  Hunk  Offset  Hunk

 _Chk_Abort                    0000000E  35  0000048C  35  0000051C  35
                               0000057C  35  000005D2  35


18. DATA.   Memory Type PUBLIC Total Size 000004.

 File: LIB:lc.lib
 Program Unit: abort
 Base: 000000  Size: 000004

 Symbol                        Offset  Hunk  Offset  Hunk  Offset  Hunk

 _Enable_Abort                 00000006  35  00000484  35  00000514  35
                               00000574  35  000005CA  35


19. BSS.    Memory Type PUBLIC

 File: LIB:lc.lib
 Program Unit: abort
 Base: 000000  Size: 000000


20. CODE.   Memory Type PUBLIC Total Size 000000.

 File: LIB:lc.lib
 Program Unit: fmode
 Base: 000000  Size: 000000


21. DATA.   Memory Type PUBLIC Total Size 000004.

 File: LIB:lc.lib
 Program Unit: fmode
```

Listing 2-4 cont.

```
Base: 000000  Size: 000004
```

Symbol	Offset	Hunk	Offset	Hunk	Offset	Hunk
__fmode	0000006A	23				

```
22. BSS.    Memory Type PUBLIC

   File: LIB:lc.lib
   Program Unit: fmode
   Base: 000000  Size: 000000


23. CODE.   Memory Type PUBLIC Total Size 0002C8.

   File: LIB:lc.lib
   Program Unit: fopen
   Base: 000000  Size: 0002C8
```

Symbol	Offset	Hunk	Offset	Hunk	Offset	Hunk
_fopen	00000046	2	00000086	2		
_freopen						
_fclose	000001D2	2	000001DE	2	00000028	14

```
24. DATA.   Memory Type PUBLIC Total Size 000000.

   File: LIB:lc.lib
   Program Unit: fopen
   Base: 000000  Size: 000000


25. BSS.    Memory Type PUBLIC

   File: LIB:lc.lib
   Program Unit: fopen
   Base: 000000  Size: 000000


26. CODE.   Memory Type PUBLIC Total Size 00014C.

   File: LIB:lc.lib
   Program Unit: fprintf
   Base: 000000  Size: 00014C
```

Symbol	Offset	Hunk	Offset	Hunk	Offset	Hunk
_fprintf	00000098	76				

```
27. DATA.   Memory Type PUBLIC Total Size 000000.
```

Listing 2-4 cont.

```
File: LIB:lc.lib
Program Unit: fprintf
Base: 000000  Size: 000000


28. BSS.    Memory Type PUBLIC

File: LIB:lc.lib
Program Unit: fprintf
Base: 000000  Size: 000000


29. CODE.   Memory Type PUBLIC Total Size 0000F0.

File: LIB:lc.lib
Program Unit: fputs
Base: 000000  Size: 0000F0

Symbol                    Offset  Hunk  Offset  Hunk  Offset  Hunk

_puts                     00000024   2   00000064   2   000000A4   2
_fputs


30. DATA.   Memory Type PUBLIC Total Size 000000.

File: LIB:lc.lib
Program Unit: fputs
Base: 000000  Size: 000000


31. BSS.    Memory Type PUBLIC

File: LIB:lc.lib
Program Unit: fputs
Base: 000000  Size: 000000


32. CODE.   Memory Type PUBLIC Total Size 000000.

File: LIB:lc.lib
Program Unit: iomode
Base: 000000  Size: 000000


33. DATA.   Memory Type PUBLIC Total Size 000004.

File: LIB:lc.lib
Program Unit: iomode
Base: 000000  Size: 000004

Symbol                    Offset  Hunk  Offset  Hunk  Offset  Hunk

__iomode                  000000C4  35
```

Listing 2-4 cont.

---

34. BSS.   Memory Type PUBLIC

  File: LIB:lc.lib
  Program Unit: iomode
  Base: 000000 Size: 000000

35. CODE.   Memory Type PUBLIC Total Size 000608.

  File: LIB:lc.lib
  Program Unit: IOS1
  Base: 000000 Size: 000608

Symbol	Offset	Hunk	Offset	Hunk	Offset	Hunk
_open	00000114	23	00000170	23	000001C6	23
_creat						
_read	00000096	38				
_write	00000200	38	000002BE	38		
_lseek	00000136	23				
_close	00000048	14	00000076	17	000002BC	23
_unlink						
_remove						
_rename						
_getch						
_getche						
_putch	00000036	17	00000050	17	0000005C	17
_ungetch						
_cgets						
_cputs						

36. DATA.   Memory Type PUBLIC Total Size 000010.

  File: LIB:lc.lib
  Program Unit: IOS1
  Base: 000000 Size: 000010

37. BSS.   Memory Type PUBLIC

  File: LIB:lc.lib
  Program Unit: IOS1
  Base: 000000 Size: 000000

38. CODE.   Memory Type PUBLIC Total Size 0003F0.

  File: LIB:lc.lib
  Program Unit: ios2
  Base: 000000 Size: 0003F0

Listing 2-4 cont.

Symbol	Offset	Hunk	Offset	Hunk	Offset	Hunk
__filbf	000000D8	2				
__flsbf	00000144	2	00000182	2	000001C0	2
	00000274	23	00000070	26	000000EA	26
	00000126	26	0000013C	26	0000004A	29
	00000088	29	000000DA	29		

39. DATA. Memory Type PUBLIC Total Size 000000.

File: LIB:lc.lib
Program Unit: ios2
Base: 000000 Size: 000000

40. BSS. Memory Type PUBLIC

File: LIB:lc.lib
Program Unit: ios2
Base: 000000 Size: 000000

41. CODE. Memory Type PUBLIC Total Size 00016C.

File: LIB:lc.lib
Program Unit: mem1
Base: 000000 Size: 00016C

Symbol	Offset	Hunk	Offset	Hunk	Offset	Hunk
_lsbrk	000000DE	44				
_sbrk						
_rbrk						
_MemCleanup	00000142	0				

42. DATA. Memory Type PUBLIC Total Size 000000.

File: LIB:lc.lib
Program Unit: mem1
Base: 000000 Size: 000000

43. BSS. Memory Type PUBLIC Total Size 00000C.

File: LIB:lc.lib
Program Unit: mem1
Base: 000000 Size: 00000C

44. CODE. Memory Type PUBLIC Total Size 000284.

File: LIB:lc.lib

Listing 2-4 cont.

```
Program Unit: mem2
Base: 000000   Size: 000284

Symbol                          Offset   Hunk   Offset   Hunk   Offset   Hunk

_sizmem
_getmem                         000003A8   38
_getml
_rlsmem                         0000029A   23
_rlsml
```

45. DATA.   Memory Type PUBLIC Total Size 000000.

```
File: LIB:lc.lib
Program Unit: mem2
Base: 000000   Size: 000000
```

46. BSS.   Memory Type PUBLIC

```
File: LIB:lc.lib
Program Unit: mem2
Base: 000000   Size: 000000
```

47. CODE.   Memory Type PUBLIC Total Size 000088.

```
File: LIB:lc.lib
Program Unit: strcat
Base: 000000   Size: 000088

Symbol                          Offset   Hunk   Offset   Hunk   Offset   Hunk

_strcat
_strncat                        00000162   76
```

48. DATA.   Memory Type PUBLIC Total Size 000000.

```
File: LIB:lc.lib
Program Unit: strcat
Base: 000000   Size: 000000
```

49. BSS.   Memory Type PUBLIC

```
File: LIB:lc.lib
Program Unit: strcat
```

50. CODE.   Memory Type PUBLIC Total Size 000024.

```
File: LIB:lc.lib
```

Listing 2-4 cont.

```
Program Unit: strlen
Base: 000000   Size: 000024
```

Symbol	Offset	Hunk	Offset	Hunk	Offset	Hunk
_strlen	000005E8	35	0000000A	47	00000044	47

51. DATA.   Memory Type PUBLIC Total Size 000000.

```
File: LIB:lc.lib
Program Unit: strlen
Base: 000000   Size: 000000
```

52. BSS.   Memory Type PUBLIC

```
File: LIB:lc.lib
Program Unit: strlen
Base: 000000   Size: 000000
```

53. CODE.   Memory Type PUBLIC Total Size 000000.

```
File: LIB:lc.lib
Program Unit: ufbs
Base: 000000   Size: 000000
```

54. DATA.   Memory Type PUBLIC Total Size 000004.

```
File: LIB:lc.lib
Program Unit: ufbs
Base: 000000   Size: 000004
```

Symbol	Offset	Hunk	Offset	Hunk	Offset	Hunk
__nufbs	0000003E	14	0000006C	17	0000001E	35
	00000072	35	0000009A	35	0000000A	56

55. BSS.   Memory Type PUBLIC Total Size 000078.

```
File: LIB:lc.lib
Program Unit: ufbs
Base: 000000   Size: 000078
```

Symbol	Offset	Hunk	Offset	Hunk	Offset	Hunk
__ufbs	00000208	23	00000030	35	0000005A	35
	00000084	35	000000BE	35	0000001E	56
	0000003A	56	00000180	76	00000186	76
	0000018E	76	00000194	76	0000019A	76
	000001D2	76	000001DE	76	000001F8	76

Listing 2-4 cont.

0000020E	76	0000021A	76	0000022A	76
00000236	76	0000023C	76	00000246	76

56. CODE.   Memory Type PUBLIC Total Size 000068.

File: LIB:lc.lib
Program Unit: \lc\library\amiga_exit
Base: 000000   Size: 000068

Symbol	Offset	Hunk	Offset	Hunk	Offset	Hunk
__exit	0000005E	14	0000008A	17		

57. DATA.   Memory Type PUBLIC Total Size 000000.

File: LIB:lc.lib
Program Unit: \lc\library\amiga_exit
Base: 000000   Size: 000000

58. BSS.   Memory Type PUBLIC

File: LIB:lc.lib
Program Unit: \lc\library\amiga_exit
Base: 000000   Size: 000000

59. CODE.   Memory Type PUBLIC Total Size 000000.

File: LIB:lc.lib
Program Unit: _iob
Base: 000000   Size: 000000

60. DATA.   Memory Type PUBLIC Total Size 000000.

File: LIB:lc.lib
Program Unit: _iob
Base: 000000   Size: 000000

61. BSS.   Memory Type PUBLIC Total Size 0001E0.

File: LIB:lc.lib
Program Unit: _iob
Base: 000000   Size: 0001E0

Symbol	Offset	Hunk	Offset	Hunk	Offset	Hunk
__iob	00000020	14	00000006	23	00000012	23
	00000030	23	0000001A	29	00000022	29
	0000002C	29	00000032	29	00000040	29

Listing 2-4 cont.

00000056	29	0000005E	29	00000068	29
0000006E	29	0000007E	29	00000092	76
00000118	76	00000120	76	00000126	76
0000012E	76	00000134	76	0000013A	76

62. CODE.   Memory Type PUBLIC Total Size 00087C.

File: LIB:lc.lib
Program Unit: _pfmt
Base: 000000 Size: 00087C

Symbol	Offset	Hunk	Offset	Hunk	Offset	Hunk
__pfmt	0000008A	26				

63. DATA.   Memory Type PUBLIC Total Size 000014.

File: LIB:lc.lib
Program Unit: _pfmt
Base: 000000 Size: 000014

64. BSS.   Memory Type PUBLIC

File: LIB:lc.lib
Program Unit: _pfmt
Base: 000000 Size: 000000

65. CODE.   Memory Type PUBLIC Total Size 000000.

File: LIB:lc.lib
Program Unit: _pool
Base: 000000 Size: 000000

66. DATA.   Memory Type PUBLIC Total Size 000010.

File: LIB:lc.lib
Program Unit: _pool
Base: 000000 Size: 000010

Symbol	Offset	Hunk	Offset	Hunk	Offset	Hunk
__pool	000000A2	41	000000AE	41		
__melt	0000009C	41	000000A8	41	00000006	44
	00000046	44	00000096	44	00000160	44
	00000166	44	000001EA	44	00000218	44

67. BSS.   Memory Type PUBLIC

Listing 2-4 cont.

```
File: LIB:lc.lib
Program Unit: _pool
Base: 000000   Size: 000000
```

68. CODE.   Memory Type PUBLIC Total Size 000044.

```
File: LIB:lc.lib
Program Unit: \lc\library\68000\cxd33
Base: 000000   Size: 000044
```

Symbol	Offset	Hunk	Offset	Hunk	Offset	Hunk
_CXD33	00000040	44	000000C6	44	0000014A	44
	000001E8	62	00000216	62	000007D4	62
	000007EE	62				

69. CODE.   Memory Type PUBLIC Total Size 000044.

```
File: LIB:lc.lib
Program Unit: \lc\library\68000\cxm33
Base: 000000   Size: 000044
```

Symbol	Offset	Hunk	Offset	Hunk	Offset	Hunk
_CXM33	00000018	14	00000200	23	00000028	35
	00000052	35	0000007C	35	000000B6	35
	000000D2	44	000000A2	62	000000F2	62

70. CODE.   Memory Type PUBLIC Total Size 000010.

```
File: LIB:lc.lib
Program Unit: cxferr
Base: 000000   Size: 000010
```

Symbol	Offset	Hunk	Offset	Hunk	Offset	Hunk
_CXFERR	000000AE	73	000000BE	73		

71. DATA.   Memory Type PUBLIC Total Size 000000.

```
File: LIB:lc.lib
Program Unit: cxferr
Base: 000000   Size: 000000
```

72. BSS.   Memory Type PUBLIC

```
File: LIB:lc.lib
Program Unit: cxferr
Base: 000000   Size: 000000
```

Listing 2-4 cont.

73. CODE.   Memory Type PUBLIC Total Size 0000D8.

File: LIB:lc.lib
Program Unit: \lc\library\68000\cxfxt5
Base: 000000   Size: 0000D8

Symbol	Offset	Hunk	Offset	Hunk	Offset	Hunk
_CXFXT5	00000016	74				
_CXFNM5	0000032C	74				

74. CODE.   Memory Type PUBLIC Total Size 000394.

File: LIB:lc.lib
Program Unit: \lc\library\68000\cxvfd
Base: 000000   Size: 000394

Symbol	Offset	Hunk	Offset	Hunk	Offset	Hunk
_CXVFD	000004F2	62				
_CXVDF						

75. CODE.   Memory Type PUBLIC Total Size 000018.

File: LIB:lc.lib
Program Unit: No Name
Base: 000000   Size: 000018

Symbol	Offset	Hunk	Offset	Hunk	Offset	Hunk
__xcovf	0000000E	2				

76. CODE.   Memory Type PUBLIC Total Size 00026C.

File: LIB:lc.lib
Program Unit: _main
Base: 000000   Size: 00026C

Symbol	Offset	Hunk	Offset	Hunk	Offset	Hunk
__main	000000D0	0	00000132	0		

77. DATA.   Memory Type PUBLIC Total Size 000050.

File: LIB:lc.lib
Program Unit: _main
Base: 000000   Size: 000050

Listing 2-4 cont.

---

78. BSS.   Memory Type PUBLIC Total Size 00008C.

   File: LIB:lc.lib
   Program Unit: _main
   Base: 000000 Size: 00008C

   Symbol   Offset   Hunk   Offset   Hunk   Offset   Hunk

   _argc
   _argv

79. CODE.   Memory Type PUBLIC Total Size 000058.

   File: LIB:lc.lib
   Program Unit: cxovf
   Base: 000000 Size: 000058

   Symbol   Offset   Hunk   Offset   Hunk   Offset   Hunk

   _cxovf   00000008   75

80. DATA.   Memory Type PUBLIC Total Size 00006C.

   File: LIB:lc.lib
   Program Unit: cxovf
   Base: 000000 Size: 00006C

   Symbol   Offset   Hunk   Offset   Hunk   Offset   Hunk

   _Text2
   _BodyText
   _ResponseText

81. BSS.   Memory Type PUBLIC Total Size 000004.

   File: LIB:lc.lib
   Program Unit: cxovf
   Base: 000000 Size: 000004

   Symbol   Offset   Hunk   Offset   Hunk   Offset   Hunk

   _IntuitionBase   00000006   86

82. CODE.   Memory Type PUBLIC Total Size 000000.
   Hunkname: _LVO

   File: LIB:amiga.lib
   Program Unit: No Name
   Base: 000000 Size: 000000

Listing 2-4 cont.

Symbol	Offset	Hunk	Offset	Hunk	Offset	Hunk
_LVOExecute						
_LVOIsInteractive						
_LVOParentDir						
_LVOWaitForChar						
_LVODelay						
_LVODateStamp						
_LVOSetProtection						
_LVOSetComment						
_LVODeviceProc						
_LVOQueuePacket						
_LVOGetPacket						
_LVOUnLoadSeg						
_LVOLoadSeg						
_LVOExit						
_LVOCreateProc						
_LVOIoErr						
_LVOCurrentDir	00000106	0				
_LVOCreateDir						
_LVOInfo						
_LVOExNext						
_LVOExamine						
_LVODupLock						
_LVOUnLock						
_LVOLock						
_LVORename						
_LVODeleteFile						
_LVOSeek						
_LVOOutput						
_LVOInput						
_LVOWrite						
_LVORead						
_LVOClose	00000158	0	00000164	0		
_LVOOpen	00000116	0				

```
File: LIB:amiga.lib
Program Unit: No Name
Base: 000000   Size: 000000
```

Symbol	Offset	Hunk	Offset	Hunk	Offset	Hunk
_LVOOpenLibrary	000001BE	0				
_LVOVacate						
_LVOProcure						
_LVOTypeOfMem						
_LVOGetCC						
_LVORawDoFmt						
_LVORawPutChar						
_LVORawMayGetChar						
_LVORawIOInit						
_LVOOpenResource						
_LVORemResource						

Listing 2-4 cont.

```
_LVOAddResource
_LVOAbortIO
_LVOWaitIO
_LVOCheckIO
_LVOSendIO
_LVODoIO
_LVOCloseDevice
_LVOOpenDevice
_LVORemDevice
_LVOAddDevice
_LVOSumLibrary
_LVOSetFunction
_LVOCloseLibrary
_LVOOldOpenLibrary
_LVORemLibrary
_LVOAddLibrary
_LVOFindPort
_LVOWaitPort            000001A8      0
_LVOReplyMsg            00000178      0
_LVOGetMsg              000001B0      0
_LVOPutMsg
_LVORemPort
_LVOAddPort
_LVOFreeTrap
_LVOAllocTrap
_LVOFreeSignal
_LVOAllocSignal
_LVOSignal
_LVOWait
_LVOSetExcept
_LVOSetSignal
_LVOSetTaskPri
_LVOFindTask            00000030      0
_LVORemTask
_LVOAddTask
_LVOFindName
_LVOEnqueue
_LVORemTail
_LVORemHead
_LVORemove
_LVOAddTail
_LVOAddHead
_LVOInsert
_LVOFreeEntry
_LVOAllocEntry
_LVOAvailMem
_LVOFreeMem
_LVOAllocAbs
_LVOAllocMem
_LVODeallocate
_LVOAllocate
_LVOCause
_LVORemIntServer
_LVOAddIntServer
```

Listing 2-4 cont.

```
_LVOSetIntVector
_LVOUserState
_LVOSuperState
_LVOSetSR
_LVOPermit
_LVOForbid                        0000016E    0
_LVOEnable
_LVODisable
_LVODebug
_LVOAlert                         00000198    0
_LVOInitResident
_LVOFindResident
_LVOMakeFunctions
_LVOMakeLibrary
_LVOInitStruct
_LVOInitCode
_LVOException
_LVODispatch
_LVOSwitch
_LVOReschedule
_LVOSchedule
_LVOExitIntr
_LVOSupervisor
```

```
83. CODE.   Memory Type PUBLIC Total Size 0000E4.
    Hunkname: dos_lib

    File: LIB:amiga.lib
    Program Unit: No Name
    Base: 000000  Size: 00001C
```

Symbol	Offset	Hunk	Offset	Hunk	Offset	Hunk
_Open	000001B6	35	00000470	35	00000178	76
	000001F0	76				

```
    File: LIB:amiga.lib
    Program Unit: No Name
    Base: 00001C  Size: 000014
```

Symbol	Offset	Hunk	Offset	Hunk	Offset	Hunk
_Close	000003D2	35	00000044	56		

```
    File: LIB:amiga.lib
    Program Unit: No Name
    Base: 000030  Size: 00001C
```

Symbol	Offset	Hunk	Offset	Hunk	Offset	Hunk
_Read	0000025E	35	000004CE	35	0000059E	35

```
    File: LIB:amiga.lib
```

Listing 2-4 cont.

```
Program Unit: No Name
Base: 00004C  Size: 00001C

Symbol                        Offset    Hunk   Offset    Hunk   Offset    Hunk

_Write                        000002E2   35    0000053C   35    000005FC   35

File: LIB:amiga.lib
Program Unit: No Name
Base: 000068  Size: 000010

Symbol                        Offset    Hunk   Offset    Hunk   Offset    Hunk

_Input                        000001CC   76

File: LIB:amiga.lib
Program Unit: No Name
Base: 000078  Size: 000010

Symbol                        Offset    Hunk   Offset    Hunk   Offset    Hunk

_Output                       000001D8   76

File: LIB:amiga.lib
Program Unit: No Name
Base: 000088  Size: 00001C

Symbol                        Offset    Hunk   Offset    Hunk   Offset    Hunk

_Seek                         0000035A   35    0000038A   35

File: LIB:amiga.lib
Program Unit: No Name
Base: 0000A4  Size: 000014

Symbol                        Offset    Hunk   Offset    Hunk   Offset    Hunk

_DeleteFile                   00000186   35    000003F0   35

File: LIB:amiga.lib
Program Unit: No Name
Base: 0000B8  Size: 00001C

Symbol                        Offset    Hunk   Offset    Hunk   Offset    Hunk

_Rename                       00000438   35

File: LIB:amiga.lib
Program Unit: No Name
Base: 0000D4  Size: 000010

Symbol                        Offset    Hunk   Offset    Hunk   Offset    Hunk

_IoErr                        000001CA   35    00000270   35    000002F4   35
```

Listing 2-4 cont.

00000368	35	000003FC	35	00000444	35

84. CODE.   Memory Type PUBLIC Total Size 000074.
Hunkname: exec_lib

File: LIB:amiga.lib
Program Unit: No Name
Base: 000000   Size: 000018

Symbol	Offset	Hunk	Offset	Hunk	Offset	Hunk
_AllocMem	00000014	41				

File: LIB:amiga.lib
Program Unit: No Name
Base: 000018   Size: 000018

Symbol	Offset	Hunk	Offset	Hunk	Offset	Hunk
_FreeMem	000000D6	41				

File: LIB:amiga.lib
Program Unit: No Name
Base: 000030   Size: 000014

Symbol	Offset	Hunk	Offset	Hunk	Offset	Hunk
_FindTask	0000005E	0	000001AA	76		

File: LIB:amiga.lib
Program Unit: No Name
Base: 000044   Size: 000018

Symbol	Offset	Hunk	Offset	Hunk	Offset	Hunk
_SetSignal	0000000E	17				

File: LIB:amiga.lib
Program Unit: No Name
Base: 00005C   Size: 000018

Symbol	Offset	Hunk	Offset	Hunk	Offset	Hunk
_OpenLibrary	0000000A	79				

85. DATA.   Memory Type PUBLIC Total Size 000000.

File: LIB:amiga.lib
Program Unit: No Name
Base: 000000   Size: 000000

Symbol	Offset	Hunk	Offset	Hunk	Offset	Hunk

Listing 2-4 cont.

```
_AbsExecBase              00000016   0   00000168   0
_cartridge
_bootrom
_romstart
_romend


86. CODE.   Memory Type PUBLIC Total Size 000034.
Hunkname: intuition_lib

File: LIB:amiga.lib
Program Unit: No Name
Base: 000000  Size: 000034


Symbol                    Offset  Hunk  Offset  Hunk  Offset  Hunk


_AutoRequest              00000042   79
```

ALINK is a simple and straightforward program. It scans its input files and library files in the order in which they appear on its command line. In most cases, this has little effect on the final outcome of the process; however, in a few cases this can have a major effect. Earlier we noted that if a symbol has multiple definitions, only the first definition is valid. Thus, if files are linked with different definitions for the same symbol, the later definitions will have no effect. This is a problem when dealing with libraries, since redefinitions here are not even tagged with a warning message.

The Amiga system software supplies two libraries which are both typically linked to all programs.

lc.lib is the most general library and contains the routines from the standard library, as well as more specialized functions.

amiga.lib contains code for the AmigaDOS functions.

It must be noted that some AmigaDOS functions have the same name as those in the standard library. If the usual practice of linking in *lc.lib* and then *amiga.lib* is followed, the standard library will mask the AmigaDOS functions. Whenever working directly with this latter operating system, it is necessary to link *amiga.lib* first or, as is more common, to make it the sole library linked.

A similar caution involves the input files. Here the system supplies two object modules that, in turn, supply start-up and initialization code.

LStartUp.obj is a general purpose start-up routine—used in most cases.

AStartUp.obj is used to access AmigaDOS.

One of these modules must be the first file in the list of input files. This is start-up code and must come at the beginning of the program. This file must be the first one read and transferred to the output. Following are some typical ALINK command lines.

```
Simple link:

    ALINK FROM LStartUp.obj+df1:demo.o TO df1:demo LIBRARY lib/lc.lib+
lib/amiga.lib

Full link:

    ALINK FROM LStartUp.obj+df1:demo.o TO df1:demo VER message LIBRARY
lib/lc.lib+lib/amiga.lib MAP df1:symbol.ref XREF df1:xref.ref

Link using a WITH file:

    ALINK FROM LStartUp.obj+df1:demo WITH df1:commands

Link for AmigaDOS:

    ALINK FROM AStartUp.obj+df1:demo.o TO df1:demo LIBRARY
lib/amiga.lib
```

Specialized Amiga Data Types

Access to the Amiga's system resource is supplied through software objects defined in terms of C syntax rules. The system also supplies a set of specialized data types to ease the programmer's plight and to enhance internal documentation. It must be emphasized that these are not really new types at all, but merely a renaming of data types standard to C. The new names help relate these types to the realities of the Amiga environment. For example, although type BOOL is really just a short integer, the word BOOL conveys that this value is a boolean, better than the more ordinary short designator. The advantage is really one of suggestion, but in a long and complex program, this can be quite valuable.

The creation of these new names is done with the *typedef* statement. The example type BOOL is created with the statement:

```
typedef  short  BOOL;
```

This is a form long familiar to C programmers. Of course, this has no effect on the data type *short*; it only alerts the system to the fact that there are now two distinct ways to declare a variable of this type.

The complete list of these special types can be found in Table 2-1. Among the more important and commonly used, we find:

LONG	long
ULONG	unsigned long
WORD	short

BYTE   char
UBYTE   unsigned char

Either form of these data types can be used in a program and the system will understand it. They may even be used interchangeably in the same file.

Table 2-1. Amiga data types

Amiga Types	Standard C Types
LONG	long
ULONG	unsigned long
LONGBITS	unsigned long
WORD	short
UWORD	unsigned short
WORDBITS	unsigned short
BYTE	char
UBYTE	unsigned char
BYTEBITS	unsigned char
STRPTR	*unsigned char
APTR	*unsigned char
SHORT	short
USHORT	unsigned short
FLOAT	float
DOUBLE	double
COUNT	short
UCOUNT	unsigned short
BOOL	short
TEXT	unsigned char

One final note involves the implementation-specific details of Lattice C on the Amiga. The C language defines its data types in terms of the basic unit of storage—the computer word—and not with any absolute value. This means that the size of specific types is implementation-dependent; therefore, it is always a good idea to ask about this dependency before writing for a particular machine. These relationships are detailed in Table 2-2.

Table 2-2. Data element sizes for Lattice C on the Amiga

Data Type	Bit Size	Range of Values
char	8	−128 to +127
unsigned char	8	0 to 255
short	16	−32768 to 32767
unsigned short	16	0 to 65535
int	32	−2,147,483,648 to 2,147,483,647
unsigned int	32	0 to 4,294,967,295
long	32	same as int
unsigned long	32	same as int
float	32	$\pm10E-37$ to $\pm10E38$
double	64	$\pm10E-307$ to $\pm10E308$

Summary

This chapter has discussed the Amiga programming environment. It has explored the way in which this system offers access to the hardware resources and software subsystems of the Amiga. It has also discussed some of the problems and benefits of a multiprocessing computer system.

The basic operation of the compiler and the linker has been covered. You have seen their basic operation and some of the important options that they offer. The system's debugging facilities have been touched upon, including:

The OMD (Object Module Disassembler)

The MAP option to ALINK

The XREF option

Examples have shown how these might help a programmer quickly diagnose and repair software problems.

Finally, this chapter has discussed the specialized data types defined with the Amiga's software system, and you have seen how they might be used to enhance the internal structure of a program.

Using Intuition   Chapter 3

I ntuition is the window-based interface most often used to access the Amiga. It serves as a standard interface within which input and output can be conveniently generated and controlled. The resources available include *screens*, *windows*, *menus*, and user-manipulable icons called *gadgets*. In this chapter, we will discuss methods for generating these objects and interfacing them to user created programs.

Intuition

The basic philosophy of Intuition is well indicated by its name. It is meant to be an interface that offers the full range of operating system services yet requires the minimum amount of off-line study to master. Every aspect of the computer is meant to be transparent and obvious to the user. The main access channel is the mouse, although it could be any similar device, such as a joystick. The main activity with this device is pointing. Access is reduced to as few actions as possible.

Intuition is a world of screens and windows. The *screen* is the main visual object, which sets certain key parameters such as font, color, and resolution. The *window* is the locus of most activity in Intuition. It handles input and output and contains the *gadgets*—specialized control objects. Both windows and screens can be freely moved around within limits set by the programmer.

The ease with which a user can manipulate the objects in Intuition, however, is not carried over to program writing. Of the three programming environments found on the Amiga—Intuition, AmigaDOS and the executive kernel—this is the most difficult one in which to develop software. It is a very complex system which requires even small, simple programs to handle many display details. However, Intuition is and is meant to be the primary user operating system, and most software will have to deal with it.

Intuition consists of a library of compiled code that contains executable copies of all of the functions that it offers as services. This library is different than the libraries commonly used by software developers to produce programs. These are typically disk files which contain the object code for useful functions. (The standard library always found with C is a good example.) Such libraries are used during the linking phase of a software translation to add the function code to the program as it is being translated into a binary object file. On the Amiga, in contrast, most of the machine specific libraries are not added to the programs that use them, but are loaded along with the program. If a function is needed, the program calls it in memory as an offset from the library's current address; this adds greater flexibility and efficiency. If two programs are both using Intuition, only a single copy need be loaded; neither program is bloated by extra code segments.

Because Intuition is a run-time library, it is necessary to load it before its functions can be accessed. A global variable is declared:

```
struct IntuitionBase *IntuitionBase
```

This variable will contain the address of the library after it is loaded into memory. Note that there is no option with this variable; it must be called IntuitionBase. The actual loading is done by a call to system open function:

```
IntuitionBase=(struct IntuitionBase *)
    OpenLibrary(intuition.library,INT_REV)
```

where

intuition.library is the name of the particular library that the function is opening.

INT__REV is the current revision number of the library.

OpenLibrary() returns the address of the loaded module or NULL if the load has failed. Since this function is used to open other libraries—the graphics one, for example—we must cast to the correct pointer type. This bit of code must be a part of any program that uses Intuition.

Windows and Screens

The *window* is the basic element in an Intuition display. It is not the most elementary—the screen underlies and contains all windows—but it is the one in which all of the action takes place.

A window, at its simplest, is a rectangular box that can be placed anywhere on the screen. This is the minimum window, not allowing for any output text or graphics. Of course you can do much more with a window. You draw pictures in it, send messages through it, and take input with it. It serves multitasking by allowing each running program to have a kind of virtual terminal of its own to work through. Thus, you can keep track of more than one process at a time, although only one window can be active for input at any given moment. Moreover, each process has sole control of its console device, so no special consideration need be given to coordinating the output of disparate programs. Because of their importance, the creation and manipulation of windows within Intuition is an optimized procedure.

A *screen* is a somewhat more limited structure. It is the background upon which windows are displayed and manipulated. Like the window, the screen shows a rectangular figure on the display. This does not mean that a screen definition is nothing more than a specification for a background display—a few colors and maybe a style of lettering. The screen contains the window not only in the sense of framing its display, but in the more profound sense of containing all of the structures and values that the window itself manipulates. It is both a tangible limit and a system work area for the windows.

There are two kinds of screens available under Intuition. The standard is the *Workbench Screen*; this is predefined and needs no specification or action on the part of an application to open or close. But Intuition also allows the option of creating a *customized screen* specialized to a particular program or set of programs. In the latter case, the screen must be specified; its values must be initialized; and it must be explicitly opened before any windows can make use of its capabilities. The Workbench Screen is the one you are already familiar with: it covers the entire display area and contains the familiar capabilities. A customized screen can be any size, within the limits set by Intuition, and can contain either a subset or superset of the features found in the Workbench Screen. The chief advantage of the Workbench Screen is that it offers a standard interface to the user—one that is the same over a variety of applications. Also, it runs in concert with the Workbench application and has available to it specialized characteristics, such as icons, which may not be easy to import to a customized screen. Figure 3-1 shows a typical Workbench Screen; Figure 3-2, a customized one.

A screen allocation not only creates the display that you see, but also sets aside a workspace within memory where you can define your windows. Each window requires not only a set of data objects to manage its changing values; but also space to perform its calculations and an area to draw any necessary graphics. In addition to this, the screen sets certain parameters that are inherited by its windows. For example, the screen sets the color registers and the default type font.

Even though a screen is a basic element in an Intuition display, there is not a single basic screen underlying all others. There can be as many screens running as is desired and can be supported by the memory resouces of the system. Each screen is a world unto itself, as there can be no direct communication between them or between their windows. Windows cannot be moved outside of their designated screens. Screens may overlay one another either wholly or partially.

In this chapter you will first explore the definition and manipulation of windows and screens. You will discover not only how to make them appear, but also how to manipulate their interrelationship to produce displays and applications.

Figure 3-1. Workbench Screen

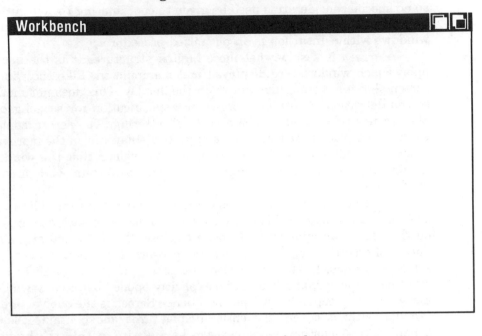

Figure 3-2. User-customized screen

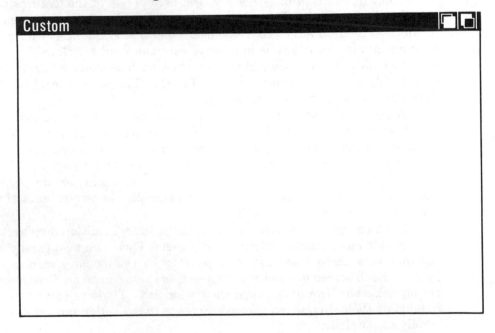

Defining a Window

Let us begin by defining some simple windows in the Workbench Screen. A great deal of programming is done within this environment, and it will allow you to focus on window-specific topics and put aside, for the moment, some of the complications generated by customized screens. Additionally, it will provide some interesting objects that you can then reimplement in custom screens, to explore these complications more fully.

Two objects are necessary to create a window. These objects are specified by a C structure. The *New Window* structure is used to specify the parameters of a window and pass those values to the Intuition function, *OpenWindow( )*, which creates the window. This function creates the second structure associated with an open window, the *window* structure; this, in turn, is used to manipulate the window.

NewWindow is a temporary structure that is only needed until the window is up and running. Its memory can then be deallocated or reused to open another window. NewWindow is a C structure with the following form:

```
struct NewWindow {
      SHORT LeftEdge,TopEdge,
            Width,Height;
      UBYTE DetailPen,BlockPen;
      USHORT IDCMPFlags;
      ULONG Flags;
      struct Gadget *FirstGadget;
      struct Image *CheckMark;
      UBYTE *Title;
      struct Screen *Screen;
      struct BitMap *BitMap;
      SHORT MinWidth,MinHeight,
            MaxWidth,MaxHeight;
      USHORT Type;
};
```

Each one of these fields controls one or more aspects of the window, but we will initially restrict ourselves to the minimal subset necessary to display a window.

LeftEdge and **TopEdge** define the coordinates of the upper left hand corner of the window, setting its initial position.

Width and **Height** set the size of the displayed window.

DetailPen and **BlockPen** contain references to the colors used to draw around and within the window;

Flags contains a series of values that set various capabilties and activities.

Text is the title of the window.

Type refers to the screen in which the window will be embedded.

For now, we will set the other fields to NULL or 0 and ignore them. The values assigned to these fields are partially dependent on the characteristics of the screen and partially on your own desire.

The initial position of the window is set in relation to the upper left-hand corner of the enclosing screen. This is always position 0,0. The units of these measurements are *pixels* or picture elements, but the size of these pixels is dependent on the resolution of the display—a screen parameter. Since initially we will be using the Workbench Screen, the resolution will be 640 horizontally by 200 vertically. Later on, when you experiment with custom screens, resolution is one of the parameters you can vary. Positioning of the window is in relation to its upper left-hand corner; so you can easily calculate where on the screen to position it, once you also decide on its *Width* and *Height*. These are also set in terms of pixels and may vary with the resolution of the underlying screen.

The other fields are straightforward. The *Title* is a character string that contains the contents of the title bar, which will appear at the top of the window. The screen type is Workbench, so the *Type* field will be set to WBENCHSCREEN. Both *DetailPen* and *BlockPen* are set to color register numbers. These are the colors that will be used to draw the window. *DetailPen* sets the color that will be used to draw the borders and the details of the window, while *BlockPen* indicates the color that will be used for the block in the window. If these fields are initialized to −1, the screen defaults will be used. The *Flags* field is one of the most important in the structure. We will use the ACTIVATE flag, which will cause the window to become active as soon as it is opened. This means that it will be the one waiting to receive input.

Listing 3-1 shows a program that will open a simple window in the Workbench Screen. You will see right away how strange this minimal display looks next to the application screens that you are used to seeing in Amiga applications. Nearly everything about the window is controlled by a variable; this is to give maximum flexibility to the programmer. Gradually we will increase the complexity of our sample windows, by filling in these other fields. By the time we discuss graphics in Chapter 5, we will have explored the full power of Intuition's window system. In this example, we declare a variable window as a pointer to a window structure. We open the Intuition library, then the window, and finally close it. The interesting action takes place in the function *make_window( )*; here all of the interesting initialization and work is done. We declare a variable *NewWindow* of type struct *NewWindow* in the function; this is an automatic variable that will disappear when the function returns to *main( )*. This will be no problem, because these values are only needed for a call to *OpenWindow( )*; once this is done, the structure can be discarded. We set the members of *NewWindow* to the values that we want for our window. In this case, it will be 300 pixels wide by 100 high and will be positioned at location 20,20 in the underlying screen. We also set the title and the colors. Many of the fields are set at defaults or common values. These will be explained later in the chapter.

**Listing 3-1. The creation of a simple window in the
Workbench Screen.**

```
*/

#include "exec/types.h"
#include "intuition/intuition.h"
```

Listing 3-1 cont.

```
struct IntuitionBase *IntuitionBase;
struct Window *Window;

#define INTUITION_REV 29


main()
{
 LONG i;

 OpenAll();

 /*    ======Open a new window=====   */

  make_window();

 /*    ======Delay for a bit to show off the window====== */

  for(i=0;i<1000000;i++)
    ;
  CloseWindow(Window);
}

OpenAll()
/*This function will open the necessary libraries */
{

  IntuitionBase=(struct IntuitionBase *)
            OpenLibrary("intuition.library",INTUITION_REV);

 if(IntuitionBase==NULL)
    exit(FALSE);
 }

make_window()
/* This function will initialize the NewWindow structure
   and open the window   */
{
  struct NewWindow NewWindow;

  NewWindow.LeftEdge=20;
  NewWindow.TopEdge=20;
  NewWindow.Width=300;
  NewWindow.Height=100;
  NewWindow.DetailPen=0;
  NewWindow.BlockPen=1;
  NewWindow.Title="A Simple Window";
  NewWindow.Flags=SMART_REFRESH|ACTIVATE|BORDERLESS;
  NewWindow.IDCMPFlags=NULL;
  NewWindow.Type=WBENCHSCREEN;
  NewWindow.FirstGadget=NULL;
  NewWindow.CheckMark=NULL;
  NewWindow.Screen=NULL;
  NewWindow.BitMap=NULL;
```

Listing 3-1 cont.

```
NewWindow.MinWidth=0;
NewWindow.MinHeight=0;
NewWindow.MaxWidth=0;
NewWindow.MaxHeight=0;

Window=(struct Window *) OpenWindow(&NewWindow);

if(Window==NULL)
  exit(FALSE);
```

The call to *OpenWindow()* is the heart of this function. Note that this system routine takes a pointer to the NewWindow structure as a parameter. It returns the address of the window structure that will be associated with this open window; it allocates the memory for this structure; and it initializes the values. If *OpenWindow()* fails, it returns a value of NULL. The program will exit in such a case.

Once the window has been successfully opened, *make_window()* returns control to *main()*. Here we set up a delay loop so that we may view our handiwork, and then we close the window. This closure is accomplished by a call to:

```
CloseWindow(Window)
```

Here *Window* is also a pointer to a currently open window. It is always important on a multiprocessing system such as the Amiga to be careful about relinquishing resources when finished with them. Failure to do this can lead to deadlock situations, where program execution comes to a halt, because memory or some necessary device is not available.

Certain key operations in this example should be noted; they will be true of all subsequent window examples. The basic steps necessary to open a window are:

- Declare a variable to represent the window. This must be a global variable of type struct *Window*.
- Declare and initialize a NewWindow structure.
- Call *OpenWindow* with the NewWindow structure as a parameter.
- Remember to close the window when it is no longer needed.

The complexity of the process is really a function of the fields set in NewWindow. For this example, we set up the minimum window. All of the fields were set with literal values. In a realistic program, some of these fields would be set with variable values.

In the examples in this book, we will be exploring a certain way of approaching particular kinds of programming problems. Intuition, in fact, poses several difficulties in relation to the kind of stylistic program designs that many programmers are used to, from more orthodox academic or technical writing. The notion of windows and screens and their interaction with an operating system that is more complex than average, requires a unique technique. Intuition is extremely complex; it requires many variables and data structures even to perform the simplest of tasks. The programmer must evolve a way to deal with that complexity, or risk writing programs that are unmaintainable and undecipherable. What we have attempted to do in these examples is to depend heavily on defining C functions for the simple, basic operations and then to build the more complex operations out of these modular building blocks. Thus, our *make__window()* function hides the New-Window structure from the main part of the program. If we were to eschew this technique and do everything in the main function—or any other function, for that matter—we would soon find ourselves with huge and completely unmanageable functions.

For the moment, ignore those fields in the NewWindow structure that have been set to the ubiquitous NULL, concentrating on those fields to which an explicit value has been given. The most important of these are: *LeftEdge*, *TopEdge*, *Width*, and *Height*. The first two locate the window on the display area. *TopEdge* specifies the window's vertical offset from the top and *LeftEdge* specifies its horizontal distance from the left-hand side. These two dictate where the window will initially appear when it comes into existence. Although the full discussion of them will come later in the chapter, these values are measured relative to the screen that encloses them. Most of the time, this means from the top and sides of the display, but it is possible to define a screen that does not cover the entire area. The *Width* and *Height* indicate what size box appears.

DetailPen and *BlockPen* tell the machine which colors to apply in displaying the window. Depending on the resolution of the display—also a parameter that can be set through software—there are sixteen or thirty-two different colors available. *DetailPen* picks the color used to produce the figures and border lines in the window, while *BlockPen* addresses the area fills. In the simple example given earlier, we specified the same choices as the screen uses.

The *Title* field requires a character string. This string will appear in the title bar at the top of the window. In the example, we put a literal string in this place. In general, a variable would go here.

The *Type* field is used to indicate the kind of screen that will enclose the window. Currently, there are only two values possible for this field: WBENCHSCREEN and CUSTOMSCREEN. The former is used when using the standard Workbench Screen. The latter value is used to create an enclosing screen to custom specifications.

Most of the values talked about so far are intuitive. Things such as the title, size, and position of a window are all sensible parameters. The *Flags* field is a little different. This field is used to specify a miscellany of important values that will shape the display of the window. In the example, there are two such values: SMART__REFRESH and BORDERLESS. SMART__RE-FRESH specifies an activity that will make more sense to you after you learn about *system gadgets* (procedures that allow the user to interactively manipulate the window and screen). This value indicates to Intuition that it must take responsibility for redrawing the window if it is moved or otherwise altered. The BORDERLESS flag indicates a display option for the window. By default, windows are drawn as a rectangle with a bar at the top and an outline drawn around the perimeter. This flag turns off that outline, although it still leaves the bar to display the title. The complete list of flag values are shown below.

ACTIVATE	Window will become active as soon as it is opened.
ACTIVEWINDOW	Enables the reporting mechanism that alerts program when its window is active.
BACKDROP	Creates a window that remains behind all other windows.
BORDERLESS	Specifies no borders when drawing the window.
INACTIVEWINDOW	Enables reporting on the Inactive condition.
NOCAREREFRESH	Indicates that the window need not be refreshed after a change.
REPORTMOUSE	Enables the mechanism to report on mouse movements.
SIMPLE_REFRESH	Indicates that window redraw is the responsibility of the application.
SMART_REFRESH	Indicates that window redraw and reformat is done automatically.
SUPER_BITMAP	Specifies that window will have a user maintained bit map.

Before continuing let's review what we have covered about creating a simple window. A window must have the following information specified:

- Its location within the screen or display
- Its display parameters: size and colors
- The kind of screen in which it is to be displayed
- Special instructions to the display system, such as the fact that the window is to be borderless

These values are common to all windows. Listing 3-2 shows another window definition similar to the initial example. This program also sets just minimal values needed to bring a window to visibility.

Listing 3-2. The creation of overlapping windows in the Workbench Screen.

```
*/

#include "exec/types.h"
#include "intuition/intuition.h"

struct IntuitionBase *IntuitionBase;
struct Window *Wind0,*Wind1,*Wind2;

#define INTUITION_REV 29


main()
{
 SHORT x,y;
 UBYTE name[20];
 VOID delay_func();
 /*    ======Open Intuition======= */

 IntuitionBase=(struct IntuitionBase *)
          OpenLibrary("intuition.library",INTUITION_REV);

 if(IntuitionBase==NULL)
    exit(FALSE);

 /*    ======Open some windows===== */

 strcpy(name,"Window 0");
 x=y=20;
 Wind0=(struct Window *)make_window(x,y,name);

 strcpy(name,"Window 1");
 x=y=40;
 Wind1=(struct Window *)make_window(x,y,name);

 strcpy(name,"Window 2");
 x=y=60;
 Wind2=(struct Window *)make_window(x,y,name);

 /*    ======Delay for a bit to show off the Windows====== */

 delay_func(1);

 /* =========Close down the windows in order========*/

 CloseWindow(Wind2);

 delay_func(1);

 CloseWindow(Wind1);

 delay_func(1);

 CloseWindow(Wind0);
```

Listing 3-2 cont.

```
}


make_window(x,y,name)
SHORT x,y;
UBYTE *name;
/* This function will initialize the NewWindow structure
   and open the window  */
{
  struct NewWindow NewWindow;

  NewWindow.LeftEdge=x;
  NewWindow.TopEdge=y;
  NewWindow.Width=300;
  NewWindow.Height=100;
  NewWindow.DetailPen=-1;
  NewWindow.BlockPen=-1;
  NewWindow.Title=name;
  NewWindow.Flags=ACTIVATE;
  NewWindow.IDCMPFlags=NULL;
  NewWindow.Type=WBENCHSCREEN;
  NewWindow.FirstGadget=NULL;
  NewWindow.CheckMark=NULL;
  NewWindow.Screen=NULL;
  NewWindow.BitMap=NULL;
  NewWindow.MinWidth=0;
  NewWindow.MinHeight=0;
  NewWindow.MaxWidth=0;
  NewWindow.MaxHeight=0;


  return(OpenWindow(&NewWindow));

}

VOID delay_func(factor)
int factor;
/* This function will cause a specified delay */
{
 int loop;

 for(loop=0;loop<factor*1000000;loop++)
    ;

 return;
}
```

Two new things should be noted about Listing 3-2. Most importantly, it opens more than a single window. In fact, it opens three: Wind0, Wind1, and Wind2. Each one of these must be represented by a window structure, and each one must be created by a separate call to *OpenWindow()*. They can, of course, share the same NewWindow structure, since it is only used during the setup process. Creating multiple windows like this is a common occurrence. Note how Intuition automatically takes care of the display problems involved with overlapping windows. Also in this example, there are two new values used in the NewWindow structure. *DetailPen* and *BlockPen* are set to −1. This value indicates to Intuition that the screen default values are also to be used for the window. We've used the Flag value ACTIVATE to insure that the window will become active as soon as it is opened. The lack of a BORDERLESS value for this field results in the appearance of the windows neatly delineated by a clean, white border.

Listing 3-3 shows one of the uses of a borderless window: it can serve as a backdrop for the activity of other windows. In this program, we first open a window specifying the BORDERLESS flag and covering the entire display area—640 by 200. Once this underlying window is in place, we open three ordinary windows that appear in front of it. This is a useful technique for creating a clean and pleasant display. It will be used to good effect during graphics programming in Chapter 5.

Listing 3-3. Creation of overlapping windows in the Workbench Screen with a borderless window in the background.

```
*/

#include "exec/types.h"
#include "intuition/intuition.h"

struct IntuitionBase *IntuitionBase;
struct Window *Wind0,*Wind1,*Wind2,*NoBorder;

#define INTUITION_REV 29


main()
{
 ULONG flags;
 SHORT x,y,w,h;
 UBYTE name[60];
 VOID delay_func();
 /*   ======Open Intuition======= */

 IntuitionBase=(struct IntuitionBase *)
          OpenLibrary("intuition.library",INTUITION_REV);

 if(IntuitionBase==NULL)
   exit(FALSE);

   /*  ======Open a borderless window======*/

 x=y=0;
 w=640;
 h=200;
 flags=ACTIVATE|BORDERLESS;
```

Listing 3-3 cont.

```
  NoBorder=(struct Window *)make_window(x,y,w,h,NULL,flags);


/*   ======Open some plain windows=====  */

strcpy(name,"Window 0");
x=y=20;
w=300;
h=100;
flags=ACTIVATE;
Wind0=(struct Window *)make_window(x,y,w,h,name,flags);

strcpy(name,"Window 1");
x=y=40;
Wind1=(struct Window *)make_window(x,y,w,h,name,flags);

strcpy(name,"Window 2");
x=y=60;
Wind2=(struct Window *)make_window(x,y,w,h,name,flags);
```

```
/*   ======Delay for a bit to show off the windows====== */

delay_func(100);

/* =========Close down the windows in order=======*/

CloseWindow(Wind2);

delay_func(10);

CloseWindow(Wind1);

delay_func(10);

CloseWindow(Wind0);

delay_func(10);

CloseWindow(NoBorder);
}


make_window(x,y,w,h,name,flags)
SHORT x,y,w,h;
UBYTE *name;
ULONG flags;
/* This function will initialize the NewWindow structure
   and open the window  */
{
  struct NewWindow NewWindow;

  NewWindow.LeftEdge=x;
  NewWindow.TopEdge=y;
  NewWindow.Width=w;
```

Listing 3-3 cont.

```
    NewWindow.Height=h;
    NewWindow.DetailPen=-1;
    NewWindow.BlockPen=-1;
    NewWindow.Title=name;
    NewWindow.Flags=flags;
    NewWindow.IDCMPFlags=NULL;
    NewWindow.Type=WBENCHSCREEN;
    NewWindow.FirstGadget=NULL;
    NewWindow.CheckMark=NULL;
    NewWindow.Screen=NULL;
    NewWindow.BitMap=NULL;
    NewWindow.MinWidth=0;
    NewWindow.MinHeight=0;
    NewWindow.MaxWidth=0;
    NewWindow.MaxHeight=0;


    return(OpenWindow(&NewWindow));

}

VOID delay_func(factor)
int factor;
/* This function will cause a specified delay */
{
 int loop;

 for(loop=0; loop<factor*1000; loop++)
    ;

 return;
}
```

Listing 3-4 shows a variation of the previous examples. The situation is the same, but each window in the foreground of the display is a different color. This is accomplished by specifying a different color register for the two color members in the NewWindow structure: *DetailPen* and *BlockPen*. The number of colors available is a function of the screen. In the case of the Workbench Screen, there are four.

Listing 3-4. Creation of overlapping windows in the Workbench Screen, with a borderless window in the background. In this program, we specify different colors for the small windows.

```
*/

#include "exec/types.h"
#include "intuition/intuition.h"

struct IntuitionBase *IntuitionBase;
```

Listing 3-4 cont.

```
struct Window *Wind0,*Wind1,*Wind2,*NoBorder;

#define INTUITION_REV 29


main()
{
 ULONG flags;
 SHORT x,y,w,h;
 UBYTE *name,c0,c1;
 VOID delay_func();

 /*   ======Open Intuition======= */

 IntuitionBase=(struct IntuitionBase *)
         OpenLibrary("intuition.library",INTUITION_REV);

 if(IntuitionBase==NULL)
    exit(FALSE);

  /*   ======Open a borderless window======*/

  x=y=0;
  w=640;
  h=200;
  c0=c1=-0x01;
  flags=ACTIVATE|BORDERLESS;
  NoBorder=(struct Window *)
     make_window(x,y,w,h,NULL,flags,c0,c1);

 /*   ======Open some plain windows=====   */

  name="Window 0";
  x=y=20;
  w=300;
  h=100;
  flags=ACTIVATE;
  c0=0x10;
  c1=0x15;

  Wind0=(struct Window *)make_window(x,y,w,h,name,flags,c0,c1);

  name="Window 1";
  x=y=40;
  c0=0x17;
  c1=0x19;

  Wind1=(struct Window *)make_window(x,y,w,h,name,flags,c0,c1);

  name="Window 2";
  x=y=60;
  c0=0x00;
  c1=0x1a;
```

Listing 3-4 cont.

```
    Wind2=(struct Window *)make_window(x,y,w,h,name,flags,c0,c1);

    /*   ======Delay for a bit to show off the windows====== */

    delay_func(100);

    /* =========Close down the windows in order========*/

    CloseWindow(Wind2);

    delay_func(10);

    CloseWindow(Wind1);

    delay_func(10);

    CloseWindow(Wind0);

    delay_func(10);

    CloseWindow(NoBorder);
}


make_window(x,y,w,h,name,flags,color0,color1)
SHORT x,y,w,h;
UBYTE *name,color0,color1;
ULONG flags;
/* This function will initialize the NewWindow structure
   and open the window  */
{
    struct NewWindow NewWindow;

    NewWindow.LeftEdge=x;
    NewWindow.TopEdge=y;
    NewWindow.Width=w;
    NewWindow.Height=h;
    NewWindow.DetailPen=color0;
    NewWindow.BlockPen=color1;
    NewWindow.Title=name;
    NewWindow.Flags=flags;
    NewWindow.IDCMPFlags=NULL;
    NewWindow.Type=WBENCHSCREEN;
    NewWindow.FirstGadget=NULL;
    NewWindow.CheckMark=NULL;
    NewWindow.Screen=NULL;
    NewWindow.BitMap=NULL;
    NewWindow.MinWidth=0;
    NewWindow.MinHeight=0;
    NewWindow.MaxWidth=0;
    NewWindow.MaxHeight=0;


    return(OpenWindow(&NewWindow));
```

Listing 3-4 cont.

```
}

VOID delay_func(factor)
int factor;
/* This function will cause a specified delay */
{
  int loop;

  for(loop=0;loop<factor*1000;loop++)
    ;

  return;
}
```

So far, all we have done with windows is to display them. But windows are the true workhorses of Intuition. Windows can move, change in size, show graphics displays and text, and can take input. But before we go on to explore these topics, we must turn our attention to the object that encloses windows—the screen.

Customizing Screens

Although windows are more versatile than screens and easier to control, there is a great deal of power and flexibility packed into the screen definitions. Customized screens combined with windows allow the programmer to create any user interface that may be desired.

A screen is defined in a way analogous to the window. There is a *New-Screen* structure that allows the specification of screen parameters. This takes the form:

```
struct NewScreen {
     SHORT LeftEdge,TopEdge,
          Height,Depth;
     UBYTE DetailPen,BlockPen;
     USHORT ViewModes,
          Type:
     struct TextAttr *Font;
     UBYTE *DefaultTitle;
     struct Gadgets *Gadgets;
     struct BitMap *CustomBitMap;
};
```

These fields are filled out with appropriate or desired values, and a pointer to the structure is passed to the Intuition function *OpenScreen()*. This, in turn, returns the address of a screen structure which can be used in subsequent interactions. A call to *CloseScreen()* removes it from the display.

Listing 3-5 illustrates the display of a simple window within a customized screen. The NewScreen structure is smaller than NewWindow, and almost all of its fields are critical and need to be initialized. Only *Font, Gadgets*, and *CustomBitMap* are optional and set to NULL. The creation of this new screen has been exported to a function, *make_screen()*. As with NewWindow, NewScreen need exist only long enough to serve as a parameter for *OpenScreen()*. This function will return a pointer to a screen structure associated with the now open and resident screen. If the call fails, NULL will be returned and the example program will exit. The function *make_screen()* returns this pointer value. Note that we must cast this value to a pointer to type struct *Screen* back in *main()*.

Listing 3-5. Creation of a window in a custom screen.

```
*/

#include "exec/types.h"
#include "intuition/intuition.h"

struct IntuitionBase *IntuitionBase;
struct Window *Window;
struct Screen *Screen;

#define INTUITION_REV 29


main()
{
 ULONG flags;
 SHORT x,y,w,h,d;
 USHORT mode;
 UBYTE *name,c0,c1;
 VOID delay_func();

 /*     ======Open Intuition======= */

 IntuitionBase=(struct IntuitionBase *)
          OpenLibrary("intuition.library",INTUITION_REV);

 if(IntuitionBase==NULL)
    exit(FALSE);
 /*  ======Open a custom screen==== */

 name="Screen";
 y=0;
 w=320;
 h=200;
 d=5;
 c0=0x00;
 c1=0x01;
 mode=NULL;

 Screen=(struct Screen *)
        make_screen(y,w,h,d,c0,c1,mode,name);
```

Listing 3-5 cont.

```
/*    ======Open windows=====  */

  name="Window";
  x=y=20;
  w=100;
  h=100;
  flags=ACTIVATE;
  c0=-0x01;
  c1=-0x01;

  Window=(struct Window *)
          make_window(x,y,w,h,name,flags,c0,c1,Screen);

/*    ======Delay for a bit to show off the windows====== */

  delay_func(100);

/* =========Close down the window then the screen=======*/

  CloseWindow(Window);


  delay_func(10);

  CloseScreen(Screen);

}


make_window(x,y,w,h,name,flags,color0,color1,screen)
SHORT x,y,w,h;
UBYTE *name,color0,color1;
ULONG flags;
struct Screen *screen;
/* This function will initialize the NewWindow structure
   and open the window  */
{
  struct NewWindow NewWindow;

  NewWindow.LeftEdge=x;
  NewWindow.TopEdge=y;
  NewWindow.Width=w;
  NewWindow.Height=h;
  NewWindow.DetailPen=color0;
  NewWindow.BlockPen=color1;
  NewWindow.Title=name;
  NewWindow.Flags=flags;
  NewWindow.IDCMPFlags=NULL;
  NewWindow.Type=CUSTOMSCREEN;
  NewWindow.FirstGadget=NULL;
  NewWindow.CheckMark=NULL;
  NewWindow.Screen=screen;
  NewWindow.BitMap=NULL;
```

Listing 3-5 cont.

```
   NewWindow.MinWidth=0;
   NewWindow.MinHeight=0;
   NewWindow.MaxWidth=0;
   NewWindow.MaxHeight=0;


   return(OpenWindow(&NewWindow));

}

make_screen(y,w,h,d,color0,color1,mode,name)
SHORT y,w,h,d;
UBYTE color0,color1,*name;
USHORT mode;
{
 struct NewScreen NewScreen;

 NewScreen.LeftEdge=0;
 NewScreen.TopEdge=y;
 NewScreen.Width=w;
 NewScreen.Height=h;
 NewScreen.Depth=d;
 NewScreen.DetailPen=color0;
 NewScreen.BlockPen=color1;
 NewScreen.ViewModes=mode;
 NewScreen.Type=CUSTOMSCREEN;
 NewScreen.Font=NULL;
 NewScreen.DefaultTitle=name;
 NewScreen.Gadgets=NULL;
 NewScreen.CustomBitMap=NULL;

 return(OpenScreen(&NewScreen));
}

VOID delay_func(factor)
int factor;
/* This function will cause a specified delay */
{
 int loop;

 for(loop=0;loop<factor*1000;loop++)
    ;

 return;
}
```

LeftEdge and *TopEdge* are meant to set the position of the screen. Under the current implementation of Intuition, however, only *TopEdge* has any meaning. *LeftEdge* is always set to 0. A screen must take up the full width of the display area. The height can be set. The screen can be smaller than the display area. *TopEdge* indicates upon which of the 200 possible lines the top of the screen will start. There is a further qualification: if the screen is less than the full height of the display, it must occupy the lower half. A small screen always goes from its top to the last possible line on the video screen. *TopEdge* must be coordinated with the *Height* field. If the screen is specified as less than 200 lines high, then *TopEdge* cannot start at the 0,0 point. The example specifies a screen that covers the full display.

Even though a screen must be as wide as the display, the *Width* field has a use: it must be set to the number of pixels across the screen. In high-resolution mode, *Width* is set to 640, while low-resolution is only 320. This field is used in conjunction with the *ViewModes* field. *ViewModes* specifies the format of the screen display. For the most part, its values deal with display resolution.

HIRES   indicates a high-resolution screen (640 x 200).

INTERLACE   indicates 400 line interlace mode.

SPRITES   allows the use of these objects in the window.

HAM   indicates hold-and-modify mode.

In the example, we are defining a low-resolution screen and have set the fields accordingly.

The *Depth* field indicates the number of colors that will be available to the screen and its objects. Its value is the number of bit planes allocated for the screen. One bit plane will give only two colors; three bit planes will give eight colors. Up to five bit planes can be specified. A complete discussion of bit planes will be deferred until Chapter 5. Each pixel has a value in each plane, and these are combined to give a color register address. The color of an individual pixel is indirectly addressed by this mechanism. *DetailPen* and *BlockPen* contain the specific color registers to be used for these functions. *Type* must be set to CUSTOMSCREEN. *DefaultTitle* points to a character string that contains the name that will appear in the screen's title bar.

One reason why screen definitions are so important is that the objects contained within screens inherit these characteristics. For example, the window created by the example is low-resolution, just as the screen is, and uses the same default colors. This consistency is absolute. There is no way a high-resolution window can be defined in a low-resolution screen.

Listing 3-6. Creation of a window in a custom screen. This time, we have altered the default colors.

```
*/

#include "exec/types.h"
#include "intuition/intuition.h"

struct IntuitionBase *IntuitionBase;
struct Window *Window;
struct Screen *Screen;

#define INTUITION_REV 29
```

Listing 3-6 cont.

```
main()
{
 ULONG flags;
 SHORT x,y,w,h,d;
 USHORT mode;
 UBYTE *name,c0,c1;
 VOID delay_func();

 /*    ======Open Intuition====== */

 IntuitionBase=(struct IntuitionBase *)
          OpenLibrary("intuition.library",INTUITION_REV);

 if(IntuitionBase==NULL)
    exit(FALSE);
 /*   ======Open a custom screen==== */

  name="Screen";
  y=0;
  w=320;
  h=200;
  d=5;
  c0=0x10;
  c1=0x11;
  mode=NULL;

  Screen=(struct Screen *)
         make_screen(y,w,h,d,c0,c1,mode,name);

 /*   ======Open windows=====  */

  name="Window";
  x=y=20;
  w=100;
  h=100;
  flags=ACTIVE;
  c0=-0x01;
  c1=-0x01;

  Window=(struct Window *)
         make_window(x,y,w,h,name,flags,c0,c1,Screen);

 /*   ======Delay for a bit to show off the windows====== */

  delay_func(100);

 /* ========Close down the window then the screen=======*/

  CloseWindow(Window);


  delay_func(10);
```

Listing 3-6 cont.

```
   CloseScreen(Screen);

}


make_window(x,y,w,h,name,flags,color0,color1,screen)
SHORT x,y,w,h;
UBYTE *name,color0,color1;
ULONG flags;
struct Screen *screen;
/* This function will initialize the NewWindow structure
   and open the window  */
{
  struct NewWindow NewWindow;

  NewWindow.LeftEdge=x;
  NewWindow.TopEdge=y;
  NewWindow.Width=w;
  NewWindow.Height=h;
  NewWindow.DetailPen=color0;
  NewWindow.BlockPen=color1;
  NewWindow.Title=name;
  NewWindow.Flags=flags;
  NewWindow.IDCMPFlags=NULL;
  NewWindow.Type=CUSTOMSCREEN;
  NewWindow.FirstGadget=NULL;
  NewWindow.CheckMark=NULL;
  NewWindow.Screen=screen;
  NewWindow.BitMap=NULL;
  NewWindow.MinWidth=0;
  NewWindow.MinHeight=0;
  NewWindow.MaxWidth=0;
  NewWindow.MaxHeight=0;


  return(OpenWindow(&NewWindow));

}

make_screen(y,w,h,d,color0,color1,mode,name)
SHORT y,w,h,d;
UBYTE color0,color1,*name;
USHORT mode;
{
 struct NewScreen NewScreen;

 NewScreen.LeftEdge=0;
 NewScreen.TopEdge=y;
 NewScreen.Width=w;
 NewScreen.Height=h;
 NewScreen.Depth=d;
 NewScreen.DetailPen=color0;
 NewScreen.BlockPen=color1;
```

Listing 3-6 cont.

```
 NewScreen.ViewModes=mode;
 NewScreen.Type=CUSTOMSCREEN;
 NewScreen.Font=NULL;
 NewScreen.DefaultTitle=name;
 NewScreen.Gadgets=NULL;
 NewScreen.CustomBitMap=NULL;

 return(OpenScreen(&NewScreen));
}

VOID delay_func(factor)
int factor;
/* This function will cause a specified delay */
{
 int loop;

 for(loop=0;loop<factor*1000;loop++)
   ;

 return;
}
```

Listing 3-6 shows a slight modification to the last example. Here we've altered the default colors. Listing 3-7 shows a somewhat more interesting variation. Here we open two overlapping screens, each with its own window. Note that we have switched to high-resolution mode. Because of this, we adjusted the *Width* field accordingly and set *ViewModes* to the flag HIRES. Screen 1 is shorter than Screen 2. Listing 3-8 shows the same two screens, but this time the smaller one is in low-resolution mode. Although all objects within a screen must share its resolution, nothing prevents us from mixing screens of different resolutions on the same display.

Listing 3-7. Creation of two overlapping custom screens, each with a window.

```
*/

#include "exec/types.h"
#include "intuition/intuition.h"

struct IntuitionBase *IntuitionBase;
struct Window *wind0,*wind1;
struct Screen *Scrn0,*Scrn1;

#define INTUITION_REV 29


main()
{
 ULONG flags;
```

Listing 3-7 cont.

```
SHORT x,y,w,h,d;
USHORT mode;
UBYTE *name,c0,c1;
VOID delay_func();

/*   ======Open Intuition======= */

IntuitionBase=(struct IntuitionBase *)
         OpenLibrary("intuition.library",INTUITION_REV);

if(IntuitionBase==NULL)
   exit(FALSE);

/*   ======Open a hi-res custom screen==== */

 name="Screen 0";
 y=0;
 w=640;
 h=200;
 d=3;
 c0=0x00;
 c1=0x01;
 mode=HIRES;

 Scrn0=(struct Screen *)
        make_screen(y,w,h,d,c0,c1,mode,name);

/*   =======And a window===============*/

 name="Window 0";
 x=20;
 y=20;
 w=300;
 h=100;
 flags=ACTIVATE;
 c0=-0x01;
 c1=-0x01;

 wind0=(struct Window *)
        make_window(x,y,w,h,name,flags,c0,c1,Scrn0);


/*   ======Open another hi-res custom screen==== */

 name="Screen 1";
 y=50;
 w=640;
 h=150;
 d=3;
 c0=0x00;
 c1=0x01;
 mode=HIRES;
```

Listing 3-7 cont.

```
Scrn1=(struct Screen *)
        make_screen(y,w,h,d,c0,c1,mode,name);

/*   =======And a window===============*/

name="Window 1";
x=20;
y=20;
w=300;
h=100;
flags=ACTIVATE;
c0=-0x01;
c1=-0x01;

wind1=(struct Window *)
        make_window(x,y,w,h,name,flags,c0,c1,Scrn1);

/*    ======Delay for a bit to show off the window====== */

delay_func(100);

/* ==========Close down the window then the screen=======*/

CloseWindow(wind1);

CloseScreen(Scrn1);

delay_func(10);

CloseWindow(wind0);

CloseScreen(Scrn0);
}


make_window(x,y,w,h,name,flags,color0,color1,screen)
SHORT x,y,w,h;
UBYTE *name,color0,color1;
ULONG flags;
struct Screen *screen;
/* This function will initialize the NewWindow structure
   and open the window  */
{
  struct NewWindow NewWindow;

  NewWindow.LeftEdge=x;
  NewWindow.TopEdge=y;
  NewWindow.Width=w;
  NewWindow.Height=h;
  NewWindow.DetailPen=color0;
  NewWindow.BlockPen=color1;
  NewWindow.Title=name;
  NewWindow.Flags=flags;
  NewWindow.IDCMPFlags=NULL;
```

Listing 3-7 cont.

```
  NewWindow.Type=CUSTOMSCREEN;
  NewWindow.FirstGadget=NULL;
  NewWindow.CheckMark=NULL;
  NewWindow.Screen=screen;
  NewWindow.BitMap=NULL;
  NewWindow.MinWidth=0;
  NewWindow.MinHeight=0;
  NewWindow.MaxWidth=0;
  NewWindow.MaxHeight=0;


  return(OpenWindow(&NewWindow));

}

make_screen(y,w,h,d,color0,color1,mode,name)
SHORT y,w,h,d;
UBYTE color0,color1,*name;
USHORT mode;
{
 struct NewScreen NewScreen;

 NewScreen.LeftEdge=0;
 NewScreen.TopEdge=y;
 NewScreen.Width=w;
 NewScreen.Height=h;
 NewScreen.Depth=d;
 NewScreen.DetailPen=color0;
 NewScreen.BlockPen=color1;
 NewScreen.ViewModes=mode;
 NewScreen.Type=CUSTOMSCREEN;
 NewScreen.Font=NULL;
 NewScreen.DefaultTitle=name;
 NewScreen.Gadgets=NULL;
 NewScreen.CustomBitMap=NULL;

 return(OpenScreen(&NewScreen));
}

VOID delay_func(factor)
int factor;
/* This function will cause a specified delay */
{
 int loop;

 for(loop=0;loop<factor*1000;loop++)
   ;

 return;
}
```

Listing 3-8. Creation of two overlapping custom screens, each with a window. One of the screens is high-resolution, the other is low-resolution.

```
*/

#include "exec/types.h"
#include "intuition/intuition.h"

struct IntuitionBase *IntuitionBase;
struct Window *wind0,*wind1;
struct Screen *Scrn0,*Scrn1;

#define INTUITION_REV 29


main()
{
 ULONG flags;
 SHORT x,y,w,h,d;
 USHORT mode;
 UBYTE *name,c0,c1;
 VOID delay_func();

 /*   ======Open Intuition======= */

 IntuitionBase=(struct IntuitionBase *)
         OpenLibrary("intuition.library",INTUITION_REV);

 if(IntuitionBase==NULL)
    exit(FALSE);

 /*   ======Open a hi-res custom screen==== */

  name="High Resolution Screen";
  y=0;
  w=640;
  h=200;
  d=3;
  c0=0x00;
  c1=0x01;
  mode=HIRES;

  Scrn0=(struct Screen *)
         make_screen(y,w,h,d,c0,c1,mode,name);

 /*   =======And a window==============*/

  name="Window";
  x=20;
  y=20;
  w=300;
  h=100;
  flags=ACTIVATE;
  c0=-0x01;
```

Listing 3-8 cont.

```
  c1=-0x01;

  wind0=(struct Window *)
          make_window(x,y,w,h,name,flags,c0,c1,Scrn0);


/*  ======Open a low-res custom screen==== */

  name="Low Resolution Screen";
  y=50;
  w=320;
  h=150;
  d=3;
  c0=0x00;
  c1=0x01;
  mode=NULL;

  Scrn1=(struct Screen *)
          make_screen(y,w,h,d,c0,c1,mode,name);

/*  =======And a window==============*/

  name="Window";
  x=20;
  y=20;
  w=150;
  h=100;
  flags=ACTIVATE;
  c0=-0x01;
  c1=-0x01;

  wind1=(struct Window *)
          make_window(x,y,w,h,name,flags,c0,c1,Scrn1);

/*    ======Delay for a bit to show off the window====== */

  delay_func(100);

/* =========Close down the window then the screen========*/

  CloseWindow(wind1);

  CloseScreen(Scrn1);

  delay_func(10);

  CloseWindow(wind0);

  CloseScreen(Scrn0);
}


make_window(x,y,w,h,name,flags,color0,color1,screen)
SHORT x,y,w,h;
```

Listing 3-8 cont.

```
UBYTE *name,color0,color1;
ULONG flags;
struct Screen *screen;
/* This function will initialize the NewWindow structure
   and open the window  */
{
  struct NewWindow NewWindow;

  NewWindow.LeftEdge=x;
  NewWindow.TopEdge=y;
  NewWindow.Width=w;
  NewWindow.Height=h;
  NewWindow.DetailPen=color0;
  NewWindow.BlockPen=color1;
  NewWindow.Title=name;
  NewWindow.Flags=flags;
  NewWindow.IDCMPFlags=NULL;
  NewWindow.Type=CUSTOMSCREEN;
  NewWindow.FirstGadget=NULL;
  NewWindow.CheckMark=NULL;
  NewWindow.Screen=screen;
  NewWindow.BitMap=NULL;
  NewWindow.MinWidth=0;
  NewWindow.MinHeight=0;
  NewWindow.MaxWidth=0;
  NewWindow.MaxHeight=0;


  return(OpenWindow(&NewWindow));

}

make_screen(y,w,h,d,color0,color1,mode,name)
SHORT y,w,h,d;
UBYTE color0,color1,*name;
USHORT mode;
{
 struct NewScreen NewScreen;

 NewScreen.LeftEdge=0;
 NewScreen.TopEdge=y;
 NewScreen.Width=w;
 NewScreen.Height=h;
 NewScreen.Depth=d;
 NewScreen.DetailPen=color0;
 NewScreen.BlockPen=color1;
 NewScreen.ViewModes=mode;
 NewScreen.Type=CUSTOMSCREEN;
 NewScreen.Font=NULL;
 NewScreen.DefaultTitle=name;
 NewScreen.Gadgets=NULL;
 NewScreen.CustomBitMap=NULL;

 return(OpenScreen(&NewScreen));
```

Listing 3-8 cont.

```
}

VOID delay_func(factor)
int factor;
/* This function will cause a specified delay */
{
 int loop;

 for(loop=0; loop<factor*1000; loop++)
   ;

 return;
}
```

Intuition supports an additional very-high-resolution mode. You can create a screen in interlaced mode that gives 400 vertical lines instead of the 200 offered by normal high-resolution. In normal high-resolution, the 200 lines of vertical movement are laid out in one cycle (Figure 3-3). In interlaced mode it takes two screen cycles to complete the picture. First one set of 200 lines is drawn on the screen. Then the hardware moves to the top and draws a second

Figure 3-3. Drawing in normal resolution

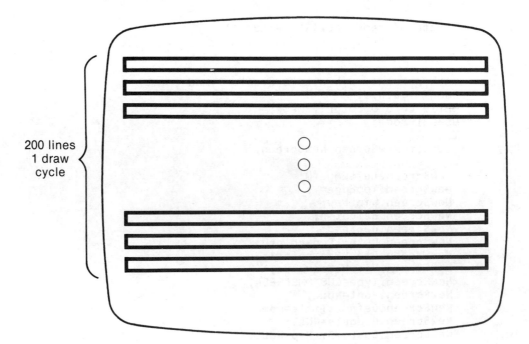

200 lines
1 draw
cycle

set of 200 lines, slightly offset from its first action. In two cycles 400 lines are drawn (Figure 3-4). Listing 3-9 illustrates a program that will put up a high-resolution interlaced screen and window. The *Height* field has been initialized to 400 and *ViewMode* is the bitwise OR of both the HIRES and the INTER-LACE flags. The interlaced screen can produce a distracting flicker on the display; this is a problem that may be solved by using a monitor with a high-persistence phosphor.

Figure 3-4. Drawing in interlace mode

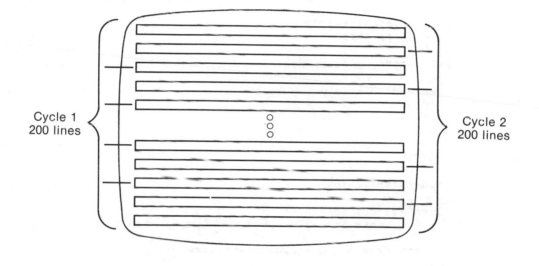

**Listing 3-9. Creation of a high-resolution interlaced
screen and window.**

```
*/

#include "exec/types.h"
#include "intuition/intuition.h"
#include "graphics/display.h"

struct IntuitionBase *IntuitionBase;
struct Window *wind;
struct Screen *Scrn;

#define INTUITION_REV 29


main()

{
  ULONG flags;
```

Listing 3-9 cont.

```
SHORT x,y,w,h,d;
USHORT mode;
UBYTE *name,c0,c1;
VOID delay_func();

/*    ======Open Intuition======= */

IntuitionBase=(struct IntuitionBase *)
          OpenLibrary("intuition.library",INTUITION_REV);

if(IntuitionBase==NULL)
    exit(FALSE);

/*    ======Open a hi-res custom screen==== */

 name="High Resolution Screen";
 y=0;
 w=640;
 h=400;
 d=3;
 c0=0x00;
 c1=0x01;
 mode=HIRES|INTERLACE;

 Scrn=(struct Screen *)
          make_screen(y,w,h,d,c0,c1,mode,name);

/*    =======And a window==============*/

 name="Window";
 x=20;
 y=20;
 w=300;
 h=100;
 flags=ACTIVATE;
 c0=-0x01;
 c1=-0x01;

 wind=(struct Window *)
          make_window(x,y,w,h,name,flags,c0,c1,Scrn);

/*    ======Delay for a bit to show off the window====== */

 delay_func(100);

/* ========Close down the window then the screen========*/

 CloseWindow(wind);

 CloseScreen(Scrn);

}
```

Listing 3-9 cont.

```
make_window(x,y,w,h,name,flags,color0,color1,screen)
SHORT x,y,w,h;
UBYTE *name,color0,color1;
ULONG flags;
struct Screen *screen;
/* This function will initialize the NewWindow structure
    and open the window  */
{
  struct NewWindow NewWindow;

  NewWindow.LeftEdge=x;
  NewWindow.TopEdge=y;
  NewWindow.Width=w;
  NewWindow.Height=h;
  NewWindow.DetailPen=color0;
  NewWindow.BlockPen=color1;
  NewWindow.Title=name;
  NewWindow.Flags=flags;
  NewWindow.IDCMPFlags=NULL;
  NewWindow.Type=CUSTOMSCREEN;
  NewWindow.FirstGadget=NULL;
  NewWindow.CheckMark=NULL;
  NewWindow.Screen=screen;
  NewWindow.BitMap=NULL;
  NewWindow.MinWidth=0;
  NewWindow.MinHeight=0;
  NewWindow.MaxWidth=0;
  NewWindow.MaxHeight=0;


  return(OpenWindow(&NewWindow));

}

make_screen(y,w,h,d,color0,color1,mode,name)
SHORT y,w,h,d;
UBYTE color0,color1,*name;
USHORT mode;
{
  struct NewScreen NewScreen;

  NewScreen.LeftEdge=0;
  NewScreen.TopEdge=y;
  NewScreen.Width=w;
  NewScreen.Height=h;
  NewScreen.Depth=d;
  NewScreen.DetailPen=color0;
  NewScreen.BlockPen=color1;
  NewScreen.ViewModes=mode;
  NewScreen.Type=CUSTOMSCREEN;
  NewScreen.Font=NULL;
  NewScreen.DefaultTitle=name;
```

Listing 3-9 cont.

```
NewScreen.Gadgets=NULL;
NewScreen.CustomBitMap=NULL;

return(OpenScreen(&NewScreen));
}

VOID delay_func(factor)
int factor;
/* This function will cause a specified delay */
{
 int loop;

 for(loop=0;loop<factor*1000;loop++)
   ;

 return;
}
```

Gadgets

One of the most difficult tasks when using a window system such as Intuition is in setting up channels of input and output. Each window and screen available to the user is a complex object with many changeable characteristics. It is not enough to send a few characters or a picture to a specific window. Things like its current position, size, and mode of activity must be known, as well as parameters such as font type and color. Getting values back from a window involves these problems as well as the additional ones of user interaction and movement around the display area. Intuition contains several subsystems that help to reduce the complexity of this problem. One of the most interesting of these is the gadget subsystem.

A *gadget* is a kind of "software machine." It is an input procedure set up to mimic some kind of physical control device. Frequently gadgets are displayed graphically to dramatically indicate their function. Other times they are rendered with text, but always with an eye to attracting the user's attention. The use of gadgets is linked to the mouse; even gadgets whose main function is to gather text frequently use the mouse to initiate a gadget session.

The "real world" orientation of these devices is underscored by the four types of gadgets that can be defined:

- Boolean gadgets ask a yes or no question; they return true or false.
- String gadgets look for a character string.
- Integer gadgets accept only a signed or unsigned string of digits.
- Proportional gadgets allow the user to specify a fraction or portion of a value.

The proportional type is the most flexible of all the gadget types. It offers a kind of input conversion that is difficult to accomplish: the translation of analog values into a form with which the computer can deal.

Gadgets are usually associated with windows, but they can also be attached to screens, outside of any particular window. This is another factor adding to their flexibility. When defined inside a window, they can be set up to share in any changes to that window. A difference in size or position will all be reflected in a proportionate change to the gadgets.

System Gadgets

Intuition offers four built-in gadgets that can be easily added to any window:

1. The Sizing Gadget allows the user to alter the size of a window dynamically.

2. The Depth Gadget adjusts the relative position of windows that overlay one another.

3. The Drag Gadget allows a window to be moved around the screen and then deposited at a new location.

4. The Close Gadget signals the owner of a window that the user wants to shut it down.

The Sizing and Depth Gadgets can be used for screens as well as windows. In fact, when a screen is opened, these two gadgets are automatically attached. System gadgets must be specifically assigned to a window, however, either at the time of window creation or through the *AddGadget()* function. Figure 3-5 illustrates these gadgets.

System gadgets always appear in the same place in the borders of a window or screen. Because of this, they represent a consistent interface to the user. No matter what application is being run:

- The Sizing Gadget is always in the lower right-hand corner of the display.

- The Depth Gadget is in the upper right-hand corner.

- The Drag Gadget is found in the title bar.

- The Close Gadget resides in the upper left-hand corner of the window or screen.

These locations are within the borders of the window or screens. These borders are adjusted to a greater width necessary for displaying them.

It is easy to add the system gadgets to a window at the time of its creation. This is done through the *Flags* field of the NewWindow structure. Each gadget has its own flag:

- WINDOWSIZING indicates a gadget that will allow the user to change the size of an open window.

Figure 3-5. Illustrating the system gadgets

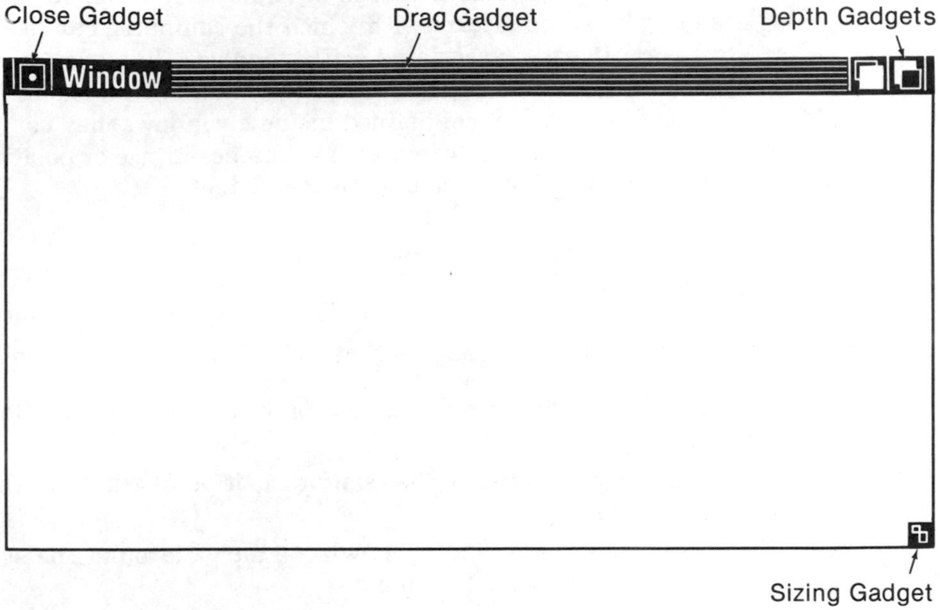

Close Gadget   Drag Gadget   Depth Gadgets

Sizing Gadget

- WINDOWDEPTH installs a gadget that will allow the user to move one window in front of another.
- WINDOWDRAG creates a gadget that will allow the window to be moved by the mouse.
- WINDOWCLOSE indicates that the user wishes to shut down a window.

By specifying one or more of these flags, the corresponding gadget will be automatically placed in the window when it is displayed.

Listing 3-10 illustrates a program that creates a window containing these system gadgets. In fact, the program opens two windows in a high-resolution custom screen; each has the full range of system gadgets. To specify these gadgets, add their appropriate flags to the *Flags* member of the NewWindow structure.

Listing 3-10. Endowment of two windows with the standard gadgets.

```
*/

#include "exec/types.h"
#include "intuition/intuition.h"

struct IntuitionBase *IntuitionBase;
struct Screen *Scrn;
struct Window *wind0,*wind1;
```

Listing 3-10 cont.

```
#define INTUITION_REV 29


main()
{
 ULONG flags;
 SHORT x,y,w,h,d;
 USHORT mode;
 UBYTE *name,c0,c1;
 VOID delay_func();

 /*    ======Open Intuition====== */

 IntuitionBase=(struct IntuitionBase *)
          OpenLibrary("intuition.library",INTUITION_REV);

 if(IntuitionBase==NULL)
    exit(FALSE);

 /*   ======Open a hi-res custom screen==== */

  name="The Gadget Screen";
  y=0;
  w=640;
  h=200;
  d=3;
  c0=0x00;
  c1=0x01;
  mode=HIRES;

  Scrn=(struct Screen *)
         make_screen(y,w,h,d,c0,c1,mode,name);

 /*   =======Open a window==============*/

  name="Window 1";
  x=20;
  y=20;
  w=300;
  h=100;
  flags=ACTIVATE|WINDOWSIZING|WINDOWDEPTH|WINDOWDRAG|
                          WINDOWCLOSE|SMART_REFRESH;
  c0=-0x01;
  c1=-0x01;

  wind0=(struct Window *)
         make_window(x,y,w,h,name,flags,c0,c1,Scrn);

 /*   =======Open another  window==============*/

  name="Window 2";
  x=330;
  y=50;
  w=300;
```

Listing 3-10 cont.

```
   h=100;
   flags=ACTIVATE|WINDOWSIZING|WINDOWDEPTH|WINDOWDRAG|
                            WINDOWCLOSE|SMART_REFRESH;
   c0=-0x01;
   c1=-0x01;

   wind1=(struct Window *)
          make_window(x,y,w,h,name,flags,c0,c1,Scrn);

/*   ======Delay for a bit to show off the window====== */

   delay_func(100);

/* =========Close down the window then the screen========*/

   CloseWindow(wind0);

   CloseWindow(wind1);

   CloseScreen(Scrn);

}


make_window(x,y,w,h,name,flags,color0,color1,screen)
SHORT x,y,w,h;
UBYTE *name,color0,color1;
ULONG flags;
struct Screen *screen;
/* This function will initialize the NewWindow structure
   and open the window  */
{
   struct NewWindow NewWindow;

   NewWindow.LeftEdge=x;
   NewWindow.TopEdge=y;
   NewWindow.Width=w;
   NewWindow.Height=h;
   NewWindow.DetailPen=color0;
   NewWindow.BlockPen=color1;
   NewWindow.Title=name;
   NewWindow.Flags=flags;
   NewWindow.IDCMPFlags=NULL;
   NewWindow.Type=CUSTOMSCREEN;
   NewWindow.FirstGadget=NULL;
   NewWindow.CheckMark=NULL;
   NewWindow.Screen=screen;
   NewWindow.BitMap=NULL;
   NewWindow.MinWidth=1;
   NewWindow.MinHeight=1;
   NewWindow.MaxWidth=640;
   NewWindow.MaxHeight=200;
```

Listing 3-10 cont.

```
   return(OpenWindow(&NewWindow));

}

make_screen(y,w,h,d,color0,color1,mode,name)
SHORT y,w,h,d;
UBYTE color0,color1,*name;
USHORT mode;
{
  struct NewScreen NewScreen;

  NewScreen.LeftEdge=0;
  NewScreen.TopEdge=y;
  NewScreen.Width=w;
  NewScreen.Height=h;
  NewScreen.Depth=d;
  NewScreen.DetailPen=color0;
  NewScreen.BlockPen=color1;
  NewScreen.ViewModes=mode;
  NewScreen.Type=CUSTOMSCREEN;
  NewScreen.Font=NULL;
  NewScreen.DefaultTitle=name;
  NewScreen.Gadgets=NULL;
  NewScreen.CustomBitMap=NULL;

  return(OpenScreen(&NewScreen));
}

VOID delay_func(factor)
int factor;
/* This function will cause a specified delay */
{
  int loop;

  for(loop=0;loop<factor*1000;loop++)
    ;

  return;
}
```

Once you create a window and specify which of the system gadgets you desire, they are—with the exception of the Close Gadget—immediately available. If you position the mouse cursor at the Sizing Gadget, select it, and move the cursor inward, the window gets smaller. An outward movement reverses the process; it gets larger. By using the Drag Gadget, you can move the window vertically and horizontally around the screen. The Depth Gadget allows you to rearrange overlapping windows. All of these functions are performed by Intuition. The commands represented by these gadgets are, in fact, trapped and never even reach the application controlling the window.

There are two exceptions: the Close Gadget and the *size verify* function. Both of these must be handled explicitly by the program that controls the window. They are not handled automatically.

The Close Gadget does not affect the display of its window. If you indicate through it that the window is to be shut down, Intuition sends a message to the controlling application that this particular gadget was selected. It never takes it upon itself to close down a window. It is always necessary—except perhaps in the case of small demonstration programs—to perform clean-up and bookkeeping operations on an application, before it can leave the screen. In any case, Intuition leaves it up to the application whether or not to actually close the window. Similarly, you can set a flag in the NewWindow structure that will perform the same kind of hold on the Sizing Gadget. This is the SIZEVERIFY flag; it goes in the *IDCMPFlags* field of the NewWindow structure. We will return to this later when we discuss the IDCMP input/output system.

Our example also shows a new parameter, which must be set to support the Sizing Gadget. You must specify both the minimum and the maximum size that a window can change. This is accomplished by setting *MinWidth*, *MinHeight*, *MaxWidth*, and *MaxHeight* in the NewWindow structure. Note that a window does not have to initially appear at its minimum size, but if you initialize the *MinWidth* or *MinHeight* fields to 0, these will be automatically set to these initial values. In the example, we have set the minimum values to 1. This will not allow the window to disappear from the screen, but it does allow the user to shrink it almost to the disappearing point.

Application Specific Gadgets

Intuition also gives you the option of creating a customized gadget to meet a special-purpose input situation. These special-purpose gadgets can take on many shapes and formats, and are frequently displayed as striking graphic images. Their form is limited only by the imagination of the programmer. Here we can only scratch the surface and talk about the technical requirements.

Custom gadgets are defined through a structure data type. This one takes the form:

```
struct Gadget {
    struct Gadget *NextGadget;
    SHORT LeftEdge,TopEdge,
        Width,Height;
    USHORT Flags,
        Activation,
        GadgetType;
    APTR GadgetRender,
        SelectRender,
    struct IntuiText *GadgetText;
    LONG MutualExclude;
    APTR SpecialInfo;
```

```
        USHORT GadgetID;
        APTR  UserData;
    }
```

Only a few of these fields concern you now. More will be of interest to you later, when we turn our attention to drawing gadgets instead of merely writing out text.

LeftEdge and *TopEdge* are concerned with positioning the gadget in the window. System gadgets are always found in the borders of windows or screens, but customized gadgets can appear anywhere. This is a manifestation of their flexibility. *Width* and *Height* must be set in concert with the two coordinate fields to get a reasonable display.

The *Flags* member controls several display characteristics of the gadget, most importantly, how it is to be highlighted when it is chosen. There are several possiblities:

- GADGHCOMP produces highlighting by turning the color of a chosen gadget to a complementary value.
- GADGHBOX draws a box around the selected item.
- GADGHIMAGE displays an alternate picture, supplied by the application, to indicate selection.
- GADGHNONE is set when no highlighting is desired.

This field controls several other characteristics. Following is a complete description of all values for the gadget *flags* field.

GADGHCOMP.	Highlighting is indicated by setting the select box to complement.
GADGHBOX.	Highlighting is indicated by a box around the select box.
GADGHIMAGE.	Highlighting is indicated by an alternate image or border.
GADGHNONE.	This specifies no highlighting.
GADGIMAGE.	This flag indicates that an image has been supplied for the gadget.
GRELBOTTOM.	This indicates that TopEdge is an offset from the bottom of the containing element.
GRELRIGHT.	This indicates that LeftEdge is be calculated from the right edge of the containing element.
GRELWIDTH.	This is set to interpret Width as an increment to the width of the containing element.
GRELHEIGHT.	This causes Height to be interpreted as an increment to the containing element's height.
SELECTED.	This indicates that the initial state of the gadget is "selected".
GADGDISABLED.	This disables the gadget.

The *Activation* field sets a similar set of characteristics for the gadget itself. TOGGLESELECT, for example, produces a gadget whose state is changed back and forth by the same select field. Each time it is selected by the user, it changes from its current state to its other state. This works much like a pushbutton switch on a lamp.

The *Gadget Type* member indicates one of three possible types:

- BOOLGADGET indicates a boolean or yes-no gadget.
- STRGADGET specifies one looking for character string input.
- PROPGADGET specifies a gadget that will accept and specify a proportional numeric value.

There is one additional type, the *integer*, which is a variant form of the string type.

The *MutualExclude* member allows you to control the interaction of individual gadgets. Specifically, this field indicates which of the other gadgets defined for the window must be de-selected when the gadget in question becomes the current one. Any gadgets that appear on this list will immediately be closed, when this gadget is selected.

Listing 3-11 shows the definition of a string gadget in a window. One additional step was necessary to bring this object to the display: the initialization of a *StringInfo* structure. This is one of two special purpose data types used to initialize the *SpecialInfo* field of the gadget structure. It has the general form:

```
struct StringInfo {
    UBYTE *Buffer,
          *UndoBuffer;
    SHORT BufferPos,
          MaxChars,
          DispPos,
          UndoPos,
          NumChars,
          DispCount,
          CLeft,CTop;
    struct Layer *LayerPtr;
    LONG  LongInt;
    struct KeyMap *AltKeyMap;
};
```

where

Buffer points to to a buffer.

UndoBuffer points to a backup buffer.

MaxChars contains the number of characters in the buffer. This includes the '\0' character.

BufferPos indicates the inital position of the cursor.

DispPos is the position of the first displayed character.

UndoPos indicates the cursor position in the undo buffer.

NumChars is the current number of characters in the buffer.

DispCount indicates the number characters visible.

CLeft, CTop is the offset of the containing.

LayerPtr points to the Layers structure.

LongInt contains the value if this is an integer gadget.

AltKeyMap points to an alternate key map.

Only a few fields need to be set to implement this object.

Buffer points to an area in the memory that is set to receive the characters that will come in from the gadget. It may be preset with a value; this preset value can be replaced by the user. If no value is entered, the preset value becomes default value. The *DispPos* field indicates which characters in this default string will be displayed. In our example, we show the entire string, so this value is 0. It is also necessary to indicate to Intuition the size of the string expected; this is done through the *MaxChar* field. *BufferPos* indicates the initial position of the cursor in this buffer. Our example puts this, too, at the beginning.

Listing 3-11. Endowment of a window with a string gadget.

```
*/

#include "exec/types.h"
#include "intuition/intuition.h"

struct IntuitionBase *IntuitionBase;
struct Screen *Scrn;
struct Window *wind0,*wind1;
struct Gadget gadget;
struct StringInfo info;

#define INTUITION_REV 29


main()
{
 ULONG flags;
 SHORT x,y,w,h,d;
 USHORT mode;
 UBYTE *name,c0,c1;
 VOID delay_func(),OpenALL();
 char dobuffer[80],undobuffer[80];

  OpenALL();

/*  ======First create a gadget========= */

 strcpy(dobuffer,"Enter New Text Here");

 info.Buffer=dobuffer;
 info.UndoBuffer=undobuffer;
 info.MaxChars=80;
```

Listing 3-11 cont.

```
info.BufferPos=0;
info.DispPos=0;

gadget.NextGadget=NULL;
gadget.LeftEdge=40;
gadget.TopEdge=40;
gadget.Width=200;
gadget.Height=75;
gadget.Flags=GADGHCOMP;
gadget.Activation=TOGGLESELECT;
gadget.GadgetType=STRGADGET;
gadget.GadgetRender=NULL;
gadget.SelectRender=NULL;
gadget.GadgetText=NULL;
gadget.MutualExclude=NULL;
gadget.SpecialInfo=(APTR)&info;
gadget.GadgetID=NULL;
gadget.UserData=NULL;
```

```
/*  ======Open a hi-res custom screen==== */

name="The Gadget Screen";
y=0;
w=640;
h=200;
d=3;
c0=0x00;
c1=0x01;
mode=HIRES;

Scrn=(struct Screen *)
        make_screen(y,w,h,d,c0,c1,mode,name);

/*  =======Open a window=============*/

name="Window 1";
x=20;
y=20;
w=400;
h=150;
flags=ACTIVATE|WINDOWSIZING|WINDOWDEPTH|WINDOWDRAG|
                        WINDOWCLOSE|SMART_REFRESH;
c0=-0x01;
c1=-0x01;

wind0=(struct Window *)
        make_window(x,y,w,h,name,flags,c0,c1,Scrn,&gadget);

/*  ======Delay for a bit to show off the window====== */

delay_func(100);

/* ========Close down the window then the screen========*/
```

Listing 3-11 cont.

```
   CloseWindow(wind0);

   CloseScreen(Scrn);

}

VOID OpenALL()
/* This function will open any necessary libraries */
{

  /*    ======Open Intuition======= */

  IntuitionBase=(struct IntuitionBase *)
            OpenLibrary("intuition.library",INTUITION_REV);

  if(IntuitionBase==NULL)
     exit(FALSE);
}

make_window(x,y,w,h,name,flags,color0,color1,screen,gadg)
SHORT x,y,w,h;
UBYTE *name,color0,color1;
ULONG flags;
struct Screen *screen;
struct Gadget *gadg;
/* This function will initialize the NewWindow structure
   and open the window   */
{
   struct NewWindow NewWindow;

   NewWindow.LeftEdge=x;
   NewWindow.TopEdge=y;
   NewWindow.Width=w;
   NewWindow.Height=h;
   NewWindow.DetailPen=color0;
   NewWindow.BlockPen=color1;
   NewWindow.Title=name;
   NewWindow.Flags=flags;
   NewWindow.IDCMPFlags=NULL;
   NewWindow.Type=CUSTOMSCREEN;
   NewWindow.FirstGadget=gadg;
   NewWindow.CheckMark=NULL;
   NewWindow.Screen=screen;
   NewWindow.BitMap=NULL;
   NewWindow.MinWidth=1;
   NewWindow.MinHeight=1;
   NewWindow.MaxWidth=640;
   NewWindow.MaxHeight=200;


   return(OpenWindow(&NewWindow));

}
```

Listing 3-11 cont.

```
make_screen(y,w,h,d,color0,color1,mode,name)
SHORT y,w,h,d;
UBYTE color0,color1,*name;
USHORT mode;
{
 struct NewScreen NewScreen;

 NewScreen.LeftEdge=0;
 NewScreen.TopEdge=y;
 NewScreen.Width=w;
 NewScreen.Height=h;
 NewScreen.Depth=d;
 NewScreen.DetailPen=color0;
 NewScreen.BlockPen=color1;
 NewScreen.ViewModes=mode;
 NewScreen.Type=CUSTOMSCREEN;
 NewScreen.Font=NULL;
 NewScreen.DefaultTitle=name;
 NewScreen.Gadgets=NULL;
 NewScreen.CustomBitMap=NULL;

 return(OpenScreen(&NewScreen));
}

VOID delay_func(factor)
int factor;
/* This function will cause a specified delay */
{
 int loop;

 for(loop=0;loop<factor*1000;loop++)
    ;

 return;
}
```

The *UndoBuffer* is an optional field. If specified with something other than NULL, it is used to save the initial string value. This initiates the built-in *undo* editing function: the right Amiga key will clear the current buffer value and return the original string of characters. The *UndoBuffer* may be shared among all the gadgets in a window, but it must be large enough to hold the largest screen. We have implemented the *UndoBuffer* in our example.

Once a gadget has been defined, it is implemented by assigning it to the *FirstGadget* field in the NewWindow structure. It is then added to the window when the window is opened. The *AddGadget()* function allows us to put new gadgets onto the list of an open window. *RemoveGadget()* performs the complementary task.

Listing 3-12 shows an example of an integer gadget. This is a string gadget whose values are restricted to strings of digits. It is set up in just the same way as our earlier example. It, too, uses a StringInfo structure. The difference is the setting of the LONGINT flag in the *Activation* field of the gadget structure.

Listing 3-12. Endowment of a window with an integer gadget.

```
*/

#include "exec/types.h"
#include "intuition/intuition.h"

struct IntuitionBase *IntuitionBase;
struct Screen *Scrn;
struct Window *wind0,*wind1;
struct Gadget gadget;
struct StringInfo info;

#define INTUITION_REV 29


main()
{
 ULONG flags;
 SHORT x,y,w,h,d;
 USHORT mode;
 UBYTE *name,c0,c1;
 VOID delay_func(),OpenALL();
 char dobuffer[80],undobuffer[80];

  OpenALL();

 /*  ======First create a gadget========= */

  strcpy(dobuffer,"0");

  info.Buffer=dobuffer;
  info.UndoBuffer=undobuffer;
  info.MaxChars=80;
  info.BufferPos=0;
  info.DispPos=0;

  gadget.NextGadget=NULL;
  gadget.LeftEdge=40;
  gadget.TopEdge=40;
  gadget.Width=200;
  gadget.Height=75;
  gadget.Flags=GADGHCOMP;
  gadget.Activation=TOGGLESELECT|LONGINT;
  gadget.GadgetType=STRGADGET;
  gadget.GadgetRender=NULL;
  gadget.SelectRender=NULL;
  gadget.GadgetText=NULL;
  gadget.MutualExclude=NULL;
  gadget.SpecialInfo=(APTR)&info;
  gadget.GadgetID=NULL;
  gadget.UserData=NULL;
```

Listing 3-12 cont.

```
/*  ======Open a hi-res custom screen==== */

 name="The Gadget Screen";
 y=0;
 w=640;
 h=200;
 d=3;
 c0=0x00;
 c1=0x01;
 mode=HIRES;

 Scrn=(struct Screen *)
         make_screen(y,w,h,d,c0,c1,mode,name);

/*  =======Open a window==============*/

 name="Window 1";
 x=20;
 y=20;
 w=400;
 h=150;
 flags=ACTIVATE|WINDOWSIZING|WINDOWDEPTH|WINDOWDRAG|
                            WINDOWCLOSE|SMART_REFRESH;
 c0=-0x01;
 c1=-0x01;

 wind0=(struct Window *)
         make_window(x,y,w,h,name,flags,c0,c1,Scrn,&gadget);

/*  ======Delay for a bit to show off the window====== */

 delay_func(100);

/* =========Close down the window then the screen=======*/

 CloseWindow(wind0);

 CloseScreen(Scrn);

}

VOID OpenALL()
/* This function will open any necessary Libraries */
{

 /*  ======Open Intuition======= */

 IntuitionBase=(struct IntuitionBase *)
         OpenLibrary("intuition.library",INTUITION_REV);

 if(IntuitionBase==NULL)
    exit(FALSE);
}
```

Listing 3-12 cont.

```
make_window(x,y,w,h,name,flags,color0,color1,screen,gadg)
SHORT x,y,w,h;
UBYTE *name,color0,color1;
ULONG flags;
struct Screen *screen;
struct Gadget *gadg;
/* This function will initialize the NewWindow structure
    and open the window  */
{
  struct NewWindow NewWindow;

  NewWindow.LeftEdge=x;
  NewWindow.TopEdge=y;
  NewWindow.Width=w;
  NewWindow.Height=h;
  NewWindow.DetailPen=color0;
  NewWindow.BlockPen=color1;
  NewWindow.Title=name;
  NewWindow.Flags=flags;
  NewWindow.IDCMPFlags=NULL;
  NewWindow.Type=CUSTOMSCREEN;
  NewWindow.FirstGadget=gadg;
  NewWindow.CheckMark=NULL;
  NewWindow.Screen=screen;
  NewWindow.BitMap=NULL;
  NewWindow.MinWidth=1;
  NewWindow.MinHeight=1;
  NewWindow.MaxWidth=640;
  NewWindow.MaxHeight=200;


  return(OpenWindow(&NewWindow));

}


make_screen(y,w,h,d,color0,color1,mode,name)
SHORT y,w,h,d;
UBYTE color0,color1,*name;
USHORT mode;
{
  struct NewScreen NewScreen;

  NewScreen.LeftEdge=0;
  NewScreen.TopEdge=y;
  NewScreen.Width=w;
  NewScreen.Height=h;
  NewScreen.Depth=d;
  NewScreen.DetailPen=color0;
  NewScreen.BlockPen=color1;
  NewScreen.ViewModes=mode;
  NewScreen.Type=CUSTOMSCREEN;
  NewScreen.Font=NULL;
  NewScreen.DefaultTitle=name;
```

Listing 3-12 cont.

```
 NewScreen.Gadgets=NULL;
 NewScreen.CustomBitMap=NULL;

 return(OpenScreen(&NewScreen));
}

VOID delay_func(factor)
int factor;
/* This function will cause a specified delay */
{
 int loop;

 for(loop=0;loop<factor*1000;loop++)
   ;

 return;
}
```

Menus

Everyone who programs is familiar with the notion of a *menu*: a list of choices that affect the flow of a program by offering the user a selection of options for program control.

The menu is one of Intuition's most basic data objects. As such it is easy to define and easy to set up for dramatic display. Unlike gadgets, which can be in a window or in a screen, the menu is solely a creature of windows. Each window may contain a linked list of such menus—the menu strip. The menu always appears in the title bar of the enclosing screen. When chosen by the right mouse button, the menu rolls down from the top.

Each menu consists of a table of choices. The user must indicate which item or items listed in this table are desired. There are several methods of choice, dependent both upon the design and the nature of the items in question. The primary methods are:

1. Toggles that stay on until explicitly turned off
2. Choices that remain as long as the mouse button is depressed

It is also possible to set up a menu so that several items can be selected by touching each in turn with the mouse cursor.

Toggled items share an important characteristic: they can be set to be mutually exclusive. Choosing one item precludes the choice of others in the prescribed list. Moreover, the choice of a mutually exclusive alternative to an item that is presently toggled *on* causes that item to be de-selected.

Although menus depend heavily on the Intuition interface of windows and screens and the convenience of pointing with the mouse, it is possible to set up a keyboard alternative for all or a selected set of menu items. These alternatives use the special Amiga keys on the keyboard to define an escape sequence of characters, which will automatically choose the menu item in question without resort to the menu. When a keyboard alternative is set up, a special mark is displayed in the visual menu to indicate that this is a possibility.

Defining Menus and Menu Items

A menu is defined by a properly initialized menu structure. Unlike the window, screen, or even the gadget structure, this is a relatively simple data object.

```
struct Menu {
    struct Menu    *NextMenu;
    SHORT   LeftEdge,TopEdge,
            Width,Height;
    USHORT  Flags;
    BYTE    *MenuName;
    struct MenuItem *FirstItem;
};
```

The first field, *NextMenu*, is the link to the next menu in the chain for this window. There is only a single string of menus in each window. Remember to set this field either to the address of the next menu or to NULL, if this is the last one.

LeftEdge sets the position of the menu header in the screen title bar; it indicates how far from the left-hand side of the display the header will appear. The *Width* field indicates the horizontal size of the menu header and its corresponding select box. In the current implementation of Intuition, both *TopEdge* and *Height* are not used. All menu headers appear at the top of the screen title bar.

The *Flags* field allows the application to communicate with Intuition. Currently two flag values are defined:

- MIDRAWN indicates the current display state of the Menu—whether or not the menu is being shown to the user.

- MENUENABLED indicates whether or not a particular menu will be available to the user.

If the MENUENABLED flag is not set, then the menu is disabled. If the flag is set, however, the menu can be controlled by the functions *OnMenu()* and *OffMenu*. The former enables, the latter disables the menu. The format for these functions is as follows:

```
OnMenu(w_ptr,m_num)
```

where

w_ptr points to a window.

m_num is a menu number.

This function activates menu, menu item, or sub-item according to the m_num identifier.

```
OffMenu(w_ptr,m_num)
```

where

w_ptr is a pointer to a window.

m_num is a menu number.

This function de-activates the corresponding object.

It is important to note that even if the menu is to be initially disabled, this flag must be set and the menu disabled through the function. Failure to do this will result in a permanently disabled function.

MenuName is a pointer to a character string that contains the text that is to appear in the menu header. It is the title of the menu. As a matter of style, it is important that this string fit nicely into the specified width of this header. The menu structure serves to set out the header and the title, and specifies the position and width of the object. In order to create a complete menu, we must also have some choices for the user to make. These choices are added through the initialization of a *MenuItem* structure. Each item in the menu is represented by one of these structures, connected together in a linked list. The *FirstItem* field in the menu structure points to the head of this list.

The MenuItem structure consists of eleven fields:

```
struct MenuItem {
    struct MenuItem  *NextItem;
    SHORT LeftEdge,TopEdge,Width,Height;
    USHORT Flags;
    LONG MutualExclude;
    APTR ItemFill;
    BYTE Command;
    struct MenuItem *SubItem;
    USHORT NextSelect;
};
```

This structure is the real workhorse of the menu subsystem. It is more complex than the menu structure itself, although many of its fields are optional. There are two pointer members in this structure.

- *NextItem* points to the next structure in the chain of items that define the menu. The last structure in this chain must set this field to NULL.

- *SubItem* defines another linked list attached to the item; these are also defined using the *Item* structure. The *SubItem* field can support its own dependent linked list.

Figure 3-6 details the relationship of items and sub-items.

Each item in the menu is displayed in its own select box. This is the area that the mouse cursor must access in order to choose the item. *LeftEdge* and *TopEdge* position the select box. As with all Intuition structures, the point

Figure 3-6. The relationship of item and sub-item

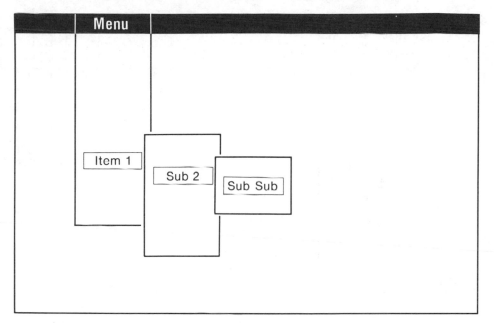

whose coordinate is represented by these two fields is relative to the left-hand corner of the enclosing structure, the menu box. The *Width* and *Height* fields round out the item select box definition. It should be noted that the select box need not have the same dimensions as the menu header.

The *MutualExclude* flag is used to specify which items in this menu are incompatible with the item being defined. Any items indicated here will be automatically de-selected whenever the user chooses this item. The field itself is a bit map defined on a long word. This puts a limit of thirty-two on the number of items that can be mutually excluded. Each bit position is assigned to a particular item number. A 1 bit in the position indicates a chosen item. Figure 3-7 illustrates this member of the structure; it is only valid for toggled items.

Itemfill contains a pointer to one of two structures:

1. If the item is to be rendered by text, it points to an *IntuiText* structure.

2. If the item is to be a graphic one, then the field must contain the address of a user-defined *BitMap*. This latter is an area of memory formatted and managed to store an image of the display.

The *SelectFill* field also points to one or the other of these structures, to specify the highlighting of a chosen item. The *Command* field allows us to specify an alternate keyboard sequence to choose the item. This is an escape sequence defined, first of all, by one of the special Amiga keys on either side of the space bar. This escape sequence allows the user to directly choose a menu and item without recourse to the screen or window display. Once this

Figure 3-7. Setting the MutualExclude flag for a menu

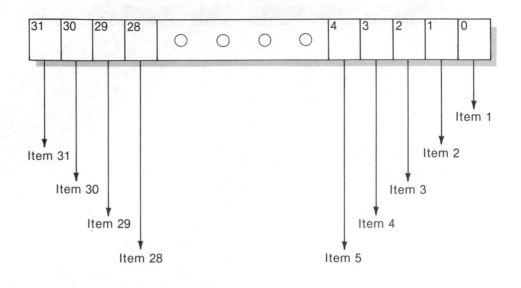

command sequence is trapped, it is treated no differently than if the menu had been accessed in the orthodox way.

As in other structures, the *Flags* field is used to communicate with Intuition on behalf of the particular item being defined. For menu items, this set of flags is correspondingly complex, since they control so many of the display parameters.

The CHECKIT flag is used to specify the kind of item being defined. If this flag is set, you are specifying a toggle item— one that is turned on and off by subsequent selections. If the flag is unset, the item is only selected momentarily while the mouse cursor is positioned over it and the button pressed. If CHECKED is also set, a check mark is displayed by the item when it is shown. It should be noted here that extra space must be left for this checkmark when declaring the dimensions of the select box for this item.

The ITEMTEXT flag is set if the item is a text-only one. This is complementary to the *ItemFill* field and indicates which structure this pointer indicates. COMMSEQ indicates that an alternative command sequence has been defined.

ITEMENABLED functions in the same way as the MENUENABLE flag. If this is not set, the item is not enabled and its status cannot be changed. The display is "ghosted" to indicate this to the user. If this flag is set, then the status of the item can be manipulated by *OnMenu()* or *OffMenu()*. These perform the same function on individual items as they do on whole menus.

When a menu item is selected, its display is highlighted. The *Flags* field contains a specification setting the form of this highlighting.

- HIGHCOMP changes the entire select box to its binary complement.
- HIGHBOX encloses the select box with an outer rectangle.
- HIGHIMAGE replaces the original display with the alternative specified in the *SelectFill* field.
- HIGHNONE turns off any highlighting of the display.

There is no default. One of these alternatives must be explicitly specified.

Intuition sets the ISDRAWN and HIGHTEM flags. The former indicates that an item's sub-items are being displayed. It is cleared when this is no longer the case. The latter flag is set to show highlighting of an item.

Creating A Menu

Once you have defined each item in the menu, combined these items into a list, and attached it to a menu definition, you still have to associate it with a particular window. This association is controlled by *SetMenuStrip()* and *ClearMenuStrip()*. These two functions allow you to dynamically create and change the menus within your applications. Two additional functions *OnMenu()* and *OffMenu()* afford even greater control by allowing you to turn specific menus or menu items on and off, without removing them from their respective lists. Finally, Intuition offers a function, *ItemAddress()*, to capture the address of a particular MenuItem structure.

SetMenuStrip() takes a pointer to a window and a pointer to a menu structure as arguments. Intuition automatically attaches the menu strip defined by this pointer to the window in question.

There may be many menus in a window—even unrelated ones—but they must all be connected together in this menu strip. Each window has only one such strip. In recognition of this fact, the *ClearMenuStrip()* function requires only a window pointer, to remove all menus. Any application that is to change a menu or item must first clear the menu strip and then make another call to *SetMenuStrip()*. This process can occur any number of times. The format of these two functions is as follows:

```
SetMenuStrip(w_ptr,m_ptr)
```

where

w__ptr points to a window.

m__ptr points to the first menu in the menu strip.

This function will install the menu strip in the window.

```
ClearMenuStrip(w_ptr)
```

where

w_ptr points to a window.

This function will remove the current menu strip from the window.

The complementary functions *OnMenu( )* and *OffMenu( )* control the menu and items once they are established in the window. Each function takes a window pointer and a *MenuNumber* as an argument, and performs its task on the object so identified. The *MenuNumber* is an Intuition variable that identifies the menu-related object currently picked; this quantity allows you to specify either an entire menu, an item, or a sub-item. An object that is disabled appears to the user with a light pattern of white dots across it to indicate its status. The format for these functions is:

```
OnMenu(w_ptr,m_number)
```

where

w_ptr points to a window.

m_nubmer is a menu item number.

This function enables the specified menu or menu item.

```
OffMenu(w_ptr,m_number)
```

where

w_ptr points to a window.

m_number is a menu item number.

This function disables the specified menu or menu item.

The *menu number* is an important parameter for all menu-related functions. You can use it to do selective enabling or disabling of particular menu objects; but it is also important for communicating choices to the controlling application. This number is sent through Intuition's IDCMP facility, a specialized communication method peculiar to Intuition. We will discuss the medium and technique for this facility in a later section. Once you have this value, it is still necessary to decode it into its exact reference.

The menu number is a composite value, giving the user's choice as:

- A particular menu
- A particular item in that menu
- A sub-item attached to the item

These values are combined into a single LONG word value. Each menu is assigned an ordinal value in the menu strip, which is the menu number. Each item is similarly numbered within its menu, and the same is true of each sub-item. Intuition supplies several macros to perform any necessary decoding.

MENUNUM( ) returns the menu number.

ITEMNUM( ) finds the item number.

SUBNUM( ) gives us the sub-item number.

You need all three of these numbers to define a reference since a sub-item is relative to an item, which in turn is relative to a menu.

The absence of a menu selection is signaled by the value MENUNULL. In addition, there are three flags which you can use to indicate a null condition to Intuition: NOMENU, NOITEM, and NOSUB. Although the reference objects of these latter flags is obvious, how they are used may not be. One important use for these constant values is in the *OnMenu()/OffMenu()* functions:

- Setting the item field to NOITEM causes the function to operate on the entire menu.

- Setting the sub-item field to NOSUB affects only the item.

- Setting none of the fields in a menu number causes the function to work only on the indicated sub-item.

Finally, the function *ItemAddress()* takes a pointer to a *MenuStrip* and a *MenuNumber* and returns a pointer to the object thus specified. These menu-related functions are summarized as follows:

```
address=ItemAddress(m_strip,m_number)
```

where

address is an address value.

m_strip points to the first menu in the menu strip.

m_number is the number of the menu or menu item.

This function will find the address of a menu item.

Now that we've talked so much about all the details involved in creating a menu, Listing 3-13 shows the definition of a single menu in a window—the most basic situation. In this example nothing can be done with the menu except display it. Even merely noting selection must wait until we cover basic window-related input/output. The function *CreateMes()* uses the IntuiText structure to create the text for each menu item. The process of the examples that follow is simple and straightforward:

- First, we defined a list of three MenuItem structures.

- We connected these structures through the *NextItem* field of each structure, taking care to set the last NextItem structure to NULL.

- We attached this linked list to our menu structure using its *FirstItem* field.

A call to *SetMenuStrip()* completed the menu processing. Note that we called *ClearMenuStrip* just before we closed the window and exited the program.

Listing 3-13. Creation of a menu in a window. This shows only the creation and display; nothing is done with the menu items.

```
*/

#include "exec/types.h"
#include "intuition/intuition.h"

struct IntuitionBase *IntuitionBase;
struct Window *Wind,*NoBorder;

#define INTUITION_REV 29


main()
{
 ULONG flags;
 SHORT x,y,w,h;
 UBYTE name[60];
 VOID delay_func(),OpenALL(),CreateMes();
 struct Menu Menu1;
 struct MenuItem m0,m1,m2;
 struct IntuiText t0,t1,t2;

  OpenALL();

   /*  ===========Set up a menu===========*/

   CreateMes(&t0,CHECKWIDTH+2,0,"Choice 0");

   m0.NextItem=&m1;
   m0.LeftEdge=5;
   m0.TopEdge=0;
   m0.Width=100;
   m0.Height=10;
   m0.Flags=CHECKIT|CHECKED|ITEMTEXT|HIGHCOMP|ITEMENABLED;
   m0.MutualExclude=NULL;
   m0.ItemFill=(APTR)&t0;
   m0.SelectFill=NULL;
   m0.Command=NULL;
   m0.SubItem=NULL;

   CreateMes(&t1,CHECKWIDTH+2,0,"Choice 1");

   m1.NextItem=&m2;
   m1.LeftEdge=5;
   m1.TopEdge=10;
   m1.Width=100;
   m1.Height=10;
   m1.Flags=CHECKIT|ITEMTEXT|HIGHCOMP|ITEMENABLED;
   m1.MutualExclude=NULL;
   m1.ItemFill=(APTR)&t1;
   m1.SelectFill=NULL;
   m1.Command=NULL;
   m1.SubItem=NULL;
```

Listing 3-13 cont.

```
CreateMes(&t2,CHECKWIDTH+2,0,"Choice 2");

m2.NextItem=NULL;
m2.LeftEdge=5;
m2.TopEdge=20;
m2.Width=100;
m2.Height=20;
m2.Flags=CHECKIT|ITEMTEXT|HIGHCOMP|ITEMENABLED;
m2.MutualExclude=NULL;
m2.ItemFill=(APTR)&t2;
m2.SelectFill=NULL;
m2.Command=NULL;
m2.SubItem=NULL;

Menu1.NextMenu=NULL;
Menu1.LeftEdge=0;
Menu1.TopEdge=0;
Menu1.Width=200;
Menu1.Height=100;
Menu1.Flags=MENUENABLED;
Menu1.MenuName="My First Menu";
Menu1.FirstItem=&m0;


/*  ======Open a borderless window======*/

x=y=0;
w=640;
h=200;
flags=ACTIVATE|BORDERLESS;
NoBorder=(struct Window *)make_window(x,y,w,h,NULL,flags);


/*  ======Open a plain window=====  */

strcpy(name,"Plain Window ");
x=y=20;
w=300;
h=100;
flags=ACTIVATE;
Wind=(struct Window *)make_window(x,y,w,h,name,flags);

/*  =============Open up the menu==================== */

SetMenuStrip(Wind,&Menu1);

/*  ======Delay for a bit to show off the windows====== */

delay_func(100);

/* ========Close down the windows in order=======*/

ClearMenuStrip(Wind);
```

Listing 3-13 cont.

```
   CloseWindow(Wind);

   delay_func(10);

   CloseWindow(NoBorder);
}

VOID OpenALL()
/* This function will open any necessary libraries */
{

   /*    ======Open Intuition======= */

   IntuitionBase=(struct IntuitionBase *)
             OpenLibrary("intuition.library",INTUITION_REV);

   if(IntuitionBase==NULL)
       exit(FALSE);
}

VOID CreateMes(x,left,top,mesg)
struct IntuiText *x;
SHORT left,top;
UBYTE *mesg;
{
  x->FrontPen=0;
  x->BackPen=1;
  x->DrawMode=JAM1;
  x->LeftEdge=left;
  x->TopEdge=top;
  x->ITextFont=NULL;
  x->IText=mesg;
  x->NextText=NULL;
}

make_window(x,y,w,h,name,flags)
SHORT x,y,w,h;
UBYTE *name;
ULONG flags;
/* This function will initialize the NewWindow structure
    and open the window  */
{
   struct NewWindow NewWindow;

   NewWindow.LeftEdge=x;
   NewWindow.TopEdge=y;
   NewWindow.Width=w;
   NewWindow.Height=h;
   NewWindow.DetailPen=-1;
   NewWindow.BlockPen=-1;
   NewWindow.Title=name;
   NewWindow.Flags=flags;
   NewWindow.IDCMPFlags=NULL;
```

Listing 3-13 cont.

```
    NewWindow.Type=WBENCHSCREEN;
    NewWindow.FirstGadget=NULL;
    NewWindow.CheckMark=NULL;
    NewWindow.Screen=NULL;
    NewWindow.BitMap=NULL;
    NewWindow.MinWidth=0;
    NewWindow.MinHeight=0;
    NewWindow.MaxWidth=0;
    NewWindow.MaxHeight=0;


    return(OpenWindow(&NewWindow));

}

VOID delay_func(factor)
int factor;
/* This function will cause a specified delay */
{
 int loop;

 for(loop=0;loop<factor*1000;loop++)
   ;

 return;
}
```

Listing 3-14 creates a slightly more complex case; it opens two menus in a window. The important differences between this and the earlier example are:

- We had to define two linked lists of MenuItem structures and attach them to the menu structure.
- We had to create a linked list of menu structures.

Listing 3-14. Creation of two menus in a window. This shows only the creation and display, nothing is done with the menu items.

```
*/

#include "exec/types.h"
#include "intuition/intuition.h"

struct IntuitionBase *IntuitionBase;
struct Window *Wind,*NoBorder;

#define INTUITION_REV 29


main()
```

Listing 3-14 cont.

```
{
 ULONG flags;
 SHORT x,y,w,h;
 UBYTE name[60];
 VOID delay_func(),OpenALL(),CreateMes(),CreateItem();
 struct Menu Menu1,Menu2;
 struct MenuItem m0,m1,m2,x0,x1;
 struct IntuiText t0,t1,t2,xt0,xt1;

  OpenALL();

    /*  ===========Set up a menu===========*/

    CreateMes(&t0,CHECKWIDTH+2,0,"Choice 0");
    CreateItem(&t0,&m0,&m1,5,0,CHECKED);

    CreateMes(&t1,CHECKWIDTH+2,0,"Choice 1");
    CreateItem(&t1,&m1,&m2,5,10,0);

    CreateMes(&t2,CHECKWIDTH+2,0,"Choice 2");
    CreateItem(&t2,&m2,NULL,5,20,0);

    Menu1.NextMenu=&Menu2;
    Menu1.LeftEdge=0;
    Menu1.TopEdge=0;
    Menu1.Width=200;
    Menu1.Height=100;
    Menu1.Flags=MENUENABLED;
    Menu1.MenuName="My First Menu";
    Menu1.FirstItem=&m0;

    /* =======Set up a second menu==========*/


    CreateMes(&xt0,CHECKWIDTH+2,0,"Choice 1");
    CreateItem(&xt0,&x0,&x1,5,10,0);

    CreateMes(&xt1,CHECKWIDTH+2,0,"Choice 2");
    CreateItem(&xt1,&x1,NULL,5,20,0);

    Menu2.NextMenu=NULL;
    Menu2.LeftEdge=220;
    Menu2.TopEdge=0;
    Menu2.Width=200;
    Menu2.Height=100;
    Menu2.Flags=MENUENABLED;
    Menu2.MenuName="My Second Menu";
    Menu2.FirstItem=&x0;


    /*  ======Open a borderless window======*/

    x=y=0;
```

Listing 3-14 cont.

```
  w=640;
  h=200;
  flags=ACTIVATE|BORDERLESS;
  NoBorder=(struct Window *)make_window(x,y,w,h,NULL,flags);


 /*    ======Open a plain window=====  */

  strcpy(name,"Plain Window ");
  x=y=20;
  w=300;
  h=100;
  flags=ACTIVATE;
  Wind=(struct Window *)make_window(x,y,w,h,name,flags);

 /*    =============Open up the menu===================== */

  SetMenuStrip(Wind,&Menu1);

 /*    ======Delay for a bit to show off the windows====== */

  delay_func(100);

 /* =========Close down the windows in order=======*/

  ClearMenuStrip(Wind);

  CloseWindow(Wind);

  delay_func(10);

  CloseWindow(NoBorder);
}

VOID OpenALL()
/* This function will open any necessary libraries */
{

  /*    ======Open Intuition====== */

  IntuitionBase=(struct IntuitionBase *)
            OpenLibrary("intuition.library",INTUITION_REV);

  if(IntuitionBase==NULL)
     exit(FALSE);
}

VOID CreateMes(x,left,top,mesg)
struct IntuiText *x;
SHORT left,top;
 UBYTE *mesg;
{
 x->FrontPen=0;
 x->BackPen=1;
```

Listing 3-14 cont.

```
  x->DrawMode=JAM1;
  x->LeftEdge=left;
  x->TopEdge=top;
  x->ITextFont=NULL;
  x->IText=mesg;
  x->NextText=NULL;
}

VOID CreateItem(name,item,next,left,top,flags)
UBYTE *name;
USHORT left,top;
ULONG flags;
struct MenuItem *item,*next;

/* This function will set up a simple MenuItem structure */
{
  item->NextItem=next;
  item->LeftEdge=left;
  item->TopEdge=top;
  item->Width=100;
  item->Height=10;
  item->Flags=CHECKIT|ITEMTEXT|HIGHCOMP|ITEMENABLED|flags;
  item->MutualExclude=NULL;
  item->ItemFill=(APTR)name;
  item->SelectFill=NULL;
  item->Command=NULL;
  item->SubItem=NULL;
}

make_window(x,y,w,h,name,flags)
SHORT x,y,w,h;
UBYTE *name;
ULONG flags;
/* This function will initialize the NewWindow structure
   and open the window  */
{
  struct NewWindow NewWindow;

  NewWindow.LeftEdge=x;
  NewWindow.TopEdge=y;
  NewWindow.Width=w;
  NewWindow.Height=h;
  NewWindow.DetailPen=-1;
  NewWindow.BlockPen=-1;
  NewWindow.Title=name;
  NewWindow.Flags=flags;
  NewWindow.IDCMPFlags=NULL;
  NewWindow.Type=WBENCHSCREEN;
  NewWindow.FirstGadget=NULL;
  NewWindow.CheckMark=NULL;
  NewWindow.Screen=NULL;
  NewWindow.BitMap=NULL;
  NewWindow.MinWidth=0;
  NewWindow.MinHeight=0;
```

Listing 3-14 cont.

```
   NewWindow.MaxWidth=0;
   NewWindow.MaxHeight=0;


   return(OpenWindow(&NewWindow));

}

VOID delay_func(factor)
int factor;
/* This function will cause a specified delay */
{
 int loop;

 for(loop=0;loop<factor*1000;loop++)
   ;

 return;
}
```

Listing 3-15 puts menus in two windows. This required that we create two disparate linked lists of menus and make two calls to *SetMenuStrip()*, as well as two to *ClearMenuStrip*.

Listing 3-15. Creation of menus in two windows. This shows only the creation and display, nothing is done with the menu items.

```
*/

#include "exec/types.h"
#include "intuition/intuition.h"

struct IntuitionBase *IntuitionBase;
struct Window *Wind,*NoBorder;

#define INTUITION_REV 29


main()
{
 ULONG flags;
 SHORT x,y,w,h;
 UBYTE *name;
 VOID delay_func(),OpenALL(),CreateMes(),CreateItem();
 struct Menu Menu1,Menu2,Menu3;
 struct MenuItem m0,m1,m2,x0,x1,p0,p1;
 struct IntuiText t0,t1,t2,xt0,xt1,pt0,pt1;

  OpenALL();
```

Listing 3-15 cont.

```
/*  ===========Set up a menu===========*/

CreateMes(&t0,CHECKWIDTH+2,0,"Choice 0");
CreateItem(&t0,&m0,&m1,5,0,CHECKED);

CreateMes(&t1,CHECKWIDTH+2,0,"Choice 1");
CreateItem(&t1,&m1,&m2,5,10,0);

CreateMes(&t2,CHECKWIDTH+2,0,"Choice 2");
CreateItem(&t2,&m2,NULL,5,20,0);

Menu1.NextMenu=&Menu2;
Menu1.LeftEdge=0;
Menu1.TopEdge=0;
Menu1.Width=200;
Menu1.Height=100;
Menu1.Flags=MENUENABLED;
Menu1.MenuName="My First Menu";
Menu1.FirstItem=&m0;

/* =======Set up a second menu==========*/


CreateMes(&xt0,CHECKWIDTH+2,0,"Choice 1");
CreateItem(&xt0,&x0,&x1,5,10,CHECKED);

CreateMes(&xt1,CHECKWIDTH+2,0,"Choice 2");
CreateItem(&xt1,&x1,NULL,5,20,0);

Menu2.NextMenu=NULL;
Menu2.LeftEdge=220;
Menu2.TopEdge=0;
Menu2.Width=200;
Menu2.Height=100;
Menu2.Flags=MENUENABLED;
Menu2.MenuName="My Second Menu";
Menu2.FirstItem=&x0;


/* =======And a third==========*/


CreateMes(&pt0,CHECKWIDTH+2,0,"Choice 1");
CreateItem(&pt0,&p0,&p1,5,10,0);

CreateMes(&pt1,CHECKWIDTH+2,0,"Choice 2");
CreateItem(&pt1,&p1,NULL,5,20,0);

Menu3.NextMenu=NULL;
Menu3.LeftEdge=0;
Menu3.TopEdge=0;
Menu3.Width=200;
Menu3.Height=100;
```

Listing 3-15 cont.

```
Menu3.Flags=MENUENABLED;
Menu3.MenuName="Second Window Menu";
Menu3.FirstItem=&p0;



   /*  ======Open a borderless window======*/
   name="A Window without Borders";
   x=y=0;
   w=640;
   h=200;
   flags=ACTIVATE|BORDERLESS;
   NoBorder=(struct Window *)make_window(x,y,w,h,name,flags);


  /*    ======Open a plain window=====   */

   name="Window: 2 Cents Plain";
   x=y=20;
   w=300;
   h=100;
   flags=ACTIVATE;
   Wind=(struct Window *)make_window(x,y,w,h,name,flags);

  /*    ==============Open up the menu===================== */

   SetMenuStrip(NoBorder,&Menu3);

   SetMenuStrip(Wind,&Menu1);

  /*    ======Delay for a bit to show off the windows====== */

   delay_func(100);

  /* =========Close down the windows in order=======*/

   ClearMenuStrip(Wind);

   ClearMenuStrip(NoBorder);

   CloseWindow(Wind);

   delay_func(10);

   CloseWindow(NoBorder);
}

VOID OpenALL()
/* This function will open any necessary libraries */
{

  /*    ======Open Intuition======= */
```

Listing 3-15 cont.

```
 IntuitionBase=(struct IntuitionBase *)
          OpenLibrary("intuition.library",INTUITION_REV);

 if(IntuitionBase==NULL)
    exit(FALSE);
}

VOID CreateMes(x,left,top,mesg)
struct IntuiText *x;
SHORT left,top;
 UBYTE *mesg;
{
 x->FrontPen=0;
 x->BackPen=1;
 x->DrawMode=JAM1;
 x->LeftEdge=left;
 x->TopEdge=top;
 x->ITextFont=NULL;
 x->IText=mesg;
 x->NextText=NULL;
}


VOID CreateItem(name,item,next,left,top,flags)
UBYTE *name;
USHORT left,top;
ULONG flags;
struct MenuItem *item,*next;

/* This function will set up a simple MenuItem structure */
{
  item->NextItem=next;
  item->LeftEdge=left;
  item->TopEdge=top;
  item->Width=100;
  item->Height=10;
  item->Flags=CHECKIT|ITEMTEXT|HIGHCOMP|ITEMENABLED|flags;
  item->MutualExclude=NULL;
  item->ItemFill=(APTR)name;
  item->SelectFill=NULL;
  item->Command=NULL;
  item->SubItem=NULL;
}


make_window(x,y,w,h,name,flags)
SHORT x,y,w,h;
UBYTE *name;
ULONG flags;
/* This function will initialize the NewWindow structure
   and open the window  */
{
  struct NewWindow NewWindow;

  NewWindow.LeftEdge=x;
  NewWindow.TopEdge=y;
```

Listing 3-15 cont.

```
NewWindow.Width=w;
NewWindow.Height=h;
NewWindow.DetailPen=-1;
NewWindow.BlockPen=-1;
NewWindow.Title=name;
NewWindow.Flags=flags;
NewWindow.IDCMPFlags=NULL;
NewWindow.Type=WBENCHSCREEN;
NewWindow.FirstGadget=NULL;
NewWindow.CheckMark=NULL;
NewWindow.Screen=NULL;
NewWindow.BitMap=NULL;
NewWindow.MinWidth=0;
NewWindow.MinHeight=0;
NewWindow.MaxWidth=0;
NewWindow.MaxHeight=0;


    return(OpenWindow(&NewWindow));

}

VOID delay_func(factor)
int factor;
/* This function will cause a specified delay */
{
 int loop;

 for(loop=0;loop<factor*1000;loop++)
    ;

 return;
}
```

There are still more things that you can do with menus. Some of these are very basic, such as getting input from them. Some are more dramatic—for example, using graphics techniques to create on screen menus.

Requesters

Intuition offers us another menu-like facility for entering values: the *requester*. Whenever a program needs a value from the user, a requester is called for. This object halts the operation of its application and waits for a reply. This is in contrast to the more passive menu, whose calling sequence is completely under the control of the user. The user must explicitly call the menu by moving the mouse cursor to the proper position and pushing the proper buttons. More importantly, a user can leave the menu without entering anything into the program—without making a choice. A requester, in contrast, demands input. Even requesters that can be explicitly controlled by the user must be satisfied once they are called.

Requesters are more flexible than menus and may be used for some menu activities to greater effect. A menu must be at the top of the screen in the title bar. It is detached from its enclosing window and, in a complicated display containing many windows, could even confuse the user. A requester appears in its associated window and, in fact, can be placed anywhere within this enclosing space. Because of this, a requester can be placed near an object that it directly affects: a request for a color change near a drawing, a frequency input adjacent to the display of its wave form. The effect is more dramatic and more appropriate to the complex displays typical of large programs— particularly those that take advantage of the Amiga's complex support software.

A requester is defined by its system defined structure.

```
struct Requester {
    struct Requester *OlderRequest;
    SHORT   LeftEdge,TopEdge,Width,Height RelLeft,RelTop;
    struct Gadget   *ReqGadget;
    struct Border   *ReqBorder;
    struct IntuiText *ReqText;
    USHORT Flags;
    UBYTE  BackFill;
    struct ClipRect  ReqCRect;
    struct BitMap   *ImageBMap;
    struct BitMap   ReqBmap;
};
```

As the structure definition shows, much of the power of this object comes from its interaction with the graphics subsystem. The system maintains a linked list of requesters in order of appearance. This supports the nesting of these objects that is a feature of Intuition. *OlderRequest* refers to this activity and is set accordingly by the operating system. *Width* and *Height* define the limits of the box that frames the requester display. This must be big enough to contain all of the text and non-text objects that will be used to create the object. The requester box can be as large as the window— but no larger—and arbitrarily small.

The positioning of the requester box refers to two sets of values. If the requester is to be placed in a fixed position within the window, then the fields *LeftEdge* and *TopEdge* will set this coordinate. However, if you initialize *RelLeft* and *RelTop* instead, the requester box will be positioned near the current position of the cursor. These two fields will set the offset. It is also necessary to set the POINTREL flag in the *Flags* field. It should be noted that *RelLeft* and *RelTop* are advisory; if the offsets specified would place the requester outside the window, the actual values are ignored and it is placed as close to them as is possible. The rest of the fields refer to the requester's interaction with the graphics subsystem.

Before leaving the subject of requesters, there is one useful function that is appropriate to discuss here: *AutoRequest()*. This function automatically creates and installs a boolean requester—one that seeks a yes or no answer. These boolean objects account for a large number of incidents of this data type. The general form of *AutoRequest()* is:

```
AutoRequest(w_ptr,b_text,p_text,n_text,p_flags,n_flags,width,height);
```

where

w__ptr points to a window.

b__text points to a character string that holds the characters to be printed in the body of the requester.

p__text is a pointer to the text associated with the positive response.

n__text is the message associated with the negative response.

p__flags and **n__flags** are IDCMP flags.

width and **height** specify the size of the requester box.

This function will automatically create a requester for the application.

Listing 3-16 shows an example that creates and opens a simple boolean requester using the *AutoRequest()* function. Again, we used the *CreateMes()* function to produce the three IntuiText messages necessary for the requester initialization:

- One to explain what the requester wants
- One to describe the positive choice
- One to describe the negative

Width and *Height* are set at 250 and 100 respectively. We set no special flags in this object. Requester input, like menu input must be through the normal I/O channels.

Listing 3-16. Creation of a very simple requester using the AutoRequest() function.

```
*/

#include "exec/types.h"
#include "intuition/intuition.h"

struct IntuitionBase *IntuitionBase;
struct Screen *Scrn;
struct Window *wind0,*wind1;

#define INTUITION_REV 29


main()
{
 ULONG flags;
 SHORT x,y,w,h,d;
 USHORT mode;
 UBYTE *name,c0,c1;
```

Listing 3-16 cont.

```
VOID delay_func(),OpenALL(),CreateMes();
struct IntuiText prompt,yprompt,nprompt;

OpenALL();

/*  ======Open a hi-res custom screen==== */

 name="Requests Now Being Taken";
 y=0;
 w=640;
 h=200;
 d=3;
 c0=0x00;
 c1=0x01;
 mode=HIRES;

 Scrn=(struct Screen *)
         make_screen(y,w,h,d,c0,c1,mode,name);

/*  =======Open a window==============*/

 name="Window 1";
 x=20;
 y=20;
 w=400;
 h=150;
 flags=ACTIVATE|WINDOWSIZING|WINDOWDEPTH|WINDOWDRAG|
                              WINDOWCLOSE|SMART_REFRESH;
 c0=-0x01;
 c1=-0x01;

 wind0=(struct Window *)
         make_window(x,y,w,h,name,flags,c0,c1,Scrn,NULL);

/*    ======Build and display a requester======  */

 CreateMes(&prompt,45,25,"Stop The Music!");
 CreateMes(&yprompt,3,3,"Yes");
 CreateMes(&nprompt,3,3,"No");

 AutoRequest(wind0,&prompt,&yprompt,&nprompt,NULL,NULL,250,100);

 delay_func(100);

/* ========Close down the window then the screen========*/

 CloseWindow(wind0);
 CloseScreen(Scrn);

}

VOID OpenALL()
/* This function will open any necessary libraries */
{
```

Listing 3-16 cont.

```
/*   ======Open Intuition====== */

IntuitionBase=(struct IntuitionBase *)
        OpenLibrary("intuition.library",INTUITION_REV);

if(IntuitionBase==NULL)
    exit(FALSE);
}

VOID CreateMes(x,left,top,mesg)
struct IntuiText *x;
SHORT left,top;
UBYTE *mesg;
/* This will prepare a message for display as IntuiText */
{
 x->FrontPen=0;
 x->BackPen=1;
 x->DrawMode=JAM1;
 x->LeftEdge=left;
 x->TopEdge=top;
 x->ITextFont=NULL;
 x->IText=mesg;
 x->NextText=NULL;
}

make_window(x,y,w,h,name,flags,color0,color1,screen,gadg)
SHORT x,y,w,h;
UBYTE *name,color0,color1;
ULONG flags;
struct Screen *screen;
struct Gadget *gadg;
/* This function will initialize the NewWindow structure
    and open the window  */
{
    struct NewWindow NewWindow;

    NewWindow.LeftEdge=x;
    NewWindow.TopEdge=y;
    NewWindow.Width=w;
    NewWindow.Height=h;
    NewWindow.DetailPen=color0;
    NewWindow.BlockPen=color1;
    NewWindow.Title=name;
    NewWindow.Flags=flags;
    NewWindow.IDCMPFlags=NULL;
    NewWindow.Type=CUSTOMSCREEN;
    NewWindow.FirstGadget=gadg;
    NewWindow.CheckMark=NULL;
    NewWindow.Screen=screen;
    NewWindow.BitMap=NULL;
    NewWindow.MinWidth=1;
    NewWindow.MinHeight=1;
    NewWindow.MaxWidth=640;
```

Listing 3-16 cont.

```
  NewWindow.MaxHeight=200;


  return(OpenWindow(&NewWindow));
}

make_screen(y,w,h,d,color0,color1,mode,name)
SHORT y,w,h,d;
UBYTE color0,color1,*name;
USHORT mode;
{
 struct NewScreen NewScreen;

 NewScreen.LeftEdge=0;
 NewScreen.TopEdge=y;
 NewScreen.Width=w;
 NewScreen.Height=h;
 NewScreen.Depth=d;
 NewScreen.DetailPen=color0;
 NewScreen.BlockPen=color1;
 NewScreen.ViewModes=mode;
 NewScreen.Type=CUSTOMSCREEN;
 NewScreen.Font=NULL;
 NewScreen.DefaultTitle=name;
 NewScreen.Gadgets=NULL;
 NewScreen.CustomBitMap=NULL;

 return(OpenScreen(&NewScreen));
}

VOID delay_func(factor)
int factor;
/* This function will cause a specified delay */
{
 int loop;

 for(loop=0;loop<factor*1000;loop++)
   ;

 return;
}
```

Alerts

Everyone who has programmed on the Amiga has come face to face with one version of the *alert* data object—the "Guru Meditation" box. Alerts are a kind of requester, but one that is reserved for extreme situations—usually, system or program faults that cannot be reversed. They represent an elegant way for the system to crash, inform the user that it is about to go down, and give whatever information it may possess about the error situation. Although the operating system is the origin of most alert messages which a user will receive, it is possible to create application specific ones.

Two kinds of alert objects are recognized by Intuition:

1. Those situations from which it may be possible to back out (RECOVERY__ALERT)

2. Those which will require a reboot of the system (DEADEND __ALERT)

Each of these situations is signaled by the appropriate flag values in a call to the system function, *DisplayAlert()*. In the case of a RECOVERY__ALERT, the application will proceed, depending on action by the user. If the left mouse button is pushed, the function returns true; otherwise it is equal to false. In either case, the normal display is returned.

Two additional parameters are necessary to *DisplayAlert()*: a string which comprises the alert message and a height value indicating how many lines it will take up on the screen. Alerts are always displayed from the top of the screen. The format of this function is:

```
DisplayAlert(AlertNumber,Text,Height)
```

where

> **AlertNumber** is either RECOVERY__ALERT or DEADEND __ALERT as appropriate; it is type LONG.
>
> **Height** indicates how many lines will be necessary for the display.
>
> **Text** is of the format:
> x coordinate (2 bytes)
> y coordinate (1 byte)
> text to appear in the alert box.
> continuation byte to indicate a possible substring.

Intuition I/O

There is an *input device* that monitors the interface to the outside world. Usually this outside world consists of the keyboard and the mouse. When either or both of these objects produce some value, the input device creates an *input event*. This is a message that reports the value that was produced. Input events can be created by other objects, both internal and external. For example, specialized input devices, a network device, or even internal software can trigger the input device to create one of these special purpose messages.

All input events are merged into an *input stream*. This stream is available to other parts of the Amiga. Individual events can be extracted by different subsystems, while the rest of the stream is ignored. Intuition acts as a filter for the applications that are running under it. Most importantly, it only passes the event stream to the active application.

Intuition provides two ways for an application to receive the input event stream:

1. Intuition can pass it directly through the Direct Communications Message Ports (IDCMP) facility. This provides unprocessed and untranslated input values.

2. Alternately, Intuition can filter this input through the console device.

The console device is a kind of virtual terminal, which will process the input values, doing some translations and reporting out well-behaved values. Values coming out of this device will be ASCII characters or well-behaved control sequences—usually ANSI standard escape sequences.

The IDCMP Facility

The IDCMP facility sends through to the application only raw events. These are completely unprocessed and uninterpreted; the application must make sense of them itself. The first thing that must be done is to choose those events in which the application is interested. Recall that most of the event stream will be passed through by Intuition, although it does trap some events in which it has a proprietary interest. Choice is exercised by setting the IDCMP flags. These flags are found in every object definition in Intuition: windows, screens, gadgets, menus, everything. Furthermore, in order to receive these messages, the application must continuously check the message port that has been provided by Intuition. These events are instances of the *IntuiMessage* object. As with other Intuition objects, this one is defined and manipulated by a specific structure.

Contrast this to the text-only display that comes through the console device. This is in the form of the ASCII character set that is so familiar to computer users. Values that are meant to be interpreted as control messages are translated into escape sequences—strings of characters preceded by the ESC character. All translating performed by the console device is under the control of the application. Translation sequences and key mapping can be altered. It is also possible to open both a console device and an IDCMP port in a single window to get both kinds of input. Similarly, a window can be opened with neither one of these facilities available. Such a window can accept no input.

The IDCMP facility will specifically inform an application about mouse, keyboard, and Intuition-generated events. IDCMP also defines a class of verification functions that allow the application to deal elegantly with asynchronous events, such as menu or requester input. In fact, the only way to access these functions is through the IDCMP.

The IDCMP itself consists of complementary message ports for both the application process and for Intuition. These ports are opened automatically whenever an IDCMP flag is set in the definition of a window. These ports can be manipulated after the window is open by the *ModifyIDCMP()* function.

```
ModifyIDCMP(w_ptr,flags)
```

where

w_ptr points to a window.

flags contains a flag value indicating the desired change.

flags:

NULL indicates whether or not the window is open and closes it.

MOUSEBUTTONS reports the state of the buttons on the mouse.

SELECTDOWN, SELECTUP, MENUDOWN, MENUUP sets Intuition to trap these events.

MOUSEMOVE reports mouse movements in absolute x,y values.

DELTAMOVE reports mouse movements as amounts of change from last position.

GADGETDOWN, GADGETUP indicates these conditions for the gadgets.

CLOSEWINDOWN indicates that this gadget has been picked.

MENUPICK, MENUVERIFY reports these events concerning menu.

REQSET, REQCLEAR indicates the first and the last requestor respectively

REQVERIFY verifies conditions before a requestor is drawn.

NEWSIZE indicates a user has resized the window.

REFRESHWINDOW reports that a window needs refreshing.

SIZEVERIFY causes a drawing to be finished before a resizing.

RAWKEY bypasses the key translator table.

NEWPREFS indicates that preferences have been changed.

DISKINSERTED, DISKREMOVED indicates that these events have occured.

This function can also be used to modify the IDCMP functions requested for the window. Messages are exchanged via an *IntuiMessage* structure initialized with the desired values.

The form of an IntuiMessage structure is:

```
struct IntuiMessage  {
    struct Message       ExecMessage;
    ULONG                Class;
    USHORT               Code,
                         Qualifier;
    APTR                 IAddress;
    SHORT                MouseX,
                         MouseY;
    ULONG                Seconds,
                         Micros;
    struct Window        *IDCMPWindow;
```

```
    struct InutiMessage  *SpecialLink;
};
```

where

ExecMessage is a link to the Exec kernel message system.

Class, Code links this message to Intuition.

Qualifier refers to the input device.

MouseX, MouseY are relative to the upper left corner of the current window.

Seconds, Micros reports the current system clock.

IAddress points to an object associated with the message.

IDCMPWindow points to the window associated with the message.

SpecialLink is used by the system.

The *ExecMessage* and *SpecialLink* fields are used by the operating system to manage and route the message. The other fields contain the information and values necessary to the calling application.

The *Class* field indicates the IDCMP flag value that is being transmitted.

The *Code* field is interpreted in terms of the class of the message. It contains special values such as a menu or MenuItem number. In the case of a RAWKEY event, it contains the generated code value.

The *Qualifier* field is set by the input device and is also useful for RAWKEY situations. It indicates if the value sent has been accompanied by a qualifying event such as a SHIFT or CTRL key value.

MouseX and *MouseY* report the coordinates of the cursor relative to the upper left-hand corner of the window.

The *Seconds* and *Micros* fields contain the current time; this can be evaluated to give the date as well.

Iaddress contains the address of an object significant to the message. *IDCMPWINDOW* is the window address for the message.

By interpreting these fields, an application can interpret the IDCMP stream.

The events that generate these IntuiMessages are set by the IDCMP flags. These include:

- MOUSEBUTTONS to report on the status of the buttons on the pointing device. Both up and down events are recognized. The code field of the structure contains either SELECTDOWN, SELECTUP, MENUDOWN, or MENUUP. The latter two are only reported if the RMBTRAP flag is set. Otherwise, Intuition deals directly with these two actions.

- MOUSEMOVE causes a set of x and y values to be reported, indicating the movement of the mouse. This is dependent on either REPORTMOUSE or some gadget's FOLLOWMOUSE flag being set simultaneously. If DELTAMOVE is also set, this report is in the form of a change from last position and not as an absolute coordinate.

Certain flags are associated with a gadget:

- GADGETDOWN is reported under appropriate circumstances if the GADGIMMEDIATE flag has been set. Gadget reports require the setting of the RELVERIFY flag.

- CLOSEWINDOW indicates that this system-defined gadget has been chosen.

There are two menu flags:

- MENUPICK indicates the selection of a menu. The number of the item or sub-item chosen will be in the *Code* field of the IntuiMessage structure.

- MENUVERIFY causes any MENUPICK operation to wait for completion, until the application has responded to the message requesting it. All windows with this flag set must respond before operation can continue. Only the active window can cancel menu operations.

The requester flags are:

- REQSET reports the first requester open in a window.

- REQCLEAR reports the last requester cleared; it is the complement to REQSET.

- REQVERIFY, like its menu counterpart holds a requester pending until a reply from the application is received. Only the first requester is kept waiting.

Window information is also reported.

- NEWSIZE indicates a resizing operation has been performed on the window.

- REFRESHWINDOW sends a message, if a refresh operation is necessary. This is only valid when SIMPLE_REFRESH or SMART_REFRESH have also been set.

- SIZEVERIFY halts a sizing operation until the application signals it to continue.

- ACTIVEWINDOW and INACTIVEWINDOW send a report, indicating that a window has gone into one of these states.

Miscellaneous flags include:

- RAWKEY sends unprocessed keycodes from the keyboard. These values are found in the *Code* field of the structure.

- NEWPREFS sends a report indicating that the system preferences have been altered. A call to *GetPrefs()* will return the new values.

- DISKINSERTED and DISKREMOVED indicate when these disk-oriented events have occurred.

The verification functions operate in a different way from the other IDCMP functions. These send a message and then go to sleep via an Exec

Wait( ) function. The activity that they request is halted pending a reply from the receiving task. The function will not proceed until this occurs. Caution is advised with this particular set of functions. There is potential for a system log jam here, as tasks are held awaiting permission to complete. One way to ameliorate this problem is to create a monitoring task to manage such potential bottlenecks.

Setting up a monitoring task involves creating and linking two ports: the window port and the monitor task's port. Intuition can open both of these. Alternatively, you can explicitly open a task message port and link it to the window port.

The monitor task will respond to each message and decide what can be done and what must be held. Whatever the decision, the message is replied to immediately, so that the message port can be cleared and a bottleneck avoided. The basic algorithm is

- Read the message.
- Copy the values from the message structure.
- *Reply( )* to the message.

The important thing is to keep the message port clear. Rather than depending on the operating system to handle these problems, the task itself must take responsibility for them.

An example program that uses the IDCMP facility to communicate with a window is found in Listing 3-17. After opening a background and a foreground window, this program sets up a read-loop that monitors the IDCMP port. Specifically, it is looking for a CLOSEWINDOW event. The loop is created by using a *Wait( )* function to suspend operation, pending the reception of signal. When that occurs, all of the queued-up messages are stripped off through the *GetMsg( )* function and properly replied to through *Reply( )*. If any of these messages contains a window close request, it is honored.

Listing 3-17. Use of the IDCMP to communicate with an open window.

```
*/

#include "exec/types.h"
#include "intuition/intuition.h"

struct IntuitionBase *IntuitionBase;
struct Window *Wind,*NoBorder;


struct IntuiMessage *mesg;


#define INTUITION_REV 29


main()
```

Listing 3-17 cont.

```c
{
 ULONG flags,iflags,mclass;
 SHORT x,y,w,h;
 VOID delay_func(),OpenALL();

 OpenALL();

  /*  ======Open a borderless window======*/

  x=y=0;
  w=640;
  h=200;
  flags=ACTIVATE|BORDERLESS;
  iflags=NULL;
  NoBorder=(struct Window *)
     make_window(x,y,w,h,NULL,flags,iflags);


  /*   ======Open a plain window=====  */

  x=y=20;
  w=300;
  h=100;
  flags=ACTIVATE|WINDOWSIZING|WINDOWCLOSE|WINDOWDRAG;
  iflags=CLOSEWINDOW;
  Wind=(struct Window *)
     make_window(x,y,w,h,"Window",flags,iflags);

 /* ===Set Up an IDCMP Read Loop ==== */

  Wait(1<<Wind->UserPort->mp_SigBit);

  while((mesg=(struct IntuiMessage *)
     GetMsg(Wind->UserPort))!=NULL)  {
       mclass=mesg->Class;
       ReplyMsg(mesg);
  }
     if(mclass==CLOSEWINDOW)  {
        CloseWindow(Wind);
        delay_func(100);
        CloseWindow(NoBorder);
      }
}


VOID OpenALL()
/* This function will open any required libraries */
{
 /*==Intuition...*/

 IntuitionBase=(struct IntuitionBase *)
          OpenLibrary("intuition.library",INTUITION_REV);

 if(IntuitionBase==NULL)
```

Listing 3-17 cont.

```
        exit(FALSE);
}

make_window(x,y,w,h,name,flags,iflags)
SHORT x,y,w,h;
UBYTE *name;
ULONG flags,iflags;
/* This function will initialize the NewWindow structure
     and open the window  */
{
  struct NewWindow NewWindow;

  NewWindow.LeftEdge=x;
  NewWindow.TopEdge=y;
  NewWindow.Width=w;
  NewWindow.Height=h;
  NewWindow.DetailPen=-1;
  NewWindow.BlockPen=-1;
  NewWindow.Title=name;
  NewWindow.Flags=flags;
  NewWindow.IDCMPFlags=iflags;
  NewWindow.Type=WBENCHSCREEN;
  NewWindow.FirstGadget=NULL;
  NewWindow.CheckMark=NULL;
  NewWindow.Screen=NULL;
  NewWindow.BitMap=NULL;
  NewWindow.MinWidth=0;
  NewWindow.MinHeight=0;
  NewWindow.MaxWidth=640;
  NewWindow.MaxHeight=200;


  return(OpenWindow(&NewWindow));

}

VOID delay_func(factor)
int factor;
/* This function will cause a specified delay */
{
 int loop;

 for(loop=0;loop<factor*1000;loop++)
    ;

 return;
}
```

The Console Device

There are three methods for putting values on the display:

1. An image can be directly created by using the graphics primitives built into the operating system kernel. This gives maximum flexibility.

2. Intuition also supplies a similar set of graphics routines, which allow an application to display values and pictures. These routines take responsibility for more of the detail work of creating images. As a result, they are easy to use.

3. If the only output is text, the console device can be used. This displays line-oriented text with all of the features of a traditional terminal display.

We will leave the graphics techniques for a later chapter and turn our attention here to text output.

The console device is the preferred medium for text-oriented output: it adds the text processing, editing, and formatting capabilities that we have come to expect from a computer terminal. Although this device exists outside of Intuition, it can easily and smoothly interface with a window to produce a pleasing and convenient user interface. There are two ways to activate the console device: as an AmigaDOS device file or directly through calls to the executive kernel.

The AmigaDOS console is the easiest to deal with, although it does involve the most operating system overhead. Under AmigaDOS, a console is treated as a kind of file—a byte stream. It is a sequential file of character strings with no further organization. Another qualification placed on this kind of console concerns the nature of the values. Raw, unprocessed input is one option, but well-behaved ASCII characters can be specified and are the rule. *Open()* is the AmigaDOS function call that sets up and starts the console. A call to the complementary *Close()* will shut it down. Access is equally simple; it, too, is byte-oriented. The controlling task must supply a buffer to hold the input characters and a count of how many are going in or out. Once these parameters are set and the console is opened, access is through an appropriate AmigaDOS function call: *Read()* or *Write()*. This topic will be covered more fully in Chapter 4, which deals with the AmigaDOS operating environment.

More flexibility is available by opening the console device directly, bypassing AmigaDOS. To do this you must access the executive kernel. The first step is to allocate an *IOStdReq* structure, but in this case you need only initialize one of the fields. The *io_Data* field is set with a pointer to the window in question. A call to *OpenDevice()* starts up the console device, connecting it to the specified window. IOStdReq is also set up for communication between these two objects. At this point, text can be sent back and forth between the console and the window.

To read from the console device, the following steps are necessary:

*   Set the *io_Data* field of *IOStdReq* to the address of a string buffer.

*   Set the *io_Length* field to the number of bytes expected in the transfer operation.

*   Finally, put the CMD_READ flag into *io_Command*.

The read will be initiated by one of the I/O functions. *DoIO()* will transmit the request and then halt the task until that request is satisfied. *SendIO()*, in contrast, will transmit the request and then return control to the calling program, even before that request has been satisfied. The field *io__Actual* will contain the number of bytes that were actually transferred.

Text is written to the window in a similar way. The *io__Data* field and *io__Length* field are initiated as before, but this time the buffer contains the message to be sent. The *io__Command* field is set equal to the flag CMD__WRITE. Either *DoIO()* or *SendIO()* begins the request. Text will be written only in the non-border area of the window; it will never overwrite the border gadgets. A line that is too long to fit into the window space will be wrapped around to the next line.

A program illustrating these functions and procedures can be found in Listing 3-18. Here the function *Send__Message()* is created to properly initialize a IOStdReq structure and use it to send a message.

Listing 3-18. Placement of text in a window using direct control of the console device.

```
*/

#include "exec/types.h"
#include "intuition/intuition.h"

struct IntuitionBase *IntuitionBase;
struct Window *Wind,*NoBorder;


#define INTUITION_REV 29


main()
{
 ULONG flags;
 SHORT x,y,w,h;
 VOID delay_func(),OpenALL();

 OpenALL();

  /*  ======Open a borderless window======*/

  x=y=0;
  w=640;
  h=200;
  flags=ACTIVATE|BORDERLESS;
  NoBorder=(struct Window *)make_window(x,y,w,h,NULL,flags);


  /*   ======Open some plain windows=====  */

  x=y=20;
  w=300;
  h=100;
```

Listing 3-18 cont.

```
    flags=ACTIVATE;
    Wind=(struct Window *)make_window(x,y,w,h,"Window",flags);

    /* ===Send a message to the window=== */

    Send_Message(Wind,"I'm seeing the world in a window");


    /*    ======Delay for a bit to show off the windows====== */

    delay_func(100);

    /* =========Close down the windows in order========*/

    delay_func(10);

    CloseWindow(Wind);

    delay_func(10);

    CloseWindow(NoBorder);
}


VOID OpenALL()
/* This function will open any required libraries */
{
  /*==Intuition...*/

  IntuitionBase=(struct IntuitionBase *)
            OpenLibrary("intuition.library",INTUITION_REV);

  if(IntuitionBase==NULL)
     exit(FALSE);
}

make_window(x,y,w,h,name,flags)
SHORT x,y,w,h;
UBYTE *name;
ULONG flags;
/* This function will initialize the NewWindow structure
   and open the window  */
{
    struct NewWindow NewWindow;

    NewWindow.LeftEdge=x;
    NewWindow.TopEdge=y;
    NewWindow.Width=w;
    NewWindow.Height=h;
    NewWindow.DetailPen=-1;
    NewWindow.BlockPen=-1;
    NewWindow.Title=name;
    NewWindow.Flags=flags;
```

Listing 3-18 cont.

```
   NewWindow.IDCMPFlags=NULL;
   NewWindow.Type=WBENCHSCREEN;
   NewWindow.FirstGadget=NULL;
   NewWindow.CheckMark=NULL;
   NewWindow.Screen=NULL;
   NewWindow.BitMap=NULL;
   NewWindow.MinWidth=0;
   NewWindow.MinHeight=0;
   NewWindow.MaxWidth=0;
   NewWindow.MaxHeight=0;


   return(OpenWindow(&NewWindow));

}

VOID delay_func(factor)
int factor;
/* This function will cause a specified delay */
{
 int loop;

 for(loop=0;loop<factor*1000;loop++)
    ;

 return;
}
```

```
Send_Message(to_window,message)
struct Window *to_window;
UBYTE *message;
{
 struct IOStdReq mesg;

 /* ===Open the console in the window=== */

 mesg.io_Data=(APTR)to_window;
 OpenDevice("console.device",0,&mesg,0);

 /* ===send the message=== */

 mesg.io_Data=message;
 mesg.io_Length=-1;
 mesg.io_Command=CMD_WRITE;
 DoIO(&mesg);

 /* ===tidy up=== */

 CloseDevice(&mesg);

}
```

With the console device comes a full range of control sequences. These sequences offer special formatting and display options that allow the console device to mimic virtually any existing terminal, or allow the user to customize to personal taste. In fact, the entire set of keyboard bindings—the values assigned to each keyboard code—can be altered by an application.

Remembering Memory

Intuition supplies a support subsystem that makes the allocation and de-allocation of memory within a task simple and straightforward. The key to this facility is the *Remember* structure.

```
struct Remember  {

    struct  Remember    *NextRemember;

    ULONG               RememberSize;

    UBYTE               *Memory;

}
```

where

NextRemember points to the next string on the chain.

RememberSize is the number of bytes in this node.

Memory points to the memory associated with this node.

NextRemember is the standard executive structure for creating linked lists of data objects. This allows the creation of links of memory nodes, which can then be managed locally. *RememberSize* keeps the number of bytes allocated for the particular node, and *Memory* is the address of the actual allocation of bytes.

To allocate a chain of memory, we have only to create a variable, *RememberKey*, that is a pointer to the Remember structure type; this must be initialized to NULL. Repeated calls to *AllocRemember()* create the node, allocate the memory requested and link it into the list anchored by *RememberKey*. A call to *FreeRemember()*, passing it this variable, returns the entire list of memory allocations to the operating system for reuse.

Accessing Preferences

The *preferences* tool allows the user to set a wide variety of system operator parameters, ranging from the shape and color of the mouse cursor to the type of printer expected. These values will sometimes have a bearing on the operation of an application task. It is possible to access these values, although only the Workbench Preferences tool can actually alter them.

All access to these values is through the *Preferences* structure, shown below.

```
struct Preferences  {
    BYTE          FontHeight;
    UBYTE         PrinterPort;
    USHORT        BaudRate;
    struct timeval KeyRptSpeed,
                  KeyRptDelay;
    struct timeval DoubleClick;
    USHORT        PointerMatrix[POINTERSIZE];
    BYTE          XOffset,
                  YOffset;
    USHORT        color17,
                  color18,
                  color19,
                  ViewXOffset,
                  ViewYOffset;
    WORD          ViewInitX,
                  ViewInitY;
    BOOL          EnableCLI;
    USHORT        PrinterType;
    UBYTE         PrinterFilename[FILENAME_SIZE];
    USHORT        PrintPitch,
                  PrintQuality,
                  PrintSpacing;
    UWORD         PrintLeftMargin,
                  PrintRightMargin;
    USHORT        PrintImage,
                  PrintAspect,
                  PrintShade;
    UWORD         PrintTheshold;
    USHORT        PaperSize;
    UWORD         PaperLength;
    USHORT        PaperType;
};
```

Each field reports specific values of various subsystems of the computer.

Access is accomplished by declaring such a structure and then using it to call the Intuition function *GetPrefs()*. This fills the structure with the current settings; fields of interest can then be inspected for new values. If the volume in question does not contain the preferences tool, the function *GetDefPref()* will return the default preferences set—those that were in effect on the boot diskette.

It should be noted that the fields are grouped in order of most-to-least commonly used. It is possible to pass either of these functions a truncated buffer. The function will return as many values as it can fit in the smaller space. This allows a more efficient method of access if the desired values are near the top.

Summary

This has been a long chapter and a difficult one to summarize. We have covered the topic of Intuition and its basic operation. This has run the gamut from the very basic notions of screens and windows, through the complex tasks of defining menus and gadgets, to input and output through a window-based operating system, ending up with the system preferences data structure. We have seen Intuition as a very complicated but very rich operating environment, which repays the extra effort required in programming with a very flexible operating system that allows us to create software that is reliable and easy to use.

Process Control
and AmigaDOS

Chapter 4

T he Amiga has a traditional operating system, AmigaDOS, which works together with Intuition. The most important task of AmigaDOS is resource management, including not only the file management system, but the all-important multiprocessing system. In this chapter, we'll discuss the use of this operating system resource to create programs that run successfully in an environment with other executing processes.

Multitasking

Most large computers—in contrast to the ubiquitous microcomputer, which has become almost a fixture in our daily lives—are scarce resources. In order to use them, you must schedule time, make a reservation for a terminal period, or even submit a program to be run. Every effort has been expended to wring the last bit of operating time out of them. To this end, these systems are invariably multitasking: they run more than one program at a time. Indeed, they are more than this; they are also multi-user, serving more than a single user at a time.

Until recently, microcomputers have not been treated in quite the same way. Because of their origin as small, general purpose machines, many of these machines have correspondingly simple operating systems. Usually, they can run only a single program at a time. Attempts have been made to create an environment in which more than one program can be in memory, but even then only one of these programs is available to the user at any given time. Switching from one to the other can be quite awkward.

The advantages of multitasking are obvious: an increased productivity in terms of number of tasks performed per unit of time. If I can run two or three programs at the same time on my computer, I can accomplish more than if I can only run one. The trade-offs may not be so obvious, however. It is not just that a multitasking operating system is more complex than a single-user system. If this were the only difference, we would have long ago seen such operating systems dominate the small computer market. The complexity of multitasking also requires hardware support: increased memory and speed of computation—things that have only recently become available for a reasonable price in small computers.

The Amiga is an ideal machine to implement this more complex system software. It has a powerful and fast microprocessor chip, capable of addressing up to 8 million bytes of memory, coupled with a set of specialized processors that ease the burden of the main CPU, leaving plenty of time for it to do the housekeeping associated with multitasking.

The Process

Most of us are used to thinking of the program as the main object of attention in a computer. We write it, compile it, swear over it, and finally, run it. This is a perfectly adequate view when dealing with a single-tasking system. The compiled program consists of a series of executable machine commands —numbers that represent instructions for the CPU or that identify locations in memory where data is stored. The object file is really an image of the memory when the program runs. Loading the program is a process of copying from the disk directly into memory. Since there is only one program, it is always loaded at the same place (Figure 4-1). Program execution is begun by a jump command to that location.

Figure 4-1. A single processing system

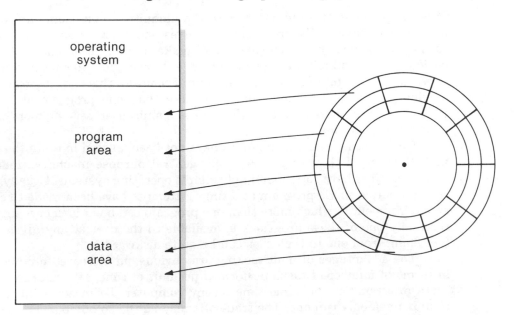

Code and data are always loaded at the same location.

This description is accurate, if a little bit simplistic. The situation is complicated by many factors, including the presence or absence of co-resident programs. These are usually loaded in memory away from the area occupied by the main program, frequently at the other end of the computer's address space. Space must be left for the operating system utilities and service routines.

In contrast, a multitasking system's program loading and memory management are more difficult. More than one task is going on at the same time, and if we wish to load a new program, where we put it is a function of which memory locations are available. It doesn't always go into the same spot. Starting the program up is also a more complex process; we can no longer rely on a simple jump command to accomplish the job.

On the Amiga—as in most multitasking environments—rather than a static landscape of memory locations, we have a more fluid situation. The resources in use and those available are in a constant state of flux. First one set of instructions is executed; then, when these are blocked (perhaps waiting for keyboard input), attention is focused on some other set of commands. You need a way to make sense out of this constant switching. You need something, too, that describes how a program is loaded and run (Figure 4-2).

In a broad sense, a program bears the same relationship to a process as the program's executable code does to the source statement that was used to produce it. A single program can give rise to many processes. Each process is an independent example of the program executing in its own memory locations, using its own resources. It is the process and not the program that is manipulated by the operating system.

A *process*, then, is an entity that lives in memory. When you or one of your programs decides to run a program, a process is spawned. When it has finished doing its job, it is removed and another one takes its place. A program can give rise to many processes because you can load the code in different locations and start it up independently. It is important to maintain this distinction between program and process.

As stated above, a process is a program—or anyway a collection of executable code—that is in the process of executing. During its time in the memory, this process must interact not only with the operating system itself, but also with other processes, both competing and cooperating. Some of these processes are put in place by the operating system itself. There is a process to control the disk drive, a process to handle output to the printer, and even one to accept keyboard input. This ability to interact is what makes a multitasking operating system convenient and powerful.

Messages

How do processes interact? What allows them to cooperate with one another and with the operating system? All of this is accomplished through the use of an elaborate message passing system. When a process is started up, the specific resources called for in the program code itself are allocated, as well as

Figure 4-2. A multiprocessing system

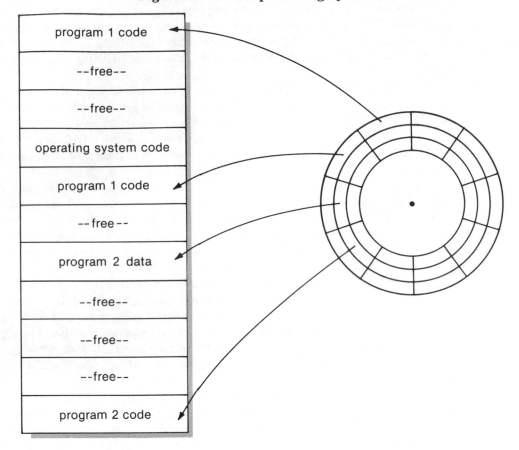

program 1 code
--free--
--free--
operating system code
program 1 code
--free--
program 2 data
--free--
--free--
--free--
program 2 code

Program code and data are loaded at different locations in the memory.

system specific resources. The most important of these is a port that allows communication with the outside world.

The most basic underlying system software, the executive kernel, maintains a message passing system that all processes can and must use for communication (Figure 4-3). The key to this system is twofold:

- A port associated with each process that sends and receives
- The messages themselves

Because this system is maintained at the lowest level of the machine—even lower than AmigaDOS or Intuition—there is a consistent interface among system resources that greatly simplifies programming.

The message consists of two main parts:

1. A section that contains the hooks that allow the executive to manipulate the message

Figure 4-3. The message-passing system

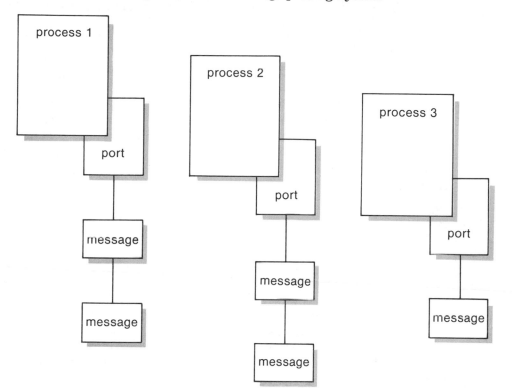

2.   The body of the message, which contains the actual values to be transmitted

The former is consistent throughout all levels of system software, while the latter is specific to the problem at hand and may be vastly different for different contexts.

The message object is implemented as a C structure; it has the general form:

```
struct Message {
    struct Node mn_Node;
    struct MsgPort *mn_ReplyPort;
    UWORD mm_Length;
};
```

where

mn_Node is an object that supplies the system connections mentioned above.

mn_ReplyPort is a pointer to the port where the sender expects a reply.

mm_Length indicates the size of the message body.

This message structure becomes the preface messages that are created for specific situations. For example, consider the following message form:

```
struct P_message }
   struct Message p_mess;
   UBYTE *line;
};
```

This allows you to send a character string as a message to a printer or other display device. The system-wide message structure allows you to tap into the operating system's message handling software—its "switchboard"—but the specific parts of the message allow you to tailor it to your own requirements. Of course, this is a simple example. There is no restriction on the complexity of a message structure.

Ports

Once you have defined your messages and put them into a useful form, you must have somewhere to send them. You need to have a specific way to address both source and destination. Keep in mind that the Amiga is a "software driven" machine. System routines and, more important, devices are not hard wired into the memory, but are loaded at various locations, which may change between runs or in the course of running a series of programs. For each object in this web of communication, you must define one or more ports.

A *port* is a multifaceted object that serves as a connecting link between communicating processes. Whenever you send a message, you include the address of a *reply port* in the body of the message. This represents the location where you expect some kind of communication from the recipient object—a reply, for example, that the message was received.

Like the message, the port is implemented as a software object and is accessed through a C structure data type. The specific form of this structure is:

```
struct MsgPort  {

    struct Node      mp_Node;

    BYTE             mp_Flags,

                     mp_SigBit;

    struct Task      *mp_SigTask;

    struct List      mp_MsgList;
}
```

where

mp_Node is creates a linked data structure for this object.

mp_Flags indicates what is to be done when a message arrives:
PA_SIGNAL, signal a particular task.
PA_SOFTINT, perform an interrupt.
PA_IGNORE, ignore the arrival.

mp_SigBit identifies a specific signal when signaling is enabled.

mp_SigTask points to the task that is to be awakened by the signal or interrupt.

mp_MsgList is a header pointing to the queue of messages that have arrived.

Unlike the message structure, except at the very lowest levels, this structure tends to be manipulated via system routines and not directly. In operation, the port—or more properly, the *mp_SigTask* member of the port—acts as head of a linked list of messages waiting to be served by whatever device or process contains the port. These messages are collected as they arrive to form a FIFO (First In First Out) queue; they are then handled in the order received. Figure 4-4 illustrates the relationship between ports and messages.

Figure 4-4. The relationship between ports and messages

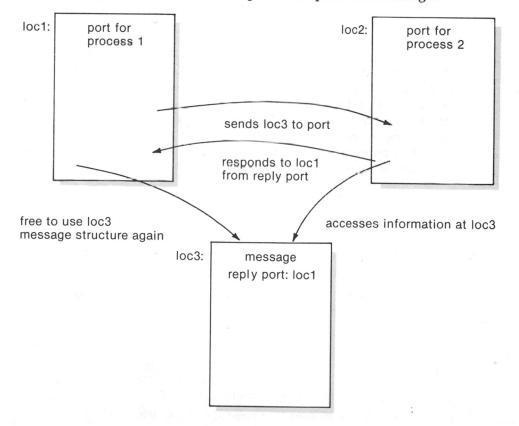

What is actually being transmitted when a message is sent between two operating system entities? How is this connection made? This can be confusing. The only thing that does any traveling is a memory address. When you send a message from process A to device B, you create the message structure in that part of memory allocated to A and then pass a pointer to this structure to B. You are implicitly giving B the means and the right to access and probably change part of A's memory. As a result, it is important that A not alter the structure until B signals that it has received the message. Nothing has been transmitted in the sense of a telephone line or a radio signal—a common but misleading metaphor used to explain message passing systems —just a reassignment of values, in this case, address or pointer values.

A *port address* is frequently sent as part of a message. This is the reply port and it has a specific function to fulfill. The receiving entity—process or device—must tell the sender that the message was received. This acknowledgment is directed to the reply port found in the message structure. However, it is also possible and sometimes desirable to have a port that is publicly available. This is accomplished by giving the port a name which can later be accessed by other processes. This access is via the name field as part of the *mp__Node* field within the message port structure.

Manipulating Ports and Messages

The executive kernel contains a variety of system functions to manipulate ports and messages. You can add ports to the system and remove them using *AddPort()* and *RemPort()*. You can even use *CreatePort()* to generate a brand new port—although this is not, strictly speaking, a system function, but is supplied as part of a library. The main interest in this chapter, however, centers around the use of this message passing system: how to send and receive messages.

The appropriate functions that allow you to use the facilities of the message passing system are listed below.

```
port_id=FindPort(name)
```

where

port__id is a pointer to a port in the message system.

name is a character string containing the port name.

This function returns a pointer to a publicly accessible, named port.

```
PutMsg(port_id,message)
```

where

port__id is a pointer to a port.

message is a pointer to a message structure.

This function sends a message to the designated port.

```
message=GetMsg(port_id)
```

where

> **port_id** is a pointer to a port.
>
> **message** is a pointer to a message structure.

This function removes the next message on the port's queue.

```
ReplyMsg(message)
```

where

> **message** is a pointer to a message structure.

This function returns a message to its point of origin.

```
message=WaitPort(port_id)
```

where

> **message** is a pointer to a message structure.
>
> **port_id** is a pointer to a port.

This function suspends a calling process until a message is returned.

PutMsg() sends an initialized message structure to a particular port. The execution of this function is asynchronous: once it is called, any action performed by the operating system is done independently of the calling program. Since the Amiga has a multitasking operating system, responsibility for carrying through on this command is left to another process. The net effect is that control immediately passes to the next statement in line.

Receiving a message is a more complex process. First, you have to know that a message has arrived at a given port. This requires an effort of synchronization between the sender and the receiver. The executive kernel has a signal allocation system to supply this synchronization. Furthermore, there is a high-level system that allows you to tap into it. The *WaitPort()* function puts the current task to sleep until a signal reaches its port.

Once you know that a message is waiting for you, you still have to remove it from the port's queue; this is done with the *GetMsg()* function. Each call of this function removes the next message from the port. Note that these messages come off their queue in FIFO order; no other form of priority scheme can be applied to them. If there are no messages available, the value zero is returned.

Finally, it is frequently, if not usually, the case that once a message is received, it must be acknowledged to the sender. This is accomplished using the *ReplyMsg()* system call. *ReplyMsg()* returns the message structure to the port mentioned in the *mm_ReplyPort* of this original data structure. If the field is set to zero, no reply is expected. *ReplyMsg()* returns the original message, so it must not be called until that message has either been acted on or copied to a local buffer. By returning the message, you lose control of it. Messages are frequently reused by processes, so even if you retained its address, you would have no guarantee of the integrity of the values you found. Before a message is answered, it is the property of the receiver. Of course, you must return the message as soon as possible, in order to speed up total system operations and increase process execution.

A kind of message receiving template is defined by the following code fragment;

```
WaitPort(Port);
While((message=GetMsg(Port))!=NULL) {
    ==>do something with the information<==
    ReplyMsg(message);
}
```

The basic command sequence appears over and over again in example programs. It illustrates the way you can use these system calls to produce coordinated message exchanges. Of course, *PutMsg()* would be initiated from the original calling process.

These four system functions—*PutMsg()*, *GetMsg()*, *WaitPort()*, and *ReplyMsg()*—are used in concert to access the message passing software made available by the executive kernel. They allow software objects not only to communicate with one another, but also to synchronize their operations. It must be emphasized that these are not the only system functions available to the user. These are the ones you will use to implement and control multitasking under AmigaDOS, but several other low-level subsystems are available to the advanced user. An entire I/O subsystem, for example, is built on top of this message passing facility; we have already seen examples of this in the earlier chapter on Intuition, particularly in the discussion of window input and output. The next step is to relate messages, ports, and processes. A process, as defined so far, is an independent piece of program code, loaded into memory. It must have some way of communicating with other processes and the outside world. The message passing subsystem supplies this venue. This capability is an important constituent of the Amiga's multitasking capability.

AmigaDOS

Of the three semi-autonomous operating environments available on the Amiga—the executive kernel, Intuition, and AmigaDOS—it is the latter that you will be primarily concerned with in creating multitasking programs. Indeed, it is within AmigaDOS that the notion of a process is formed. These other two operating systems lend support and background services, but the tools needed to create a multiprogram environment are found in AmigaDOS.

The executive kernel supplies the underlying software support for process creation. It defines the message passing system and also a management system for low-level tasks. Each task is a software object that can be created or removed by the operating system. These tasks can be further manipulated, and themselves represent executable code modules. However, a task is not a process; it is a much more primitive entity. These are only the barest beginnings of a multitasking system.

An AmigaDOS process is, like most Amiga software objects, defined by a C structure definition:

```
struct Process {
    struct Task pr_Task;
    struct MsgPort    pr_MsgPort;
    WORD              pr_Pad;
    BPTR              pr_SegList;
    LONG              pr_TaskNum;
    BPTR              pr_StackBase;
    LONG              pr_Result2;
    BPTR              pr_CurrentDir,
                      pr_CIS,
                      pr_COS;
    APTR              pr_ConsoleTask,
                      pr_FileSystemTask;
    BPTR              pr_CLI;
    APTR              pr_ReturnAddr,
                      pr_PktWait,
                      pr_WindowPtr;
};
```

This is a long and complex definition, but fortunately, most of these fields are set by the AmigaDOS system calls that you make to set up and use a process. One important thing that you can see immediately is that a process has a message header for access to the system of ports and messages. Also note that a process is also part of the task manipulation system; entry here is via the Task structure at the very beginning of the definition.

The remaining fields are, for the most part, straightforward, if not always obvious. The *pr_SegList* points to the memory locations where the process code currently resides. *pr_StackSize* indicates the number of bytes in this resource. Process identification is through *pr_TaskNum*; this relates the process to a task number relative to the calling CLI. There are also hooks to the current disk directory (*pr_CurrentDir*), the standard input and output for this process (*pr_CIS* and *pr_COS*), as well as pointers to the various subsidiary and support processes and functions. These fields are rarely manipulated directly by a user process.

The tasking system is responsible for the process once it is in memory. It manages the CPU and other resources. This system takes primary responsiblity for scheduling and moving between the various states associated with an executing process. One of its primary jobs is to switch between the various competing processes, giving each one a quantum of access to the system and then moving to the next. It is this switching that allows many programs to run simultaneously.

Although the tasking subsystem is directly available to the programmer through the executive kernel, it is not necessary to access it to accomplish multiprocessing operation. Direct access to these low-level routines has advantages and disadvantages. The most important benefit is one of speed. By accessing the tasking system directly, you eliminate the overhead inherent when going through AmigaDOS. Furthermore, direct access gives you routines that are unique to your particular application and not general purpose ones. The disadvantage is that the application itself must handle all of the details of operation; the benefits of dealing with a high-level construct such as a process are lost. In a complex application this can pose a problem.

Calling AmigaDOS

Calling an AmigaDOS function from a C application is a simple procedure. You simply treat the system call that you want as any other C function. You invoke its name, pass it whatever parameters it expects, and take whatever return value it wants to give you. From the programmer's point of view, a system function is really no different from any of the other built-in functions found in the various C libraries.

Listing 4-1 shows a simple call to an AmigaDOS function. In this case, we are accessing the system clock to extract the date and time. The function that we are interested in is:

```
DateStamp(d_ptr);
```

Once called, this function will accept a pointer to a *Datestamp* structure; it will fill this structure with current values:

d__ptr->ds__Days indicates the number of days since 1 January 1978.

d__ptr->ds__Minute is the number of minutes since midnight.

d__ptr->ds__Tick is the number of ticks since the beginning of the minute.

This latter measure is potentially confusing; it refers to a measure that divides a single minute. In the case of the Amiga, there are 50 ticks in a single minute.

Listing 4-1. DateStamp AmigaDOS call.

```
*/

#include "exec/types.h"
#include "exec/nodes.h"
#include "exec/lists.h"
#include "exec/libraries.h"
#include "exec/ports.h"
#include "exec/interrupts.h"
#include "exec/io.h"
#include "exec/memory.h"
```

Listing 4-1 cont.

```
#include "libraries/dos.h"
#include "libraries/dosextens.h"

main()
{
    struct DateStamp v;

    DateStamp(&v);

    printf("days (since 1/78)..............%ld\n",v.ds_Days);
    printf("minutes (since midnight).......%ld\n",v.ds_Minute);
    printf("ticks (from start of minute)...%ld\n",v.ds_Tick);
}
```

DateStamp() is an example of an AmigaDOS system call. It does not directly participate in any multitasking, although it is an important function in its own right, but it does serve to illustrate the calling sequence. Remember, too, the discussion in Chapter 2. In calling AmigaDOS functions, you must link the source code to *amiga.lib* rather than *lc.lib*, and it is imperative that you disable stack checking with the *-v* option. The complete explanation is found in Chapter 2.

Calling Processes From the CLI

If Intuition is the user interface, then the CLI or command interpreter is the programmer's interface. Most program development proceeds from this familiar TTY-like interface. Editors and compilers work from it, and it gives access to most system support utilities. The CLI is perhaps the easiest environment within which to run programs. You have seen in Chapter 3 the many details that must be attended to in writing applications for Intuition. In the CLI, the program interface is familiar and straightforward.

Any program that you run under these circumstances is really a daughter process to the CLI from which you begin. Such processes inherit input/output streams and windows from the parent although they can open their own resources as well. These daughter processes are started up and the CLI goes dormant until the executing process is finished; then it takes control again. The same thing is true for processes spawned by other processes within this environment. Process A begins process B, and then goes to sleep until process B is finished executing.

One way to accomplish this simple form of multiprocessing is to use the *Execute()* system call. The general form of this function is:

```
Execute(string,input,output);
```

Here, the function returns a boolean value to indicate whether or not it was successful. It takes as parameters:

- A string indicating the name of the program to be run
- Input and output streams to be used to display results

If you set input and output to zero, the current assignments for these files is used.

Listing 4-2. A simple example of the AmigaDOS Execute call.

```
*/

#include "exec/types.h"
#include "exec/nodes.h"
#include "exec/lists.h"
#include "exec/libraries.h"
#include "exec/ports.h"
#include "exec/interrupts.h"
#include "exec/io.h"
#include "exec/memory.h"
#include "libraries/dos.h"
#include "libraries/dosextens.h"

main()
{

    Execute("dir df1:source",0,0);

}
```

A very simple use of *Execute()* is illustrated in Listing 4-2. Here you have a *main()* function whose sole purpose is to call this function to execute a *dir* command on a particular subdirectory. The function is set up so that it uses the current window as output; there is no input value. Listing 4-3 shows a slight variation on this same program. Here we call two different commands from *main()*. We also program a delay into the program by reference to the *Delay()* system call. This accepts a duration, measured in ticks, as a parameter and waits the specified time.

Listing 4-3. A simple example of the AmigaDOS Delay call. It is used in conjunction with the Execute call.

```
*/

#include "exec/types.h"
#include "exec/nodes.h"
#include "exec/lists.h"
#include "exec/libraries.h"
#include "exec/ports.h"
#include "exec/interrupts.h"
```

Listing 4-3 cont.

```
#include "exec/io.h"
#include "exec/memory.h"
#include "libraries/dos.h"
#include "libraries/dosextens.h"

main()
{

    Execute("dir df1:source",0,0);

    Delay(1500);

    Execute("info",0,0);

}
```

The *Execute()* system function can be used in the manner illustrated in Listing 4-4. By passing the function an empty string, you can create a new interactive CLI just as if you had called NEWCLI from the command level. In order to accomplish this you must specify a window for the new CLI. The example does this with the declaration:

```
struct FileHandle *wind;
```

This filehandle type will be explained in greater detail in Chapter 0, when we turn our attention to the file management system. Accept it here as a designator for a new input window. By setting the final parameter to zero, the output stream will be associated with this new window.

**Listing 4-4. This program starts a new CLI,
using the Execute() function.**

```
*/

#include "exec/types.h"
#include "exec/nodes.h"
#include "exec/lists.h"
#include "exec/libraries.h"
#include "exec/ports.h"
#include "exec/interrupts.h"
#include "exec/io.h"
#include "exec/memory.h"
#include "libraries/dos.h"
#include "libraries/dosextens.h"

struct FileHandle input;
```

Listing 4-4 cont.

```
main()
{
  static char cmd[]="";

  Execute(cmd,&input,0);

  Delay(1500);


}
```

Using Workbench To Start a Process

You are now familiar with Workbench from the recent discussion of Intuition. The Workbench Screen is one of the standard screens that comes up in this user interface. In some ways, it is the primary standard screen, certainly the most commonly seen. But Workbench is also a system utility program that defines other operating environments. That's what we will explore here.

Actually, Workbench defines two environments:

1. The iconic interface that allows you to choose programs visually via the mouse and an Intuition screen

2. An interface that allows you to start up programs as complete independent processes

It is this latter capability that is most interesting here, for you can tap it from the CLI interface, bypassing Intuition. Workbench allows you to create the most complete form of multiprocessing—totally independent executing processes.

Before plunging into examples, consider what is necessary to set up an independent process:

1. First, you must load the code that is to execute into the memory of the computer.

2. Second, you must alert the system that you are starting up a new process.

3. You must signal the loaded and initialized code that it can begin executing.

The first of these requirements is self-evident. You cannot run anything until it resides in memory. Configuring code as a process involves taking care of all overhead that is necessary for the system to treat the program as a process. This includes activities such as putting the program in the process queue and initializing its process structure values. Finally, the code itself needs some kind of indication that all is well and that it can begin doing whatever it was meant to do.

Loading program code into memory is controlled by two complementary AmigaDOS functions: *LoadSeg()* and *UnLoadSeg()*. The first of these takes the object file produced by the compiler and linker and loads it into whatever free locations it finds in memory. It has the general form:

```
segment_id=LoadSeg(file_name);
```

Segment__id points to the head of a chain of segments that contains the code. *File__name* is the name of the file as it appears in the disk directory. Note here that the program will not necessarily reside in contiguous memory locations. This is why the *segment_id* is a pointer to a linked list. Once you are finished with the program, you must remove it from memory and return its resources to the free memory pool. This is accomplished by:

```
UnLoadSeg(segment_id);
```

Segment__id points to a linked list of locations to be returned to the system. It is very important to perform these un-do operations. Under AmigaDOS, no automatic reclamation of resources is performed. If you forget to unload memory, it remains unavailable to the system.

Now that you have your program code loaded, you need to turn it into a process. Do this with:

```
process_id=CreateProc(proc_name,pri,segment_id,stack);
```

This system call takes the code that is stored under *segment__id* and creates a new process. *Pri* sets the priority of the process. The value *stack* sets the size of this resource. *Proc__name* is a character string variable that contains a name for the process. *CreateProc()* returns a *process__id* which is of type struct *Process*. If the operation fails, zero is returned.

CreateProc() actually starts up the process. It puts in any necessary queues, does all the overhead necessary to start the process up, and enters the code at the first segment. This segment is expected to contain some initialization routine to get the program started. The easiest way to accomplish this start-up task is to arrange your code so that it accepts a start-up message from its initiating task. Using the Workbench environment and, more specifically the Workbench start-up message, is a very convenient way to accomplish this.

The Workbench start-up message is a software object defined by the structure *WBStartup* found in *workbench/startup.h* shown below.

```
struct WBStartup  {

    struct Message    sm_Message;

    struct MsgPort    sm_Process;

    BPTR              sm_Segment;
```

```
        LONG              sm_NumArgs;

        char              *sm_ToolWindow;

        struct WBArg      sm_ArgList;

    }
```

where

sm_Message is an entry to the message passing system.

sm_Process connects the start-up message to a process.

sm_Segment points to the memory resident code of a process.

sm_NumArgs indicates the number of arguments being passed.

sm_ToolWindow is a pointer to support window.

sm_ArgList contains the arguments being passed in this message.

Many of these fields relate to the iconic interface. In our examples, we will only be using this structure as a start-up message and so will do the barest minimum of initialization. You should know that there is much more versatility built into this interface than we will utilize now.

Listings 4-5 and 4-6 illustrate a simple process creation. The first program loads the object code from the second, creates a process, sends it a start-up message, and then sends it an additional message with more instructions. The first process then goes to sleep until the second is finished. In Listing 4-6, the program receives the message, executes the request, and then sends a reply message back to the first. This example illustrates one of the simplest systems, where a process spawns another process.

Listing 4-5. A simple process creation, using LoadSeg( ),
UnloadSeg( ), and CreateProc( ).

```
*/

#include "exec/types.h"
#include "exec/nodes.h"
#include "exec/lists.h"
#include "exec/libraries.h"
#include "exec/ports.h"
#include "exec/interrupts.h"
#include "exec/io.h"
#include "exec/memory.h"
#include "libraries/dos.h"
#include "libraries/dosextens.h"

#include "workbench/startup.h"

extern struct Message *GetMsg();
extern int LoadSeg();
extern struct MsgPort *CreateProc();
```

Listing 4-5 cont.

```c
struct P_Mess  {
   struct Message message;
   char *title;
   int files[3];
 };

extern int stdin;
extern int stdout;
extern int stderr;

struct MsgPort *NewProc;
int NewSeg;

main()
{
 struct Message *reply;
 struct Process *o_proc;

 struct WBStartup st;
 struct P_Mess pmes;

 struct MsgPort *o_rp;

 if(init_proc("p1_test","New Process")==0)
   Exit();

 o_proc=(struct Process *)FindTask(0);
 o_rp=&o_proc->pr_MsgPort;

 make_startup(&st);
 PutMsg(NewProc,&st);

 make_message(&pmes,"CON:100/10/320/150/New Process");

 PutMsg(NewProc,&pmes);

 WaitPort(o_rp);

 reply=GetMsg(o_rp);
 WaitPort(o_rp);
 reply=GetMsg(o_rp);

 UnLoadSeg(NewSeg);

}

init_proc(fname,pname)
char *fname,*pname;
{

   if((NewSeg=LoadSeg(fname))==0)  {
     printf("Can't Create a Segment\n");
     return(0);
   }
```

 # pmes ?

Listing 4-5 cont.

```
   if((NewProc=CreateProc(pname,0,NewSeg,5000))==0)  {
      printf("Can't Create a Process\n");
      UnLoadSeg(NewSeg);
      return(0);
   }
   return(1);
}

make_startup(x,reply_port)
struct WBStartup *x;
struct MsgPort *reply_port;
{
    x->sm_Message.mn_ReplyPort=reply_port;
    x->sm_Message.mn_Length=sizeof(struct WBStartup);
    x->sm_Message.mn_Node.ln_Name="startup";
    x->sm_ArgList=NULL;
    x->sm_ToolWindow=NULL;
}
make_message(y,gist_of_it,reply_port)
struct P_Mess *y;
char *gist_of_it;
struct MsgPort *reply_port;
{
    y->message.mn_ReplyPort=reply_port;
    y->message.mn_Length=sizeof(struct P_Mes);
    y->message.mn_Node.ln_Name="p0_test";
    y->title=gist_of_it;
    y->files[0]=(int)stdin;
    y->files[1]=(int)stdout;
    y->files[2]=(int)stderr;
}
```

First, look at Listing 4-5, the parent process. The required initialization is taken care of by three functions. The first, *init_proc()*, loads the daughter process code into memory and transforms it into a process. The example uses a stack size of 5000 bytes and an arbitrary priority of 0. *Pname* contains the name of the process, but the more important process is contained in the global variable *NewProc*. Once the new process is created, you are ready to set up the communication links between it and its parent. First you must find the reply port attached to the current process. *FindTask()* is a function that returns process identification if you pass it the process name. If zero is passed, it returns the current process. Once you have the process, it is easy to grab hold of the message port. These jobs are accomplished in the example by the lines:

```
o_proc=(struct Process *)FindTask(0);
o_rp=&o_proc->pr_MsgPort;
```

The next step is to utilize this information by passing some messages to the new process.

The *make—startup()* function initializes the WBStartup structure to contain the start-up message. There are no surprises here. The reply port and the size are initialized and the name of this message is set to "startup". Everything else is set to NULL. Back in the *main()* function, we use *PutMsg()* to send the message to its intended recipient.

Finally, *make—message()* is invoked to create a command message to the child process. Again you must initialize the reply port and the size of the message, and give it a name. The actual information that you want to transmit to the other process is contained in the character string "title". Once you have initialized this message, send it again using *PutMsg()*, but this time put the program to sleep with a *WaitPort()*.

Clean-up consists of removing the returning message from the queue with a *GetMsg()*, another *WaitPort()* and another call to *GetMsg()*. In the first instance, you are waiting for the return of the start-up message; the second wait is for a reply to the command message. Finally, you unload the new process segment.

Listing 4-6. A simple process, using LoadSeg( ), UnloadSeg( ), and CreateProc( ). This is the companion to p0—test.c.

```
*/

#include "exec/types.h"
#include "exec/nodes.h"
#include "exec/lists.h"
#include "exec/libraries.h"
#include "exec/ports.h"
#include "exec/interrupts.h"
#include "exec/io.h"
#include "exec/memory.h"
#include "libraries/dos.h"
#include "libraries/dosextens.h"
#include "workbench/startup.h"

extern struct Message *GetMsg();
extern struct Task *FindTask();
extern struct FileHandle *Open();

struct P_Mess {
   struct Message Message;
   char *title;
   int files[3];
 };

extern int stdout;
extern int stderr;

main()
{
  struct P_Mess *pmes;
```

Listing 4-6 cont.

```
struct MsgPort *cur_rp;
struct Process *cur_proc;
struct FileHandle *new_outp,*stdin;
char ch[40],*get_string();

cur_proc=(struct Process *)FindTask(0);
cur_rp=&cur_proc->pr_MsgPort;

WaitPort(cur_rp);

pmes=(struct P_Mess *)GetMsg(cur_rp);

stdout=pmes->files[1];

if((new_outp=Open(pmes->title,MODE_NEWFILE))==0)  {
  ReplyMsg(pmes);
  exit(0);
 }
else  {
  stdout=(int)new_outp;
  stdin=new_outp;
  printf("enter anything==>");
  get_string(stdin,ch);
  printf("%s\n",ch);
  stdout=pmes->files[1];
  Close(new_outp);
  ReplyMsg(pmes);
 }
}

char *get_string(fp,buffer)
struct FileHandle *fp;
char *buffer;
{
 int len;

 len=Read(fp,buffer,39);
 buffer+=(len+1);
 *buffer='\0';
}
```

Listing 4-6 contains a simple program. It, too, figures out the address of its own port and waits for a message from the parent process. Note that the activity of the start-up message has already been handled by the time these statements are executed. A reply has already been sent. This program is waiting for the second command message. Once the second message is received, it is executed by the statement:

```
new_outp=Open(pmes->title,MODE_NEWFILE);
```

This statement—embedded in an *if* statement—opens the window indicated in the character string *pmes->title*. Although the new process does not inherit any I/O streams from the parent—it is a totally independent process—we do send over the *stdin* and *stdout*. Here we are creating a new set of I/O streams. Once we do this, we ask for some input from the keyboard, then return to the other process.

The finishing code for this smaller process is correspondingly simple. We close the new window, reply to the command message, and then stop execution. One final note—since we are using *amiga.lib* and not *lc.lib*, it is necessary to create *getstring()* in order to do simple input from a window. We do not have *scanf()* available to us in this particular library.

The two remaining examples are variations on this first pair of programs. Listing 4-7 contains a more realistic version of Listing 4-5; it uses *AllocMem()* to dynamically allocate memory and does some additional error checking. Listing 4-8 is, however, significantly different. Here we start up two independent processes from the parent. Each daughter process is given a slightly different command message. Both of these programs use the code in Listing 4-6 to produce child processes.

**Listing 4-7. A more complex process creation, using LoadSeg( ),
UnloadSeg( ), and CreateProc( ).**

```
*/

#include "exec/types.h"
#include "exec/nodes.h"
#include "exec/lists.h"
#include "exec/libraries.h"
#include "exec/ports.h"
#include "exec/interrupts.h"
#include "exec/io.h"
#include "exec/memory.h"
#include "libraries/dos.h"
#include "libraries/dosextens.h"

#include "workbench/startup.h"

extern struct Message *GetMsg();
extern int LoadSeg();
extern struct MsgPort *CreateProc();

struct P_Mess {
   struct Message message;
   char *title;
   int files[3];
 };

extern int stdin;
extern int stdout;
extern int stderr;

struct MsgPort *NewProc;
int NewSeg;
```

Listing 4-7 cont.

```
main()
{
 struct Message *reply;
 struct Process *o_proc;

 struct WBStartup *st;
 struct P_Mess *pmes;

 struct MsgPort *o_rp;

 if(init_proc("p1_test","New Process")==0)
   Exit();

 o_proc=(struct Process *)FindTask(0);
 o_rp=&o_proc->pr_MsgPort;

 if((st=(struct WBStartup *)
    AllocMem(sizeof (struct WBStartup),MEMF_CLEAR))!=0)  {

   make_startup(st);
   PutMsg(NewProc,st);
 }
 else  {
   FreeMem(st,sizeof(struct WBStartup));
   Exit();
 }

 if((pmes=(struct P_Mess *)
    AllocMem(sizeof(struct P_Mess),MEMF_CLEAR))!=0)  {

   make_message(pmes,"CON:100/10/320/150/New Process");

   PutMsg(NewProc,pmes);

   WaitPort(o_rp);

   reply=GetMsg(o_rp);
   WaitPort(o_rp);
   reply=GetMsg(o_rp);
 }

   UnLoadSeg(NewSeg);

   FreeMem(pmes,sizeof(struct P_Mess));
   FreeMem(st,sizeof(struct WBStartup));
}

init_proc(fname,pname)
char *fname,*pname;
{

   if((NewSeg=LoadSeg(fname))==0)  {
      printf("Can't Create a Segment\n");
```

Listing 4-7 cont.

```
      return(0);
   }

   if((NewProc=CreateProc(pname,0,NewSeg,5000))==0)   {
      printf("Can't Create a Process\n");
      UnLoadSeg(NewSeg);
      return(0);
   }
   return(1);
}

make_startup(x,reply_port)
struct WBStartup *x;
struct MsgPort *reply_port;
{
   x->sm_Message.mn_ReplyPort=reply_port;
   x->sm_Message.mn_Length=sizeof(struct WBStartup);
   x->sm_Message.mn_Node.ln_Name="startup";
   x->sm_ArgList=NULL;
   x->sm_ToolWindow=NULL;
}
make_message(y,gist_of_it,reply_port)
struct P_Mess *y;
char *gist_of_it;
struct MsgPort *reply_port;
{
   y->message.mn_ReplyPort-reply_port;
   y->message.mn_Length=sizeof(struct P_Mes);
   y->message.mn_Node.ln_Name="p0_test",
   y->title=gist_of_it;
   y->files[0]=(int)stdin;
   y->files[1]=(int)stdout;
   y->files[2]=(int)stderr;
}
```

Listing 4-8. The creation of two processes.

```
*/

#include "exec/types.h"
#include "exec/nodes.h"
#include "exec/lists.h"
#include "exec/libraries.h"
#include "exec/ports.h"
#include "exec/interrupts.h"
#include "exec/io.h"
#include "exec/memory.h"
#include "libraries/dos.h"
#include "libraries/dosextens.h"
#include "workbench/startup.h"
```

Listing 4-8 cont.

```c
extern struct Message *GetMsg();
extern int LoadSeg();
extern struct MsgPort *CreateProc();

struct P_Mess  {
   struct Message message;
   char *title;
   int files[3];
 };

extern int stdin;
extern int stdout;
extern int stderr;

struct MsgPort *NewProc,*Proc1,*Proc2;
int NewSeg,Seg1,Seg2;

main()
{
 struct Message *reply;
 struct Process *o_proc;

 struct WBStartup st1,st2;
 struct P_Mess pmes1,pmes2;

 struct MsgPort *o_rp;

 if(init_proc("p1_test","Process 1")==0)
   Exit();

 Seg1=NewSeg;
 Proc1=NewProc;

 if(init_proc("p1_test","Process 2")==0)
   Exit();

 Seg2=NewSeg;
 Proc2=NewProc;

 o_proc=(struct Process *)FindTask(0);
 o_rp=&o_proc->pr_MsgPort;

/**** startup first message ****/

 make_startup(&st1,o_rp);
 PutMsg(Proc1,&st1);

 make_message(&pmes1,"CON:10/10/320/150/New Process 1");

 PutMsg(Proc1,&pmes1);

/***** startup second process ****/

 make_startup(&st2,o_rp);
```

Listing 4-8 cont.

```
    PutMsg(Proc2,&st2);

    make_message(&pmes2,"CON:100/10/320/150/New Process 2");

    PutMsg(Proc2,&pmes2);

    WaitPort(o_rp);
    reply=GetMsg(o_rp);
    WaitPort(o_rp);
    reply=GetMsg(o_rp);
    UnLoadSeg(Seg1);

    WaitPort(o_rp);
    reply=GetMsg(o_rp);
    WaitPort(o_rp);
    reply=GetMsg(o_rp);
    UnLoadSeg(Seg2);
}

init_proc(fname,pname)
char *fname,*pname;
{

    if((NewSeg=LoadSeg(fname))==0)  {
       printf("Can't Create a Segment\n");
       return(0);
     }

    if((NewProc=CreateProc(pname,0,NewSeg,5000))==0)  {
       printf("Can't Create a Process\n");
       UnLoadSeg(NewSeg);
       return(0);
     }
    return(1);
}

make_startup(x,reply_port)
struct WBStartup *x;
struct MsgPort *reply_port;
{
    x->sm_Message.mn_ReplyPort=reply_port;
    x->sm_Message.mn_Length=sizeof(struct WBStartup);
    x->sm_Message.mn_Node.ln_Name="startup";
    x->sm_ArgList=NULL;
    x->sm_ToolWindow=NULL;
}
make_message(y,gist_of_it,reply_port)
struct P_Mess *y;
char *gist_of_it;
struct MsgPort *reply_port;
{
    y->message.mn_ReplyPort=reply_port;
```

Listing 4-8 cont.

```
    y->message.mn_Length=sizeof(struct P_Mes);
    y->message.mn_Node.ln_Name="p0_test";
    y->title=gist_of_it;
    y->files[0]=(int)stdin;
    y->files[1]=(int)stdout;
    y->files[2]=(int)stderr;
}
```

Summary

This has been a full chapter. We started out with a discussion of multiprocessing—running more than one program at a time. This led us to the notion of a process as opposed to a simple program. A process is program code that is executing in the machine or about to execute. Dealing with processes is a necessary step in creating multiprocessing environments, but it is not all that you need to know to implement these on the Amiga. It was necessary to take a digression into the message passing subsystem supplied by the executive kernel. We talked about ports and messages, and discussed how to create messages and pass them about within the machine.

Finally, we were able to talk about the details of implementing multiprocessing. There are two kinds available:

1. One process can spin off another and then wait for it to finish using the *Execute()* call in AmigaDOS.

2. You can produce wholly independent processes through a combination of the AmigaDOS system functions—*LoadSeg()*, *UnLoadSeg()*, and *CreateProc()*—and the Workbench start-up message.

Through a series of simple examples, we explored the techniques of these two methods.

Drawing in Intuition  Chapter 5

A s you saw in Chapter 3, Intuition offers an interface system that is both intuitive to the user and simple to set up and use. In this chapter we will continue to explore the services offered by this window-oriented system. Here we will concentrate on the graphics facilities offered. Intuition makes it possible to create sophisticated displays with little more effort than it would take to set up a menu or gadget.

In the course of the chapter, we will return to some of the Intuition topics covered earlier. Then, we used relatively simple examples, because you did not yet have the capabilities to create a fully visual object. Once you understand the many graphics functions, however, you will be able to create truly striking menus, gadgets, and requestors.

Finally, we will discuss the graphics functions found at the very core of the Amiga, in the executive ROM kernel. Intuition provides a convenient backdrop for exhibiting the full power of the graphics engine that is built into the Amiga hardware. You can do moves, draw lines and polygons, and do area fill at an amazing speed, because of the specialized graphics hardware. The specialized windows and screens that we briefly touched on in Chapter 3 will come into their own.

Intuition-Supported Graphics Functions

Intuition itself offers a useful selection of graphics functions. These are closely tied to its system of screens and windows, and support the auxiliary functions of menus, gadgets, and requestors. Although their main purpose is to manipulate the Intuition environment, these functions are by no means restricted to this secondary role. Frequently, the roles seem to be reversed, and a window may be opened so that a picture can be rendered by the drawing routines. At other times, it is the drawing that is subservient to a menu or a requestor. No special preparation is required to use these functions. Since they are supported by Intuition, they can be brought up by opening Intuition itself. Intuition takes care of any initialization necessary, brings in any special header files, and opens the appropriate libraries, making these functions even more attractive. As you will shortly see, much can be done with just these functions.

There are three kinds of graphics output associated with the Intuition graphics system.

1. Borders are lines or polygons drawn on the display area.

2. Images are pictures produced by altering the values of each pixel in the display area.

3. IntuiText is a character display rendered in a supplied or user-customized font.

The only apparent surprise in this list is the IntuiText object; however, a character display is really nothing more than a specialized picture. By treating it as straight graphics, Intuition offers a flexibility that is not available in many, otherwise powerful microcomputers. Text may be displayed in any font style you choose. This graphic treatment of text also facilitates the integration of traditional pictorial information in a document.

There is consistency among these basic graphics outputs. Each one shares a common form of construction and a common set of functions. There is a unique structure associated with each form—border, image, and IntuiText—yet there is a great similarity between these structures. The direct implementation of each form is also similar: *DrawBorder()*, *DrawImage()*, and *PrintIText()*. Each of these functions produces a display according to its appropriate form, yet each is similar to the other, having the same kind of setup specifications and parameters. In fact these functions are so alike that if you know how to create one of these objects, you can create the others. Of course, each of these data structures can be indirectly created through one of the other Intuition objects, such as a menu. Here there is a greater diversity of method, but still the underlying data structures are similar.

One final note before plunging into the definition and manipulation of Intuition graphics: with each of these objects, Intuition allows you to create a string of similar objects that can be dealt with in a single function call. You can create not only one Intuitext message, one set of lines or one single image with a function call, you can also create a whole screen full of these objects with that one call. This alone can greatly increase the effectiveness of graphic displays.

Setting a Border

Perhaps the most straightforward of these graphics objects is the border. The name is a historical accident; what you are really dealing with here is a generalized polygon drawing structure. A border can be:

- A single line

- An arbitrary collection of lines
- A true polygon

Of course, a border can be used to render the rectangular area around a window or screen. These basic configurations are illustrated in Figure 5-1.

Figure 5-1. Different kinds of borders

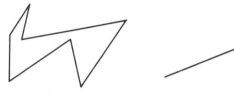 

An arbitrary collection   A single line   A true polygon
of lines

A border is defined by its corresponding structure.

```
struct Border  {
    SHORT LeftEdge,TopEdge,
          FrontPen,BackPen,
          DrawMode,
          Count,
          *XY;
    struct Border *NextBorder;
};
```

Each border structure is associated with an array of integers (the actual data type is SHORT), that define the end points of the lines that will make up this particular object.

LeftEdge and *TopEdge* define where the figure will appear within the enclosing structure. There is a natural tendency to see these two coordinates as the upper left-hand vertex of the proposed polygon. This may not be the case. *LeftEdge* and *TopEdge* actually define a reference point that sets the actual vertices of the figure: that is, those contained in the defining array. The point defined by these two values may, in fact, not even be a part of the drawn figure, and can even be enclosed by the figure it is used to measure. Figure 5-2 delineates the important relationships between this point and the rest of the drawing.

FrontPen is a pointer to a color register. It selects the color that will be used to draw the lines on the display. These colors must come from the current palette specified during the creation of the all-encompassing screen. This value will be further affected by the *DrawMode* field, which controls the way in which lines are painted on the display. Currently, the *BackPen* field is not used for drawing a border.

DrawMode selects one of two possible ways of drawing the lines that will trace out a desired figure. A value of JAM1 causes the display to trace between the various vertices, using the color specified in the *FrontPen* field. These lines are laid over the background color without changing it. In con-

**Figure 5-2. The relationship of LeftEdge and TopEdge
to the border figure**

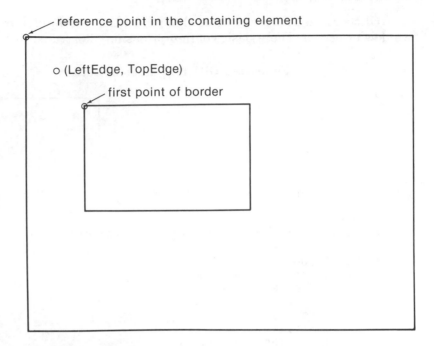

trast, if this field is set with the COMPLEMENT flag, the border object will change the background to its binary complement along the figure lines.

The field *XY* is a pointer to the array that contains the points that define the figure. The *Count* field indicates how many sides the figure has. It is important to note that the *Count* field is not the number of vertices, but is actually the number of pairs of coordinate points in the drawing. A mistake here or a change in this field can cause the same set of data to draw very different figures.

NextBorder is a pointer that allows a link to another border structure. Intuition enables such structures to form chains that will be given to the display, one after the other, by a single function call. This linked list of borders makes it possible to create efficient and complex displays. The last border structure in the chain must set this field to NULL.

Once defined and initialized, the border structure can be used in a variety of contexts to create a figure for display. You can use it in conjunction with one of the other Intuition objects—menus or gadgets, for example—to enhance the appearance and effectiveness of these constructions. You can also send it directly to the window or screen; this is done via the *DrawBorder()* function. This border output function has the general form:

```
DrawBorder(RPort,Border,L_Offset,T_Offset)
```

RPort is a pointer to the Raster Port address associated with the window or screen in which our drawing is to take place. *Border* is a pointer to the defined and initialized border structure. *L__Offset* and *T__Offset* are values that will be added to the specified points in the vertex array. They allow a translation of the figure either up, down, or sideways in the display. The last two values can be zero.

Listing 5-1. The creation of a simple border structure in a window.

```
*/

#include "exec/types.h"
#include "intuition/intuition.h"

struct IntuitionBase *IntuitionBase;
struct Window *NoBorder;
struct GfxBase *GfxBase;
struct RastPort *r;

#define INTUITION_REV 29
#define GRAPHICS_REV 29

SHORT points[]={10,10,
                400,10,
                400,100,
                10,100,
                10,10};


struct Border lines={0,0,
                     5,0,
                     JAM1,
                     5,
                     NULL,
                     NULL};
main()
{
 ULONG flags;
 SHORT x,y,w,h;
 VOID delay_func(),OpenALL();

 OpenALL();

  /*  ======Open a borderless window======*/

  x=y=0;
  w=640;
  h=200;
  flags=ACTIVATE|SMART_REFRESH|BORDERLESS;
  NoBorder=(struct Window *)make_window(x,y,w,h,NULL,flags);

 /*  ======Create a border structure========== */

  lines.XY=points;
```

Listing 5-1 cont.

```
  r=NoBorder->RPort;

  DrawBorder(r,&lines,0,0);


 /*   ======Delay for a bit to show off the windows====== */

  delay_func(100);

 /* =========Close down the windows in order========*/

  delay_func(10);


  CloseWindow(NoBorder);
}


VOID OpenALL()
/* This function will open any required libraries */
{
 /*==Intuition...*/

  IntuitionBase=(struct IntuitionBase *)
           OpenLibrary("intuition.library",INTUITION_REV);

  if(IntuitionBase==NULL)
     exit(FALSE);

 /* ====Open the Graphics Library=== */

  GfxBase=(struct GfxBase *)
           OpenLibrary("graphics.library",GRAPHICS_REV);

  if(GfxBase==NULL)
     exit(FALSE);
}

make_window(x,y,w,h,name,flags)
SHORT x,y,w,h;
UBYTE *name;
ULONG flags;
/* This function will initialize the NewWindow structure
   and open the window   */
{
  struct NewWindow NewWindow;

  NewWindow.LeftEdge=x;
  NewWindow.TopEdge=y;
  NewWindow.Width=w;
  NewWindow.Height=h;
  NewWindow.DetailPen=-1;
  NewWindow.BlockPen=-1;
```

Listing 5-1 cont.

```
    NewWindow.Title=name;
    NewWindow.Flags=flags;
    NewWindow.IDCMPFlags=NULL;
    NewWindow.Type=WBENCHSCREEN;
    NewWindow.FirstGadget=NULL;
    NewWindow.CheckMark=NULL;
    NewWindow.Screen=NULL;
    NewWindow.BitMap=NULL;
    NewWindow.MinWidth=0;
    NewWindow.MinHeight=0;
    NewWindow.MaxWidth=0;
    NewWindow.MaxHeight=0;


    return(OpenWindow(&NewWindow));

}

VOID delay_func(factor)
int factor;
/* This function will cause a specified delay */
{
 int loop;

 for(loop=0;loop<factor*1000;loop++)
   ;

 return;
}
```

Listing 5-1 shows a simple example of a directly rendered border. For the sake of simplicity, we pre-initialize an array of type SHORT to contain five pairs of coordinate values. Our border structure is also initialized to indicate the following characteristics for the figure:

FrontPen set to register 5

DrawingMode set to JAM1—a simple line output

Count set to 5, to reflect the number of lines that make up the figure

Figure 5-3 shows the output from this example program. Listing 5-2 shows a somewhat more ambitious undertaking. This program contains a set of linked border structures. These structures create a more complex figure, but with only a single call to the function *DrawBorder()*. Notice how the *FrontPen* field of each border object has been assigned a different color to produce a more striking display. Note, too, that the *NextBorder* field of the last structure in the chain has been set to NULL. Figure 5-4 displays the output of this program.

The border structure can actually serve as a model for the other two objects. As you will see, Intuition is remarkably consistent in these operations. This situation makes life much easier for the programmer who wants to create very complex user interfaces and displays.

Figure 5-3. The output of Listing 5-1

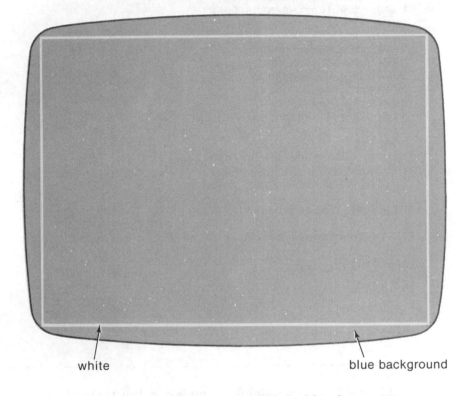

white   blue background

**Listing 5-2. The creation of several linked border structures
in a window.**

```
*/

#include "exec/types.h"
#include "intuition/intuition.h"

struct IntuitionBase *IntuitionBase;
struct Window *NoBorder;
struct GfxBase *GfxBase;
struct RastPort *r;

#define INTUITION_REV 29
#define GRAPHICS_REV 29

SHORT points[][10]={{0,0,600,0,600,150,0,150,0,0},
                    {10,10,590,10,590,140,10,140,10,10},
                    {20,20,580,20,580,130,20,130,20,20},
                    {30,30,570,30,570,120,30,120,30,30}};
```

Listing 5-2 cont.

```
struct Border lines[4];

main()
{
 ULONG flags;
 SHORT x,y,w,h;
 VOID delay_func(),OpenALL();

 OpenALL();

  /*  ======Open a borderless window======*/

  x=y=0;
  w=640;
  h=200;
  flags=ACTIVATE|SMART_REFRESH|BORDERLESS;
  NoBorder=(struct Window *)make_window(x,y,w,h,NULL,flags);

 /*     ======Create a border structure========== */

  lines[0].LeftEdge=0;
  lines[0].TopEdge=0;
  lines[0].FrontPen=1;
  lines[0].BackPen=0;
  lines[0].DrawMode=JAM1;
  lines[0].Count=5;
  lines[0].XY=&points[0][0];
  lines[0].NextBorder=&lines[1];

  lines[1].LeftEdge=0;
  lines[1].TopEdge=0;
  lines[1].FrontPen=2;
  lines[1].BackPen=0;
  lines[1].DrawMode=JAM1;
  lines[1].Count=5;
  lines[1].XY=&points[1][0];
  lines[1].NextBorder=&lines[2];

  lines[2].LeftEdge=0;
  lines[2].TopEdge=0;
  lines[2].FrontPen=3;
  lines[2].BackPen=0;
  lines[2].DrawMode=JAM1;
  lines[2].Count=5;
  lines[2].XY=&points[2][0];
  lines[2].NextBorder=&lines[3];

  lines[3].LeftEdge=0;
  lines[3].TopEdge=0;
  lines[3].FrontPen=4;
  lines[3].BackPen=0;
  lines[3].DrawMode=JAM1;
  lines[3].Count=5;
  lines[3].XY=&points[3][0];
```

Listing 5-2 cont.

```
 lines[3].NextBorder=NULL;

 r=NoBorder->RPort;

 DrawBorder(r,&lines[0],10,10);


 /*   ======Delay for a bit to show off the windows====== */

  delay_func(100);

 /* ========Close down the windows in order========*/

  delay_func(10);


  CloseWindow(NoBorder);
}


VOID OpenALL()
/* This function will open any required libraries */
{
 /*==Intuition...*/

 IntuitionBase=(struct IntuitionBase *)
          OpenLibrary("intuition.library",INTUITION_REV);

 if(IntuitionBase==NULL)
     exit(FALSE);

 /* ====Open the Graphics Library=== */

 GfxBase=(struct GfxBase *)
          OpenLibrary("graphics.library",GRAPHICS_REV);

 if(GfxBase==NULL)
     exit(FALSE);
}
make_window(x,y,w,h,name,flags)
SHORT x,y,w,h;
UBYTE *name;
ULONG flags;
/* This function will initialize the NewWindow structure
    and open the window   */
{
   struct NewWindow NewWindow;

   NewWindow.LeftEdge=x;
   NewWindow.TopEdge=y;
   NewWindow.Width=w;
   NewWindow.Height=h;
   NewWindow.DetailPen=-1;
```

Listing 5-2 cont.

```
    NewWindow.BlockPen=-1;
    NewWindow.Title=name;
    NewWindow.Flags=flags;
    NewWindow.IDCMPFlags=NULL;
    NewWindow.Type=WBENCHSCREEN;
    NewWindow.FirstGadget=NULL;
    NewWindow.CheckMark=NULL;
    NewWindow.Screen=NULL;
    NewWindow.BitMap=NULL;
    NewWindow.MinWidth=0;
    NewWindow.MinHeight=0;
    NewWindow.MaxWidth=0;
    NewWindow.MaxHeight=0;


    return(OpenWindow(&NewWindow));

}

VOID delay_func(factor)
int factor;
/* This function will cause a specified delay */
{
 int loop;

 for(loop=0;loop<factor*1000;loop++)
    ;

 return;
}
```

IntuiText

Although Intuition offers specialized functions and support routines, along with data structures for putting text onto the display screen, it is still just another type of graphics object. Remembering this will help you to keep straight the steps needed for this kind of display. Like the border, text has its own structure—*IntuiText*. It is necessary to create and initialize this structure before you can render text. The IntuiText structure has the form:

```
struct IntuiText {
    UBYTE FrontPen,BackPen,
          DrawMode;
    SHORT LeftEdge,TopEdge;
    struct TextAttr *ITextFont;
    UBYTE *IText;
    struct IntuiText *NextText;
};
```

Figure 5-4. Output of Listing 5-2

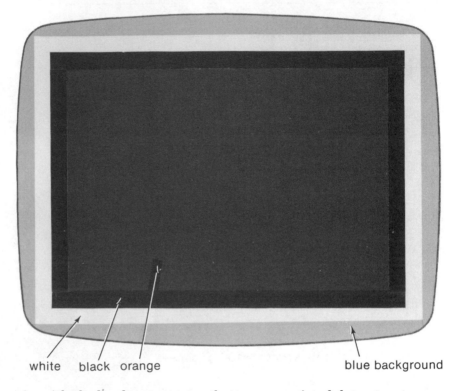

white   black   orange   blue background

As with the border structure, there are associated data structures peculiar to the IntuiText structure, as well as some that are common to all of Intuition's graphics objects.

ITextFont points to a structure that defines a particular type font. If you set this parameter to NULL, the text is rendered in the default style for that window or screen. Several fonts are available in the Font Library, and the Amiga allows the creation of new ones. *IText* is another pointer, this time to a character string—an array of characters terminated by the '\0' character. This string contains the actual characters that make up this IntuiText structure.

LeftEdge and *TopEdge* perform the same function here as they do with the border. These two values form a reference coordinate from which the text position will be measured.

FrontPen and *BackPen* each contain the value of a color register. *DrawMode* sets the way in which text will be presented. The rendering of text on a display is somewhat more intricate with text than with the simpler border structure. As a result, the relationship between *DrawMode*, *FrontPen* and *BackPen* is correspondingly more complex. The simplest case is set by choosing JAM1 as the *DrawMode*. The text is rendered in the chosen font, in the color set by *FrontPen*, on the background of the display window or screen. A mode of JAM2 causes the characters to be displayed in the color indicated by *FrontPen*, but the background underneath will be changed by the *BackPen* reference. COMPLEMENT mode draws the characters, by tracing their outlines in the binary complement of the background color.

Finally, *NextText* allows you to set up a string of IntuiText structures. You can produce several lines of output with a single function call.

The system call that translates your initialized structure to a display is:

```
PrintIText(RPort,IText,L_Offset,T_Offset)
```

Where *RPort* is a pointer to the enclosing objects RastPort, *IText* is a pointer to the IntuiText structure, and *L__Offset* and *T__Offset* are translation values. These last two are added to the position values created by the structure itself. They allow you to reposition the text anywhere in the display without altering the structure. This translation capability is particularly handy if you are displaying the same text in a number of different objects within the display. You can have independent control of the text location in each object. You can also change text positions in one object without affecting the display elsewhere.

A useful function unique to the IntuiText structure is:

```
IntuiTextLength(IText);
```

IText is a pointer to an IntuiText structure. This function returns the length of the structure in pixels. This function is necessary whenever you need to know how much space a text display will require. Since text can be rendered in different fonts, the actual size of a given line of text can vary over a wide range. In any case, the pixel is a more appropriate unit of measure than the character.

Listing 5-3 shows an example of a simple IntuiText structure in a window. We create the structure, initialize it, and use it as a parameter in a call to *PrintIText()*. We use the simplest situation and draw the text using the color pointed to by *FrontPen*. Note that we use an offset value of 0,0 in the function call. In this particular case, *r* is a pointer to the window's RastPort. Figure 5-5 shows the resulting display.

**Listing 5-3. The creation of a simple IntuiText structure
in a window.**

```
*/

#include "exec/types.h"
#include "intuition/intuition.h"

struct IntuitionBase *IntuitionBase;
struct Window *NoBorder;
struct GfxBase *GfxBase;
struct RastPort *r;

#define INTUITION_REV 29
#define GRAPHICS_REV 29
```

Listing 5-3 cont.

```
struct IntuiText mesg;

main()
{
 ULONG flags;
 SHORT x,y,w,h;
 VOID delay_func(),OpenALL();

 OpenALL();

  /*  ======Open a borderless window======*/

 x=y=0;
 w=640;
 h=200;
 flags=ACTIVATE|SMART_REFRESH|BORDERLESS;
 NoBorder=(struct Window *)make_window(x,y,w,h,NULL,flags);

  /*   ======Create an IntuiText structure========== */

 mesg.FrontPen=5;
 mesg.BackPen=1;
 mesg.DrawMode=JAM1;
 mesg.LeftEdge=10;
 mesg.TopEdge=10;
 mesg.ITextFont=NULL;
 mesg.IText=(UBYTE *)"This is only a Test!!!";
 mesg.NextText=NULL;
 r=NoBorder->RPort;

 PrintIText(r,&mesg,0,0);

  /*   ======Delay for a bit to show off the windows====== */

 delay_func(100);

  /* ========Close down the windows in order========*/

 delay_func(10);


 CloseWindow(NoBorder);
}


VOID OpenALL()
/* This function will open any required libraries */
{
 /*==Intuition...*/

 IntuitionBase=(struct IntuitionBase *)
```

Listing 5-3 cont.

```
                   OpenLibrary("intuition.library",INTUITION_REV);

  if(IntuitionBase==NULL)
     exit(FALSE);

  /* ====Open the Graphics Library=== */

  GfxBase=(struct GfxBase *)
             OpenLibrary("graphics.library",GRAPHICS_REV);

  if(GfxBase==NULL)
     exit(FALSE);
}

make_window(x,y,w,h,name,flags)
SHORT x,y,w,h;
UBYTE *name;
ULONG flags;
/* This function will initialize the NewWindow structure
    and open the window  */
{
  struct NewWindow NewWindow;

  NewWindow.LeftEdge=x;
  NewWindow.TopEdge=y;
  NewWindow.Width=w;
  NewWindow.Height=h;
  NewWindow.DetailPen=-1;
  NewWindow.BlockPen=-1;
  NewWindow.Title=name;
  NewWindow.Flags=flags;
  NewWindow.IDCMPFlags=NULL;
  NewWindow.Type=WBENCHSCREEN;
  NewWindow.FirstGadget=NULL;
  NewWindow.CheckMark=NULL;
  NewWindow.Screen=NULL;
  NewWindow.BitMap=NULL;
  NewWindow.MinWidth=0;
  NewWindow.MinHeight=0;
  NewWindow.MaxWidth=0;
  NewWindow.MaxHeight=0;


  return(OpenWindow(&NewWindow));

}

VOID delay_func(factor)
int factor;
/* This function will cause a specified delay */
{
 int loop;

 for(loop=0;loop<factor*1000;loop++)
```

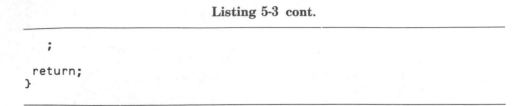

Listing 5-3 cont.

```
    ;

  return;
}
```

Figure 5-5. Output of Listing 5-3

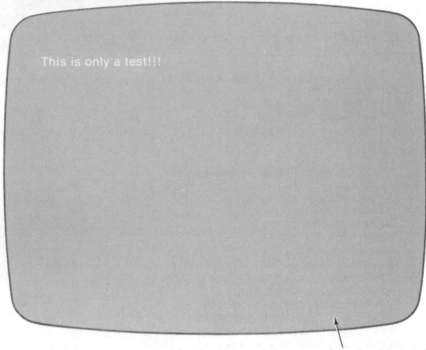

This is only a test!!!

blue background

Listing 5-4 is a more ambitious program. Here we display several linked IntuiText structures. Again, we use the simple JAM1 *DrawMode*. The result of this program is shown in Figure 5-6.

**Listing 5-4. Creation of linked IntuiText structures
in a window.**

```
*/

#include "exec/types.h"
#include "intuition/intuition.h"

struct IntuitionBase *IntuitionBase;
struct Window *NoBorder;
struct GfxBase *GfxBase;
struct RastPort *r;
```

Listing 5-4 cont.

```
#define INTUITION_REV 29
#define GRAPHICS_REV 29


struct IntuiText mesg[3];

main()
{
 ULONG flags;
 SHORT x,y,w,h;
 VOID delay_func(),OpenALL();

 OpenALL();

   /*  ======Open a borderless window======*/

   x=y=0;
   w=640;
   h=200;
   flags=ACTIVATE|SMART_REFRESH|BORDERLESS;
   NoBorder=(struct Window *)make_window(x,y,w,h,NULL,flags);

   /*   ======Create an IntuiText structure========= */

   mesg[0].FrontPen=5;
   mesg[0].BackPen=1;
   mesg[0].DrawMode=JAM1;
   mesg[0].LeftEdge=0;
   mesg[0].TopEdge=0;
   mesg[0].ITextFont=NULL;
   mesg[0].IText=(UBYTE *)"This is only a Test.";
   mesg[0].NextText=&mesg[1];

   mesg[1].FrontPen=6;
   mesg[1].BackPen=1;
   mesg[1].DrawMode=JAM1;
   mesg[1].LeftEdge=30;
   mesg[1].TopEdge=10;
   mesg[1].ITextFont=NULL;
   mesg[1].IText=(UBYTE *)"Nothing can go wrong...";
   mesg[1].NextText=&mesg[2];

   mesg[2].FrontPen=7;
   mesg[2].BackPen=1;
   mesg[2].DrawMode=JAM1;
   mesg[2].LeftEdge=60;
   mesg[2].TopEdge=20;
   mesg[2].ITextFont=NULL;
   mesg[2].IText=(UBYTE *)"...go wrong...go wrong...";
   mesg[2].NextText=NULL;

   r=NoBorder->RPort;

   PrintIText(r,&mesg,0,20);
```

Listing 5-4 cont.

```
/*    ======Delay for a bit to show off the windows====== */

  delay_func(100);

/* =========Close down the windows in order========*/

  delay_func(10);


  CloseWindow(NoBorder);
}


VOID OpenALL()
/* This function will open any required libraries */
{
 /*==Intuition...*/

  IntuitionBase=(struct IntuitionBase *)
          OpenLibrary("intuition.library",INTUITION_REV);

  if(IntuitionBase==NULL)
     exit(FALSE);

 /* ====Open the Graphics Library=== */

  GfxBase=(struct GfxBase *)
          OpenLibrary("graphics.library",GRAPHICS_REV);

  if(GfxBase==NULL)
     exit(FALSE);
}
make_window(x,y,w,h,name,flags)
SHORT x,y,w,h;
UBYTE *name;
ULONG flags;
/* This function will initialize the NewWindow structure
   and open the window  */
{
   struct NewWindow NewWindow;

   NewWindow.LeftEdge=x;
   NewWindow.TopEdge=y;
   NewWindow.Width=w;
   NewWindow.Height=h;
   NewWindow.DetailPen=-1;
   NewWindow.BlockPen=-1;
   NewWindow.Title=name;
   NewWindow.Flags=flags;
   NewWindow.IDCMPFlags=NULL;
   NewWindow.Type=WBENCHSCREEN;
```

Listing 5-4 cont.

```
NewWindow.FirstGadget=NULL;
NewWindow.CheckMark=NULL;
NewWindow.Screen=NULL;
NewWindow.BitMap=NULL;
NewWindow.MinWidth=0;
NewWindow.MinHeight=0;
NewWindow.MaxWidth=0;
NewWindow.MaxHeight=0;


   return(OpenWindow(&NewWindow));

}

VOID delay_func(factor)
int factor;
/* This function will cause a specified delay */
{
 int loop;

 for(loop=0;loop<factor*1000;loop++)
   ;

 return;
}
```

In this section, we have been concerned with creating and directly displaying text in a window or screen. But text can also be part of menus, gadgets, alerts, and requesters. The procedures are different in these more complicated cases, but they still utilize the IntuiText structure to define that part of the display. Some examples of these topics in Chapter 3 used this kind of structure without fully explaining it. We will turn our attention back to these objects and their relationship to text display later in this chapter.

Images

The most primitive of all Intuition graphics objects is the *image*. The image creates a display by specifying the color information contained in each pixel of a proposed figure. Rather than creating a picture with a series of lines, you interact at the level of the display itself, indicating which areas will be light and dark, and putting a specific color at a specific location. Intuition still shields you from the many details necessary to produce such a display. It gives you the capability of creating an image and displaying it anywhere on the display surface ... even rendering the same image in more than one object.

As with a border, an image is defined in two parts. The image structure carries the information needed to find a place for the object and to render it successfully. Contained in the image structure is a pointer to the actual pixel-

Figure 5-6. Output of Listing 5-4

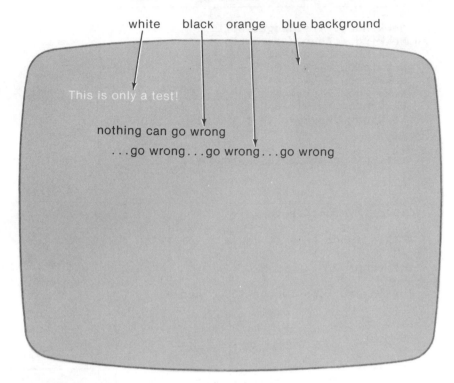

by-pixel information that specifies the shape and the colors of the displayed image. This information is contained in an array, but the situation is more complex than with the straightforward border array.

The image-defining structure is deceptively short:

```
struct Image  {
    SHORT LeftEdge, TopEdge,
          Width, Height, Depth,
          *ImageData;
    UBYTE PlanePick, PlaneOnOff;
    struct Image *NextImage;
};
```

This structure maintains the same consistent design found in the two earlier structures: the positioning information and the pointer to the next graphic object. But there are some significant differences.

Once you have created an object, *LeftEdge* and *TopEdge* allow you to move it around and position it anywhere within the visible display area. These two values represent a reference coordinate from which the painting of the image can be done. This is similar to the situation with border or even IntuiText objects. The *width* and *height* fields, in contrast, have a more active role to play in the creation of an object. These two values indicate roughly the size of the object; they define a rectangular region within which your design is created.

NextImage is a pointer to another image structure. With this, you can maintain the Intuition tradition of specifying a chain of images that can be controlled by a single function call. This adds to the efficiency and elegance of graphics under Intuition. It also cancels out any overhead that might have been incurred by using this high-level interface to the system. *ImageData* is another pointer; this one refers to an array that contains a series of 16-bit words. These words are logically manipulated into a rectangular display area —a bit map which, in turn, is translated by the hardware into an image on the display screen. The height and width fields are used to make this translation. Each bit in each word is associated with a different pixel on the screen. By manipulating the value of the bit, you can alter the display of the corresponding pixel.

A single rectangular area allows you to produce a monochrome display. Either the pixel is on or off. The *Depth* field allows you to specify more than one of these bit planes. With more bit planes, you open up the possibility of multiple colors in the display. This color production on the Amiga is not something new. However, the image structure allows extra flexibility with the *PlanePick* and *PlaneOnOff* fields. By manipulating these fields, you can easily change the display characteristics of an image object. The *PlanePick* field allows you to match the bit planes of the image structure with the bit planes of the enclosing window or screen (Figure 5-7). *PlaneOnOff* lets Intuition know what to do with the bit planes that are not matched to the image. *Depth* specifies directly the number of bit planes used in the picture and thus, indirectly, the colors available to your pixels.

Figure 5-7. The bit mask relationships for PlanePick

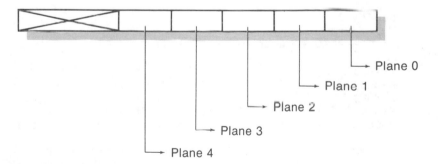

The final stage in the process is a call to the Intuition function:

```
DrawImage(RPort,ImagePtr,Xoffset,Yoffset);
```

RPort points to the RastPort structure for the window or screen that displays the image. *ImagePtr* points to the current image structure. *Xoffset* and *Yoffset* provide displacement values for the object's position on the display surface.

**Listing 5-5. Creation of a simple image structure in
a window.**

```
*/

#include "exec/types.h"
#include "intuition/intuition.h"

struct IntuitionBase *IntuitionBase;
struct Window *NoBorder;
struct GfxBase *GfxBase;
struct RastPort *r;

#define INTUITION_REV 29
#define GRAPHICS_REV 29

USHORT imagepts[]={0xffff,0x4ffe,0x3ffc,0x1ff8,
                   0x0ff0,0x07e0,0x03c0,0x03c0,
                   0x03c0,0x03c0,0x07f0,0x0ff0,
                   0x1ff8,0x3ffc,0x4ffe,0xffff};
```

```
struct Image picture={0,0,
                      16,16,
                      3,
                      NULL,
                      0x0001,0x0000,
                      NULL};
```

```
main()
{
 ULONG flags;
 SHORT x,y,w,h;
 VOID delay_func(),OpenALL();

 OpenALL();

  /* ======Open a borderless window======*/

  x=y=0;
  w=640;
  h=200;
  flags=ACTIVATE|SMART_REFRESH|BORDERLESS;
  NoBorder=(struct Window *)make_window(x,y,w,h,NULL,flags);
```

```
 /* ======Create a border structure========== */

  picture.ImageData=imagepts;

  r=NoBorder->RPort;

  DrawImage(r,&picture,0,0);
```

```
  /* ======Delay for a bit to show off the windows====== */
```

Listing 5-5 cont.

```
   delay_func(100);

 /* =========Close down the windows in order========*/

   delay_func(10);


   CloseWindow(NoBorder);
}


VOID OpenALL()
/* This function will open any required libraries */
{
 /*==Intuition...*/

  IntuitionBase=(struct IntuitionBase *)
            OpenLibrary("intuition.library",INTUITION_REV);

  if(IntuitionBase==NULL)
     exit(FALSE);

 /* ====Open the Graphics Library=== */

  GfxBase=(struct GfxBase *)
            OpenLibrary("graphics.library",GRAPHICS_REV);

 if(GfxBase==NULL)
     exit(FALSE);
}

make window(x,y,w,h,name,flags)
SHORT x,y,w,h;
UBYTE *name;
ULONG flags;
/* This function will initialize the NewWindow structure
   and open the window  */
{
   struct NewWindow NewWindow;

   NewWindow.LeftEdge=x;
   NewWindow.TopEdge=y;
   NewWindow.Width=w;
   NewWindow.Height=h;
   NewWindow.DetailPen=-1;
   NewWindow.BlockPen=-1;
   NewWindow.Title=name;
   NewWindow.Flags=flags;
   NewWindow.IDCMPFlags=NULL;
   NewWindow.Type=WBENCHSCREEN;
   NewWindow.FirstGadget=NULL;
   NewWindow.CheckMark=NULL;
   NewWindow.Screen=NULL;
   NewWindow.BitMap=NULL;
```

Listing 5-5 cont.

```
  NewWindow.MinWidth=0;
  NewWindow.MinHeight=0;
  NewWindow.MaxWidth=0;
  NewWindow.MaxHeight=0;


  return(OpenWindow(&NewWindow));

}

VOID delay_func(factor)
int factor;
/* This function will cause a specified delay */
{
 int loop;

 for(loop=0;loop<factor*1000;loop++)
   ;

 return;
}
```

Figure 5-8. Output of Listing 5-5

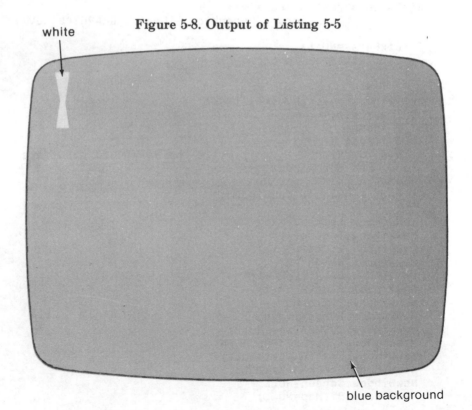

white

blue background

Listing 5-5 illustrates some of these points. We initialize an array, *imagepts[]*, with the values that will render our image. Also initialized is an image structure. The offset is 0, the size of the image is 16 by 16, and all other fields are set to the defaults for the enclosing display object. A call to *DrawImage()* finishes the action. The result is shown in Figure 5-8. Note that the offset in both the image structure and in the function call is 0,0.

As with the previous two graphics objects, it is possible to create a string of images with a single call to *DrawImage()*. The image structures are connected in a linked list and the first one on this list is sent to the function as a parameter. Note that the offset values that are also sent as parameters will be applied to each image, not just to the first one. It is best to use the *LeftEdge* and *TopEdge* fields in the individual structures in this situation. Listing 5-6 shows this procedure in action. Here we create an array of image structures, link them together, and finally call *DrawImage()*. Notice how we use the same set of points for each structure. As with our earlier example, we use *LeftEdge* and *TopEdge* to set the displacement for each object.

**Listing 5-6. The creation of several image structures
in a window.**

```
*/

#include "exec/types.h"
#include "intuition/intuition.h"

struct IntuitionBase *IntuitionBase;
struct Window *NoBorder;
struct GfxBase *GfxBase;
struct RastPort *r;

#define INTUITION_REV 29
#define GRAPHICS_REV 29

USHORT imagepts[]={0xffff,0x4ffe,0x3ffc,0x1ff8,
                   0x0ff0,0x07e0,0x03c0,0x03c0,
                   0x03c0,0x03c0,0x07f0,0x0ff0,
                   0x1ff8,0x3ffc,0x4ffe,0xffff};
```

```
struct Image picture[3];

main()
{
 ULONG flags;
 SHORT x,y,w,h;
 VOID delay_func(),OpenALL();

 OpenALL();
```

```
  /*  ======Open a borderless window======*/

  x=y=0;
```

doesn't seem to work

Listing 5-6 cont.

```
w=640;
h=200;
flags=ACTIVATE|SMART_REFRESH|BORDERLESS;
NoBorder=(struct Window *)make_window(x,y,w,h,NULL,flags);

/*    ======Create image structures========== */

picture[0].LeftEdge=0;
picture[0].TopEdge=0;
picture[0].Width=16;
picture[0].Height=16;
picture[0].Depth=1;
picture[0].ImageData=imagepts;
picture[0].PlanePick=0x0001;
picture[0].PlaneOnOff=0x0000;
picture[0].NextImage=&picture[1];

picture[1].LeftEdge=50;
picture[1].TopEdge=10;
picture[1].Width=16;
picture[1].Height=16;
picture[1].Depth=1;
picture[1].ImageData=imagepts;
picture[1].PlanePick=0x0001;
picture[1].PlaneOnOff=0x0000;
picture[1].NextImage=&picture[2];

picture[2].LeftEdge=100;
picture[2].TopEdge=20;
picture[2].Width=16;
picture[2].Height=16;
picture[2].Depth=1;
picture[2].ImageData=imagepts;
picture[2].PlanePick=0x0001;
picture[2].PlaneOnOff=0x0000;
picture[2].NextImage=NULL;

r=NoBorder->RPort;

DrawImage(r,&picture,300,50);


/*    ======Delay for a bit to show off the windows====== */

delay_func(100);

/* =========Close down the windows in order========*/

delay_func(10);


CloseWindow(NoBorder);
}
```

Listing 5-6 cont.

```
VOID OpenALL()
/* This function will open any required libraries */
{
 /*==Intuition...*/

 IntuitionBase=(struct IntuitionBase *)
          OpenLibrary("intuition.library",INTUITION_REV);

 if(IntuitionBase==NULL)
    exit(FALSE);

 /* ====Open the Graphics Library=== */

 GfxBase=(struct GfxBase *)
          OpenLibrary("graphics.library",GRAPHICS_REV);

 if(GfxBase==NULL)
    exit(FALSE);
}

make_window(x,y,w,h,name,flags)
SHORT x,y,w,h;
UBYTE *name;
ULONG flags;
/* This function will initialize the NewWindow structure
   and open the window  */
{
  struct NewWindow NewWindow;

  NewWindow.LeftEdge=x;
  NewWindow.TopEdge=y;
  NewWindow.Width=w;
  NewWindow.Height=h;
  NewWindow.DetailPen=-1;
  NewWindow.BlockPen=-1;
  NewWindow.Title=name;
  NewWindow.Flags=flags;
  NewWindow.IDCMPFlags=NULL;
  NewWindow.Type=WBENCHSCREEN;
  NewWindow.FirstGadget=NULL;
  NewWindow.CheckMark=NULL;
  NewWindow.Screen=NULL;
  NewWindow.BitMap=NULL;
  NewWindow.MinWidth=0;
  NewWindow.MinHeight=0;
  NewWindow.MaxWidth=0;
  NewWindow.MaxHeight=0;


  return(OpenWindow(&NewWindow));

}
```

Listing 5-6 cont.

```
VOID delay_func(factor)
int factor;
/* This function will cause a specified delay */
{
 int loop;

 for(loop=0;loop<factor*1000;loop++)
   ;

 return;
}
```

Using Graphics with Gadgets

User-defined gadgets without some striking display on the screen are not particularly effective; those that do draw pictures are extremely so. System-defined gadgets clearly illustrate this point. In Chapter 3, we talked at length about these devices and how to set them up, but our examples were universally disappointing. Here, we will remedy that defect with a series of graphics-oriented examples.

Listing 5-7. Window with a string gadget rendered with a
complex double border.

```
*/

#include "exec/types.h"
#include "intuition/intuition.h"

struct IntuitionBase *IntuitionBase;
struct Screen *Scrn;
struct Window *wind0,*wind1;
struct Gadget gadget;
struct StringInfo info;

SHORT brd0[]={0,0,200,0,200,12,0,12,0,0},
      brd1[]={0,0,210,0,210,16,0,16,0,0};

struct Border border0={-2,-2,1,0,JAM1,5,brd0,NULL},
              border1={-7,-4,2,0,JAM1,5,brd1,NULL};

#define INTUITION_REV 29

main()
{
 ULONG flags;
 SHORT x,y,w,h,d;
```

Listing 5-7 cont.

```
USHORT mode;
UBYTE *name,c0,c1;
VOID delay_func(),OpenALL();
char dobuffer[80],undobuffer[80];

 OpenALL();
/* ======First create a gadget========= */

 strcpy(dobuffer,"Enter New Text Here");
 border0.NextBorder=&border1;

 info.Buffer=dobuffer;
 info.UndoBuffer=undobuffer;
 info.MaxChars=80;
 info.BufferPos=0;
 info.DispPos=0;

 gadget.NextGadget=NULL;
 gadget.LeftEdge=40;
 gadget.TopEdge=40;
 gadget.Width=199;
 gadget.Height=15;
 gadget.Flags=GADGHBOX;
 gadget.Activation=TOGGLESELECT;
 gadget.GadgetType=STRGADGET;
 gadget.GadgetRender=(APTR)&border0;
 gadget.SelectRender=NULL;
 gadget.GadgetText=NULL;
 gadget.MutualExclude=NULL;
 gadget.SpecialInfo=(APTR)&info;
 gadget.GadgetID=NULL;
 gadget.UserData=NULL;

/* ======Open a hi-res custom screen==== */

 name="The Gadget Screen";
 y=0;
 w=640;
 h=200;
 d=3;
 c0=0x00;
 c1=0x01;
 mode=HIRES;

 Scrn=(struct Screen *)
        make_screen(y,w,h,d,c0,c1,mode,name);

/* ======Open a window==============*/

 name="Window 1";
 x=20;
 y=20;
 w=400;
 h=150;
```

Listing 5-7 cont.

```
    flags=ACTIVATE|WINDOWSIZING|WINDOWDEPTH|WINDOWDRAG|
                              WINDOWCLOSE|SMART_REFRESH;
    c0=-0x01;
    c1=-0x01;

    wind0=(struct Window *)
            make_window(x,y,w,h,name,flags,c0,c1,Scrn,&gadget);

 /*   ======Delay for a bit to show off the window====== */

    delay_func(100);

 /* =========Close down the window then the screen========*/

    CloseWindow(wind0);

    CloseScreen(Scrn);

}

VOID OpenALL()
/* This function will open any necessary Libraries */
{

 /*   ======Open Intuition====== */

    IntuitionBase=(struct IntuitionBase *)
            OpenLibrary("intuition.library",INTUITION_REV);

    if(IntuitionBase==NULL)
        exit(FALSE);
}

make_window(x,y,w,h,name,flags,color0,color1,screen,gadg)
SHORT x,y,w,h;
UBYTE *name,color0,color1;
ULONG flags;
struct Screen *screen;
struct Gadget *gadg;
/* This function will initialize the NewWindow structure
    and open the window  */
{
    struct NewWindow NewWindow;

    NewWindow.LeftEdge=x;
    NewWindow.TopEdge=y;
    NewWindow.Width=w;
    NewWindow.Height=h;
    NewWindow.DetailPen=color0;
    NewWindow.BlockPen=color1;
    NewWindow.Title=name;
    NewWindow.Flags=flags;
    NewWindow.IDCMPFlags=NULL;
    NewWindow.Type=CUSTOMSCREEN;
```

Listing 5-7 cont.

```
    NewWindow.FirstGadget=gadg;
    NewWindow.CheckMark=NULL;
    NewWindow.Screen=screen;
    NewWindow.BitMap=NULL;
    NewWindow.MinWidth=1;
    NewWindow.MinHeight=1;
    NewWindow.MaxWidth=640;
    NewWindow.MaxHeight=200;


    return(OpenWindow(&NewWindow));

}

make_screen(y,w,h,d,color0,color1,mode,name)
SHORT y,w,h,d;
UBYTE color0,color1,*name;
USHORT mode;
{
  struct NewScreen NewScreen;

  NewScreen.LeftEdge=0;
  NewScreen.TopEdge=y;
  NewScreen.Width=w;
  NewScreen.Height=h;
  NewScreen.Depth=d;
  NewScreen.DetailPen=color0;
  NewScreen.BlockPen=color1;
  NewScreen.ViewModes=mode;
  NewScreen.Type=CUSTOMSCREEN;
  NewScreen.Font=NULL;
  NewScreen.DefaultTitle=name;
  NewScreen.Gadgets=NULL;
  NewScreen.CustomBitMap=NULL;

  return(OpenScreen(&NewScreen));
}

VOID delay_func(factor)
int factor;
/* This function will cause a specified delay */
{
  int loop;

  for(loop=0;loop<factor*1000;loop++)
    ;

  return;
}
```

Listing 5-7 shows a string gadget rendered with a double border around its select box. The result is shown in Figure 5-9. To accomplish this display, we first create two border structures: *border0* and *border1*. There is something new with this definition; we specify *LeftEdge* and *TopEdge* as negative quantities. The enclosing object in this case is the select box of the gadget. By using a negative offset, we can position our border figure outside of this select box, even though our reference is this figure. *Border0* and *border1* are connected together into a linked list, but instead of a call to the *DrawBorder()* function, we set the *GadgetRender* field to the address of *border0*. When the gadget is summoned, the figure will be automatically drawn. The same techniques can be used with an integer or a boolean gadget.

Figure 5-9. Output of Listing 5-7

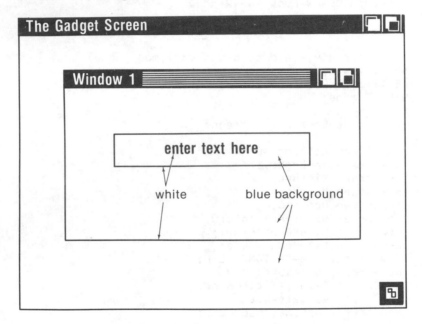

In Listing 5-8, we have a more complex kind of gadget, the proportional gadget. As you saw in Chapter 3, this simulates the kind of control found with an analog device in the real world—such as a control knob. Without a graphics interface, it is impossible to create an effective gadget of this type.

Listing 5-8. A window with a proportional gadget.

```
*/

#include "exec/types.h"
#include "intuition/intuition.h"

struct IntuitionBase *IntuitionBase;
struct Screen *Scrn;
struct Window *wind0,*wind1;
struct Gadget gadget;
struct PropInfo info;
```

Listing 5-8 cont.

```
struct Image image;
struct IntuiText message={1,0,
                          JAM1,
                          -2,-9,
                          NULL,
                          "This is only a test!",
                          NULL};


#define INTUITION_REV 29


main()
{
 ULONG flags;
 SHORT x,y,w,h,d;
 USHORT mode;
 UBYTE *name,c0,c1;
 VOID delay_func(),OpenALL();

  OpenALL();

 /*  ======First create a gadget========= */

  info.Flags=AUTOKNOB|FREEHORIZ|KNOBHIT;
  info.HorizPot=0;
  info.VertPot=0;
  info.HorizBody=0x0001;
  info.VertBody=0x0001;

  gadget.NextGadget=NULL;
  gadget.LeftEdge=40;
  gadget.TopEdge=40;
  gadget.Width=199;
  gadget.Height=10;
  gadget.Flags=GADGHCOMP;
  gadget.Activation=NULL;
  gadget.GadgetType=PROPGADGET;
  gadget.GadgetRender=(APTR)&image;
  gadget.SelectRender=NULL;
  gadget.GadgetText=&message;
  gadget.MutualExclude=NULL;
  gadget.SpecialInfo=(APTR)&info;
  gadget.GadgetID=NULL;
  gadget.UserData=NULL;

 /*  ======Open a hi-res custom screen==== */

  name="The Gadget Screen";
  y=0;
  w=640;
  h=200;
  d=3;
  c0=0x00;
```

Listing 5-8 cont.

```
  c1=0x01;
  mode=HIRES;

  Scrn=(struct Screen *)
          make_screen(y,w,h,d,c0,c1,mode,name);

/*  =======Open a window==============*/

  name="Window 1";
  x=20;
  y=20;
  w=400;
  h=150;
  flags=ACTIVATE|WINDOWSIZING|WINDOWDEPTH|WINDOWDRAG|
                             WINDOWCLOSE|SMART_REFRESH;
  c0=-0x01;
  c1=-0x01;

  wind0=(struct Window *)
          make_window(x,y,w,h,name,flags,c0,c1,Scrn,&gadget);

/*   ======Delay for a bit to show off the window====== */

  delay_func(100);

/* =========Close down the window then the screen=======*/

  CloseWindow(wind0);

  CloseScreen(Scrn);

}

VOID OpenALL()
/* This function will open any necessary Libraries */
{

/*   ======Open Intuition======= */

  IntuitionBase=(struct IntuitionBase *)
          OpenLibrary("intuition.library",INTUITION_REV);

  if(IntuitionBase==NULL)
     exit(FALSE);
}

make_window(x,y,w,h,name,flags,color0,color1,screen,gadg)
SHORT x,y,w,h;
UBYTE *name,color0,color1;
ULONG flags;
struct Screen *screen;
struct Gadget *gadg;
/* This function will initialize the NewWindow structure
   and open the window  */
```

Listing 5-8 cont.

```
{
  struct NewWindow NewWindow;

  NewWindow.LeftEdge=x;
  NewWindow.TopEdge=y;
  NewWindow.Width=w;
  NewWindow.Height=h;
  NewWindow.DetailPen=color0;
  NewWindow.BlockPen=color1;
  NewWindow.Title=name;
  NewWindow.Flags=flags;
  NewWindow.IDCMPFlags=NULL;
  NewWindow.Type=CUSTOMSCREEN;
  NewWindow.FirstGadget=gadg;
  NewWindow.CheckMark=NULL;
  NewWindow.Screen=screen;
  NewWindow.BitMap=NULL;
  NewWindow.MinWidth=1;
  NewWindow.MinHeight=1;
  NewWindow.MaxWidth=640;
  NewWindow.MaxHeight=200;


  return(OpenWindow(&NewWindow));

}

make_screen(y,w,h,d,color0,color1,mode,name)
SHORT y,w,h,d;
UBYTE color0,color1,*name;
USHORT mode;
{
  struct NewScreen NewScreen;

  NewScreen.LeftEdge=0;
  NewScreen.TopEdge=y;
  NewScreen.Width=w;
  NewScreen.Height=h;
  NewScreen.Depth=d;
  NewScreen.DetailPen=color0;
  NewScreen.BlockPen=color1;
  NewScreen.ViewModes=mode;
  NewScreen.Type=CUSTOMSCREEN;
  NewScreen.Font=NULL;
  NewScreen.DefaultTitle=name;
  NewScreen.Gadgets=NULL;
  NewScreen.CustomBitMap=NULL;

  return(OpenScreen(&NewScreen));
}

VOID delay_func(factor)
int factor;
/* This function will cause a specified delay */
```

Listing 5-8 cont.

```
{
 int loop;

 for(loop=0;loop<factor*1000;loop++)
    ;

 return;
}
```

Figure 5-10. Output of Listing 5-8

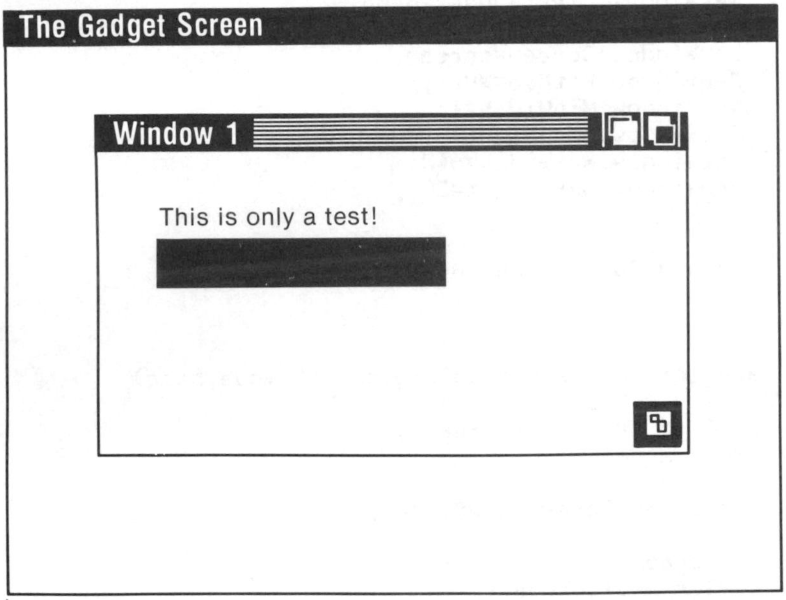

Recall that a proportional gadget requires a Special Info structure in addition to the gadget structure itself. This Info structure defines the values of the control interface portion of the gadget. In this structure, besides initializing the values of the control fields, you must also set certain key values that affect the display of the gadget. These values are set in the *Flags* field of this structure and include:

FREEHORIZ or FREEVERT to indicate the direction of movement of the control device

PROPBORDERLESS to display the gadget without a border around the container of the control device

AUTOKNOB to indicate the default control device shape

It is possible to create your own control object, but AUTOKNOB is a convenient default that produces an effective display. It shows the control surface as a rectangle within an outer rectangle that serves as a containing surface. In Listing 5-8, we have a control device that moves in the horizontal direction. There are two further things to note about the example in Listing 5-8. Even though we are using the default AUTOKNOB object, we must declare an image structure and assign its address to the *GadgetRender* field of the gadget structure. This area is used by Intuition to build the AUTOKNOB object. This example also uses an IntuiText structure to place text into the gadget display. The gadget's *GadgetText* field is set to the address of this structure. This gadget is displayed in Figure 5-10.

In Listing 5-9, we take our proportional gadget a step further. Here we define two complementary gadgets: one moves horizontally; the other, vertically. Notice that the two gadgets are also elegantly connected in a linked list. The result is visible in Figure 5-11.

Listing 5-9. A window with two proportional gadgets.

```
*/

#include "exec/types.h"
#include "intuition/intuition.h"

struct IntuitionBase *IntuitionBase;
struct Screen *Scrn;
struct Window *wind0,*wind1;
struct Gadget gadget0,gadget1;
struct PropInfo info0,info1;
struct Image image0,image1;
struct IntuiText message={1,0,
                          JAM1,
                          -2,-9,
                          NULL,
                          "This is only a test!",
                          NULL};


#define INTUITION_REV 29


main()
{
 ULONG flags;
 SHORT x,y,w,h,d;
 USHORT mode;
 UBYTE *name,c0,c1;
 VOID delay_func(),OpenALL();

  OpenALL();

/*  ======First create a gadget========= */

  info0.Flags=AUTOKNOB|FREEHORIZ|KNOBHIT;
  info0.HorizPot=0;
```

Listing 5-9 cont.

```
info0.VertPot=0;
info0.HorizBody=0x0001;
info0.VertBody=0x0001;

gadget0.NextGadget=(APTR)&gadget1;
gadget0.LeftEdge=40;
gadget0.TopEdge=40;
gadget0.Width=199;
gadget0.Height=10;
gadget0.Flags=GADGHCOMP;
gadget0.Activation=NULL;
gadget0.GadgetType=PROPGADGET;
gadget0.GadgetRender=(APTR)&image0;
gadget0.SelectRender=NULL;
gadget0.GadgetText=&message;
gadget0.MutualExclude=NULL;
gadget0.SpecialInfo=(APTR)&info0;
gadget0.GadgetID=NULL;
gadget0.UserData=NULL;


info1.Flags=AUTOKNOB|FREEVERT|KNOBHIT;
info1.HorizPot=0;
info1.VertPot=0;
info1.HorizBody=0x0001;
info1.VertBody=0x0001;

gadget1.NextGadget=NULL;
gadget1.LeftEdge=40;
gadget1.TopEdge=55;
gadget1.Width=20;
gadget1.Height=75;
gadget1.Flags=GADGHCOMP;
gadget1.Activation=NULL;
gadget1.GadgetType=PROPGADGET;
gadget1.GadgetRender=(APTR)&image1;
gadget1.SelectRender=NULL;
gadget1.GadgetText=NULL;
gadget1.MutualExclude=NULL;
gadget1.SpecialInfo=(APTR)&info1;
gadget1.GadgetID=NULL;
gadget1.UserData=NULL;

/*  ======Open a hi-res custom screen==== */

name="The Gadget Screen";
y=0;
w=640;
h=200;
d=3;
c0=0x00;
c1=0x01;
mode=HIRES;
```

Listing 5-9 cont.

```
    Scrn=(struct Screen *)
            make_screen(y,w,h,d,c0,c1,mode,name);

 /*  =======Open a window==============*/

    name="Window 1";
    x=20;
    y=20;
    w=400;
    h=150;
    flags=ACTIVATE|WINDOWSIZING|WINDOWDEPTH|WINDOWDRAG|
                                WINDOWCLOSE|SMART_REFRESH;
    c0=-0x01;
    c1=-0x01;

    wind0=(struct Window *)
            make_window(x,y,w,h,name,flags,c0,c1,Scrn,&gadget0);

 /*   ======Delay for a bit to show off the window====== */

    delay_func(100);

 /* =========Close down the window then the screen=======*/

    CloseWindow(wind0);

    CloseScreen(Scrn);

}

VOID OpenALL()
/* This function will open any necessary libraries */
{

  /*   ======Open Intuition======= */

  IntuitionBase=(struct IntuitionBase *)
            OpenLibrary("intuition.library",INTUITION_REV);

  if(IntuitionBase==NULL)
     exit(FALSE);
}

make_window(x,y,w,h,name,flags,color0,color1,screen,gadg)
SHORT x,y,w,h;
UBYTE *name,color0,color1;
ULONG flags;
struct Screen *screen;
struct Gadget *gadg;
/* This function will initialize the NewWindow structure
   and open the window  */
{
  struct NewWindow NewWindow;
```

Listing 5-9 cont.

```
   NewWindow.LeftEdge=x;
   NewWindow.TopEdge=y;
   NewWindow.Width=w;
   NewWindow.Height=h;
   NewWindow.DetailPen=color0;
   NewWindow.BlockPen=color1;
   NewWindow.Title=name;
   NewWindow.Flags=flags;
   NewWindow.IDCMPFlags=NULL;
   NewWindow.Type=CUSTOMSCREEN;
   NewWindow.FirstGadget=gadg;
   NewWindow.CheckMark=NULL;
   NewWindow.Screen=screen;
   NewWindow.BitMap=NULL;
   NewWindow.MinWidth=1;
   NewWindow.MinHeight=1;
   NewWindow.MaxWidth=640;
   NewWindow.MaxHeight=200;


   return(OpenWindow(&NewWindow));

}

make_screen(y,w,h,d,color0,color1,mode,name)
SHORT y,w,h,d;
UBYTE color0,color1,*name;
USHORT mode;
{
 struct NewScreen NewScreen;

 NewScreen.LeftEdge=0;
 NewScreen.TopEdge=y;
 NewScreen.Width=w;
 NewScreen.Height=h;
 NewScreen.Depth=d;
 NewScreen.DetailPen=color0;
 NewScreen.BlockPen=color1;
 NewScreen.ViewModes=mode;
 NewScreen.Type=CUSTOMSCREEN;
 NewScreen.Font=NULL;
 NewScreen.DefaultTitle=name;
 NewScreen.Gadgets=NULL;
 NewScreen.CustomBitMap=NULL;

 return(OpenScreen(&NewScreen));
}

VOID delay_func(factor)
int factor;
/* This function will cause a specified delay */
{
 int loop;
```

Listing 5-9 cont.

```
for(loop=0;loop<factor*1000;loop++)
  ;

return;
}
```

Figure 5-11. Output of Listing 5-9

ROM Kernel Graphics Commands

Beneath Intuition, underlying it and supporting it, is the executive kernel. This contains the most basic system calls and the essential multitasking support routines. This collection of software is often called the ROM kernel or the Exec kernel—although, in contrast to most microcomputers, it is actually contained in a protected area of memory called a *writable control store*. Among the system services provided by this low-level kernel is a complete set of graphics and display routines. These are functions that directly interact with the specialized graphics chips that are a unique feature of the Amiga: the *blitter* and the *copper*. These routines work independently of Intuition— indeed they support it—but they can also be used within Intuition to create more efficient graphics displays.

The connecting link between Intuition and these routines is a basic structure of the Exec kernel, the *RastPort*. This is a specialized message port that allows communication with individual display areas. The RastPort is a fairly complex structure and a more basic one than a screen or a window, although in operation it is similar. Fortunately, Intuition opens and initializes a RastPort for each screen and window that it opens. Access to these is found in the respective Intuition structures:

- For screens this is the *RastPort* field.
- For windows, it is *RPort*.

This greatly simplifies life for the programmer. It allows the creation of elaborate graphics displays without having to manage all the details of the display. What is more important, these graphics displays exist under the well-behaved rules of the Intuition interface. This is also a situation where a GIMMEZEROZERO or a backdrop window can be used to good effect.

Setting Up the RastPort

Each window or screen has its own RastPort structure. Within this structure are a number of fields which relate to the action of specific Exec kernel functions. It is sometimes necessary to set these fields and then pass the RastPort structure as a parameter to a particular function. These fields refer to certain actions within the graphics hardware, or set default values.

The first such set of values contains the drawing pens defined in the RastPort structure. These pens are pointers to one of the thirty-two color registers maintained by the Amiga to control the display. There are three pens:

- *FgPen* sets the primary drawing color.
- *BgPen* is the background color.
- *AOlPen* is the color used for area outlining.

Each one of these is set by a specific system function: *SetAPen()*, *SetBPen()*, and *SetOPen()* respectively. The format of each of these is identical. For example, to set the *FgPen*, call:

```
SetAPen(RPort,Color);
```

Here *RPort* is a pointer to a RastPort structure, and *Color* is a value which indicates a color register. The range over which *Color* can vary is dependent on the depth of the structure attached to *RPort*.

The format of a graphics display is set by the drawing mode. As with the Intuition-specific functions, this specifies the interplay between foreground and background colors. Four are possible:

- JAM1 replaces each pixel indicated by the color of the *FgPen*.
- JAM2 is more complicated, utilizing both *FgPen* and *BgPen* to produce a pattern.

- COMPLEMENT sets the pixels to their complement value.
- INVERSEVID draws text in a way that inverts its normal appearance.

These modes are set by a call to *SetDrMd()*. This has the general form:

```
SetDrMd(RPort,Mode);
```

Again, *RPort* is a pointer to a RastPort structure. *Mode* is one of the legal modes mentioned above—except in the case of INVERSVID, which can be combined with either JAM1 or JAM2 to produce different effects.

Drawing Support

Several Exec kernel functions are available to facilitate line drawing on the display.

```
Move(RPort,x,y)
```

repositions the drawing cursor from its current position to coordinates defined by x and y. *RPort* points to the RastPort of the object in which this movement is to take place. This is a positioning function; no output is shown. To draw a line between two points, use:

```
Draw(RPort,x,y);
```

Note that this has precisely the same form as the *Move()* function, but in this case a line is drawn connecting the current position with the new one. The cursor is also moved to the new point.

Draw() sketches its line in the color set by *FgPen*. To produce a series of multicolored lines, it is only necessary to combine this function with *SetAPen()*. Listing 5-10 illustrates a program that uses this combination to create bars of color in a window. The function *makebar()* draws a series of lines in a single color across the display. The number of vertical lines drawn is set by the parameter *lin*. The color of the line is also a parameter. The main program loops through sixteen colors, calling *makebar()* for each iteration.

**Listing 5-10. The use of ROM kernel graphics routines
in a window (running in Intuition).**

```
*/

#include "exec/types.h"
#include "intuition/intuition.h"

struct IntuitionBase *IntuitionBase;
struct Window *NoBorder;
struct GfxBase *GfxBase;
struct RastPort *r;
```

Listing 5-10 cont.

```
struct Screen *Scrn;

#define INTUITION_REV 29
#define GRAPHICS_REV 29

main()
{
 ULONG flags;
 SHORT x,y,w,h,d,c0,c1;
 USHORT mode;
 VOID delay_func(),OpenALL();
 int i,j;

 OpenALL();

 /*  ======Open a hi-res custom screen==== */

  y=0;
  w=640;
  h=400;
  d=4;
  c0=0x00;
  c1=0x01;
  mode=HIRES;

  Scrn=(struct Screen *)
         make_screen(y,w,h,d,c0,c1,mode,NULL);

  /*  ======Open a borderless window======*/

  x=y=0;
  w=640;
  h=200;
  flags=ACTIVATE|SMART_REFRESH|BORDERLESS;
  NoBorder=(struct Window *)
            make_window(x,y,w,h,NULL,flags,Scrn);

  /*   ======Draw some lines========= */

   r=NoBorder->RPort;

   j=0;

   for(i=0;i<=16;i++)  {
     make_bar(i,10,r,j);
     j+=10;
   }

  /*  ======Delay for a bit to show off the windows====== */

   delay_func(100);

  /* ========Close down the windows in order========*/
```

Listing 5-10 cont.

```
   delay_func(10);


   CloseWindow(NoBorder);

   CloseScreen(Scrn);
}

VOID OpenALL()
/* This function will open any required libraries */
{
 /*==Intuition...*/

  IntuitionBase=(struct IntuitionBase *)
           OpenLibrary("intuition.library",INTUITION_REV);

  if(IntuitionBase==NULL)
     exit(FALSE);

 /* ====Open the Graphics Library=== */

  GfxBase=(struct GfxBase *)
           OpenLibrary("graphics.library",GRAPHICS_REV);

  if(GfxBase==NULL)
     exit(FALSE);
}

make_window(x,y,w,h,name,flags,screen)
SHORT x,y,w,h;
UBYTE *name;
ULONG flags;
struct Screen *screen;

/* This function will initialize the NewWindow structure
   and open the window  */
{
   struct NewWindow NewWindow;

   NewWindow.LeftEdge=x;
   NewWindow.TopEdge=y;
   NewWindow.Width=w;
   NewWindow.Height=h;
   NewWindow.DetailPen=-1;
   NewWindow.BlockPen=-1;
   NewWindow.Title=name;
   NewWindow.Flags=flags;
   NewWindow.IDCMPFlags=NULL;
   NewWindow.Type=CUSTOMSCREEN;
   NewWindow.FirstGadget=NULL;
   NewWindow.CheckMark=NULL;
   NewWindow.Screen=screen;
   NewWindow.BitMap=NULL;
   NewWindow.MinWidth=0;
```

Listing 5-10 cont.

```
   NewWindow.MinHeight=0;
   NewWindow.MaxWidth=0;
   NewWindow.MaxHeight=0;


   return(OpenWindow(&NewWindow));

}

VOID delay_func(factor)
int factor;
/* This function will cause a specified delay */
{
 int loop;

 for(loop=0;loop<factor*1000;loop++)
    ;

 return;
}


make_screen(y,w,h,d,color0,color1,mode,name)
SHORT y,w,h,d;
UBYTE color0,color1,*name;
USHORT mode;
{
 struct NewScreen NewScreen;


 NewScreen.LeftEdge=0;
 NewScreen.TopEdge=y;
 NewScreen.Width=w;
 NewScreen.Height=h;
 NewScreen.Depth=d;
 NewScreen.DetailPen=color0;
 NewScreen.BlockPen=color1;
 NewScreen.ViewModes=mode;
 NewScreen.Type=CUSTOMSCREEN;
 NewScreen.Font=NULL;
 NewScreen.DefaultTitle=name;
 NewScreen.Gadgets=NULL;
 NewScreen.CustomBitMap=NULL;

 return(OpenScreen(&NewScreen));
}

make_bar(col,lin,rast,y)
int col,lin;
struct RastPort *rast;
SHORT y;
{
 int j;
```

Listing 5-10 cont.

```
SetAPen(rast,col);
for(j=0;j<lin;j++) {
    Move(rast,10,y+j);
    Draw(rast,600,y+j);
  }
}
```

To draw a series of connected lines (a polygon), use:

```
PolyDraw(RPort, count, array);
```

This functions much as the *DrawBorder()* function found in Intuition. The coordinate for each vertex is placed in an array. This array is passed to the function, along with a count of the number of sides and a pointer to the RastPort structure of the enclosing device. This function uses *FgPen* to render the lines.

Listing 5-11. The PolyDraw() function, using ROM kernel graphics routines in a window (running in Intuition).

```
*/

#include "exec/types.h"
#include "intuition/intuition.h"

struct IntuitionBase *IntuitionBase;
struct Window *NoBorder;
struct GfxBase *GfxBase;
struct RastPort *r;
struct Screen *Scrn;

#define INTUITION_REV 29
#define GRAPHICS_REV 29

main()
{
 ULONG flags;
 SHORT x,y,w,h,d,c0,c1;
static SHORT poly[]={450,10,
                     600,75,
                     450,150,
                     150,150,
                      10,75,
                     150,10};
 USHORT mode;
 VOID delay_func(),OpenALL();

 OpenALL();

/*  ======Open a hi-res custom screen==== */
```

Listing 5-11 cont.

```
y=0;
w=640;
h=400;
d=4;
c0=0x00;
c1=0x01;
mode=HIRES;

Scrn=(struct Screen *)
        make_screen(y,w,h,d,c0,c1,mode,NULL);

/*  ======Open a borderless window======*/

x=y=0;
w=640;
h=200;
flags=ACTIVATE|SMART_REFRESH|BORDERLESS;
NoBorder=(struct Window *)
            make_window(x,y,w,h,NULL,flags,Scrn);

/*   ======Draw some lines========= */

 r=NoBorder->RPort;

 SetAPen(r,5);
 Move(r,150,10);
 PolyDraw(r,6,poly);

/*   ======Delay for a bit to show off the windows====== */

 delay_func(100);

/* ========Close down the windows in order========*/

 delay_func(10);


 CloseWindow(NoBorder);

 CloseScreen(Scrn);
}

VOID OpenALL()
/* This function will open any required libraries */
{
/*==Intuition...*/

 IntuitionBase=(struct IntuitionBase *)
            OpenLibrary("intuition.library",INTUITION_REV);

 if(IntuitionBase==NULL)
    exit(FALSE);
```

Listing 5-11 cont.

```
/* ====Open the Graphics Library=== */

GfxBase=(struct GfxBase *)
           OpenLibrary("graphics.library",GRAPHICS_REV);

if(GfxBase==NULL)
    exit(FALSE);
}

make_window(x,y,w,h,name,flags,screen)
SHORT x,y,w,h;
UBYTE *name;
ULONG flags;
struct Screen *screen;

/* This function will initialize the NewWindow structure
   and open the window  */
{
   struct NewWindow NewWindow;

   NewWindow.LeftEdge=x;
   NewWindow.TopEdge=y;
   NewWindow.Width=w;
   NewWindow.Height=h;
   NewWindow.DetailPen=-1;
   NewWindow.BlockPen=-1;
   NewWindow.Title=name;
   NewWindow.Flags=flags;
   NewWindow.IDCMPFlags=NULL;
   NewWindow.Type=CUSTOMSCREEN;
   NewWindow.FirstGadget=NULL;
   NewWindow.CheckMark=NULL;
   NewWindow.Screen=screen;
   NewWindow.BitMap=NULL;
   NewWindow.MinWidth=0;
   NewWindow.MinHeight=0;
   NewWindow.MaxWidth=0;
   NewWindow.MaxHeight=0;


   return(OpenWindow(&NewWindow));

}

VOID delay_func(factor)
int factor;
/* This function will cause a specified delay */
{
 int loop;

 for(loop=0;loop<factor*1000;loop++)
   ;

 return;
```

Listing 5-11 cont.

```
}

make_screen(y,w,h,d,color0,color1,mode,name)
SHORT y,w,h,d;
UBYTE color0,color1,*name;
USHORT mode;
{
 struct NewScreen NewScreen;

 NewScreen.LeftEdge=0;
 NewScreen.TopEdge=y;
 NewScreen.Width=w;
 NewScreen.Height=h;
 NewScreen.Depth=d;
 NewScreen.DetailPen=color0;
 NewScreen.BlockPen=color1;
 NewScreen.ViewModes=mode;
 NewScreen.Type=CUSTOMSCREEN;
 NewScreen.Font=NULL;
 NewScreen.DefaultTitle=name;
 NewScreen.Gadgets=NULL;
 NewScreen.CustomBitMap=NULL;

 return(OpenScreen(&NewScreen));
}
```

In Listing 5-11 we use *PolyDraw()* to produce a figure in a window. The array *poly* contains the coordinate points for each vertex in our figure. We position the cursor at position 150,10 through a *Move()* function. *PolyDraw()* takes our initialized RastPort structure, the array of vertices, and the count of the sides of our figure, and draws it.

Figure 5-12 shows the result.

With these three functions—*Move()*, *Draw()*, and *PolyDraw()*—it is necessary that the application do its own boundary checking. In each of these functions, if a point is specified that lies outside the bit map supplied by the RastPort structure, the results will be unpredictable.

In addition to the above functions, there are a pair of function calls that give you a handle on individual pixels:

```
ReadPixel(RPort,x,y);
```

This function returns an integer value—the value of the color found at that position—ranging from 0 to 255. If you specify a point outside the area defined as the display, a value of −1 is returned. The complementary function is:

```
WritePixel(RPort,x,y)
```

Figure 5-12. Output of Listing 5-11

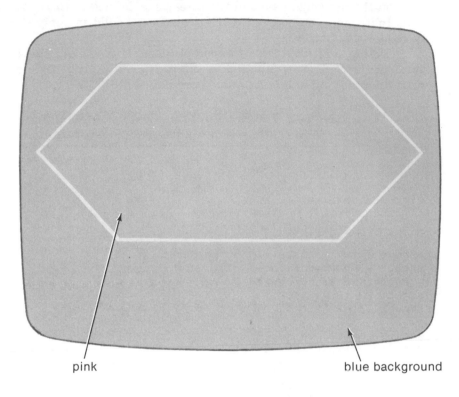

pink   blue background

This puts a pixel at the specified *x,y* coordinate. *FgPen* supplies the color. A value of −1 returned by this function indicates an out-of-bounds condition for the coordinates. If the function call is successful, 0 is returned.

Area Fill

One of the most important of all graphics operations is filling an arbitrary polygon on the display with either a color or a pattern. The Amiga has this capability built into its hardware—a feature which it shares with very expensive graphics work stations. This means that fill operations are done significantly faster than with systems where the work must be done in software. Access to this specialized hardware is through several system calls. Each of these calls allows you to do the fill operation in a slightly different way. The simplest fill operation allocates and fills a rectangle in the display with a specified color. The necessary function call for this operation is:

```
RectFill(Rport,xmin,ymin,xmax,ymax);
```

RPort is a pointer to the RastPort of the enclosing figure. *Xmin, ymin, xmax*, and *ymax* define a rectangle by specifying its upper left-hand and lower right-hand coordinates. The color used for the fill operation is dependent on the drawing mode and the three pens defined in the RastPort structure. In its simplest mode—JAM1—the color is a solid and only *FgPen* is used to render the display.

Listing 5-12 illustrates this simple case. Here we set the *FgPen* color through the *SetAPen()* function. A call to *RectFill()* produces a filled square with its upper left-hand corner at coordinate 10,10.

Listing 5-12. The RectFill() function, using ROM kernel graphics routines in a window (running in Intuition).

```
*/

#include "exec/types.h"
#include "intuition/intuition.h"
#include "graphics/gfxmacros.h"

struct IntuitionBase *IntuitionBase;
struct Window *NoBorder;
struct GfxBase *GfxBase;
struct RastPort *r;
struct Screen *Scrn;

#define INTUITION_REV 29
#define GRAPHICS_REV 29

main()
{
 ULONG flags;
 SHORT x,y,w,h,d,c0,c1;
 USHORT mode;
 VOID delay_func(),OpenALL();

 OpenALL();

 /*  ======Open a hi-res custom screen==== */

  y=0;
  w=640;
  h=400;
  d=4;
  c0=0x00;
  c1=0x01;
  mode=HIRES;

  Scrn=(struct Screen *)
          make_screen(y,w,h,d,c0,c1,mode,NULL);

 /*  ======Open a borderless window======*/

 x=y=0;
 w=640;
 h=200;
 flags=ACTIVATE|SMART_REFRESH|BORDERLESS;
```

Listing 5-12 cont.

```
    NoBorder=(struct Window *)
            make_window(x,y,w,h,NULL,flags,Scrn);

    /*    ======Draw some lines========= */

    r=NoBorder->RPort;

    SetAPen(r,2);
    SetOPen(r,3);

    RectFill(r,10,10,100,100);

  /*    ======Delay for a bit to show off the windows====== */

   delay_func(100);

  /* =========Close down the windows in order========*/

   delay_func(10);


   CloseWindow(NoBorder);

   CloseScreen(Scrn);
}

VOID OpenALL()
/* This function will open any required libraries */
{
 /*==Intuition...*/

  IntuitionBase=(struct IntuitionBase *)
            OpenLibrary("intuition.library",INTUITION_REV);

  if(IntuitionBase==NULL)
     exit(FALSE);

  /* ====Open the Graphics Library=== */

  GfxBase=(struct GfxBase *)
            OpenLibrary("graphics.library",GRAPHICS_REV);

  if(GfxBase==NULL)
     exit(FALSE);
}

make_window(x,y,w,h,name,flags,screen)
SHORT x,y,w,h;
UBYTE *name;
ULONG flags;
struct Screen *screen;

/* This function will initialize the NewWindow structure
   and open the window  */
```

Listing 5-12 cont.

```
{
  struct NewWindow NewWindow;

  NewWindow.LeftEdge=x;
  NewWindow.TopEdge=y;
  NewWindow.Width=w;
  NewWindow.Height=h;
  NewWindow.DetailPen=-1;
  NewWindow.BlockPen=-1;
  NewWindow.Title=name;
  NewWindow.Flags=flags;
  NewWindow.IDCMPFlags=NULL;
  NewWindow.Type=CUSTOMSCREEN;
  NewWindow.FirstGadget=NULL;
  NewWindow.CheckMark=NULL;
  NewWindow.Screen=screen;
  NewWindow.BitMap=NULL;
  NewWindow.MinWidth=0;
  NewWindow.MinHeight=0;
  NewWindow.MaxWidth=0;
  NewWindow.MaxHeight=0;


  return(OpenWindow(&NewWindow));

}

VOID delay_func(factor)
int factor;
/* This function will cause a specified delay */
{
 int loop;

 for(loop=0;loop<factor*1000;loop++)
   ;

 return;
}


make_screen(y,w,h,d,color0,color1,mode,name)
SHORT y,w,h,d;
UBYTE color0,color1,*name;
USHORT mode;
{
 struct NewScreen NewScreen;


 NewScreen.LeftEdge=0;
 NewScreen.TopEdge=y;
 NewScreen.Width=w;
 NewScreen.Height=h;
 NewScreen.Depth=d;
 NewScreen.DetailPen=color0;
```

Listing 5-12 cont.

```
NewScreen.BlockPen=color1;
NewScreen.ViewModes=mode;
NewScreen.Type=CUSTOMSCREEN;
NewScreen.Font=NULL;
NewScreen.DefaultTitle=name;
NewScreen.Gadgets=NULL;
NewScreen.CustomBitMap=NULL;

 return(OpenScreen(&NewScreen));
}
```

True polygon fill can be accomplished by using the *AreaMove()* and *AreaDraw()* functions, but these, in turn, are dependent on two structures associated with the RastPort of the enclosing object—either screen or window. The first of these is *AreaInfo*. This structure sets up a buffer to store information about the figure that is being created by the fill functions. It is initialized by a call to:

```
InitArea(AInfo,buffer,count);
```

AInfo points to an AreaInfo structure; *buffer* is a pointer to a storage area for the figure being drawn, and *count* indicates the size of the figure in question. *Buffer* holds, temporarily, the coordinates of the vertices that define the polygon. As a rule of thumb, you need to set aside about five bytes of storage space per vertex. *AInfo* is assigned to the *AreaInfo* field of the RastPort structure.

Once you have a storage space for the parameters of your figure, you must allocate a workspace for the drawing routines themselves. This is accomplished by declaring a TmpRas structure. This is usually set to the full size of the screen—200 by 320 in low-resolution and 200 by 640 in high-resolution mode. This space is set aside by a call to:

```
InitTmpRas(TRas,buffer,size);
```

Here *TRas* is a pointer to a TmpRas structure, *buffer* points to a block of memory; and *size* is an integer indicating the size of the buffer area. The *TmpRas* field of the RastPort structure is set to the address returned by this function.

With the initialization of these two workspaces, it is possible to define an arbitrary area to be filled. The first function to be called is:

```
AreaMove(RPort,x,y);
```

This function performs a dual service. It closes any pending polygon by connecting its last drawn coordinate to its initial point. The position *x,y* is recorded in the previously defined buffer and a new figure is started. A call to:

```
AreaDraw(RPort,x,y)
```

stores new *x,y* coordinates in this buffer. Note that nothing has been rendered on the display at this point. A final call to:

```
AreaEnd(RPort)
```

terminates the figure and also causes it to appear on the display monitor.

Listing 5-13. Area fill, using ROM kernel graphics routines in a window (running in Intuition).

```
*/

#include "exec/types.h"
#include "intuition/intuition.h"
#include "graphics/gfxmacros.h"

struct IntuitionBase *IntuitionBase;
struct Window *NoBorder;
struct GfxBase *GfxBase;
struct RastPort *r;
struct Screen *Scrn;
struct TmpRas TRas;
struct AreaInfo AInfo;

#define INTUITION_REV 29
#define GRAPHICS_REV 29

main()
{
 ULONG flags;
 SHORT x,y,w,h,d,c0,c1;
 static SHORT Buffer[500];

 USHORT mode;
 VOID delay_func(),OpenALL();

 OpenALL();

 /*  ======Open a hi-res custom screen==== */

 y=0;
 w=640;
 h=400;
 d=4;
 c0=0x00;
 c1=0x01;
 mode=HIRES;

 Scrn=(struct Screen *)
        make_screen(y,w,h,d,c0,c1,mode,NULL);

 /*  ======Open a borderless window======*/
```

Listing 5-13 cont.

```
   x=y=0;
   w=640;
   h=200;
   flags=ACTIVATE|SMART_REFRESH|BORDERLESS;
   NoBorder=(struct Window *)
            make_window(x,y,w,h,NULL,flags,Scrn);

/*    ======Draw some lines========= */

  r=NoBorder->RPort;

  InitArea(&AInfo,Buffer,200);

  r->AreaInfo=&AInfo;
  r->TmpRas=(struct TmpRas *)
       InitTmpRas(&TRas,AllocRaster(320,200),RASSIZE(320,200));

  AreaMove(r,0,0);
  AreaDraw(r,75,0);
  AreaDraw(r,75,75);
  AreaDraw(r,0,75);
  AreaEnd(r);


  /*    ======Delay for a bit to show off the windows====== */

   delay_func(100);

  /* =========Close down the windows in order========*/

   delay_func(10);


   CloseWindow(NoBorder);

   CloseScreen(Scrn);
}

VOID OpenALL()
/* This function will open any required libraries */
{
 /*==Intuition...*/

  IntuitionBase=(struct IntuitionBase *)
           OpenLibrary("intuition.library",INTUITION_REV);

  if(IntuitionBase==NULL)
     exit(FALSE);

  /* ====Open the Graphics Library=== */

  GfxBase=(struct GfxBase *)
           OpenLibrary("graphics.library",GRAPHICS_REV);
```

Listing 5-13 cont.

```
 if(GfxBase==NULL)
    exit(FALSE);
}

make_window(x,y,w,h,name,flags,screen)
SHORT x,y,w,h;
UBYTE *name;
ULONG flags;
struct Screen *screen;

/* This function will initialize the NewWindow structure
   and open the window  */
{
  struct NewWindow NewWindow;

  NewWindow.LeftEdge=x;
  NewWindow.TopEdge=y;
  NewWindow.Width=w;
  NewWindow.Height=h;
  NewWindow.DetailPen=-1;
  NewWindow.BlockPen=-1;
  NewWindow.Title=name;
  NewWindow.Flags=flags;
  NewWindow.IDCMPFlags=NULL;
  NewWindow.Type=CUSTOMSCREEN;
  NewWindow.FirstGadget=NULL;
  NewWindow.CheckMark=NULL;
  NewWindow.Screen=screen;
  NewWindow.BitMap=NULL;
  NewWindow.MinWidth=0;
  NewWindow.MinHeight=0;
  NewWindow.MaxWidth=0;
  NewWindow.MaxHeight=0;


  return(OpenWindow(&NewWindow));

}

VOID delay_func(factor)
int factor;
/* This function will cause a specified delay */
{
 int loop;

 for(loop=0;loop<factor*1000;loop++)
   ;

 return;
}


make_screen(y,w,h,d,color0,color1,mode,name)
```

Listing 5-13 cont.

```
SHORT y,w,h,d;
UBYTE color0,color1,*name;
USHORT mode;
{
 struct NewScreen NewScreen;


 NewScreen.LeftEdge=0;
 NewScreen.TopEdge=y;
 NewScreen.Width=w;
 NewScreen.Height=h;
 NewScreen.Depth=d;
 NewScreen.DetailPen=color0;
 NewScreen.BlockPen=color1;
 NewScreen.ViewModes=mode;
 NewScreen.Type=CUSTOMSCREEN;
 NewScreen.Font=NULL;
 NewScreen.DefaultTitle=name;
 NewScreen.Gadgets=NULL;
 NewScreen.CustomBitMap=NULL;

 return(OpenScreen(&NewScreen));
}
```

Listing 5-13 shows the production of a simple figure. We use the RastPort pointer supplied by the open window, and we set aside 200 bytes to draw a four-sided figure—more than enough. A series of *AreaDraw()* function calls, bracketed by an *AreaMove()* and an *AreaEnd()*, complete the picture.

Listing 5-14. Area fill with outlining, using ROM kernel graphics routines in a window (running in Intuition).

```
*/

#include "exec/types.h"
#include "intuition/intuition.h"
#include "graphics/gfxmacros.h"

struct IntuitionBase *IntuitionBase;
struct Window *NoBorder;
struct GfxBase *GfxBase;
struct RastPort *r;
struct Screen *Scrn;
struct TmpRas TRas;
struct AreaInfo AInfo;

#define INTUITION_REV 29
#define GRAPHICS_REV 29

main()
{
```

Listing 5-14 cont.

```
ULONG flags;
SHORT x,y,w,h,d,c0,c1;
static SHORT Buffer[500];

USHORT mode;
VOID delay_func(),OpenALL();

OpenALL();

/*  ======Open a hi-res custom screen==== */

 y=0;
 w=640;
 h=400;
 d=4;
 c0=0x00;
 c1=0x01;
 mode=HIRES;

 Scrn=(struct Screen *)
        make_screen(y,w,h,d,c0,c1,mode,NULL);

 /*  ======Open a borderless window======*/

 x=y=0;
 w=640;
 h=200;
 flags=ACTIVATE|SMART_REFRESH|BORDERLESS;
 NoBorder=(struct Window *)
            make_window(x,y,w,h,NULL,flags,Scrn);

/*   ======Draw some lines========= */

 r=NoBorder->RPort;

 InitArea(&AInfo,Buffer,200);

 r->AreaInfo=&AInfo;
 r->TmpRas=(struct TmpRas *)
     InitTmpRas(&TRas,AllocRaster(320,200),RASSIZE(320,200));

 SetOPen(r,3);

 AreaMove(r,0,0);
 AreaDraw(r,75,0);
 AreaDraw(r,75,75);
 AreaDraw(r,0,75);
 AreaEnd(r);

/*   ======Delay for a bit to show off the windows====== */

 delay_func(100);
```

Listing 5-14 cont.

```
/* =========Close down the windows in order=======*/

  delay_func(10);


  CloseWindow(NoBorder);

  CloseScreen(Scrn);
}

VOID OpenALL()
/* This function will open any required libraries */
{
 /*==Intuition...*/

  IntuitionBase=(struct IntuitionBase *)
           OpenLibrary("intuition.library",INTUITION_REV);

  if(IntuitionBase==NULL)
     exit(FALSE);

 /* ====Open the Graphics Library=== */

  GfxBase=(struct GfxBase *)
           OpenLibrary("graphics.library",GRAPHICS_REV);

  if(GfxBase==NULL)
     exit(FALSE);
}

make_window(x,y,w,h,name,flags,screen)
SHORT x,y,w,h;
UBYTE *name;
ULONG flags;
struct Screen *screen;

/* This function will initialize the NewWindow structure
   and Open the Window  */
{
  struct NewWindow NewWindow;

  NewWindow.LeftEdge=x;
  NewWindow.TopEdge=y;
  NewWindow.Width=w;
  NewWindow.Height=h;
  NewWindow.DetailPen=-1;
  NewWindow.BlockPen=-1;
  NewWindow.Title=name;
  NewWindow.Flags=flags;
  NewWindow.IDCMPFlags=NULL;
  NewWindow.Type=CUSTOMSCREEN;
  NewWindow.FirstGadget=NULL;
  NewWindow.CheckMark=NULL;
  NewWindow.Screen=screen;
```

Listing 5-14 cont.

```
    NewWindow.BitMap=NULL;
    NewWindow.MinWidth=0;
    NewWindow.MinHeight=0;
    NewWindow.MaxWidth=0;
    NewWindow.MaxHeight=0;


    return(OpenWindow(&NewWindow));
}

VOID delay_func(factor)
int factor;
/* This function will cause a specified delay */
{
 int loop;

 for(loop=0;loop<factor*1000;loop++)
    ;

 return;
}


make_screen(y,w,h,d,color0,color1,mode,name)
SHORT y,w,h,d;
UBYTE color0,color1,*name;
USHORT mode;
{
 struct NewScreen NewScreen;


 NewScreen.LeftEdge=0;
 NewScreen.TopEdge=y;
 NewScreen.Width=w;
 NewScreen.Height=h;
 NewScreen.Depth=d;
 NewScreen.DetailPen=color0;
 NewScreen.BlockPen=color1;
 NewScreen.ViewModes=mode;
 NewScreen.Type=CUSTOMSCREEN;
 NewScreen.Font=NULL;
 NewScreen.DefaultTitle=name;
 NewScreen.Gadgets=NULL;
 NewScreen.CustomBitMap=NULL;

 return(OpenScreen(&NewScreen));
}
```

Listing 5-14 shows an interesting variation. By setting the *AOlPen* to a contrasting color, we produce a filled figure that is also outlined. Figures 5-13 and 5-14 show the results of these two examples.

Figure 5-13. Output of Listing 5-13

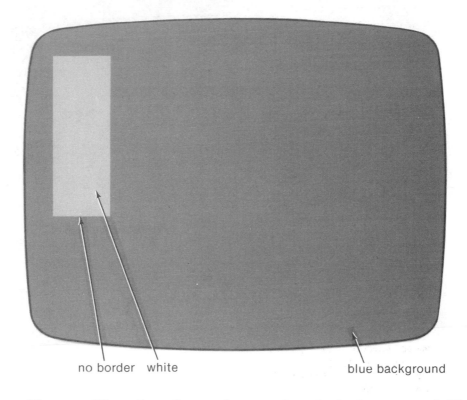

no border white   blue background

The area fill routines that we have used so far both create and fill a figure with color. It is sometimes necessary to draw a figure so that it appears on the screen or window in outline form, and then fill it. This is accomplished by using the *Flood()* function of the ROM kernel. This function has the form:

```
Flood(RPort,mode,x,y)
```

Here *x* and *y* define a point within an already drawn figure, and *mode* specifies one of two filling modes.

- If mode is equal to 0, each pixel in the area encompassed by the figure is compared to the color in the *AOlPen*. If it is different from this color, it is changed to that of the *FgPen*. This is *Outline Mode*.
- *Color Mode* is indicated by a value of 1 for the mode variable. This takes the color at the *x* and *y* coordinates used as a parameter. Each pixel with the same color as this initial point is replaced with the color in *FgPen*.

Flood() is illustrated by Listing 5-15. Here we use the *Draw()* and *Move* commands to create a rectangle in the NoBorder Window. We use the *Flood()*

Figure 5-14. Output of Listing 5-14

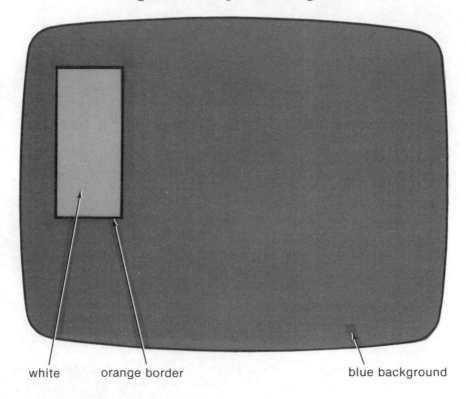

white   orange border   blue background

function to fill that rectangle. Figure 5-15 shows the output from this program.

Listing 5-15. Flood fill, using ROM kernel graphics routines in a window (running in Intuition).

```
*/

#include "exec/types.h"
#include "intuition/intuition.h"
#include "graphics/gfxmacros.h"

struct IntuitionBase *IntuitionBase;
struct Window *NoBorder;
struct GfxBase *GfxBase;
struct RastPort *r;
struct Screen *Scrn;

#define INTUITION_REV 29
#define GRAPHICS_REV 29

main()
{
 ULONG flags;
```

Listing 5-15 cont.

```
SHORT x,y,w,h,d,c0,c1;
USHORT mode;
VOID delay_func(),OpenALL();
BYTE Fpen;

OpenALL();

/*  ======Open a hi-res custom screen==== */

 y=0;
 w=640;
 h=400;
 d=4;
 c0=0x00;
 c1=0x01;
 mode=HIRES;

 Scrn=(struct Screen *)
        make_screen(y,w,h,d,c0,c1,mode,NULL);

 /*  ======Open a borderless window======*/

 x=y=0;
 w=640;
 h=200;
 flags=ACTIVATE|SMART_REFRESH|BORDERLESS;
 NoBorder=(struct Window *)
          make_window(x,y,w,h,NULL,flags,Scrn);

 /*  ======Draw some lines========= */

 r=NoBorder->RPort;
 SetOPen(r,3);

 SetAPen(r,r->AOlPen);
 Move(r,0,0);
 Draw(r,100,0);
 Draw(r,100,100);
 Draw(r,0,100);
 Draw(r,0,0);
 SetAPen(r,3);
 Flood(r,0,10,50);

/*  ======Delay for a bit to show off the windows====== */

 delay_func(100);

/* ========Close down the windows in order=======*/

 delay_func(10);


 CloseWindow(NoBorder);
```

Listing 5-15 cont.

```
  CloseScreen(Scrn);
}

VOID OpenALL()
/* This function will open any required libraries */
{
 /*==Intuition...*/

  IntuitionBase=(struct IntuitionBase *)
            OpenLibrary("intuition.library",INTUITION_REV);

  if(IntuitionBase==NULL)
     exit(FALSE);

  /* ====Open the Graphics Library=== */

  GfxBase=(struct GfxBase *)
            OpenLibrary("graphics.library",GRAPHICS_REV);

  if(GfxBase==NULL)
     exit(FALSE);
}

make_window(x,y,w,h,name,flags,screen)
SHORT x,y,w,h;
UBYTE *name;
ULONG flags;
struct Screen *screen;

/* This function will initialize the NewWindow structure
   and open the window  */
{
   struct NewWindow NewWindow;

   NewWindow.LeftEdge=x;
   NewWindow.TopEdge=y;
   NewWindow.Width=w;
   NewWindow.Height=h;
   NewWindow.DetailPen=-1;
   NewWindow.BlockPen=-1;
   NewWindow.Title=name;
   NewWindow.Flags=flags;
   NewWindow.IDCMPFlags=NULL;
   NewWindow.Type=CUSTOMSCREEN;
   NewWindow.FirstGadget=NULL;
   NewWindow.CheckMark=NULL;
   NewWindow.Screen=screen;
   NewWindow.BitMap=NULL;
   NewWindow.MinWidth=0;
   NewWindow.MinHeight=0;
   NewWindow.MaxWidth=0;
   NewWindow.MaxHeight=0;
```

Listing 5-15 cont.

```
   return(OpenWindow(&NewWindow));

}

VOID delay_func(factor)
int factor;
/* This function will cause a specified delay */
{
 int loop;

 for(loop=0;loop<factor*1000;loop++)
    ;

 return;
}


make_screen(y,w,h,d,color0,color1,mode,name)
SHORT y,w,h,d;
UBYTE color0,color1,*name;
USHORT mode;
{
 struct NewScreen NewScreen;

 NewScreen.LeftEdge=0;
 NewScreen.TopEdge=y;
 NewScreen.Width=w;
 NewScreen.Height=h;
 NewScreen.Depth=d;
 NewScreen.DetailPen=color0;
 NewScreen.BlockPen=color1;
 NewScreen.ViewModes=mode;
 NewScreen.Type=CUSTOMSCREEN;
 NewScreen.Font=NULL;
 NewScreen.DefaultTitle=name;
 NewScreen.Gadgets=NULL;
 NewScreen.CustomBitMap=NULL;

 return(OpenScreen(&NewScreen));
}
```

Filling with a Pattern

The RastPort structure contains two fields that support the use of patterns with graphics objects.

1. You can specify a line drawing pattern that will allow you to create various forms of dotted or dashed lines.

Figure 5-15. Output of Listing 5-15

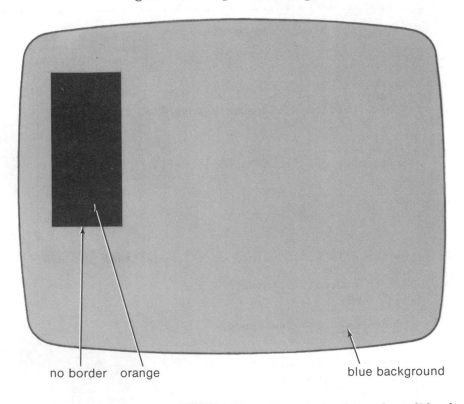

no border   orange   blue background

2. You can specify an area fill pattern and use it in place of a solid color during a fill operation.

These capabilities are controlled by two macros: *SetDrPt( )* and *SetAfPt( )*. These macros are found in the header file *graphics/gfxmacros.h*. This file must be explicitly included before the definition of any function or program that is to do pattern fill.

The simplest form of pattern drawing is that of a line. The line pattern is a 16-bit quantity, applied to all lines controlled by the RastPort. The pattern can be set or reset at any time via the macro command:

```
SetDrPt(RPort,pattern);
```

Pattern is a number, usually specified in hexadecimal, which indicates the form of the line pattern. For example, *0xffff* represents the bit pattern, 1111111111111111. This is a solid line, the default condition when the RastPort is initially opened. A value of 1 in a bit position forces the line drawing routines to put in a solid section; a 0, a blank space. The bit pattern 0101111101011111, indicates a more complex pattern; it would be specified by the number *0x5f5f*. Area pattern fill requires a more complex operation. An area pattern is a rectangle sixteen bits wide, but it can be any height as long as the height is a power of two. Thus, you can create a pattern that is 1, 2, 4,

8, or any higher power of two. This pattern can then be used to fill a figure in place of the solid color used above.

An area fill pattern is defined in an array. Each member of the array represents one line of the pattern. A 1 bit indicates that a pixel will be drawn. A 0 bit defines that space as an empty area. Once you have defined this pattern, you can call the macro:

```
SetAfPt(RPort,PatArray,Size);
```

PatArray is a pointer to the array just defined containing the pattern, and *Size* indicates indirectly how many lines you have defined within the pattern. This value is the power of two that indicates this quantity. Once you have executed this setup procedure, whenever you specify a fill operation, this pattern will be used.

Listing 5-16. The RectFill() function with a pattern, using ROM kernel graphics routines in a window (running in Intuition).

```
*/

#include "exec/types.h"
#include "intuition/intuition.h"
#include "graphics/gfxmacros.h"

struct IntuitionBase *IntuitionBase;
struct Window *NoBorder;
struct GfxBase *GfxBase;
struct RastPort *r;
struct Screen *Scrn;

USHORT pat[]={ 0xff00,
               0xff00,
               0x00ff,
               0x00ff,
               0xf0f0,
               0xf0f0,
               0x0f0f,
               0x0f0f};

#define INTUITION_REV 29
#define GRAPHICS_REV 29

main()
{
 ULONG flags;
 SHORT x,y,w,h,d,c0,c1;
 USHORT mode;
 VOID delay_func(),OpenALL();

 OpenALL();

 /*  ======Open a hi-res custom screen==== */
```

Listing 5-16 cont.

```
y=0;
w=640;
h=400;
d=4;
c0=0x00;
c1=0x01;
mode=HIRES;

Scrn=(struct Screen *)
        make_screen(y,w,h,d,c0,c1,mode,NULL);

/*   ======Open a borderless window======*/

x=y=0;
w=640;
h=200;
flags=ACTIVATE|SMART_REFRESH|BORDERLESS;
NoBorder=(struct Window *)
        make_window(x,y,w,h,NULL,flags,Scrn);

/*    ======Draw some lines========= */

r=NoBorder->RPort;

SetAPen(r,2);
SetOPen(r,3);
SetBPen(r,4);

SetAfPt(r,pat,3);
SetDrMd(r,JAM2);

RectFill(r,10,10,100,100);

/*   ======Delay for a bit to show off the windows====== */

delay_func(100);

/* ========Close down the windows in order========*/

delay_func(10);


CloseWindow(NoBorder);

CloseScreen(Scrn);
}

VOID OpenALL()
/* This function will open any required libraries */
{
/*==Intuition...*/

IntuitionBase=(struct IntuitionBase *)
        OpenLibrary("intuition.library",INTUITION_REV);
```

Listing 5-16 cont.

```
    if(IntuitionBase==NULL)
       exit(FALSE);

   /* ====Open the Graphics Library=== */

   GfxBase=(struct GfxBase *)
              OpenLibrary("graphics.library",GRAPHICS_REV);

   if(GfxBase==NULL)
       exit(FALSE);
}

make_window(x,y,w,h,name,flags,screen)
SHORT x,y,w,h;
UBYTE *name;
ULONG flags;
struct Screen *screen;

/* This function will initialize the NewWindow structure
      and open the window  */
{
   struct NewWindow NewWindow;

   NewWindow.LeftEdge=x;
   NewWindow.TopEdge=y;
   NewWindow.Width=w;
   NewWindow.Height=h;
   NewWindow.DetailPen=-1;
   NewWindow.BlockPen=-1;
   NewWindow.Title=name;
   NewWindow.Flags=flags;
   NewWindow.IDCMPFlags=NULL;
   NewWindow.Type=CUSTOMSCREEN;
   NewWindow.FirstGadget=NULL;
   NewWindow.CheckMark=NULL;
   NewWindow.Screen=screen;
   NewWindow.BitMap=NULL;
   NewWindow.MinWidth=0;
   NewWindow.MinHeight=0;
   NewWindow.MaxWidth=0;
   NewWindow.MaxHeight=0;


   return(OpenWindow(&NewWindow));

}

VOID delay_func(factor)
int factor;
/* This function will cause a specified delay */
{
 int loop;
```

Listing 5-16 cont.

```
 for(loop=0;loop<factor*1000;loop++)
    ;

 return;
}


make_screen(y,w,h,d,color0,color1,mode,name)
SHORT y,w,h,d;
UBYTE color0,color1,*name;
USHORT mode;
{
 struct NewScreen NewScreen;


 NewScreen.LeftEdge=0;
 NewScreen.TopEdge=y;
 NewScreen.Width=w;
 NewScreen.Height=h;
 NewScreen.Depth=d;
 NewScreen.DetailPen=color0;
 NewScreen.BlockPen=color1;
 NewScreen.ViewModes=mode;
 NewScreen.Type=CUSTOMSCREEN;
 NewScreen.Font=NULL;
 NewScreen.DefaultTitle=name;
 NewScreen.Gadgets=NULL;
 NewScreen.CustomBitMap=NULL;

 return(OpenScreen(&NewScreen));
}
```

Pattern fill is shown in Listing 5-16 and Figure 5-16. Here we set up a pattern using the *SetAfPt()* macro and do a rectangle fill. Note that we set the drawing mode to JAM2; this will render the pattern using the *FgPen* to color the 1 bits and the *BgPen* to draw the 0 bit positions.

Some Miscellaneous Functions

We will close out this chapter by turning attention to two functions that are simple to use, yet offer a high level of convenience to the graphics programmer.

```
 SetRast(RPort,Pen)
```

sets the entire raster display to the color of the pen specified by the *Pen* parameter. Listing 5-17 illustrates the use of this function. We set *FgPen* to point to a specific color register and pass it to the function, along with a pointer to the RastPort structure. The result, shown in Figure 5-17, is a

Figure 5-16. Output of Listing 5-16

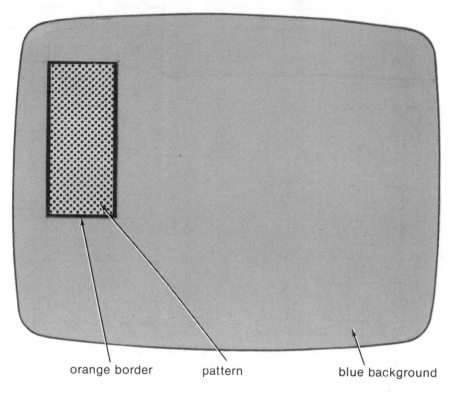

orange border   pattern   blue background

change to that color for the entire display. This function can be used to make such a global change quickly.

Listing 5-17. SetRast() function, using ROM kernel graphics routines in a window (running in Intuition).

```
*/

#include "exec/types.h"
#include "intuition/intuition.h"
#include "graphics/gfxmacros.h"

struct IntuitionBase *IntuitionBase;
struct Window *NoBorder;
struct GfxBase *GfxBase;
struct RastPort *r;
struct Screen *Scrn;

#define INTUITION_REV 29
#define GRAPHICS_REV 29

main()
{
 ULONG flags;
```

Listing 5-17 cont.

```
SHORT x,y,w,h,d,c0,c1;
USHORT mode;
VOID delay_func(),OpenALL();

OpenALL();

/*  ======Open a hi-res custom screen==== */

 y=0;
 w=640;
 h=400;
 d=4;
 c0=0x00;
 c1=0x01;
 mode=HIRES;

 Scrn=(struct Screen *)
         make_screen(y,w,h,d,c0,c1,mode,NULL);

 /*  ======Open a borderless window======*/

 x=y=0;
 w=640;
 h=200;
 flags=ACTIVATE|SMART_REFRESH|BORDERLESS;
 NoBorder=(struct Window *)
             make_window(x,y,w,h,NULL,flags,Scrn);

 /*  ======Draw some lines========= */

 r=NoBorder->RPort;

 SetAPen(r,3);
 SetRast(r,r->FgPen);

 /*  ======Delay for a bit to show off the windows====== */

 delay_func(100);

 /* ========Close down the windows in order=======*/

 delay_func(10);


 CloseWindow(NoBorder);

 CloseScreen(Scrn);
}

VOID OpenALL()
/* This function will open any required libraries */
{
 /*==Intuition...*/
```

Listing 5-17 cont.

```
   IntuitionBase=(struct IntuitionBase *)
            OpenLibrary("intuition.library",INTUITION_REV);

   if(IntuitionBase==NULL)
      exit(FALSE);

   /* ====Open the Graphics Library=== */

   GfxBase=(struct GfxBase *)
            OpenLibrary("graphics.library",GRAPHICS_REV);

   if(GfxBase==NULL)
      exit(FALSE);
}

make_window(x,y,w,h,name,flags,screen)
SHORT x,y,w,h;
UBYTE *name;
ULONG flags;
struct Screen *screen;

/* This function will initialize the NewWindow structure
   and open the window  */
{
   struct NewWindow NewWindow;

   NewWindow.LeftEdge=x;
   NewWindow.TopEdge=y;
   NewWindow.Width=w;
   NewWindow.Height=h;
   NewWindow.DetailPen=-1;
   NewWindow.BlockPen=-1;
   NewWindow.Title=name;
   NewWindow.Flags=flags;
   NewWindow.IDCMPFlags=NULL;
   NewWindow.Type=CUSTOMSCREEN;
   NewWindow.FirstGadget=NULL;
   NewWindow.CheckMark=NULL;
   NewWindow.Screen=screen;
   NewWindow.BitMap=NULL;
   NewWindow.MinWidth=0;
   NewWindow.MinHeight=0;
   NewWindow.MaxWidth=0;
   NewWindow.MaxHeight=0;


   return(OpenWindow(&NewWindow));

}

VOID delay_func(factor)
int factor;
/* This function will cause a specified delay */
```

Listing 5-17 cont.

```
{
 int loop;

 for(loop=0;loop<factor*1000;loop++)
    ;

 return;
}


make_screen(y,w,h,d,color0,color1,mode,name)
SHORT y,w,h,d;
UBYTE color0,color1,*name;
USHORT mode;
{
 struct NewScreen NewScreen;


 NewScreen.LeftEdge=0;
 NewScreen.TopEdge=y;
 NewScreen.Width=w;
 NewScreen.Height=h;
 NewScreen.Depth=d;
 NewScreen.DetailPen=color0;
 NewScreen.BlockPen=color1;
 NewScreen.ViewModes=mode;
 NewScreen.Type=CUSTOMSCREEN;
 NewScreen.Font=NULL;
 NewScreen.DefaultTitle=name;
 NewScreen.Gadgets=NULL;
 NewScreen.CustomBitMap=NULL;

 return(OpenScreen(&NewScreen));
}
```

Listing 5-18 illustrates another simple yet powerful function:

```
ScrollRaster(RPort,delta_x,delta_y,xmin,ymin,xmax,ymax)
```

This causes a section of the display attached to the specified RastPort structure to scroll in either a horizontal direction, a vertical direction, or both. The area over which this scrolling takes place is defined by the variables *xmin,ymin,xmax,ymax*. *Delta_x* and *delta_y* indicate the incremental change in the position of the display. Areas vacated by the objects in the display are replaced by the background color. Figure 5-18 shows the output from this example.

Figure 5-17. Output of Listing 5-17

orange

Listing 5-18. The ScrollRaster( ) function, using ROM kernel graphics routines in a window (running in Intuition).

```
*/

#include "exec/types.h"
#include "intuition/intuition.h"

struct IntuitionBase *IntuitionBase;
struct Window *NoBorder;
struct GfxBase *GfxBase;
struct RastPort *r;

#define INTUITION_REV 29
#define GRAPHICS_REV 29

USHORT imagepts[]={0xffff,0x4ffe,0x3ffc,0x1ff8,
                   0x0ff0,0x07e0,0x03c0,0x03c0,
                   0x03c0,0x03c0,0x07f0,0x0ff0,
                   0x1ff8,0x3ffc,0x4ffe,0xffff};


struct Image picture={0,0,
                      16,16,
                      3,
                      NULL,
```

Listing 5-18 cont.

```
                              0x0001,0x0000,
                              NULL};

main()
{
 ULONG flags;
 SHORT x,y,w,h;
 VOID delay_func(),OpenALL();
 int i;

 OpenALL();

 /*  ======Open a borderless window===== */

  x=y=0;
  w=640;
  h=200;
  flags=ACTIVATE|SMART_REFRESH|BORDERLESS;
  NoBorder=(struct Window *)make_window(x,y,w,h,NULL,flags);


 /*  ======Create an image structure============== */

  picture.ImageData=imagepts;

  r=NoBorder->RPort;

  DrawImage(r,&picture,50,50);

  delay_func(10);

  for(i=0;i<50;i++)
    ScrollRaster(r,0,1,10,10,100,100);


 /* =======Delay for a bit to show off the windows======== */

  delay_func(100);

 /* =======Close down the windows in order=========*/

  delay_func(10);


  CloseWindow(NoBorder);
}


VOID OpenALL()
/* This function will open any required libraries */
{
 /*==Intuition...*/

  IntuitionBase=(struct IntuitionBase *)
            OpenLibrary("intuition.library",INTUITION_REV);
```

Listing 5-18 cont.

```
  if(IntuitionBase==NULL)
     exit(FALSE);

 /* ====Open the Graphics Library=== */

 GfxBase=(struct GfxBase *)
            OpenLibrary("graphics.library",GRAPHICS_REV);

 if(GfxBase==NULL)
    exit(FALSE);
}

make_window(x,y,w,h,name,flags)
SHORT x,y,w,h;
UBYTE *name;
ULONG flags;
/* This function will initialize the NewWindow structure
   and open the window  */
{
  struct NewWindow NewWindow;

  NewWindow.LeftEdge=x;
  NewWindow.TopEdge=y;
  NewWindow.Width=w;
  NewWindow.Height=h;
  NewWindow.DetailPen=-1;
  NewWindow.BlockPen=-1;
  NewWindow.Title=name;
  NewWindow.Flags=flags;
  NewWindow.IDCMPFlags=NULL;
  NewWindow.Type=WBENCHSCREEN;
  NewWindow.FirstGadget=NULL;
  NewWindow.CheckMark=NULL;
  NewWindow.Screen=NULL;
  NewWindow.BitMap=NULL;
  NewWindow.MinWidth=0;
  NewWindow.MinHeight=0;
  NewWindow.MaxWidth=0;
  NewWindow.MaxHeight=0;


  return(OpenWindow(&NewWindow));

}

VOID delay_func(factor)
int factor;
/* This function will cause a specified delay */
{
 int loop;

 for(loop=0;loop<factor*1000;loop++)
   ;
```

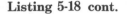
Listing 5-18 cont.

```
 return;
}
```

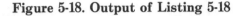
Figure 5-18. Output of Listing 5-18

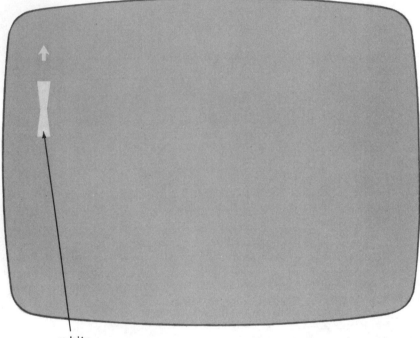

white

Summary

In this chapter, we have explored the graphics capability of the Amiga, available to the programmer through Intuition. We have discussed the three graphics objects directly defined within the window interface: borders, IntuiText, and images. This represents a well-behaved interface that is both powerful and easy to use. With these objects and their corresponding functions, powerful graphics displays can be produced.

The Amiga does not stop with Intuition graphics. The underlying operating system software—the Exec ROM kernel—offers a complete graphics system, including drawing commands, area fill, and area pattern fill. We have explored these graphics functions, as they are accessible through the high-level interface Intuition.

Animating the Sprites Chapter 6

T he Amiga offers hardware support for animation; this comes in the form of *sprites*, graphics-oriented displays that can be moved independent of other objects in the display field. The format or the color of sprites can also be changed while they are being displayed. Although there are some restrictions on the shape and colors that constitute them, sprites offer a flexible alternative for movement and animation in a video display. In addition to these hardware resources, there is a software subsystem that facilitates the manipulation of the hardware resource.

Sprites

A sprite is a hardware object on the Amiga. There are eight special purpose DMA (direct memory access) channels that are used to define these graphics objects. This means that the drawing of these objects on the screen is independent of the main processor. Sprites can be drawn, moved, changed, and redrawn while the CPU is dealing with other tasks. Because they are supported directly this way and not built up through layers of software, sprites are fast, easy to program, and flexible in their use.

One of the most striking uses of a sprite—and one that well displays its flexibility—is the mouse cursor; this is sprite 0. Using a sprite as the cursor is necessary, because the cursor must be available across the entire display and not be stopped at window or screen boundaries. The hardware cursor is defined outside of all the Intuition objects, so that it can easily move between them. This is one example of sprite versatility. Other uses for these objects span the obvious and the not-so-obvious. Sprites are available for their traditional uses in video games, representing rockets, missiles, and the usual panoply of deadly devices. Since the shape of a sprite can be changed while it is being displayed, explosions and other forms of mayhem can easily be programmed into the display. Sprites can also have more mundane uses. They can serve as "paint brush" objects in drawing programs or "follow the bouncing ball" pointers in a program devoted to music. There are many unanticipated applications wherein this kind of object can be used to effect. You are limited only by imagination.

Defining a Sprite

One restriction on the definition of a sprite is that its basic measurements are specified in terms of the normal or low-resolution display. The pixel is defined as:

1/320th the width of the screen; and

1/200th the height of the screen

However, since these objects are independently supported in hardware, their resolution is unaffected by that of any other objects that are on the display at the same time. Even if these objects change, the sprite remains the same. This is not hard to understand if you remember that a sprite is really only appearing in front of windows and screens, and is never really a part of them.

The width of a sprite is also restricted: it may be no more than sixteen pixels wide. A corresponding restriction is not in effect for height, which can be any value up to the full height of the display. Actually, a sprite can be higher than any screen or window that might be displayed behind it. In this case, the sprite must be scrolled to discover its full shape. Beyond these two restrictions, any shape that can be rendered into a space sixteen pixels wide can be implemented as a sprite.

The shape of a sprite is specified in memory as a set of contiguous 16-bit locations (Figure 6-1). The first two locations are reserved for hardware control instructions and represent the values to be put into the hardware registers associated with the sprite. The last two locations are also used for control. The body of this array is used to define the shape of the sprite. Each line is represented by two locations in memory. Each pixel in the display is defined by a pair of bits—one from each of the two words (Figure 6-2). This pair of bits indicates the color that a particular pixel will be. The color is specified indirectly through one or more color registers; these kinds of color specification will be discussed in more detail later.

The memory locations that define the sprite image are accessible through an array of 16-bit integers; either USHORT or UWORD will work. Typically, the appropriate values are indicated using hexadecimal numbers, since these make it easy to translate from bit positions to a numeric form that the system can understand. Figure 6-3 shows a typical way to create a sprite. First you create the figure in some convenient form such as graph paper. Once you have a form that you like, you can then translate each line of your drawing into a four-digit hexadecimal number (recall that four bits translate to one hexadecimal digit). Specification of the second word defining the line is a function of the color that you want for the individual pixel.

We mentioned earlier that the mouse cursor is actually a sprite. Intuition offers a function that allows you to change the shape of this cursor. This

Figure 6-1. The format of a sprite definition in memory

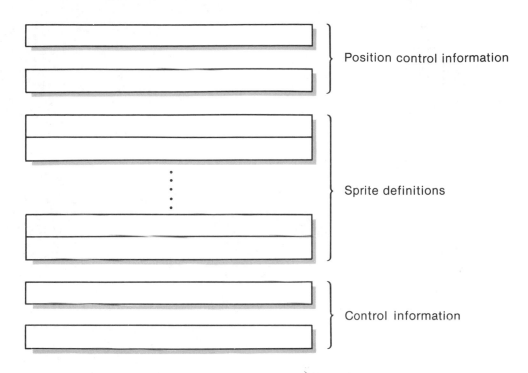

Position control information

Sprite definitions

Control information

Figure 6-2. Defining the sprite image

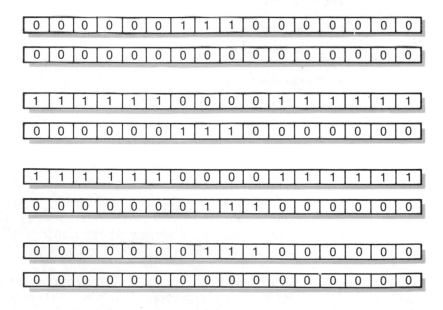

0	0	0	0	0	0	1	1	1	0	0	0	0	0	0	0
0	0	0	0	0	0	0	0	0	0	0	0	0	0	0	0

1	1	1	1	1	1	0	0	0	0	1	1	1	1	1	1
0	0	0	0	0	0	1	1	1	0	0	0	0	0	0	0

1	1	1	1	1	1	0	0	0	0	1	1	1	1	1	1
0	0	0	0	0	0	0	1	1	1	0	0	0	0	0	0

0	0	0	0	0	0	0	1	1	1	0	0	0	0	0	0
0	0	0	0	0	0	0	0	0	0	0	0	0	0	0	0

Figure 6-3. Translating a sprite image from graph paper to array

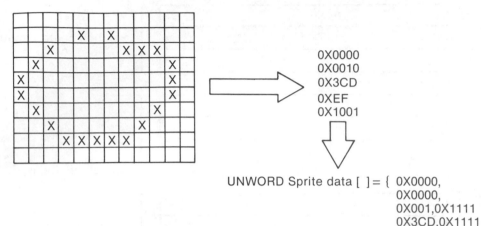

```
0X0000
0X0010
0X3CD
0XEF
0X1001
```

```
UNWORD Sprite data [ ] = { 0X0000,
                           0X0000,
                           0X001,0X1111
                           0X3CD,0X1111
                           0XEF,0X1111
                           0X1001,0X1111} ;
```

function, *SetPointer( )* is tied to a particular window. Whenever the window is active, the new definition governs the shape of this cursor; when the window is deactivated, the cursor reverts to its original form. This is consistent with our claim that the sprite is independent of windows. The Intuition operating system senses the boundaries of software defined objects, such as windows, and in this case, changes the definition associated with the sprite. This can also be done under program command, which will be covered later.

The form of the command to alter the cursor is:

```
SetPointer(window,s_data,height,width,x,y)
```

where

> **window** is a pointer to an open window.
>
> **s_data** points to an array of 16-bit words.
>
> **height** indicates the number of pixels in the y axis.
>
> **width** indicates the size along the horizontal dimension.
>
> **x and y** are the offsets from the cursor position box.

These last two parameters need some clarification. The action of the cursor is dependent on the position of a particular spot—called the *hot spot*—over the object to be chosen. The x and y value indicate the relationship of the shape of the cursor to this spot. Values of 0,0 place it at the upper left-hand corner (Figure 6-4). Note that any changes specified by *SetPointer( )* occur immediately.

Listing 6-1 contains a program that uses the *SetPointer( )* function. After opening a high-resolution screen and window, we use *SetPointer( )* to change the shape of the cursor from its default value. The shape is defined in the

Figure 6-4. The hot spot and its relationship to xoffset and yoffset

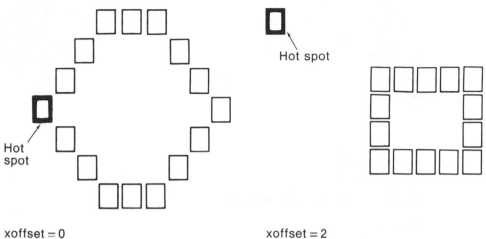

xoffset = 0
xoffset = 0

xoffset = 2
xoffset = 2

array *imp_data*. For the sake of simplicity, we define a single color cursor. Note that the *x* and *y* offsets are both 0.

Listing 6-1. Use of SetPointer( ) to change the window pointer.

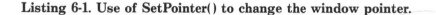

```
*/

#include "exec/types.h"
#include "intuition/intuition.h"
#include "graphics/sprite.h"

struct IntuitionBase *IntuitionBase;
struct GfxBase *GfxBase;
struct Screen *Scrn;
struct Window *wind;

USHORT imp_data[]= {
    0x0000,0x0000,
    0x0180,0x0180,
    0x03c0,0x03c0,
    0x07e0,0x07e0,
    0x0e70,0x0e70,
    0x1c38,0x1c38,
    0x381c,0x381c,
    0x718e,0x718e,
    0xc3c3,0xc3c3,
    0xc3c3,0xc3c3,
    0x718e,0x718e,
    0x381c,0x381c,
    0x1c38,0x1c38,
    0x0e70,0x0e70,
```

doesn't show anything

Listing 6-1 cont.

```
   0x07e0,0x07e0,
   0x03c0,0x03c0,
   0x0180,0x0180,
   0x0000,0x0000,
   0x0000,0x0000 };

#define INTUITION_REV 29
#define GRAPHICS_REV 29

main()
{
 SHORT x,y,w,h,d;
 USHORT mode;
 ULONG flags;
 UBYTE c0,c1;
 VOID delay_func(),OpenALL();

  OpenALL();

 /*  ======Open a hi-res custom screen==== */

  y=0;
  w=640;
  h=200;
  d=3;
  c0=0x00;
  c1=0x01;
  mode=HIRES;

  Scrn=(struct Screen *)
          make_screen(y,w,h,d,c0,c1,mode,"TEST SCREEN");


 /* ===Open a window=== */

  x=10;
  y=10;
  w=300;
  h=150;
flags=ACTIVATE|SMART_REFRESH|WINDOWSIZING|WINDOWCLOSE|WINDOWDRAG;
  c0=-1;
  c1=-1;

  wind=(struct Window *)
          make_window(x,y,w,h,"Window 0",flags,c0,c1,Scrn,NULL);

 /* ===Create and set a new pointer=== */

  SetPointer(wind,imp_data,16,16,0,0);

  Delay(500);

 /* =========Close down the window then the screen==========*/
```

Listing 6-1 cont.

```
  CloseScreen(Scrn);

}

VOID OpenALL()
/* This function will open any necessary Libraries */
{

  /*    ======Open Intuition======= */

  IntuitionBase=(struct IntuitionBase *)
           OpenLibrary("intuition.library",INTUITION_REV);

  if(IntuitionBase==NULL)
     exit(FALSE);

  GfxBase=(struct GfxBase *)                 
           OpenLibrary("graphics.library",GRAPHICS_REV);

  if(GfxBase==NULL)
     exit(FALSE);
}
make_screen(y,w,h,d,color0,color1,mode,name)
SHORT y,w,h,d;
UBYTE color0,color1,*name;
USHORT mode;
{
  struct NewScreen NewScreen;

  NewScreen.LeftEdge=0;
  NewScreen.TopEdge=y;
  NewScreen.Width=w;
  NewScreen.Height=h;
  NewScreen.Depth=d;
  NewScreen.DetailPen=color0;
  NewScreen.BlockPen=color1;
  NewScreen.ViewModes=mode;
  NewScreen.Type=CUSTOMSCREEN;
  NewScreen.Font=NULL;
  NewScreen.DefaultTitle=name;
  NewScreen.Gadgets=NULL;
  NewScreen.CustomBitMap=NULL;

  return(OpenScreen(&NewScreen));
}
make_window(x,y,w,h,name,flags,color0,color1,screen,gadg)
SHORT x,y,w,h;
UBYTE *name,color0,color1;
ULONG flags;
struct Screen *screen;
struct Gadget *gadg;
/* This function will initialize the NewWindow structure
   and open the window */
{
```

Listing 6-1 cont.

```
struct NewWindow NewWindow;

NewWindow.LeftEdge=x;
NewWindow.TopEdge=y;
NewWindow.Width=w;
NewWindow.Height=h;
NewWindow.DetailPen=color0;
NewWindow.BlockPen=color1;
NewWindow.Title=name;
NewWindow.Flags=flags;
NewWindow.IDCMPFlags=NULL;
NewWindow.Type=CUSTOMSCREEN;
NewWindow.FirstGadget=gadg;
NewWindow.CheckMark=NULL;
NewWindow.Screen=screen;
NewWindow.BitMap=NULL;
NewWindow.MinWidth=1;
NewWindow.MinHeight=1;
NewWindow.MaxWidth=640;
NewWindow.MaxHeight=200;

return(OpenWindow(&NewWindow));
}


VOID delay_func(factor)
int factor;
/* This function will cause a specified delay */
{
 int loop;

 for(loop=0;loop<factor*1000;loop++)
   ;

 return;
}
```

Color and the Sprites

We alluded to the fact that each pixel in the sprite is assigned a value that points to a color register. This indirect color addressing is the same throughout the Amiga for any kind of graphic image rendering. There is, however, a limitation on the sprite that is not found in the pure graphics routines. Each particular sprite is associated with a specific set of four-color registers. Each pixel in the sprite can take on one of three colors, or it can be transparent. In this latter case, the appearance of the sprite—or parts of the sprite—allow other objects to show through it. This allows the designer to make the sprite appear as if it were going behind an object. Recall that this object type is completely independent of windows and screens, and can contain no gadgets.

Transparency is a way to capture the same kind of action that a window or screen provides with the Depth Arrangement Gadget.

Figure 6-5. Indirect addressing of color registers

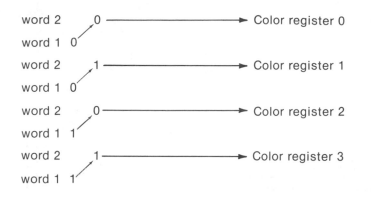

The color register identifier is encoded in the 2-bit specification for each pixel. (Recall that the sprite data array required two integers to define a single line of the figure.) The 0 bits of each word are taken together, the 1 bits, and so on down to the sixteenth position. Within the three-color constraint, each pixel's color is independent of its neighbors. Figure 6-5 indicates how these color values are encoded. Techniques such as *artifacting*—where adjacent colors produce the illusion of a third—may be used to produce more than the three colors available.

Thirty-two color registers are available on the Amiga, numbered from 0 to 31. Each of these registers may specify any of the 4096 possible colors that can be produced. Any or all of the registers may be used by the graphics objects found in the display; this is a function of the specified depth of these objects. Sprites are assigned to the color registers 16 through 31; they do not necessarily have exclusive use of these registers. This is dependent on what is being displayed concurrently and the number of bit planes allocated. Some registers have to be shared with windows, screens, or pictures. Figure 6-6 indicates the specific assignment of registers to sprites.

There is a further complication. Sprites are divided into pairs, and each pair must share a register set. Setting a particular set of colors for sprite 0, for example, means that you are also setting the same colors for sprite 1.

The Simple Sprite

So far, you have seen how to specify the shape of a sprite, how to set the colors of its pixels, and what kind of memory organization the hardware expects. The Amiga also offers a software subsystem that lets you easily set up and manipulate these objects through C programs, without requiring access of the hardware register locations or even assembly language pro-

Figure 6-6. Sprite color register map

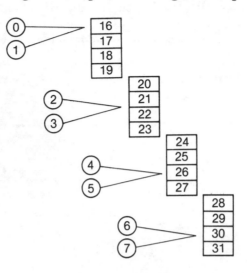

gramming. This subsystem consists of the SimpleSprite structure and a series of system functions that manipulate it. This structure exists in addition to the array definition already used to good effect in the *SetPointer()* function. There are two system macros:

ON__SPRITE

OFF__SPRITE

These macros switch the sprite display circuitry on and off. The default condition is ON__SPRITE, so this need never be explicitly mentioned unless a previous execution of OFF__SPRITE has made the sprites invisible. These, along with other necessary declarations, are found in the header file *graphics/sprite.h*.

A SimpleSprite is defined by its structure declaration:

```
struct SimpleSprite {
    UWORD  *posctldata,
            height,
            x,y,
            num;
};
```

where

posctldata points to position control values in memory.

height indicates the number of lines in the sprite.

x,y set the sprite's current position in the display area.

num also contains hardware-specific information.

This is a very simple data type, particularly since only *height*, *x*, and *y* are set by the user. The other two members of the structure are set solely by the machine.

Once you have declared a SimpleSprite variable, you must ask the system to allocate a sprite for your use. This, too, is done through a system function:

```
sprite_id=GetSprite(s_ptr,s_number);
```

where

sprite_id is the number of the sprite allocated by this function.

s_ptr points to a SimpleSprite structure.

s_number indicates the number of the sprite desired.

A call to this function initializes the structure and prepares it to participate in the other sprite functions. If you specify -1 for the *s_number* parameter, the system assigns the next available sprite. In contrast, if you ask for a specific sprite, that one is allocated. If it is not available, the functions return -1 to indicate an error condition. This value is also returned if there are no sprites left to allocate.

Once a sprite has been allocated, it is necessary to set the desired values into the defining structure and to attach it to the image data. Setting the initial values is easily accomplished by explicitly assigning values to the *x,y*, and *height* members. The *x* and *y* assignment set the initial position of the sprite. The *height* assignment must be consistent with the layout of the image data. Once you have made the *height* assignment—this is the only one that is strictly necessary—you can call the system to attach the data and sprite. This is done with:

```
ChangeSprite(v_port,s_struct,s_data)
```

where

v_port is a pointer to the ViewPort of the display area. This is commonly set to 0 to indicate the current value.

s_struct points to the SimpleSprite structure.

s_data is a pointer to the image data.

This function can be used again to change an existing sprite, by attaching a new image data array to it. The shape, the color, or both may be changed. The new sprite is visible immediately.

Besides adjusting a sprite's shape and color, it is also necessary to move it around the display. This is done by a call to:

```
MoveSprite(v_port,s_num,x,y)
```

V_port is a pointer to the ViewPort of the display area or to 0 to indicate the current one. This function moves the sprite to the location *x,y* on the display area. These coordinates are relative to the overall coordinates of the displayed ViewPort; this can be either a window or a screen. Figure 6-7 illustrates this

Figure 6-7. The position of a sprite relative to a ViewPort

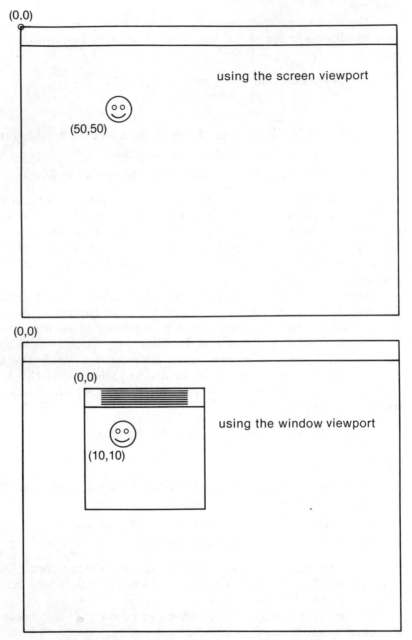

relationship. Again, even if you specify a location in relation to a window, the sprite is still an independent hardware object, not really a part of that window.

Listing 6-2 produces a multicolored sprite and causes it to move back and forth diagonally on the display screen. After calling *GetSprite( )* to allocate the next available sprite, we check to make sure that the function was successful; if it was not, we exit. Next we initialize the SimpleSprite structure, *imp*. Here the critical value is setting *imp.height* to 9 to make it compatible with the data in the *imp_data* array. The *switch* statement is set up to discover which sprite was assigned to the *s_id* variable. This variable sets the variable *k* to the corresponding color register value.

Listing 6-2. Allocating and playing with a hardware sprite.

```
*/

#include "exec/types.h"
#include "intuition/intuition.h"
#include "graphics/sprite.h"

struct IntuitionBase *IntuitionBase;
struct GfxBase *GfxBase;
struct Screen *Scrn;
struct Window wind;
struct SimpleSprite imp;

UWORD imp_data[]= {
    0,0,
    0x0fc3,0x0000,
    0x3ff3,0x0000,
    0x30c3,0x0000,
    0x0000,0x3c03,
    0x0000,0x3fc3,
    0x0000,0x03c3,
    0xc033,0xc033,
    0xffc0,0xffc0,
    0x3f03,0x3f03,
    0,0 };

#define INTUITION_REV 29
#define GRAPHICS_REV 29

main()
{
  SHORT x,y,w,h,d,s_id,k,xmove,ymove,n,i;
  USHORT mode;
  ULONG flags;
  UBYTE *name,c0,c1;
  VOID delay_func(),OpenALL();

  OpenALL();

  /*   ======Open a hi-res custom screen==== */

  y=0;
  w=640;
  h=200;
  d=3;
  c0=0x00;
```

CRASH ~ 3. ~

Listing 6-2 cont.

```
c1=0x01;
mode=HIRES;

Scrn=(struct Screen *)
        make_screen(y,w,h,d,c0,c1,mode,NULL);

ShowTitle(Scrn,FALSE);

/* ===Open a backdrop window=== */

name=NULL;
x=0;
y=0;
w=640;
h=200;
flags=ACTIVATE|SMART_REFRESH|BORDERLESS|BACKDROP;
c0=-1;
c1=-1;

wind=(struct Window *)
        make_window(x,y,w,h,name,flags,c0,c1,Scrn,NULL);

/* ===Create and play with a simple hardware sprite=== */

if((s_id=GetSprite(&imp,-1))==-1)
  exit();

imp.x=0;
imp.y=0;
imp.height=9;

switch(s_id)  {
  case 0:
  case 1: k=16;
          break;
  case 2:
  case 3: k=20;
          break;
  case 4:
  case 5: k=24;
          break;
  case 6:
  case 7: k=28;
          break;

 }


SetRGB4(&Scrn->ViewPort,k+1,12,3,8);
SetRGB4(&Scrn->ViewPort,k+2,13,13,13);
SetRGB4(&Scrn->ViewPort,k+3,4,4,15);

ChangeSprite(&Scrn->ViewPort,&imp,&imp_data);
```

Listing 6-2 cont.

```
  MoveSprite(0,&imp,30,0);

  xmove=1;
  ymove=1;

  for(n=0;n<4;n++)  {
    i=0;
    while(i++< 185)  {
      MoveSprite(0,&imp,imp.x+xmove,imp.y+ymove);
      WaitTOF();
     }
    ymove=-ymove;
    xmove=-xmove;
   }

 FreeSprite(s_id);

  /* =========Close down the window then the screen=======*/


  CloseScreen(Scrn);

}

VOID OpenALL()
/* This function will open any necessary libraries */
{

  /*    ======Open Intuition======= */

  IntuitionBase=(struct IntuitionBase *)
          OpenLibrary("intuition.library",INTUITION_REV);

  if(IntuitionBase==NULL)
     exit(FALSE);

  GfxBase=(struct GfxBase *)
          OpenLibrary("graphics.library",GRAPHICS_REV);

  if(GfxBase==NULL)
     exit(FALSE);
}
make_screen(y,w,h,d,color0,color1,mode,name)
SHORT y,w,h,d;
UBYTE color0,color1,*name;
USHORT mode;
{
 struct NewScreen NewScreen;

 NewScreen.LeftEdge=0;
 NewScreen.TopEdge=y;
 NewScreen.Width=w;
 NewScreen.Height=h;
 NewScreen.Depth=d;
```

Listing 6-2 cont.

```
   NewScreen.DetailPen=color0;
   NewScreen.BlockPen=color1;
   NewScreen.ViewModes=mode;
   NewScreen.Type=CUSTOMSCREEN;
   NewScreen.Font=NULL;
   NewScreen.DefaultTitle=name;
   NewScreen.Gadgets=NULL;
   NewScreen.CustomBitMap=NULL;

  return(OpenScreen(&NewScreen));
}
make_window(x,y,w,h,name,flags,color0,color1,screen,gadg)
SHORT x,y,w,h;
UBYTE *name,color0,color1;
ULONG flags;
struct Screen *screen;
struct Gadget *gadg;
/* This function will initialize the NewWindow structure
   and open the window */
{
  struct NewWindow NewWindow;

  NewWindow.LeftEdge=x;
  NewWindow.TopEdge=y;
  NewWindow.Width=w;
  NewWindow.Height=h;
  NewWindow.DetailPen=color0;
  NewWindow.BlockPen=color1;
  NewWindow.Title=name;
  NewWindow.Flags=flags;
  NewWindow.IDCMPFlags=NULL;
  NewWindow.Type=CUSTOMSCREEN;
  NewWindow.FirstGadget=gadg;
  NewWindow.CheckMark=NULL;
  NewWindow.Screen=screen;
  NewWindow.BitMap=NULL;
  NewWindow.MinWidth=1;
  NewWindow.MinHeight=1;
  NewWindow.MaxWidth=640;
  NewWindow.MaxHeight=200;

  return(OpenWindow(&NewWindow));
}


    VOID delay_func(factor)
    int factor;
```

Listing 6-2 cont.

```
/* This function will cause a specified delay */
{
 int loop;

 for(loop=0;loop<factor*1000;loop++)
   ;

 return;
}
```

Once our program has completed its initialization, we are ready to be creative with the sprite. We first set the colors of the three registers associated with our current choice; this is done by a call to:

```
SetRGB(v_port,c_reg,red,green,blue);
```

where

v__port is a pointer to the active ViewPort.

c__reg identifies the particular color register.

red, green, and **blue** set the values for these respective colors in that register.

The three primary color variables take on values between 0 and 15. These values represent the proportion of that particular color that will be mixed into the color to be associated with a particular register. In our example, we use the screen ViewPort.

Once we have set the colors that the sprite data will use, we execute *ChangeSprite()* to associate these colors with the data defined in *imp__data[ ]*. We initially move the sprite to location 30,0 by a call to *MoveSprite()*, and enter a loop. The loop continues to move the sprite by an increment of one through the variables *xmove* and *ymove*. By changing the sign of *ymove* on every loop, we cause the sprite to move back and forth. The heart of this inner loop is the *MoveSprite()* function call, but we also include a *WaitTOF()* command. This command is an executive kernel call; it suspends the move until the next draw cycle (actually the video blanking period). This delay tends to make a smoother appearing program. The *FreeSprite()* function takes the sprite identifier as a parameter and de-allocates the memory assigned to it. It is always necessary, when using the Amiga, to relinguish resources no longer needed.

**Listing 6-3. Allocating and playing
with improved hardware sprites.**

```
*/

#include "exec/types.h"
```

DOES NOTHING

Listing 6-3 cont.

```
#include "intuition/intuition.h"
#include "graphics/sprite.h"

struct IntuitionBase *IntuitionBase;
struct GfxBase *GfxBase;
struct Screen *Scrn;
struct Window wind;
struct SimpleSprite imp;

UWORD imp_data[]= {
   0,0,
   0x0180,0x0000,
   0x03c0,0x0000,
   0x07e0,0x0000,
   0x0e70,0x0000,
   0x1c38,0x0000,
   0x381c,0x0000,
   0x718e,0x0000,
   0xc3c3,0x0000,
   0xc3c3,0x0000,
   0x718e,0x0000,
   0x381c,0x0000,
   0x1c38,0x0000,
   0x0e70,0x0000,
   0x07e0,0x0000,
   0x03c0,0x0000,
   0x0180,0x0000,
   0,0 };

#define INTUITION_REV 29
#define GRAPHICS_REV 29

main()
{
 SHORT s_id,x,y,w,h,d,xmove,ymove,n,i;
 USHORT mode;
 ULONG flags;
 UBYTE *name,c0,c1;
 VOID delay_func(),OpenALL();

   OpenALL();

   /*  ======Open a hi-res custom screen==== */

   y=0;
   w=640;
   h=200;
   d=3;
   c0=0x00;
   c1=0x01;
   mode=HIRES;
```

Listing 6-3 cont.

```
Scrn=(struct Screen *)
        make_screen(y,w,h,d,c0,c1,mode,NULL);

ShowTitle(Scrn,FALSE);

/* ===Open a backdrop window=== */

name=NULL;
x=0;
y=0;
w=640;
h=200;
flags=ACTIVATE|SMART_REFRESH|BORDERLESS|BACKDROP;
c0=-1;
c1=-1;

wind=(struct Window *)
        make_window(x,y,w,h,name,flags,c0,c1,Scrn,NULL);

/* ===Create and play with a simple hardware sprite=== */

init_sprite(&imp,&s_id);

ChangeSprite(&Scrn->ViewPort,&imp,&imp_data);

MoveSprite(0,&imp,30,0);

xmove=1;
ymove=1;

for(n=0;n<4;n++)  {
    i=0;
    while(i++< 185)  {
        MoveSprite(0,&imp,imp.x+xmove,imp.y+ymove);
        WaitTOF();
    }
    ymove=-ymove;

}

FreeSprite(s_id);

/* ========Close down the window then the screen=======*/


CloseScreen(Scrn);

}

VOID OpenALL()
/* This function will open any necessary libraries */
{

/*    ======Open Intuition====== */
```

Listing 6-3 cont.

```
IntuitionBase=(struct IntuitionBase *)
          OpenLibrary("intuition.library",INTUITION_REV);

if(IntuitionBase==NULL)
    exit(FALSE);

GfxBase=(struct GfxBase *)
          OpenLibrary("graphics.library",GRAPHICS_REV);

if(GfxBase==NULL)
    exit(FALSE);
}
make_screen(y,w,h,d,color0,color1,mode,name)
SHORT y,w,h,d;
UBYTE color0,color1,*name;
USHORT mode;
{
 struct NewScreen NewScreen;

 NewScreen.LeftEdge=0;
 NewScreen.TopEdge=y;
 NewScreen.Width=w;
 NewScreen.Height=h;
 NewScreen.Depth=d;
 NewScreen.DetailPen=color0;
 NewScreen.BlockPen=color1;
 NewScreen.ViewModes=mode;
 NewScreen.Type=CUSTOMSCREEN;
 NewScreen.Font=NULL;
 NewScreen.DefaultTitle=name;
 NewScreen.Gadgets=NULL;
 NewScreen.CustomBitMap=NULL;

 return(OpenScreen(&NewScreen));
}
make_window(x,y,w,h,name,flags,color0,color1,screen,gadg)
SHORT x,y,w,h;
UBYTE *name,color0,color1;
ULONG flags;
struct Screen *screen;
struct Gadget *gadg;
/* This function will initialize the NewWindow structure
   and open the window */
{
  struct NewWindow NewWindow;

  NewWindow.LeftEdge=x;
  NewWindow.TopEdge=y;
  NewWindow.Width=w;
  NewWindow.Height=h;
  NewWindow.DetailPen=color0;
  NewWindow.BlockPen=color1;
  NewWindow.Title=name;
```

Listing 6-3 cont.

```
   NewWindow.Flags=flags;
   NewWindow.IDCMPFlags=NULL;
   NewWindow.Type=CUSTOMSCREEN;
   NewWindow.FirstGadget=gadg;
   NewWindow.CheckMark=NULL;
   NewWindow.Screen=screen;
   NewWindow.BitMap=NULL;
   NewWindow.MinWidth=1;
   NewWindow.MinHeight=1;
   NewWindow.MaxWidth=640;
   NewWindow.MaxHeight=200;

   return(OpenWindow(&NewWindow));
}
init_sprite(imp,s_id)
struct SimpleSprite *imp;
SHORT *s_id;
{
  SHORT k;

  if((*s_id=GetSprite(&imp,-1))==-1)
    exit();

  imp->x=0;
  imp->y=0;
  imp->height=16;

  switch(*s_id)  {
    case 0:
    case 1: k=16;
            break;
    case 2:
    case 3: k=20;
            break;
    case 4:
    case 5: k=24;
            break;
    case 6:
    case 7: k=28;
            break;
  }

  SetRGB4(&Scrn->ViewPort,k+1,12,3,8);
  SetRGB4(&Scrn->ViewPort,k+2,13,13,13);
  SetRGB4(&Scrn->ViewPort,k+3,4,4,15);

}



VOID delay_func(factor)
int factor;
```

Listing 6-3 cont.

```
/* This function will cause a specified delay */
{
 int loop;

 for(loop=0;loop<factor*1000;loop++)
   ;

 return;
}
```

The code in Listing 6-3 produces a display similar to the first example. The program is improved in two ways:

1. All initialization has been gathered together in a single function, *init__sprite( )*.

2. The sprite image has been redesigned to a more pleasant form and increased in size to 16 by 16.

The function definition makes this example a more modular program in comparison to Listing 6-2.

In Listing 6-4, we allocate and manipulate two separate sprites. Notice that we use the same image data to define each one, but we initialize them independently and have two sets of commands for each. The program moves the sprite around on the display screen. There must be a separate call to *FreeSprite( )* for each sprite defined.

Listing 6-4. Allocating and playing with two hardware sprites.

```
*/

#include "exec/types.h"
#include "intuition/intuition.h"
#include "graphics/sprite.h"

struct IntuitionBase *IntuitionBase;
struct GfxBase *GfxBase;
struct Screen *Scrn;
struct Window wind;
struct SimpleSprite imp0,imp1;

UWORD imp_data[]= {
    0,0,
    0x0180,0x0000,
    0x03c0,0x0000,
    0x07e0,0x0000,
    0x0e70,0x0000,
    0x1c38,0x0000,
    0x381c,0x0000,
```

Listing 6-4 cont.

```
   0x718e,0x0000,
   0xc3c3,0x0000,
   0xc3c3,0x0000,
   0x718e,0x0000,
   0x381c,0x0000,
   0x1c38,0x0000,
   0x0e70,0x0000,
   0x07e0,0x0000,
   0x03c0,0x0000,
   0x0180,0x0000,
   0,0 };
```

```c
#define INTUITION_REV 29
#define GRAPHICS_REV 29

main()
{
 SHORT s_id0,s_id1,x,y,w,h,d,xmove0,ymove0,xmove1,ymove1,n,i;
 USHORT mode;
 ULONG flags;
 UBYTE *name,c0,c1;
 VOID delay_func(),OpenALL();

  OpenALL();

 /*  ======Open a hi-res custom screen==== */

  y=0;
  w=640;
  h=200;
  d=3;
  c0=0x00;
  c1=0x01;
  mode=HIRES;

  Scrn=(struct Screen *)
        make_screen(y,w,h,d,c0,c1,mode,NULL);

  ShowTitle(Scrn,FALSE);

 /* ===Open a backdrop window=== */

  name=NULL;
  x=0;
  y=0;
  w=640;
  h=200;
  flags=ACTIVATE|SMART_REFRESH|BORDERLESS|BACKDROP;
  c0=-1;
  c1=-1;

  wind=(struct Window *)
        make_window(x,y,w,h,name,flags,c0,c1,Scrn,NULL);
```

Listing 6-4 cont.

```
/* ===Create and play with a simple hardware sprite=== */

 init_sprite(&imp0,&s_id0);

 ChangeSprite(&Scrn->ViewPort,&imp0,&imp_data);

 MoveSprite(0,&imp0,30,0);

 init_sprite(&imp1,&s_id1);

 ChangeSprite(&Scrn->ViewPort,&imp1,&imp_data);

 MoveSprite(0,&imp1,35,10);

 xmove0=1;
 ymove0=1;
 xmove1=1;
 xmove1=1;

 for(n=0;n<4;n++)  {
   i=0;
   while(i++< 185)  {
     MoveSprite(0,&imp0,imp0.x+xmove0,imp0.y+ymove0);
     WaitTOF();
     MoveSprite(0,&imp1,imp1.x+xmove1,imp1.y+ymove1);
     WaitTOF();
    }
   ymove0=(-ymove0);
   ymove1=(-ymove1);

 }

FreeSprite(s_id0);
FreeSprite(s_id1);

   /* =========Close down the window then the screen========*/


   CloseScreen(Scrn);

}

VOID OpenALL()
/* This function will open any necessary libraries */
{

   /*   ======Open Intuition====== */

IntuitionBase=(struct IntuitionBase *)
          OpenLibrary("intuition.library",INTUITION_REV);

if(IntuitionBase==NULL)
   exit(FALSE);
```

Listing 6-4 cont.

```
GfxBase=(struct GfxBase *)
          OpenLibrary("graphics.library",GRAPHICS_REV);

 if(GfxBase==NULL)
    exit(FALSE);
}
make_screen(y,w,h,d,color0,color1,mode,name)
SHORT y,w,h,d;
UBYTE color0,color1,*name;
USHORT mode;
{
 struct NewScreen NewScreen;

 NewScreen.LeftEdge=0;
 NewScreen.TopEdge=y;
 NewScreen.Width=w;
 NewScreen.Height=h;
 NewScreen.Depth=d;
 NewScreen.DetailPen=color0;
 NewScreen.BlockPen=color1;
 NewScreen.ViewModes=mode;
 NewScreen.Type=CUSTOMSCREEN;
 NewScreen.Font=NULL;
 NewScreen.DefaultTitle=name;
 NewScreen.Gadgets=NULL;
 NewScreen.CustomBitMap=NULL;

 return(OpenScreen(&NewScreen));
}
make_window(x,y,w,h,name,flags,color0,color1,screen,gadg)
SHORT x,y,w,h;
UBYTE *name,color0,color1;
ULONG flags;
struct Screen *screen;
struct Gadget *gadg;
/* This function will initialize the NewWindow structure
   and open the window */
{
  struct NewWindow NewWindow;

  NewWindow.LeftEdge=x;
  NewWindow.TopEdge=y;
  NewWindow.Width=w;
  NewWindow.Height=h;
  NewWindow.DetailPen=color0;
  NewWindow.BlockPen=color1;
  NewWindow.Title=name;
  NewWindow.Flags=flags;
  NewWindow.IDCMPFlags=NULL;
  NewWindow.Type=CUSTOMSCREEN;
  NewWindow.FirstGadget=gadg;
  NewWindow.CheckMark=NULL;
  NewWindow.Screen=screen;
```

Listing 6-4 cont.

```
NewWindow.BitMap=NULL;
NewWindow.MinWidth=1;
NewWindow.MinHeight=1;
NewWindow.MaxWidth=640;
NewWindow.MaxHeight=200;

return(OpenWindow(&NewWindow));
}
init_sprite(imp,s_id)
struct SimpleSprite *imp;
SHORT *s_id;
{
  SHORT k;

  if((*s_id=GetSprite(&imp,-1))==-1)
    exit();

  imp->x=0;
  imp->y=0;
  imp->height=16;

  switch(*s_id)  {
    case 0:
    case 1: k=16;
            break;
    case 2:
    case 3: k=20;
            break;
    case 4:
    case 5: k=24;
            break;
    case 6:
    case 7: k=28;
            break;
  }


  SetRGB4(&Scrn->ViewPort,k+1,12,3,8);
  SetRGB4(&Scrn->ViewPort,k+2,13,13,13);
  SetRGB4(&Scrn->ViewPort,k+3,4,4,15);

}



VOID delay_func(factor)
int factor;
/* This function will cause a specified delay */
{
  int loop;

  for(loop=0;loop<factor*1000;loop++)
```

Listing 6-4 cont.

```
    ;

  return;
}
```

Up until now the only thing you have done with sprites is to move them around the screen. You are not restricted to this activity. By creating a loop, you can continuously change any of the parameters of the object. In Listing 6-5, we not only move a sprite, but we periodically change its shape. Notice that we have two independent image data arrays. Each array defines a different shape for the sprite. To make a shape change, all we need to do is call *ChangeSprite()* and pass it the new image data array. Our example makes such a shape change controlled by the outer *for* loop. Each time this loop is incremented, a call to *ChangeSprite()* switches the sprite from its current shape to that defined by the other image data array. On even-numbered loops, we use *imp__data1*, and on odd-numbered loops, *imp__data0*. The inner loop merely moves the sprite around the display.

Listing 6-5. Changing the shape of a hardware sprite.

does nothing, doesn't come back

```
*/

#include "exec/types.h"
#include "intuition/intuition.h"
#include "graphics/sprite.h"

struct IntuitionBase *IntuitionBase;
struct GfxBase *GfxBase;
struct Screen *Scrn;
struct Window wind;
struct SimpleSprite imp0,imp1;

UWORD imp_data0[]= {
    0,0,
    0x07e0,0x0000,
    0x0810,0x0000,
    0x1008,0x0000,
    0x2004,0x0000,
    0x4c32,0x0000,
    0x9e79,0x0000,
    0x8c31,0x0000,
    0x8001,0x0000,
    0x8001,0x0000,
    0x8001,0x0000,
    0x9009,0x0000,
    0x4812,0x0000,
    0x27e4,0x0000,
    0x1008,0x0000,
    0x0810,0x0000,
```

Listing 6-5 cont.

```
0x07e0,0x0000,
0,0 },
imp_data1[]={
0,0,
0x07e0,0x0000,
0x0810,0x0000,
0x1008,0x0000,
0x2004,0x0000,
0x4c32,0x0000,
0x9e79,0x0000,
0x8c31,0x0000,
0x8001,0x0000,
0x8001,0x0000,
0x87e1,0x0000,
0x8811,0x0000,
0x500a,0x0000,
0x2004,0x0000,
0x1008,0x0000,
0x0810,0x0000,
0x07e0,0x0000,
0,0};
```

```
#define INTUITION_REV 29
#define GRAPHICS_REV 29

main()
{
 SHORT s_id,x,y,w,h,d,xmove0,ymove0,n,i;
 USHORT mode;
 ULONG flags;
 UBYTE *name,c0,c1;
 VOID delay_func(),OpenALL();

  OpenALL();

 /*  ======Open a hi-res custom screen==== */

  y=0;
  w=640;
  h=200;
  d=3;
  c0=0x00;
  c1=0x01;
  mode=HIRES;

  Scrn=(struct Screen *)
        make_screen(y,w,h,d,c0,c1,mode,NULL);

  ShowTitle(Scrn,FALSE);

 /* ===Open a backdrop window=== */

  name=NULL;
```

Listing 6-5 cont.

```
    x=0;
    y=0;
    w=640;
    h=200;
    flags=ACTIVATE|SMART_REFRESH|BORDERLESS|BACKDROP;
    c0=-1;
    c1=-1;

    wind=(struct Window *)
            make_window(x,y,w,h,name,flags,c0,c1,Scrn,NULL);

   /* ===Create and play with a simple hardware sprite=== */

    init_sprite(&imp0,&s_id,0,0,0,0);

    ChangeSprite(0,&imp0,&imp_data0);

    MoveSprite(0,&imp1,35,10);

    xmove0=1;
    ymove0=1;

    for(n=0;n<4;n++)  {
      i=0;
      while(i++< 185)  {
        MoveSprite(0,&imp0,imp0.x+xmove0,imp0.y+ymove0);
        WaitTOF();
       }
      if((n%2)==0)
        ChangeSprite(0,&imp0,&imp_data1);
      else
        ChangeSprite(0,&imp0,&imp_data0);
      ymove0=(-ymove0);

    }

FreeSprite(s_id);

   /* =========Close down the window then the screen========*/


   CloseScreen(Scrn);

}

VOID OpenALL()
/* This function will open any necessary libraries */
{

 /*    ======Open Intuition====== */

  IntuitionBase=(struct IntuitionBase *)
            OpenLibrary("intuition.library",INTUITION_REV);
```

Listing 6-5 cont.

```
 if(IntuitionBase==NULL)
    exit(FALSE);

 GfxBase=(struct GfxBase *)
           OpenLibrary("graphics.library",GRAPHICS_REV);

 if(GfxBase==NULL)
    exit(FALSE);
}
make_screen(y,w,h,d,color0,color1,mode,name)
SHORT y,w,h,d;
UBYTE color0,color1,*name;
USHORT mode;
{
 struct NewScreen NewScreen;

 NewScreen.LeftEdge=0;
 NewScreen.TopEdge=y;
 NewScreen.Width=w;
 NewScreen.Height=h;
 NewScreen.Depth=d;
 NewScreen.DetailPen=color0;
 NewScreen.BlockPen=color1;
 NewScreen.ViewModes=mode;
 NewScreen.Type=CUSTOMSCREEN;
 NewScreen.Font=NULL;
 NewScreen.DefaultTitle=name;
 NewScreen.Gadgets=NULL;
 NewScreen.CustomBitMap=NULL;

 return(OpenScreen(&NewScreen));
}

make_window(x,y,w,h,name,flags,color0,color1,screen,gadg)
SHORT x,y,w,h;
UBYTE *name,color0,color1;
ULONG flags;
struct Screen *screen;
struct Gadget *gadg;
/* This function will initialize the NewWindow structure
   and open the window */
{
  struct NewWindow NewWindow;

  NewWindow.LeftEdge=x;
  NewWindow.TopEdge=y;
  NewWindow.Width=w;
  NewWindow.Height=h;
  NewWindow.DetailPen=color0;
  NewWindow.BlockPen=color1;
  NewWindow.Title=name;
  NewWindow.Flags=flags;
  NewWindow.IDCMPFlags=NULL;
  NewWindow.Type=CUSTOMSCREEN;
```

Listing 6-5 cont.

```
    NewWindow.FirstGadget=gadg;
    NewWindow.CheckMark=NULL;
    NewWindow.Screen=screen;
    NewWindow.BitMap=NULL;
    NewWindow.MinWidth=1;
    NewWindow.MinHeight=1;
    NewWindow.MaxWidth=640;
    NewWindow.MaxHeight=200;

    return(OpenWindow(&NewWindow));
}
```

```
init_sprite(imp,s_id,s_num,r,g,b)
struct SimpleSprite *imp;
SHORT *s_id,s_num;
USHORT r,b,g;
{
  SHORT k;

  if((*s_id=GetSprite(&imp,s_num))==-1)
    exit();

  imp->x=0;
  imp->y=0;
  imp->height=16;

  switch(*s_id)  {
    case 0:
    case 1: k=16;
            break;
    case 2:
    case 3: k=20;
            break;
    case 4:
    case 5: k=24;
            break;
    case 6:
    case 7: k=28;
            break;
  }


  SetRGB4(&Scrn->ViewPort,k+1,r,g,b);
  SetRGB4(&Scrn->ViewPort,k+2,r,g,b);
  SetRGB4(&Scrn->ViewPort,k+3,r,g,b);

}
```

```
VOID delay_func(factor)
int factor;
```

Listing 6-5 cont.

```
/* This function will cause a specified delay */
{
 int loop;

 for(loop=0;loop<factor*1000;loop++)
   ;

 return;
}
```

Summary

In this short chapter, we have explored programming with the sprites, hardware controlled objects that can coexist in the display area with windows, screens, and other graphic objects. The sprites are independent of any enclosing structure and can move freely. The mouse cursor is a sprite—sprite 0, to be specific.

Controlling these useful objects is easy through a software support system offered by the Amiga. You can access the hardware parameters through the SimpleSprite structure and define its shape with an array of 16-bit words. Manipulation of sprites is facilitated by a series of system functions that allow you to initialize, change, and move them.

Programming Sound   Chapter 7

T he Amiga has the capability to produce high quality, stereophonic sound. Four independent audio channels in the hardware support a flexible and easily programmed subsystem. The audio channels are general-purpose, digital-to-analog converters rather than specialized music producing chips. This allows a wide variety of sounds, from special effects to rich and complex musical notes.

In this chapter, we will explore the important features of this subsystem. Multiple channels will be used to produce both monaural and stereophonic sound. Each example will treat, as much as possible, a single aspect of this important resource.

Creating Sounds

Sound is composed of compression waves in a physical medium, usually air. The source—a musical instrument, stereo speaker, etc.—produces compresssions and rarefactions of the air. These are received by our ears and translated into sounds (Figure 7-1). Two important points should be noted:

1. Sound is defined by a series of parameters.
2. The perception of sound is largely determined by a psychological component.

The scope of this chapter does not allow us to do much more than mention these important aspects of sound, but we must always keep them in mind as we start to experiment with sound generation. The psychological component of sound is especially difficult to pinpoint, even in a single occurrence. Consider the distinction between pleasant and unpleasant sounds. One person's music is another's noise. Even a particular sound takes its coloration from the circumstances: the raucous clang of the city may be pleasant after a long sojourn in the country, or unpleasant and distracting under different circumstances. More practically, certain sounds can affect their mutual perception, producing something more than the mere sum of their parts. The Amiga's extensive sound subsystem makes this kind of experimentation easy and fun.

Figure 7-1. Sound is transmitted via a compression wave in air and then interpreted by the human ear

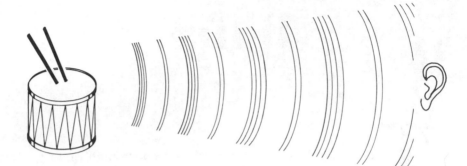

The physical components of sound are of more immediate interest to us. We need to understand which aspects of a sound wave vary to produce perceptible differences to our ears. Unfortunately, there are a great many parameters that affect sound, such as the temperature of the air and the acoustic properties of the space in which we are hearing the sound. However, there are three main properties which represent the key to producing any sound:

1. The frequency of the wave
2. The amplitude of the wave
3. The tone quality or timbre

We need to establish a working definition of these qualities before proceeding much further.

The *frequency* of a sound wave is the basic parameter; waves of different frequency are perceived as different tones. Middle C on the piano, for example, is about 523 cycles per second. By varying this parameter, we can produce notes of different tone. Complex sounds—such as noise—are made up of a combination of many of such pure tones. Figure 7-2 lists frequencies for some of the most common musical tones.

The *amplitude* of a sound is another attribute whose effect is obvious; this represents the loudness of a sound. Varying this attribute makes a sound more or less faint, going to quiet on one end of the spectrum and painfully loud on the other. Less obvious is the fact that this, too, is a component in the creation of complex sounds. A mixture of different frequencies, where each has a different amplitude, sounds different than a mixture where each of the tones is at the same level of loudness.

The most difficult parameter to explain is *timbre*. This can be loosely described as the "quality of sound." The frequency dictates what tone is

Figure 7-2. Approximate frequencies of selected common musical notes

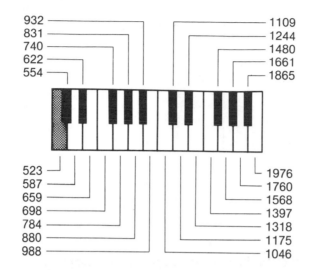

being created, but the same tone can be perceived in a variety of different ways. An example can be taken from the musical scale. An "A" note sounded on a violin and the very same note on a piano are recognizably the same note, but each also has a perceptibly different quality. You are not likely to mistake one for the other. There are a number of factors involved in defining this quality; a complete discussion is beyond the scope of this chapter. The timbre is a kind of general purpose parameter which allows us to get a handle on the complexity of a sound.

Computerized Sounds

With this general picture of the factors that go to make up a sound, we must turn our attention to the techniques for creating sounds on the Amiga. You have seen that sound is a recurring object, which may be described mathematically; this is also the way to approach sound creation from the computer side. You simulate the sound mathematically and then depend on the Amiga's circuitry to reproduce this simulation through the speakers.

The big problem in creating sound on the Amiga or any other computer is one of translation between the analog physical world and the internal digital representations used by the computer. This basic dichotomy—digital vs. analog—is illustrated in Figure 7-3. Analog quantities, such as sound, are continuous, one value merging into the next with nothing in between. Digital values, in contrast, are discrete: there is a definite transition between two adjacent values.

How can you represent a continuous value in terms of a discrete representation? The solution to this problem is a technique known as *sampling* (Figure 7-4). A continuous quantity, such as a sound, exists over a certain

Figure 7-3. A continuous function compared to an incremental one

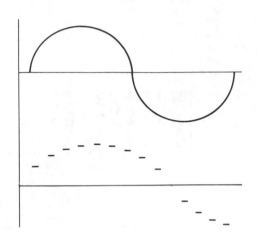

time period. In the case of a sound, this time period represents one portion, or cycle, of a recurring quantity. During one of these intervals, you can note, or sample, the value present at various points in the interval. Each time you take a sample, you convert it to a number. This collection of numbers represents a discrete description of the quantity at a particular moment. A collection of numbers is easy for a computer to store and manipulate.

Figure 7-4. Sampling an analog waveform

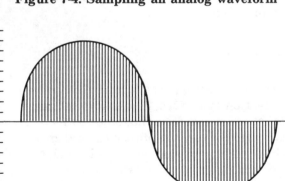

Once this conversion from continuous values to a collection of numbers is complete, you are free to manipulate the numbers just as you would any numeric quantity in the computer. This kind of representation gives a great deal of flexibility, for not only dealing with well-behaved sounds—such as musical notes—but also for creating interesting combinations of sounds, even some that never existed in nature. This is where the power of the Amiga's sound subsystem becomes obvious.

Creating Sound on the Amiga

The specific capabilities of the Amiga to produce sound set it apart from most computers with a sound component. First of all, the Amiga produces stereo sound. Notice that on the back of the system box are both a left and a right speaker output plug; this is an unusual capability for a computer in the Amiga's price range. Each stereo channel consists of two virtual channels; these are independent sound producing circuits. It is also possible to combine these four virtual channels into a single speaker to produce a monaural sound with four components.

The fact that you are dealing with straight digital-to-analog converters and not a specialized sound chip also increases flexibility. Not only can you produce virtually any known sound within the machine's freqency range, but you can also create brand new sounds. This straight conversion also allows more accurate reproduction of musical tones. The Amiga can produce rich and pleasing notes that have none of the "computer sound" found in so many other microcomputers.

Access to the sound circuitry is through the *audio device*. This is primarily a software object that interfaces with the hardware components of the sound subsystem. Like the other driver software found on the Amiga, it runs in the multitasking environment, concurrently with any calling software. The audio device simplifies access to the hardware parameters.

Communication between a user application and the audio device is through the message system. This device has its own specialized message node that is transmitted through one of the I/O system calls; the primary ones involved here are *BeginIO()*, *WaitIO()*, and *CheckIO()*. *SendIO()* and *DoIO()* are rarely used because they interfere with some of the initialized fields in the audio device message node—they "de-initialize" the *io_Flags* field of the node.

Messages are sent:

- To initialize the sound device
- To start up a sound
- To alter the parameters of a sound
- To terminate a sound

In addition to I/O messages, the *OpenDevice()* and *CloseDevice()* system functions are used to attach or remove the audio device to a program.

The message structure type for the audio device has the following form:

```
struct IOAudio {
    struct IORequest ioa_Request;
    WORD   ioa_AllocKey;
    UBYTE *ioa_Data;
    ULONG ioa_Length;
    UWORD ioa_Period,
          ioa_Volume,
          ioa_Cycles;
    struct Message ioa_WriteMsg;
};
```

You can see the usual message structure bracketing the device-specific information fields, and you can also see that the important sound parameters each have a dedicated field in the structure. This structure definition is found in *devices/audio.h*.

Many of these fields require lengthy discussion in order to understand them fully. For now, we will briefly describe each one, so that we can begin a more complete discussion with the entire picture in mind. In the IORequest structure, the following fields will be important to our use of the audio device:

ioa__Request.io__Unit indicates which of the four possible channels is being addressed.

ioa__Request.io__Command indicates which operation the audio device is to perform.

ioa__Request.io__Flags indicates specific modifications to the commands issued to the device.

There are a number of options available for each one of these fields.

The next field, *ioa__AllocKey*, is a unique identifier returned by the device after successful allocation of one or more audio channels. This value helps tie together channels that have been allocated together. Prior allocation of the sound channels makes audio access consistent with a multitasking environment, since there is no chance that two tasks will try to simultaneously access the device. You can, however, directly call the device and have it sound immediately, without worrying about conflicts with other programs or tasks. In this latter case the *ioa__AllocKey* field is ignored.

The *ioa__Data* field serves two functions. When the audio device is initially being opened, this field holds a map of the proposed channel allocations—which are to be opened and which are not. In subsequent messages, it is a pointer to the representation of the waveform that is to be sounded. The *ioa__Length* field contains the size of the *ioa__Data* field.

The frequency of a sound is specified, not in the familiar units of cycles per second, but as its inverse, the period. There is an easy mathematical relationship between the two: the period is the reciprocal of the frequency. This value is set in *ioa__Period*. The loudness is set in *ioa__Volume*; and *ioa__Cycles* tells the device how many times to repeat the sound—how many cycles to actually play.

Sound Data Representation

The first area to explore is the actual representation of the sound values in the machine. We noted earlier that sampling is the technique for generating a numeric representation of a continuous sound wave. A sample of a particular waveform is a series of values taken across time; that is to say, you measure the waveform at regular intervals and note its actual value. In the case of the Amiga, you measure the amplitude (loudness). This set of values can be sent to the sound subsystem, which reproduces the original sound by converting these numbers back into a series of varying voltages. These voltages, in turn, drive the speakers. The frequency of the sound is set by specifying the sampling interval.

It is possible to actually sample sounds with the Amiga and some specialized out-board circuitry; however, because the intermediate step in the "equation" is an array of numbers, you can create your own sounds mathematically, simply by specifying these numbers. A very convenient way to do this is to fill the array using the *sin()* function. The resulting sine curve produces a pleasingly pure tone. You can just as easily initialize the values arbitrarily. There is a restriction on the range of values for this data: −127 to 127.

More realistic sounds can be generated using more complex waveforms. Figure 7-5 illustrates some other commonly used shapes, such as the sawtooth waveform. To create arbitrarily complex sounds, combinations of waveforms are used. The sample size need not be very large. Even as few as two values will yield some kind of sound. There is also no set sample size; the *ioa_Length* field tells the audio device how many values to expect.

Figure 7-5. Waveforms used to represent sound data

Sawtooth Waveform

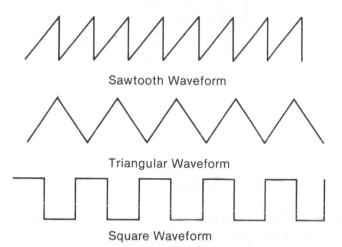

Triangular Waveform

Square Waveform

The frequency of a tone is set by placing a value into the period field of the IOAudio structure—*ioa_Period*. The period is the inverse of the frequency and actually specifies the time interval needed for a sample. The time unit is clock ticks, the lowest measurable interval on the computer. The mathematical relationship between the desired frequency and the period specified is calculated by the formula:

$$\text{period} = (\text{microseconds per sample}) \div 0.279.$$

The number of microseconds per sample is a function of the number of items in the data, and the desired frequency. For example, if you have a data set with thirty-two items and you want a frequency of 5000 Hz., then each cycle is 1/5000 second. With thirty-two samples per cycle, each sampling interval is approximately six microseconds. The period for this frequency is approximately 23. Figure 7-6 contains the period values for some musical notes. It should be noted here that the higher the period value, the lower the frequency of the sound.

Figure 7-6. Period values for some common musical notes

C	428	214
C#	404	202
D	381	190
E	339	170
F	320	160
F#	302	151
G	285	143
G#	269	135
A	254	
A#	240	
B	226	

Accessing the Audio Device

The audio device is one of many such devices on the Amiga. As such, it is a shared resource and its usage must be allocated among the tasks and processes that need to use it. A user application must indicate to the operating system that it needs to use this device. This is accomplished by the *OpenDevice()* function. You have seen this function before in dealing with other system devices and device drivers; therefore, a lengthy discussion is not necessary. Here we will concentrate on those operations and specifications that are unique to the audio device.

The general form of a call to open the audio device takes the form:

```
OpenDevice(AUDIONAME,OL,audio_struct,OL)
```

where

AUDIONAME is a global constant designating the official name of the device.

audio_struct is an object of type struct IOAudio, set up to initialize the device.

The global value AUDIONAME is used to protect the programmer against future changes in the operating system environment. Right now, if you were to look in *audio.h,* you would find that this has the assigned value "audio.device"; but there is no guarantee against future operating system revisions. Most of our attention then will focus on the structure and how it must be set up to open the device properly.

The first thing to do with the audio structure is to attach a reply port so that you can receive return messages from the operating device. This is done by a simple call to the system function *CreatePort().* Once you have set up the reply mechanism, only three fields need to be initialized to open the device:

ioa_Request.io_Message.mn_Node.ln_Pri to set the priority of your proposed access

ioa_Data to indicate which of the four audio channels is to be opened

ioa_Length to show the size of the data field

The first of these fields sets the priority of the request within the multitasking environment; it should be set to a value consistent with the importance of the application. What this value should be is specific to the type of program and the circumstances of the operating environment. We use the value 10 for most of the examples in this chapter.

The *ioa_Data* field must contain a bit map indicating the channels which are to be opened by the succeeding function call. Each unit of the audio device is assigned one of the bits in this map. To indicate an open channel, its corresponding bit is set to 1. A 0 bit indicates an unused channel. Figure 7-7 indicates the relationship of bits to units.

Figure 7-7. The relationship of bits and channels in ioa_Data

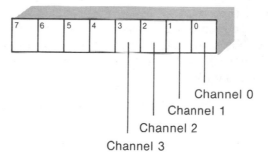

The code fragment:

```
sound.ioa_Request.io_Message.mn_Node.ln_Pri=10;
sound.ioa_Data=&sunit;
sound.ioa_Length=(ULONG)sizeof(sunit);
if((OpenDevice(AUDIONAME,)oL,&sound,OL))!=NULL exit(FALSE)
```

contains the statements necessary for opening the audio device. *Sound* is a previously declared IOAudio structure and *sunit* is a UBYTE variable initialized to *0x0f*. Notice that we use the *address-of* operator with sunit to assign it to *ioa__Data*. Remember, this field is doing double duty; usually it contains a pointer to the sound data. It is necessary to respect its pointer data type by sending it the address of the bit map and not merely the value. Notice, too, that *ioa__Length* is set by using the *sizeof* operator rather than by trying to figure out the correct size of the data and then initializing this field with a number. The *OpenDevice()* command expects the name of the audio device and a pointer to this newly intialized structure. The function's *flag* and *unitNumber* parameters are not used and are set to 0; these values set by corresponding fields in the IOAudio structure. *OpenDevice* returns a NULL if the device cannot be opened.

Audio Device Commands

Like the other devices on the Amiga, the audio device supports a full range of commands. Among the most important of these are:

> CMD__WRITE. This sends a message to the device to start a sound on a channel or unit.
>
> ADCMD__FINISH. This message stops a sound.
>
> ADCMD__PERVOL. This command alters the volume or period of an executing sound.

These commands are set in the *io__Command* field of the *ioa__Request* field within the audio structure. These are not the full range of available commands, but they are the ones that are used most frequently in sound programming.

In addition to the *ioa__Request.io__Command* field in the IOAudio structure, there is also an *io__Flags* field. Values placed in this latter field allow you to modify the basic command to fit a variety of circumstances. For example, IOF__QUICK instructs the system to give priority to your request and to bypass some of the multitasking overhead. Among the possiblities for this field beside IOF__QUICK are:

> ADIOF__SYNCCYCLE. This delays execution of the command until the end of the current cycle.
>
> ADIOF__PERVOL. This loads the values for the period and the volume set in the IOAudio structure.

One or more of these flags is used with each specific command message.

In the simplest case, a single channel is accessed to play a sound for a set period of time. This situation is illustrated in Listing 7-1. Notice that we have incorporated our earlier fragment of code that opened the audio device, and have added the necessary declarations. A simple "for" loop creates our waveform, a sawtooth (Figure 7-8); this information is stored in the array *sound__data[ ]*.

Listing 7-1. The simplest use of the audio device. The cycle field is set to specify the number of cycles.

```c
*/

#include "exec/types.h"
#include "exec/memory.h"
#include "hardware/custom.h"
#include "hardware/dmabits.h"
#include "libraries/dos.h"
#include "devices/audio.h"



extern struct MsgPort *CreatePort();
struct IOAudio sound;

UBYTE sunit=0x0f,sound_data[128];

main()
{
 UBYTE i;

 if((sound.ioa_Request.io_Message.mn_ReplyPort=CreatePort("p3",0))==NULL)
   exit(FALSE);


 sound.ioa_Request.io_Message.mn_Node.ln_Pri=10;
 sound.ioa_Data=&sunit;
 sound.ioa_Length=(ULONG)sizeof(sunit);

 if((OpenDevice(AUDIONAME,0L,&sound,0L))!=NULL)  {
  printf("Can't open Audio Device\n");
  exit(FALSE);
 }

 for(i=0;i<127;i++)
   sound_data[i]=i;
 sound_data[127]=0;


 sound.ioa_Request.io_Command=CMD_WRITE;
 sound.ioa_Request.io_Flags=ADIOF_PERVOL|IOF_QUICK;
 sound.ioa_Data=sound_data;
 sound.ioa_Cycles=100;
 sound.ioa_Length=sizeof(sound_data);
 sound.ioa_Period=508;
 sound.ioa_Volume=64;

 BeginIO(&sound);
 WaitIO(&sound);

 CloseDevice(&sound);
}
```

Figure 7-8. Sawtooth waveform used to represent sound data in Listing 7-1

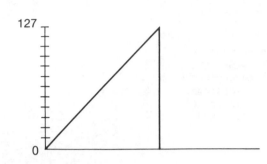

The final step requires an initialization of the IOAudio structure sound and the call to the I/O subsystem. Besides setting the CMD_WRITE command, we have to set the ADIOF_PERVOL flag to ensure that our sound data gets transmitted and used by the audio device. IOF_QUICK insures that our request will be transmitted and acted on immediately. The *ioa_Data* field is given the address of the *sound_data* array, and its length is assigned to *ioa_Length*. We have set the *ioa_Period* field to 508, middle C on the piano, and *ioa_Volume* to 64, the highest setting. We have a new field displayed here, *ioa_Cycles*; this sets the number of times the sampling operation will be repeated and the sound produced. We set this value to 100, a very short time. If we set this field to 0, the sound will continue until an explicit stop command is issued.

Once we have the desired values in an IOAudio structure, we send it to the device with a call to *BeginIO()*. *WaitIO()* puts our program to sleep until the device is finished and returns our io message structure. A call to *CloseDevice* is prudent, since in a multitasking environment, a device driver may not be unloaded at the time a program is finished. In fact, it cannnot be unloaded, unless all open requests have been balanced by a corresponding *CloseDevice()* call.

Controlling the Audio Device

In our first example, we set up the audio device, specified a tone and a duration, and started the sound. A more realistic sound generating program needs to exercise more control over this device. The first measure of control is the ability to start a sound and stop it explicitly, rather than specifying a duration through the *ioa_Cycles* field. The ACDMP_FINISH command replaces the CMD_Write in the *io_Command* field to stop an executing sound. Listing 7-2 shows a simple program that implements this finish command.

The interesting design feature of this program is the creation of two IOAudio structures, *sound* and *finish*, attached to the audio device. The

Listing 7-2. Simple use of the audio device, sending an explicit finish command to stop the tone.

```
*/

#include "exec/types.h"
#include "exec/memory.h"
#include "hardware/custom.h"
#include "hardware/dmabits.h"
#include "libraries/dos.h"
#include "devices/audio.h"
#include "lattice/stdio.h"
#include "lattice/math.h"

extern struct MsgPort *CreatePort();
struct IOAudio finish,sound;

UBYTE sound_data[32],sunit=0x0f;
main()
{

  if((sound.ioa_Request.io_Message.mn_ReplyPort=CreatePort("p3",0))==NULL)
    exit(FALSE);

  if((finish.ioa_Request.io_Message.mn_ReplyPort=CreatePort("p2",0))==NULL)
    exit(FALSE);

  sound.ioa_Request.io_Message.mn_Node.ln_Pri=10;
  sound.ioa_Data=&sunit;
  sound.ioa_Length=(ULONG)sizeof(sunit);

  if((OpenDevice(AUDIONAME,0L,&sound,0L))!=NULL)  {
   printf("Can't open Audio Device\n");
   exit(FALSE);
  }

/* ===Set up the command structures=== */

  finish=sound;

  finish.ioa_Request.io_Flags=IOF_QUICK;
  finish.ioa_Request.io_Command=ADCMD_FINISH;

/*================Finished with the initialization======*/

  fill_data(sound_data);

  sound.ioa_Request.io_Command=CMD_WRITE;
  sound.ioa_Request.io_Flags=ADIOF_PERVOL|IOF_QUICK;
  sound.ioa_Data=sound_data;
  sound.ioa_Cycles=0;
  sound.ioa_Length=sizeof(sound_data);
  sound.ioa_Period=508;
  sound.ioa_Volume=10;

  BeginIO(&sound);
```

Listing 7-2 cont.

```
delay(100000);

BeginIO(&finish);
WaitIO(&sound);

CloseDevice(&sound);
}

fill_data(sound)
UBYTE *sound;
{
 double x;

 for(x=-(PI/2);x<=PI/2;x+=.1)
   *sound=(UBYTE)floor(100*sin(x));
}

delay(x)
long x;
{
 long i;
 for(i=0;i<x;i++)
   ;
}
```

sound structure is used to initialize and start up the note. The finish structure, in contrast, is reserved for device control. We set up an audio structure and open the device. Once this has been successfully completed we copy the now initialized fields over to the remaining structure. At this point, we have two structures that are keyed to both the audio device and the same specific channel. Once this is done, we initialize first the sound structure to produce the tone and the finish structure to end it. This latter is accomplished by setting the *io__Command* field. We then call *BeginIO()*, passing it the sound structure; but instead of pausing our program and waiting for this command to run its course, after a suitable delay, we again call *BeginIO()*. This time we pass it the finish structure and then do a *WaitIO()*.

For the sake of simplicity, our delay function is primitive —just a large loop. However, this program illustrates a general form that can be used in larger and more complex applications. A sound generating program does not have to go to sleep after creating a note, but can do other things—perhaps set up the next note—while the audio device is processing its request.

This example program uses a generated sine curve to produce a more pleasing tone. The sine is easily computed and is a well-behaved mathematical object. Listing 7-3 and 7-4 are identical to our current example except in the waveform data; the first uses a square wave and the latter, a triangular one (Figure 7-9). These three programs serve to illustrate the differences introduced by using different waveform data.

Listing 7-3. Simple use of the audio device with a square wave.

```
*/

#include "exec/types.h"
#include "exec/memory.h"
#include "hardware/custom.h"
#include "hardware/dmabits.h"
#include "libraries/dos.h"
#include "devices/audio.h"
#include "lattice/stdio.h"
#include "lattice/math.h"

extern struct MsgPort *CreatePort();
struct IOAudio finish,sound;

UBYTE sound_data[32],sunit=0x0f;
main()
{

  if((sound.ioa_Request.io_Message.mn_ReplyPort=CreatePort("p3",0))==NULL)
    exit(FALSE);

  if((finish.ioa_Request.io_Message.mn_ReplyPort=CreatePort("p2",0))==NULL)
    exit(FALSE);

  sound.ioa_Request.io_Message.mn_Node.ln_Pri=10;
  sound.ioa_Data=&sunit;
  sound.ioa_Length=(ULONG)sizeof(sunit);

  if((OpenDevice(AUDIONAME,0L,&sound,0L))!=NULL)  {
   printf("Can't open Audio Device\n");
   exit(FALSE);
  }

/* ===Set up the command structures=== */

  finish=sound;

  finish.ioa_Request.io_Flags=IOF_QUICK;
  finish.ioa_Request.io_Command=ADCMD_FINISH;

/*================Finished with the initialization======*/

  fill_data(sound_data);

  sound.ioa_Request.io_Command=CMD_WRITE;
  sound.ioa_Request.io_Flags=ADIOF_PERVOL|IOF_QUICK;
  sound.ioa_Data=sound_data;
  sound.ioa_Cycles=0;
  sound.ioa_Length=sizeof(sound_data);
  sound.ioa_Period=508;
  sound.ioa_Volume=10;

  BeginIO(&sound);
```

Listing 7-3 cont.

```
delay(100000);

BeginIO(&finish);
WaitIO(&sound);

CloseDevice(&sound);
}

fill_data(sound)
UBYTE *sound;
{
 int x;

*sound=0;
  sound++;
 for(x=1;x<31;x++)   {
   *sound=(x<16)?100:-100;
   sound++;
  }
 *sound=0;
}

delay(x)
long x;
{
 long i;
 for(i=0;i<x;i++)
    ;
}
```

**Listing 7-4. Simple use of the audio device
with a triangular wave.**

```
*/

#include "exec/types.h"
#include "exec/memory.h"
#include "hardware/custom.h"
#include "hardware/dmabits.h"
#include "libraries/dos.h"
#include "devices/audio.h"
#include "lattice/stdio.h"
#include "lattice/math.h"

extern struct MsgPort *CreatePort();
struct IOAudio finish,sound;

UBYTE sound_data[32],sunit=0x0f;
main()
{
```

Listing 7-4 cont.

```
   if((sound.ioa_Request.io_Message.mn_ReplyPort=CreatePort("p3",0))==NULL)
     exit(FALSE);

   if((finish.ioa_Request.io_Message.mn_ReplyPort=CreatePort("p2",0))==NULL)
     exit(FALSE);

   sound.ioa_Request.io_Message.mn_Node.ln_Pri=10;
   sound.ioa_Data=&sunit;
   sound.ioa_Length=(ULONG)sizeof(sunit);

   if((OpenDevice(AUDIONAME,0L,&sound,0L))!=NULL)  {
    printf("Can't open Audio Device\n");
    exit(FALSE);
   }

/* ===Set up the command structures=== */

   finish=sound;

   finish.ioa_Request.io_Flags=IOF_QUICK;
   finish.ioa_Request.io_Command=ADCMD_FINISH;

/*===============Finished with the initialization=====*/

   fill_data(sound_data);

   sound.ioa_Request.io_Command=CMD_WRITE;
   sound.ioa_Request.io_Flags=ADIOF_PERVOL|IOF_QUICK;
   sound.ioa_Data=sound_data;
   sound.ioa_Cycles=0;
   sound.ioa_Length=sizeof(sound_data);
   sound.ioa_Period=508;
   sound.ioa_Volume=10;

   BeginIO(&sound);

   delay(100000);

   BeginIO(&finish);
   WaitIO(&sound);

   CloseDevice(&sound);
}

fill_data(sound)
UBYTE *sound;
{
 int x;

 for(x=0;x<=100;x+=20)  {
   *sound=x;
   sound++;
  }
```

Listing 7-4 cont.

```
for(x=80;x>=0;x-=20)   {
   *sound=x;
   sound++;
 }
for(x=1;x<=100;x+=20)   {
   *sound=-x;
   sound++;
   }
for(x=80;x>=0;x-=20)   {
   *sound=(x!=0)?-x:0;
   sound++;
   }
}

delay(x)
long x;
{
  long i;
  for(i=0;i<x;i++)
     ;
}
```

Figure 7-9. Waveforms for Listings 7-3 and 7-4

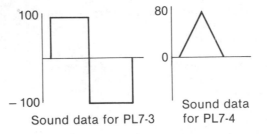

Sound data for PL7-3

Sound data for PL7-4

In the previous examples, we specify all of the audio channels in the IOAudio structure that was used to open the audio device. Whenever we specify a command, it is executed on the first available of the four channels. It is also desirable, however, to be able to use a single specific channel. Listing 7-5 illustrates one technique for accomplishing this goal. The bit map, *sunit*, is initialized to *0x01*; this sets the bit assigned to channel 0 in the audio device. The device is opened with only this channel active. The risk is that if that channel is in use and a process with a higher priority wants that particular channel, the call to *OpenDevice( )* will fail. We will have more to say about this topic when we turn our attention to multichannel usage.

Listing 7-5. Use of a single channel of the audio device.

```
*/

#include "exec/types.h"
#include "exec/memory.h"
#include "hardware/custom.h"
#include "hardware/dmabits.h"
#include "libraries/dos.h"
#include "devices/audio.h"
#include "lattice/stdio.h"
#include "lattice/math.h"

extern struct MsgPort *CreatePort();
struct IOAudio control,finish,sound;

UBYTE sound_data[32],sunit=0x01;
main()
{
 int i;
 long d;
 UWORD period=1000,loudness=64;

  if((control.ioa_Request.io_Message.mn_ReplyPort=CreatePort("p1",0))==NULL)
    exit(FALSE);

  if((finish.ioa_Request.io_Message mn_ReplyPort=CreatePort("p2",0))==NULL)
    exit(FALSE);

  if((sound.ioa_Request.io_Message.mn_ReplyPort=CreatePort("p3",0))==NULL)
    exit(FALSE);


  control.ioa_Request.io_Message.mn_Node.ln_Pri=10;
  control.ioa_Data=&sunit;
  control.ioa_Length=(ULONG)sizeof(sunit);

  if((OpenDevice(AUDIONAME,0L,&control,0L))!=NULL)  {
   printf("Can't open Audio Device\n");
   exit(FALSE);
  }

/* ===Set up the command structures=== */

  finish=control;
  sound=control;


  finish.ioa_Request.io_Flags=IOF_QUICK;
  finish.ioa_Request.io_Command=ADCMD_FINISH;

  control.ioa_Request.io_Flags=IOF_QUICK;
  control.ioa_Request.io_Command=ADCMD_PERVOL;

/*===============Finished with the initialization======*/
```

Listing 7-5 cont.

```
fill_data(sound_data);

sound.ioa_Request.io_Command=CMD_WRITE;
sound.ioa_Request.io_Flags=ADIOF_PERVOL|IOF_QUICK;
sound.ioa_Data=sound_data;
sound.ioa_Cycles=0;
sound.ioa_Length=sizeof(sound_data);
sound.ioa_Period= period;
sound.ioa_Volume=loudness;
```

```
BeginIO(&sound);

for(i=0;i<30;i++)  {
  for(d=0;d<250;d++)
    if(d<60)
        printf("*");
  printf("\n");
  period-=5;
  loudness--;
  change_sound(&control,loudness,period);
 }

BeginIO(&finish);
WaitIO(&sound);

CloseDevice(&control);
}

fill_data(sound)
UBYTE *sound;
{
 double x;

 for(x=-(PI/2);x<=PI/2;x+=.1)
   *sound=(UBYTE)floor(100*sin(x));
}

change_sound(loudness,period)
UWORD loudness,period;
{
 control.ioa_Period=period;
 control.ioa_Volume=loudness;
 BeginIO(&control);
}
```

Once a sound is executed, it is possible to change its operating parameters. Both the volume and the period can be altered. This change is accomplished through a control message to the active audio device. This message is an IOAudio structure, initialized with both the new values and the control information, and attached to the executing channel. The *io_Command* field is set to ADCMP_PERVOL to indicate the nature of the command. The *io_Flags* field should be set to IOF_QUICK, but it also may include the ADIOF_SYNCCYCLE. The use of this latter flag ensures that the changes requested will not occur until the end of a sampling cycle. Without this parameter, the changes become effective immediately.

Listing 7-6. Starting a note, then varying its period via messages sent to the audio device.

```
*/

#include "exec/types.h"
#include "exec/memory.h"
#include "hardware/custom.h"
#include "hardware/dmabits.h"
#include "libraries/dos.h"
#include "devices/audio.h"
#include "lattice/stdio.h"
#include "lattice/math.h"

extern struct MsgPort *CreatePort();
UBYTE s_data0[32],sunit=0x0f;
```

```
main()
{
 int x,y;
 struct IOAudio control,finish,sound0;

 setup(&control,&finish);

 sound0=control;

 grab_channel(&sound0,&control,"c1");

 fill_data(s_data0);

 for(;;)  {

   printf("enter period->");
   scanf("%d",&x);
   if(x==-1)
      break;
   printf("enter volume->");
   scanf("%d",&y);

   sound_note(&sound0,(UWORD)x,(UWORD)y);

   BeginIO(&sound0);
   for(;x>=135;x-=28)  {
      delay();
      printf("new note\n");
      change_sound((UWORD)y,(UWORD)x,&control);
    }
   BeginIO(&finish);
   WaitIO(&sound0);
}
```

Listing 7-6 cont.

```
 CloseDevice(&control);
}
setup(control,finish)
struct IOAudio *control,*finish;
{

if((control->ioa_Request.io_Message.mn_ReplyPort=CreatePort("p1",0))==NULL)
   exit(FALSE);

 if((finish->ioa_Request.io_Message.mn_ReplyPort=CreatePort("p2",0))==NULL)
   exit(FALSE);

 control->ioa_Request.io_Message.mn_Node.ln_Pri=10;
 control->ioa_Data=&sunit;
 control->ioa_Length=(ULONG)sizeof(sunit);

 if((OpenDevice(AUDIONAME,0L,control,0L))!=NULL)  {
  printf("Can't open Audio Device\n");
  exit(FALSE);
 }

/* ===Set up the command structures=== */

 *finish=*control;

 finish->ioa_Request.io_Flags=IOF_QUICK;
 finish->ioa_Request.io_Command=ADCMD_FINISH;

 control->ioa_Request.io_Flags=IOF_QUICK;
 control->ioa_Request.io_Command=ADCMD_PERVOL;
}

fill_data(s0)
UBYTE *s0;
{
 double x;

 for(x=-(PI/2);x<=PI/2;x+=.1)  {
   *s0=(UBYTE)floor(100*sin(x));
   s0++;
  }
}

change_sound(loudness,period,control)
UWORD loudness,period;
struct IOAudio *control;
{
 control->ioa_Period=period;
 control->ioa_Volume=loudness;
 BeginIO(control);
 WaitIO(control);
}
```

Listing 7-6 cont.

```
sound_note(chnl,period,loudness)
struct IOAudio *chnl;
UWORD period,loudness;
{
  chnl->ioa_Request.io_Command=CMD_WRITE;
  chnl->ioa_Request.io_Flags=ADIOF_PERVOL|IOF_QUICK;
  chnl->ioa_Data=s_data0;
  chnl->ioa_Cycles=0;
  chnl->ioa_Length=sizeof(s_data0);
  chnl->ioa_Period= period;
  chnl->ioa_Volume=loudness;
}

grab_channel(sound,control,name)
struct IOAudio *sound,*control;
char *name;
{
 if((sound->ioa_Request.io_Message.mn_ReplyPort=CreatePort(name,0))==NULL)
 *sound=*control;
}
delay()
{
 int i;
 for(i=0;i<1000;i++);
}
```

Listing 7-6 illustrates a program that will start up a sound and then vary its period in steps. Since this is a demonstration program, a message is displayed on the screen each time the period is changed. In this program, we have created three audio structures:

sound—to start up the initial note on the device

finish—to stop the note

control—to carry intermediate messages to the audio device

The latter two structures are not strictly necessary. One general control structure could serve both functions; however, having both increases the flexibility of control. At least one structure besides sound is needed; otherwise the note cannot be stopped once it is started. A *WaitIO()* on an IOAudio structure, where the *ioa_Cycle* field has been set to 0, is infinite, at least until you lose patience and reboot. When juggling multiple channels, the separate structures for control and finish become even more attractive.

The process of changing a sound's period is simple. Notice the function *change_sound()*. We simply set the new period value and call a *BeginIO()* followed by a *WaitIO()*. This function is a general purpose function; it is also used to change the volume of the sounded note. A program to change the volume over a range going down to a value of 0 is shown in Listing 7-7.

Listing 7-7. Starting a note and varying loudness via messages sent to the audio device.

```
*/

#include "exec/types.h"
#include "exec/memory.h"
#include "hardware/custom.h"
#include "hardware/dmabits.h"
#include "libraries/dos.h"
#include "devices/audio.h"
#include "lattice/stdio.h"
#include "lattice/math.h"

extern struct MsgPort *CreatePort();
UBYTE s_data0[32],sunit=0x0f;

main()
{
 int x,y;
 struct IOAudio control,finish,sound0;

 setup(&control,&finish);

 sound0=control;

 grab_channel(&sound0,&control,"c1");

 fill_data(s_data0);

 for(;;)  {

   printf("enter period->");
   scanf("%d",&x);
   if(x==-1)
      break;
   printf("enter volume->");
   scanf("%d",&y);

   sound_note(&sound0,(UWORD)x,(UWORD)y);

   BeginIO(&sound0);
   for(;y>=0;y--)  {
      delay();
      printf("new loudness level\n");
      change_sound((UWORD)y,(UWORD)x,&control);
    }
   BeginIO(&finish);
   WaitIO(&sound0);
 }

 CloseDevice(&control);
}
setup(control,finish)
struct IOAudio *control,*finish;
{
```

Listing 7-7 cont.

```
if((control->ioa_Request.io_Message.mn_ReplyPort=CreatePort("p1",0))==NULL)
   exit(FALSE);

 if((finish->ioa_Request.io_Message.mn_ReplyPort=CreatePort("p2",0))==NULL)
   exit(FALSE);

 control->ioa_Request.io_Message.mn_Node.ln_Pri=10;
 control->ioa_Data=&sunit;
 control->ioa_Length=(ULONG)sizeof(sunit);

 if((OpenDevice(AUDIONAME,0L,control,0L))!=NULL)  {
  printf("Can't open Audio Device\n");
  exit(FALSE);
 }

/* ===Set up the command structures=== */

 *finish=*control;

 finish->ioa_Request.io_Flags=IOF_QUICK;
 finish->ioa_Request.io_Command=ADCMD_FINISH;

 control->ioa_Request.io_Flags=IOF_QUICK;
 control->ioa_Request.io_Command=ADCMD_PERVOL;
}

fill_data(sU)
UBYTE *sU;
{
 double x;

 for(x=-(PI/2);x<=PI/2;x+=.1)  {
   *sU=(UBYTE)floor(100*sin(x));
   sU++;
  }
}

change_sound(loudness,period,control)
UWORD loudness,period;
struct IOAudio *control;
{
 control->ioa_Period=period;
 control->ioa_Volume=loudness;
 BeginIO(control);
 WaitIO(control);
}

sound_note(chnl,period,loudness)
struct IOAudio *chnl;
UWORD period,loudness;
{
  chnl->ioa_Request.io_Command=CMD_WRITE;
  chnl->ioa_Request.io_Flags=ADIOF_PERVOL|IOF_QUICK;
```

Listing 7-7 cont.

```
  chnl->ioa_Data=s_data0;
  chnl->ioa_Cycles=0;
  chnl->ioa_Length=sizeof(s_data0);
  chnl->ioa_Period= period;
  chnl->ioa_Volume=loudness;
}

grab_channel(sound,control,name)
struct IOAudio *sound,*control;
char *name;
{
 if((sound->ioa_Request.io_Message.mn_ReplyPort=CreatePort(name,0))==NULL)
 *sound=*control;
}
delay()
{
 int i;
 for(i=0;i<1000;i++);
}
```

As might be expected, a volume of 0 shuts off the sound. Listings 7-8 and 7-9 illustrate some interesting variations on these earlier examples. In the former, we vary the volume of a sound using values in an array. This array has been filled using a *sine* function. In Listing 7-9, the period is varied in the same way. These examples serve to illustrate the kind of experimentation that is possible with the Amiga's sound subsystem.

**Listing 7-8. Varying the loudness of a note. Loudness values
are taken from an array of values.**

```
*/

#include "exec/types.h"
#include "exec/memory.h"
#include "hardware/custom.h"
#include "hardware/dmabits.h"
#include "libraries/dos.h"
#include "devices/audio.h"
#include "lattice/stdio.h"
#include "lattice/math.h"

extern struct MsgPort *CreatePort();
UBYTE s_data0[32],sunit=0x0f;

main()
{
 int x,j,vol[315];
 struct IOAudio control,finish,sound0;

 setup(&control,&finish);
```

Listing 7-8 cont.

```
   sound0=control;

   grab_channel(&sound0,&control,"c1");

   fill_data(s_data0);
   fill_array(vol);

   for(;;)  {

      printf("enter period->");
      scanf("%d",&x);
      if(x==-1)
         break;

      sound_note(&sound0,(UWORD)x,(UWORD)vol[0]);

      BeginIO(&sound0);
      for(j=1;j<315;j++)  {
         delay();
         printf("vol[%d]=%d\n",j,vol[j]);
         change_sound((UWORD)vol[j],(UWORD)x,&control);
       }
      BeginIO(&finish);
      WaitIO(&sound0);
   }

  CloseDevice(&control);
}
setup(control,finish)
struct IOAudio *control,*finish;
{

if((control->ioa_Request.io_Message.mn_ReplyPort=CreatePort("p1",0))==NULL)
   exit(FALSE);

  if((finish->ioa_Request.io_Message.mn_ReplyPort=CreatePort("p2",0))==NULL)
    exit(FALSE);

  control->ioa_Request.io_Message.mn_Node.ln_Pri=10;
  control->ioa_Data=&sunit;
  control->ioa_Length=(ULONG)sizeof(sunit);

  if((OpenDevice(AUDIONAME,0L,control,0L))!=NULL)  {
   printf("Can't open Audio Device\n");
   exit(FALSE);
  }

/* ====Set up the command structures=== */

  *finish=*control;

  finish->ioa_Request.io_Flags=IOF_QUICK;
  finish->ioa_Request.io_Command=ADCMD_FINISH;
```

Listing 7-8 cont.

```
 control->ioa_Request.io_Flags=IOF_QUICK;
 control->ioa_Request.io_Command=ADCMD_PERVOL;
}

fill_data(s0)
UBYTE *s0;
{
 double x;

 for(x=-(PI/2);x<=PI/2;x+=.1)  {
   *s0=(UBYTE)floor(100*sin(x));
   s0++;
   }
}
```

```
change_sound(loudness,period,control)
UWORD loudness,period;
struct IOAudio *control;
{
 control->ioa_Period=period;
 control->ioa_Volume=loudness;
 BeginIO(control);
 WaitIO(control);
}

sound_note(chnl,period,loudness)
struct IOAudio *chnl;
UWORD period,loudness;
{
  chnl->ioa_Request.io_Command=CMD_WRITE;
  chnl->ioa_Request.io_Flags=ADIOF_PERVOL|IOF_QUICK;
  chnl->ioa_Data=s_data0;
  chnl->ioa_Cycles=0;
  chnl->ioa_Length=sizeof(s_data0);
  chnl->ioa_Period= period;
  chnl->ioa_Volume=loudness;
}

grab_channel(sound,control,name)
struct IOAudio *sound,*control;
char *name;
{
 if((sound->ioa_Request.io_Message.mn_ReplyPort=CreatePort(name,0))==NULL)
 *sound=*control;
}
delay()
{
 int i;
 for(i=0;i<1000;i++);
}

fill_array(s0)
int *s0;
```

Listing 7-8 cont.

```
{
 double x;

 for(x=-PI;x<=PI;x+=.02)  {
   *s0=(int)floor(25*sin(x)+25);
   s0++;
   }
}
```

Listing 7-9. Varying the period of a note. Period values are
taken from an array of values.

```
*/

#include "exec/types.h"
#include "exec/memory.h"
#include "hardware/custom.h"
#include "hardware/dmabits.h"
#include "libraries/dos.h"
#include "devices/audio.h"
#include "lattice/stdio.h"
#include "lattice/math.h"

extern struct MsgPort *CreatePort();
UBYTE s_data0[32],sunit=0x0f;

main()
{
 int x,y,j,vol[63];
 struct IOAudio control,finish,sound0;

 setup(&control,&finish);

 sound0=control;

 grab_channel(&sound0,&control,"c1");

 fill_data(s_data0);
 fill_array(vol);

 for(;;)  {

   printf("enter period->");
   scanf("%d",&x);
   if(x==-1)
      break;
   printf("enter volume->");
   scanf("%d",&y);

   sound_note(&sound0,(UWORD)x,(UWORD)y);
```

Listing 7-9 cont.

```
  BeginIO(&sound0);
  for(j=1;j<63;j++)  {
     delay();
     printf("vol[%d]=%d\n",j,vol[j]);
     change_sound((UWORD)y,(UWORD)vol[j],&control);
   }
  BeginIO(&finish);
  WaitIO(&sound0);
}

CloseDevice(&control);
}
setup(control,finish)
struct IOAudio *control,*finish;
{

if((control->ioa_Request.io_Message.mn_ReplyPort=CreatePort("p1",0))==NULL)
   exit(FALSE);

if((finish->ioa_Request.io_Message.mn_ReplyPort=CreatePort("p2",0))==NULL)
   exit(FALSE);

control->ioa_Request.io_Message.mn_Node.ln_Pri=10;
control->ioa_Data=&sunit;
control->ioa_Length=(ULONG)sizeof(sunit);

if((OpenDevice(AUDIONAME,0L,control,0L))!=NULL)  {
 printf("Can't open Audio Device\n");
 exit(FALSE);
}

/* ===Set up the command Structures=== */

*finish=*control;

finish->ioa_Request.io_Flags=IOF_QUICK;
finish->ioa_Request.io_Command=ADCMD_FINISH;

control->ioa_Request.io_Flags=IOF_QUICK;
control->ioa_Request.io_Command=ADCMD_PERVOL;
}
```

```
fill_data(s0)
UBYTE *s0;
{
 double x;

 for(x=-(PI/2);x<=PI/2;x+=.1)  {
   *s0=(UBYTE)floor(100*sin(x));
   s0++;
  }
}
```

Listing 7-9 cont.

```
change_sound(loudness,period,control)
UWORD loudness,period;
struct IOAudio *control;
{
 control->ioa_Period=period;
 control->ioa_Volume=loudness;
 BeginIO(control);
 WaitIO(control);
}

sound_note(chnl,period,loudness)
struct IOAudio *chnl;
UWORD period,loudness;
{
  chnl->ioa_Request.io_Command=CMD_WRITE;
  chnl->ioa_Request.io_Flags=ADIOF_PERVOL|IOF_QUICK;
  chnl->ioa_Data=s_data0;
  chnl->ioa_Cycles=0;
  chnl->ioa_Length=sizeof(s_data0);
  chnl->ioa_Period= period;
  chnl->ioa_Volume=loudness;
}

grab_channel(sound,control,name)
struct IOAudio *sound,*control;
char *name;
{
 if((sound->ioa_Request.io_Message.mn_ReplyPort=CreatePort(name,0))==NULL)
 *sound=*control;
}
delay()
{
 int i;
 for(i=0;i<1000;i++);
}

fill_array(s0)
int *s0;
{
 double x;

 for(x=-PI;x<=PI;x+=.1)  {
   *s0=(int)floor(50*sin(x)+50);
   s0++;
  }
}
```

Multichannel Sound

The Amiga has four independent sound channels attached to two output jacks. More complex sound-oriented programming involves the manipulation of more than one of these channels at a time. This added level of complexity requires careful consideration of coordination and synchronization.

When you open the audio device, you specify which of the four channels you require. These channels are specified in the bit map that is assigned to the *ioa_Data* field. Once this has been done, however, you can still send command messages to this device, that are specifically aimed at a particular channel. This information is specified in the *ioa_Request.io_Unit* field of the audio structure. By exercising this control, you can produce interesting effects, such as stereo sound.

Listing 7-10 contains a program that illustrates this kind of control. This program requires the attachment of two speakers to the two audio jacks on the Amiga. It sounds a note first on the left speaker and then moves it to the right speaker.

Listing 7-10. Playing a note first on the left channel, then on the right.

```
*/
#include "exec/types.h"
#include "exec/memory.h"
#include "hardware/custom.h"
#include "hardware/dmabits.h"
#include "libraries/dos.h"
#include "devices/audio.h"
#include "lattice/stdio.h"
#include "lattice/math.h"

extern struct MsgPort *CreatePort();
UBYTE s_data0[32],s_data1[32],sunit=0x0f,
      mapleft=0x09,mapright=0x06;

main()
{
 int x,y,j;
 UBYTE unit0,unit1;
 struct IOAudio control,finish,sound0,sound1;

 setup(&control,&finish,&unit0,&unit1);

 sound0=control;
 sound0.ioa_Request.io_Unit=unit0;

 sound1=control;
 sound1.ioa_Request.io_Unit=unit1;


 grab_channel(&sound0,&control,"c1");
 grab_channel(&sound1,&control,"c2");

 fill_data(s_data0);
 fill_data(s_data1);
```

Listing 7-10 cont.

```
  for(;;)  {

    printf("enter period->");
    scanf("%d",&x);
    if(x==-1)
       break;
    printf("enter volume->");
    scanf("%d",&y);

    sound_note(&sound0,(UWORD)x,(UWORD)y);
    sound_note(&sound1,(UWORD)x,(UWORD)y);

    BeginIO(&sound0);
    WaitIO(&sound0);

    BeginIO(&sound1);
    WaitIO(&sound1);
  }

  CloseDevice(&control);
}
setup(control,finish,unit0,unit1)
struct IOAudio *control,*finish;
UBYTE *unit0,*unit1;
{

if((control->ioa_Request.io_Message.mn_ReplyPort
   =CreatePort("p1",0))==NULL)exit(FALSE);

 if((finish->ioa_Request.io_Message.mn_ReplyPort
   =CreatePort("p2",0))==NULL)exit(FALSE);

 control->ioa_Request.io_Message.mn_Node.ln_Pri=10;
 control->ioa_Data=&sunit;
 control->ioa_Length=(ULONG)sizeof(sunit);

 if((OpenDevice(AUDIONAME,0L,control,0L))!=NULL)  {
  printf("Can't open Audio Device\n");
  exit(FALSE);
 }
 *unit0=((UBYTE)control->ioa_Request.io_Unit & mapleft);
 *unit1=((UBYTE)control->ioa_Request.io_Unit & mapright);

/* ===Set up the command structures=== */

 *finish=*control;

 finish->ioa_Request.io_Flags=IOF_QUICK;
 finish->ioa_Request.io_Command=ADCMD_FINISH;

 control->ioa_Request.io_Flags=IOF_QUICK;
 control->ioa_Request.io_Command=ADCMD_PERVOL;
}
```

Listing 7-10 cont.

```
fill_data(s0)
UBYTE *s0;
{
 double x;

 for(x=-(PI/2);x<=PI/2;x+=.1)  {
   *s0=(UBYTE)floor(100*sin(x));
   s0++;
   }
}

change_sound(loudness,period,control)
UWORD loudness,period;
struct IOAudio *control;
{
 control->ioa_Period=period;
 control->ioa_Volume=loudness;
 BeginIO(control);
 WaitIO(control);
}

sound_note(chnl,period,loudness)
struct IOAudio *chnl;
UWORD period,loudness;
{
   chnl->ioa_Request.io_Command=CMD_WRITE;
   chnl->ioa_Request.io_Flags=ADIOF_PERVOL|IOF_QUICK;
   chnl->ioa_Data=s_data0;
   chnl->ioa_Cycles=1000;
   chnl->ioa_Length=sizeof(s_data0);
   chnl->ioa_Period= period;
   chnl->ioa_Volume=loudness;
}

grab_channel(sound,control,name)
struct IOAudio *sound,*control;
char *name;
{
 if((sound-
>ioa_Request.io_Message.mn_ReplyPort=CreatePort(name,0))==NULL)
 *sound=*control;
}
delay()
{
 int i;
 for(i=0;i<1000;i++);
}
```

In this program, we have allocated a separate audio structure for each speaker—*sound0* and *sound1*. As before, we open the device along with all four channels. Once we have done this, we need a way to get a handle on the specific channels. We do this through the bit maps *mapleft* and *mapright*. Each of these serves as a mask to block out all but those bits that refer to the channels on their respective sides of the stereo setup (Figure 7-10). The bitwise "and" operator combines each of these bits maps to the corresponding *io__Unit* field to extract the appropriate unit identification. At the end of this procedure, each audio structure contains a unit number identical to one that would result from opening the device and specifying only those channels.

Figure 7-10. Values for the variables mapleft and mapright

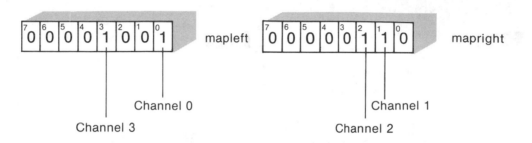

Once we have properly initialized our two structures, we can begin our sound. First we call *BeginIO()* and pass it *sound0*. The program does a *WaitIO()* until this note is finished, then does a *BeginIO()* and a *WaitIO()* on sound1. To simplify this example, we set the *ioa__Cycles* field rather than creating a continuous sound and using a *finish* command.

In Listing 7-11, we have a more complex situation. Here we start a note on the left speaker, as before, then play it on both speakers simultaneously. Finally, we finish it up on the right speaker. We create the standard audio structures: control, finish, sound0, and sound1. We set the period and volume as before. We initiate the sound by doing a *BeginIO()*, using sound0, but, instead of performing a *WaitIO()* on this command, we delay for a set period and do another *BeginIO()* with sound1. After another delay, we send a finish message to stop the sound in the left speaker. Finally, after a third delay, we send a finish command to the remaining channel.

Listing 7-11. Playing a note first on the left channel, then on both, then on the right channel. The finish command is used.

```
*/

#include "exec/types.h"
#include "exec/memory.h"
#include "hardware/custom.h"
#include "hardware/dmabits.h"
#include "libraries/dos.h"
#include "devices/audio.h"
#include "lattice/stdio.h"
#include "lattice/math.h"

extern struct MsgPort *CreatePort();
```

Listing 7-11 cont.

```
UBYTE s_data0[32],s_data1[32],sunit=0x0f,
      mapleft=0x09,mapright=0x06;

main()
{
 int x,y,j;
 UBYTE unit0,unit1;
 struct IOAudio control,finish,sound0,sound1;

 setup(&control,&finish,&unit0,&unit1);

 sound0=control;
 sound0.ioa_Request.io_Unit=unit0;

 sound1=control;
 sound1.ioa_Request.io_Unit=unit1;


 grab_channel(&sound0,&control,"c1");
 grab_channel(&sound1,&control,"c2");

 fill_data(s_data0);
 fill_data(s_data1);

 for(;;)  {

   printf("enter period->");
   scanf("%d",&x);
   if(x==-1)
      break;
   printf("enter volume->");
   scanf("%d",&y);

   sound_note(&sound0,(UWORD)x,(UWORD)y);
   sound_note(&sound1,(UWORD)x,(UWORD)y);

   BeginIO(&sound0);
   delay(100000);
   BeginIO(&sound1);
   delay(100000);
   finish.ioa_Request.io_Unit=unit0;
   BeginIO(&finish);
   WaitIO(&finish);
   delay(100000);
   finish.ioa_Request.io_Unit=unit1;
   BeginIO(&finish);
   WaitIO(&finish);
 }

 CloseDevice(&control);
}
setup(control,finish,unit0,unit1)
struct IOAudio *control,*finish;
UBYTE *unit0,*unit1;
```

Listing 7-11 cont.

```
{
    if((control->ioa_Request.io_Message.mn_ReplyPort
      =CreatePort("p1",0))==NULL)exit(FALSE);

    if((finish->ioa_Request.io_Message.mn_ReplyPort
      =CreatePort("p2",0))==NULL)exit(FALSE);

    control->ioa_Request.io_Message.mn_Node.ln_Pri=10;
    control->ioa_Data=&sunit;
    control->ioa_Length=(ULONG)sizeof(sunit);

    if((OpenDevice(AUDIONAME,0L,control,0L))!=NULL)  {
     printf("Can't open Audio Device\n");
     exit(FALSE);
    }
    *unit0=((UBYTE)control->ioa_Request.io_Unit & mapleft);
    *unit1=((UBYTE)control->ioa_Request.io_Unit & mapright);

/* ===Set up the command structures=== */

    *finish=*control;

    finish->ioa_Request.io_Flags=IOF_QUICK;
    finish->ioa_Request.io_Command=ADCMD_FINISH;

    control->ioa_Request.io_Flags=IOF_QUICK;
    control->ioa_Request.io_Command=ADCMD_PERVOL;
}

fill_data(s0)
UBYTE *s0;
{
 double x;

 for(x=-(PI/2);x<=PI/2;x+=.1)  {
   *s0=(UBYTE)floor(100*sin(x));
   s0++;
  }
}

change_sound(loudness,period,control)
UWORD loudness,period;
struct IOAudio *control;
{
 control->ioa_Period=period;
 control->ioa_Volume=loudness;
 BeginIO(control);
 WaitIO(control);
}

sound_note(chnl,period,loudness)
struct IOAudio *chnl;
UWORD period,loudness;
```

Listing 7-11 cont.

```
{
  chnl->ioa_Request.io_Command=CMD_WRITE;
  chnl->ioa_Request.io_Flags=ADIOF_PERVOL|IOF_QUICK;
  chnl->ioa_Data=s_data0;
  chnl->ioa_Cycles=0;
  chnl->ioa_Length=sizeof(s_data0);
  chnl->ioa_Period= period;
  chnl->ioa_Volume=loudness;
}

grab_channel(sound,control,name)
struct IOAudio *sound,*control;
char *name;
{
  if((sound->ioa_Request.io_Message.mn_ReplyPort
    =CreatePort(name,0))==NULL)*sound=*control;
}
delay(intv)
long intv;
{
  long i;
  for(i=0;i<=intv;i++)
      ;
}
```

In our last example, Listing 7-12, we produce a sound using all four sound channels. This produces a full, rich, and complex tone. Two channels— 0 and 2—sound from the left speaker, while the two remaining ones—1 and 3 —are attached to the right speaker. Our complement of audio structures includes control and finish, as well as four sound structures: s0, s1, s2, and s3. Each of these latter structures is attached to a particular unit of the audio device. Once we initialize each one with the note we wish to play, we begin them one at a time. For effect, we start s0 then s2, and finally s1 and s3. The channels are shut down with a finish command, specifically sent to each unit in reverse order.

Listing 7-12. Using all four channels to produce sound.

```
*/

#include "exec/types.h"
#include "exec/memory.h"
#include "hardware/custom.h"
#include "hardware/dmabits.h"
#include "libraries/dos.h"
#include "devices/audio.h"
#include "lattice/stdio.h"
#include "lattice/math.h"

extern struct MsgPort *CreatePort();
```

Listing 7-12 cont.

```
UBYTE s_data0[32],s_data1[32],s_data2[32],s_data3[32],
      sunit=0x0f;

main()
{
 int x,y,j;
 UBYTE u0=0x01,u1=0x02,u2=0x08,u3=0x04;
 struct IOAudio control,finish,s0,s1,s2,s3;

 setup(&control,&finish);

 s0=control;
 s0.ioa_Request.io_Unit=u0;

 s1=control;
 s1.ioa_Request.io_Unit=u1;

 s2=control;
 s2.ioa_Request.io_Unit=u2;

 s3=control;
 s3.ioa_Request.io_Unit=u3;


 grab_channel(&s0,&control,"c1");
 grab_channel(&s1,&control,"c2");
 grab_channel(&s2,&control,"c3");
 grab_channel(&s3,&control,"c4");

 fill_data(s_data0);
 fill_data(s_data1);
 fill_data(s_data2);
 fill_data(s_data3);

/* left channel setup */

 sound_note(&s0,(UWORD)508,(UWORD)30);
 sound_note(&s2,(UWORD)254,(UWORD)30);

/* right channel setup */

 sound_note(&s1,(UWORD)428,(UWORD)30);
 sound_note(&s3,(UWORD)214,(UWORD)30);

 BeginIO(&s0);
 delay(100000);
 BeginIO(&s2);
 delay(100000);
 BeginIO(&s1);
 delay(100000);
 BeginIO(&s3);
 delay(500000);

 finish.ioa_Request.io_Unit=u3;
```

Listing 7-12 cont.

```
 BeginIO(&finish);
 WaitIO(&finish);

 finish.ioa_Request.io_Unit=u1;
 BeginIO(&finish);
 WaitIO(&finish);

 finish.ioa_Request.io_Unit=u2;
 BeginIO(&finish);
 WaitIO(&finish);

 finish.ioa_Request.io_Unit=u0;
 BeginIO(&finish);
 WaitIO(&finish);

 CloseDevice(&control);
}

setup(control,finish)
struct IOAudio *control,*finish;
{

if((control->ioa_Request.io_Message.mn_ReplyPort
   =CreatePort("p1",0))==NULL)exit(FALSE);

 if((finish->ioa_Request.io_Message.mn_ReplyPort
   =CreatePort("p2",0))==NULL)exit(FALSE);

 control->ioa_Request.io_Message.mn_Node.ln_Pri=10;
 control->ioa_Data=&sunit;
 control->ioa_Length=(ULONG)sizeof(sunit);

 if((OpenDevice(AUDIONAME,0L,control,0L))!=NULL)  {
  printf("Can't open Audio Device\n");
  exit(FALSE);
 }
```

```
/* ===Set up the command structures=== */

 *finish=*control;

 finish->ioa_Request.io_Flags=IOF_QUICK;
 finish->ioa_Request.io_Command=ADCMD_FINISH;

 control->ioa_Request.io_Flags=IOF_QUICK;
 control->ioa_Request.io_Command=ADCMD_PERVOL;
}

fill_data(s0)
UBYTE *s0;
{
 double x;

 for(x=-(PI/2);x<=PI/2;x+=.1)  {
```

Listing 7-12 cont.

```
    *s0=(UBYTE)floor(100*sin(x));
    s0++;
   }
 }

change_sound(loudness,period,control)
UWORD loudness,period;
struct IOAudio *control;
{
 control->ioa_Period=period;
 control->ioa_Volume=loudness;
 BeginIO(control);
 WaitIO(control);
}

sound_note(chnl,period,loudness)
struct IOAudio *chnl;
UWORD period,loudness;
{
  chnl->ioa_Request.io_Command=CMD_WRITE;
  chnl->ioa_Request.io_Flags=ADIOF_PERVOL|IOF_QUICK;
  chnl->ioa_Data=s_data0;
  chnl->ioa_Cycles=0;
  chnl->ioa_Length=sizeof(s_data0);
  chnl->ioa_Period= period;
  chnl->ioa_Volume=loudness;
}

grab_channel(sound,control,name)
struct IOAudio *sound,*control;
char *name;
{
 if((sound->ioa_Request.io_Message.mn_ReplyPort
  =CreatePort(name,0))==NULL)*sound=*control;
}
delay(intv)
long intv;
{
 long i;
 for(i=0;i<=intv;i++)
    ;
}
```

Summary

Through the examples in this chapter, you have seen several ways to access the sound subsystem on the Amiga. You can go from the very simple—sounding a note on a single channel—to the complex—using all channels to produce a full, stereophonic sound. Because these channels are accessed through a standard device, they are readily available in the Amiga's multitasking environment. Thus, sound can be added as an incidental effect to an application (e.g., a game), or it can be added to a graphics program to produce an enhanced multimedia effect.

There are other capabilities of the sound subsystem that are beyond the scope of this chapter's discussion. For the programmer willing to go deep into the hardware level, it is possible to set up the sound circuitry so that one channel's output will modulate another. Both amplitude and frequency modulation are possible. In addition, as with all devices that can participate in the Amiga's multitasking, you can coordinate the audio device among competing tasks. It is possible to lock the channels and use allocation commands to arbitrate between users of different priorities. It is even possible, with some add-on hardware, to use the Amiga in a MIDI network where it can function as both a controller and as another instrument.

The sound capabilities of the Amiga make it an outstanding machine for any kind of music programming tasks. As we have seen, it is a powerful programming tool, yet that power is easy to access.

Artificial Speech   Chapter 8

T he Amiga talks! Included in the operating system software is a complete speech synthesis system that works in conjunction with the sound circuitry and the audio device to produce high quality easily understood speech. This offers an important alternative output to the more traditional monitor or printer. Using this feature is a simple operation and one that is consistent with the Amiga's other I/O devices.

The Nature of Speech

Human speech is created by the use of the vocal track system. A complete explanation would be impossible here and no more than a cursory glance need be given. Basically, the human voice starts out as a tone rich in harmonics. This tone is modulated to produce the different sounds that are recognized as human language. The original tone is produced by the vocal chords, but the throat, mouth, teeth, and tongue also have an important part to play in speaking.

There are several important parameters that are involved in any act of speaking. However, it is not necessary to create a complete simulation of the upper human anatomy to produce an intelligible sound. Certain standard sets of frequencies, the *formants*, are used in various combinations to produce nearly all the sounds of human speech. A computer simulation need only be concerned with these. You can create these formant values mathematically in the computer and end up with quite intelligible language. This is precisely what the Amiga does.

The Amiga's unique sound creation subsystem makes the simulation of human formant values not just practical, but easy as well. Recall that the sound circuitry consists, not of specialized music creation chips, but of general purpose digital- to-analog converters. Any sound can be easily mimicked using this system. The sound requirements for speech are less stringent than those for music synthesis and are well within the capabilities of these specialized chips.

Although it is possible to create speech just by manipulating the Amiga's sound subsystem, the necessity for such direct and low-level access has been obviated by the creation within the operating system of a "speech synthesis" subsystem. This is yet another example of the advanced nature of the Amiga. The speech device is on the same level of access as the more mundane printer drivers!

Phonemes and Syllables

Human speech is a function of the physical characteristics which produce it— the hardware, as it were. It is necessary to create a simulation of this hardware to create the oscillating current that drives the loudspeakers, which finally allow you to hear the sounds. However, first you need some kind of connection with the printed word that will drive this synthesis. What you want is the ability to type a line or a paragraph of text and have the Amiga speak it. The connecting link is the *phoneme*; this is a higher level construction than the actual sounds themselves.

A phoneme is a basic unit of linguistic sound, which is peculiar to and defines a particular language. The human vocal tract can make a large variety of noises, tones, and other sonic objects. Each human language restricts itself to a very small subset of these sounds; these are the phonemes. Speech synthesizers, then, need only be able to generate a small set to create intelligible speech.

The phoneme is also related to the written word. There is not necessarily a one-to-one correspondence between syllables and phonemes, but there is often at least a rough correlation. Besides creating the sounds, a speech synthesis system must be able to translate the written text, syllable by syllable, into proper phonemes, which can then be handled by the sound generator subsystem.

Each of these problems—translation and speech—is a significant one. The algorithms are not trivial, and, in fact, there is a great deal of controversy over which approaches are most proper. The Amiga tackles translation and speech by creating two related subsystems:

1. The *translator library* handles the encoding of the written word into phonemes.
2. The *narrator device* produces the speech.

In the following pages we will concentrate on how to use these two devices, both independently and together.

The Translator Library

The first task of the speech producing process is to divide the written word into its constituent phonemes. The translator library is a disk-resident object that can help accomplish this job. It takes as input a string of text and produces as output a string of text translated into a phonetic language that can be used by the narrator device. This translation is based on a number of factors. Essentially, the string is divided into words and syllables, and the syllables are matched with their corresponding phonetic equivalents. However, the spelling of English is not fully phonetic, so some exception checking is also completed. The stress on individual words and the sentence intonation are partially controlled by various punctuation marks recognized by the speech subsystem.

You are free to use your own translation functions and bypass the translator library altogether. There are circumstances where this is an attractive alternative. But realize that accurate translation is not a simple proposition. There are many homophones in English and even more words that do not sound as they are spelled. On top of all this, speed is essential; any algorithm must be relatively quick, to carry on even a simulated conversation.

The translator library has but a single function to accomplish its task:

```
Translate(in,in_length,out,out_length);
```

where

> **in** points to a character string containing the line to be translated.
>
> **in_length** indicates the number of characters in the text string.
>
> **out** is a character array that accepts the phonetic equivalent.
>
> **out_length** is the number of characters in the output string.

Although we will talk more about using the phonetic alphabet later, when we discuss its direct application, note here that, in general, the phonetic string is significantly longer than the initial text.

Before you can use the services of the translator library, you must open it and load its contents into memory. You must also tell the operating system where it resides in memory. All of this is accomplished by the same *Open-Library()* function, which you have used already to gain access to other system resources. This function returns the address of the newly available library. The value must be stored in the global variable:

```
struct Library *TranslatorBase;
```

This is similar to both Intuition and the graphics libraries. Once the library is open, calls to *Translate()* can be made repeatedly. When all translation activity is finished, a call to *CloseLibrary()* allows the operating system to regain the used memory. One further note: the system expects to find the translator library in the virtual directory LIBS:. It may be necessary to reassign this directory to whatever physical directory actually contains the library.

Listing 8-1 illustrates a simple program that translates a single line of text into a single phonetic line. The phonetic line is then printed out as a character string rather than being sent to the narrator device. This program only demonstrates how this library can be used. It is for instructional purposes only. One function, *get_phoneme()*, takes the same set of parameters as the

Listing 8-1. Use of the translator library to convert a string of characters into a string of phonemes.

```
*/

#define ERR 1
#define SUCCESS 0

#include "exec/types.h"
#include "exec/exec.h"
#include "exec/nodes.h"
#include "exec/lists.h"
#include "exec/memory.h"
#include "exec/interrupts.h"
#include "exec/ports.h"
#include "exec/libraries.h"
#include "exec/io.h"
#include "exec/tasks.h"
#include "exec/execbase.h"
#include "libraries/translator.h"
#include "lattice/stdio.h"

struct Library *TranslatorBase;
extern struct Library *OpenLibrary();

main()
{

  UBYTE in_string[80],out_string[300];

  printf("enter string ");
  scanf("%s",in_string);



  if(get_phoneme(in_string,strlen(in_string),out_string,300)==ERR)
    exit(FALSE);

  printf("\n\nThe phoneme translation of %s is %s\n",in_string,out_string);


}

get_phoneme(in,inlen,out,outlen)
UBYTE *in,*out;
SHORT inlen,outlen;
{

  TranslatorBase=(struct Library *)
              OpenLibrary("translator.library",1);

  if(TranslatorBase==NULL)
    return(ERR);

  if((Translate(in,inlen,out,outlen))!=0)
```

Listing 8-1 cont.

```
    return(ERR);

  CloseLibrary(TranslatorBase);

  return(SUCCESS);

}
```

Translate( ) function itself—in and out strings and their respective lengths. The translator library is opened within the scope of the function, the translation is made, and then the library is closed. The error checking in the *get_phoneme( )* function is minimal; it returns an integer value indicating success or failure. In the program example, we close the library immediately after the translation into phonemes, because it is a good idea to keep hold of a resource such as a library for as little time as possible. This increases the efficiency of memory usage, which, in a multitasking environment, in turn makes for fewer delays and faster program execution. In fact, closing a library doesn't necessarily mean that the library code is swapped out to disk. If the space in memory is not needed, it remains there, waiting for its next use.

There are a few points that may not be obvious from either the discussion of the *Translate( )* function or its program example. *Translate( )* always works on a sentence—a string of text. If a single word or even a single sound is translated, it is translated as a sentence. This has an effect on the intonation of the word when it is finally produced by the narrator device. Once a string of phonemes has been produced by this function, the string can be edited as any other text string; thus, you can fine tune the speech that is finally uttered without having to create your own translation algorithms.

The Narrator Device

The next step, once you have translated text into a phonetic representation, is to call up the Amiga's hardware, in order to pronounce each one of the phonemes. This capability is contained in a specialized device driver, the *Narrator*. There are many advantages in making this a device driver; a major one is that, as a device driver, the Narrator can participate fully in the Amiga's multitasking environment. The processes producing speech can run in the background in concert with other system processes rather than taking over the entire machine. Possibilities are endless, but a particular combination that comes readily to mind is the integration of sound with the fine graphics displays available on the Amiga.

Aside from the somewhat flashy (and practical) graphics and sound shows possible, other more stolid (but no less important) possibilities become apparent. Sound can be wedded to a database program and thus can tell you what is found in a search. Speech in conjunction with a program help facility can add an important dimension of performance to an application program. The narrator device, although simple in operation, is an important subsystem on the Amiga and one that is not often found on microcomputers.

Splitting the two functions—speech and translation—is yet another indication of the sophistication of the Amiga. This allows a great degree of flexibility. For example, if you have a need to say only a few phrases or repeated sentences, you can save yourself the overhead of the translator library, and hard code the phonetic representation into your program. If you need an overall conversion facility, it is available. You can also replace the translation facility with one of your own design, or even add layers of preprocessing.

Since the Narrator is a device, access is through the Amiga's message facility. You command the device by sending messages, and it returns messages to indicate the completion of the required task or to report important status information. The first level of access is through a modified message structure:

```
struct narrator_rb {
    struct IOStdReq message;
    UWORD   rate,
            pitch,
            mode,
            sex;
    UBYTE   *ch_masks;
    UWORD   nm_masks,
            volume,
            sampfreq;
    UBYTE   mouths,
            chanmask,
            numchan,
            fill;
};
```

Message is a standard I/O structure to interface with the message passing system. The *ch_masks* and *nm_masks* are concerned with channel allocation in the audio device. Note that *chanmask* and *numchan* are set by the system rather than the program. The *mouths* field is used in conjunction with the related mouth_rb structure; we will talk more about this in a moment.

The *rate* field sets the speed of the uttered speech; it is measured in words per minute. The range of this parameter varies from 40 to 400 words per minute. The default rate is set at 150. The *volume* field ranges from 0 to 64 and affects the loudness of the speech sounds. The default value is 64, while a value of 0 indicates the device is turned off.

The *mode* field affects the intonation and stress of the artificial speech produced. There are two defined modes:

NATURALF0 produces an inflected speech that attempts to model an ordinary English speaker's natural intonations.

ROBOTICF0 sets the Narrator to produce speech in a monotone—a steady, unvarying pitch with no inflection.

The default mode is NATURALF0.

Three fields can affect the sound quality of the Amiga's synthetic speech. The *pitch* field sets the base line frequency of the narrator device. Inflected speech varies around this value as a center point. If the mode is set to produce a monotone voice, this frequency is used without any variation. The range of the *pitch* field is from 65 to 320. The *sex* field takes either MALE or FEMALE; these defined constants cause the narrator device to produce speech that is characteristic of a man or a woman. The practical effect of this field is the production of a sound that is higher or lower. The *sex* field sets the overall frequency of the sound; the *pitch* value is a type of fine tuning control that varies the sound within this range.

Finally, *sampfreq* sets the sampling frequency of the audio device when it is rendering the speech sounds. Varying this between its extremes of 5000 and 28000 also indirectly affects the overall sound. Some interesting effects can be produced by playing with this field, but bear in mind that this is not the main purpose for the field. Its default value is 22200.

Listing 8-2 illustrates a program that converts a single line of text into an utterance. It consists of two functions.

1. **get_phoneme( )** accesses the translator library.
2. **talk_to_me( )** activates the narrator device.

The former has been imported from an earlier example (Listing 8-1); it translates the entered string into a phonetic representation and returns the result in the string variable *out_string*.

Listing 8-2. Use of the translator library and the narrator device to produce speech phonemes.

```
*/

#define ERR 1
#define SUCCESS 0
#define REV 0

#include "exec/types.h"
#include "exec/exec.h"
#include "exec/nodes.h"
#include "exec/lists.h"
#include "exec/memory.h"
#include "exec/interrupts.h"
#include "exec/ports.h"
#include "exec/libraries.h"
#include "exec/io.h"
#include "exec/tasks.h"
#include "exec/execbase.h"
#include "libraries/translator.h"
#include "devices/audio.h"
#include "devices/narrator.h"
#include "lattice/stdio.h"

struct Library *TranslatorBase=NULL;
```

Listing 8-2 cont.

```
extern struct Library *OpenLibrary();
struct MsgPort *WPort,*RPort;
extern struct IORequest *CreateExtIO();
extern struct Library *OpenLibrary();
struct narrator_rb *wmes;
struct mouth_rb *rmes;

BYTE audChanMasks[]={3,5,10,12};

main()
{

 UBYTE in_string[80],out_string[300];

 printf("enter string ");
 gets(in_string);

 if(get_phoneme(in_string,strlen(in_string),out_string,300)==ERR)
   exit(FALSE);

 if(talk_to_me(out_string)==ERR)
   exit(FALSE);

 CloseDevice(wmes);

}

get_phoneme(in,inlen,out,outlen)
UBYTE *in,*out;
SHORT inlen,outlen;
{

 TranslatorBase=(struct Library *)
                OpenLibrary("translator.library",REV);

 if(TranslatorBase==NULL)
   return(ERR);

 if((Translate(in,inlen,out,outlen))!=0)
   return(ERR);

 CloseLibrary(TranslatorBase);

 return(SUCCESS);

}

talk_to_me(speech)
UBYTE *speech;
{

  if((WPort=(struct MsgPort *)CreatePort(0,0))==NULL)
    return(ERR);
```

Listing 8-2 cont.

```
if((RPort=(struct MsgPort *)CreatePort(0,0))==NULL)
  return(ERR);

if((wmes=(struct narrator_rb *)
  CreateExtIO(WPort,sizeof(struct narrator_rb)))==NULL)
  return(ERR);

if((rmes=(struct mouth_rb *)
  CreateExtIO(RPort,sizeof(struct narrator_rb)))==NULL)
  return(ERR);


wmes->message.io_Command=CMD_WRITE;
wmes->message.io_Data=(APTR)speech;
wmes->message.io_Length=strlen(speech);
wmes->ch_masks=audChanMasks;
wmes->nm_masks=sizeof(audChanMasks);


if(OpenDevice("narrator.device",0,wmes,0)!=0)
  return(ERR);

wmes->mouths=0;
wmes->volume=32;
wmes->rate=20;
wmes->sex=MALE;
wmes->pitch=DEFPITCH;

DoIO(wmes);

return(SUCCESS);

}
```

The function *talk_to_me()* performs all the necessary steps to set up and use the narrator device. First we create a port to the device and attach the narrator_rb structure to it; this is accomplished by a call to *CreatePort()* and a subsequent call to *CreateExtIO()*. Both of these functions are general purpose system calls that are used whenever it is necessary to interact with the Exec kernel's underlying message passing system. The next step is to initialize the *wmes*, our narrator_rb struct, to properly interact with the narrator device. Most importantly, we set the *message.io_Command* field to CMD_WRITE, to indicate that we desire an output operation rather than input. This is a necessary prior step to the use of *OpenDevice()* to set the process in motion.

Once you have opened the narrator device, you are free to send command messages to it and wait for its activity; however, before you send a message, you must initialize it to the values on which you want it to operate. Foremost of these values is the string of phonemes that is to be pronounced; this goes into the *message.io__Data* field. This field should be cast to an absolute address data type—APTR. The length of this field is put into *message.io__Length*. These two fields, along with the *message.io__Command* field, are part of the standard message structure. The other fields that need to be set are peculiar to the narrator__rb structure itself. These are explained above, and the example contains typical values.

Once you have translated a line of text, done the setup, and opened the device, you are ready to send an I/O request to the Narrator. In the example, we use the simplest call, *DoIO()*. This sends the command structure with its variables to the device, and then stops and waits for a reply. Once that reply has been obtained, we return to the main program and execute a call to *CloseDevice()*, before stopping the program. As we have noted before, it is very important to close unused resources with the Amiga; otherwise, you may run out of a most important resource—main memory.

The example in Listing 8-3 is a modification of the previous program. This program is set up to deal with more than one line of input. The primary modification is the creation of a third function, *set__to__talk()*, which handles all setup for the narrator device. This step is necessary, because we are going to send multiple messages to this device, but we need only open it once. Note that we call *set__to__talk()* outside the main program loop.

Listing 8-3. Use of Set__to__talk() function to allow an unlimited number of spoken lines. Speech is produced using the translator library and narrator device.

```
*/

#define ERR 1
#define SUCCESS 0
#define REV 0

#include "exec/types.h"
#include "exec/exec.h"
#include "exec/nodes.h"
#include "exec/lists.h"
#include "exec/memory.h"
#include "exec/interrupts.h"
#include "exec/ports.h"
#include "exec/libraries.h"
#include "exec/io.h"
#include "exec/tasks.h"
#include "exec/execbase.h"
#include "libraries/translator.h"
#include "devices/audio.h"
#include "devices/narrator.h"
#include "lattice/stdio.h"

struct Library *TranslatorBase=NULL;
extern struct Library *OpenLibrary();
```

Listing 8-3 cont.

```
struct MsgPort *WPort,*RPort;
extern struct IORequest *CreateExtIO();
extern struct Library *OpenLibrary();
struct narrator_rb *wmes;
struct mouth_rb *rmes;

BYTE audChanMasks[]={3,5,10,12};

main()
{

  UBYTE in_string[80],out_string[300];

  if(set_to_talk()==ERR)
    exit(FALSE);

  for(;;)  {
    printf("enter string ");
    gets(in_string);

    if(!strcmp(in_string,"%halt"))
      break;

if(get_phoneme(in_string,strlen(in_string),out_string,300)==ERR)
      exit(FALSE);

    if(talk_to_me(out_string)==ERR)
      exit(FALSE);
  }

  CloseDevice(wmes);

}

get_phoneme(in,inlen,out,outlen)
UBYTE *in,*out;
SHORT inlen,outlen;
{

  TranslatorBase=(struct Library *)
                 OpenLibrary("translator.library",REV);

  if(TranslatorBase==NULL)
    return(ERR);

  if((Translate(in,inlen,out,outlen))!=0)
    return(ERR);

  CloseLibrary(TranslatorBase);

  return(SUCCESS);

}
```

Listing 8-3 cont.

```
talk_to_me(speech)
UBYTE *speech;
{
 wmes->message.io_Data=(APTR)speech;
 wmes->message.io_Length=strlen(speech);
 wmes->ch_masks=audChanMasks;
 wmes->nm_masks=sizeof(audChanMasks);


 wmes->mouths=0;
 wmes->volume=32;
 wmes->rate=20;
 wmes->sex=MALE;
 wmes->pitch=DEFPITCH;



 DoIO(wmes);



}


set_to_talk()
{
 if((WPort=(struct MsgPort *)CreatePort(0,0))==NULL)
   return(ERR);

 if((wmes=(struct narrator_rb *)
   CreateExtIO(WPort,sizeof(struct narrator_rb)))==NULL)
   return(ERR);

 wmes->message.io_Command=CMD_WRITE;

 if(OpenDevice("narrator.device",0,wmes,0)!=0)
   return(ERR);

 return(SUCCESS);
}
```

One important flaw in the two previous examples is that they do not take full advantage of the multitasking capabilities of the Amiga. Whenever a message is sent to the narrator device, the current program goes into a wait state until the message has been received and a reply sent. Since the driver for this device is independent of the calling program, it would make more sense to send the message and then continue processing. Earlier discussions of multitasking have shown that there are a number of ways to accomplish this. Listings 8-4 and 8-5 illustrate a multitasking format commonly used with the speech synthesis subsystem.

Listing 8-4. Multitasking format used with the speech synthesis subsystem. A single line is converted to phonemes, then spoken.

```
*/

#define ERR 1
#define SUCCESS 0
#define REV 0

#include "exec/types.h"
#include "exec/exec.h"
#include "exec/nodes.h"
#include "exec/lists.h"
#include "exec/memory.h"
#include "exec/interrupts.h"
#include "exec/ports.h"
#include "exec/libraries.h"
#include "exec/io.h"
#include "exec/tasks.h"
#include "exec/execbase.h"
#include "libraries/translator.h"
#include "devices/audio.h"
#include "devices/narrator.h"
#include "lattice/stdio.h"

struct Library *TranslatorBase=NULL;
extern struct Library *OpenLibrary();
struct MsgPort *WPort,*RPort;
extern struct IORequest *CreateExtIO();
extern struct Library *OpenLibrary();
struct narrator_rb *wmes;
struct mouth_rb *rmes;

BYTE audChanMasks[]={3,5,10,12};

main()
{

  UBYTE in_string[80],out_string[300];

  printf("enter string ");
  gets(in_string);

  if(get_phoneme(in_string,strlen(in_string),out_string,300)==ERR)
    exit(FALSE);

  if(talk_to_me(out_string)==ERR)
    exit(FALSE);

  CloseDevice(wmes);
```

Listing 8-4 cont.

```
}

get_phoneme(in,inlen,out,outlen)
UBYTE *in,*out;
SHORT inlen,outlen;
{

 TranslatorBase=(struct Library *)
                 OpenLibrary("translator.library",REV);

 if(TranslatorBase==NULL)
    return(ERR);

 if((Translate(in,inlen,out,outlen))!=0)
    return(ERR);

 CloseLibrary(TranslatorBase);

 return(SUCCESS);

}

talk_to_me(speech)
UBYTE *speech;
{


 if((WPort=(struct MsgPort *)CreatePort(0,0))==NULL)
   return(ERR);

 if((RPort=(struct MsgPort *)CreatePort(0,0))==NULL)
   return(ERR);

 if((wmes=(struct narrator_rb *)
   CreateExtIO(WPort,sizeof(struct narrator_rb)))==NULL)
   return(ERR);

 if((rmes=(struct mouth_rb *)
   CreateExtIO(RPort,sizeof(struct narrator_rb)))==NULL)
   return(ERR);


 wmes->message.io_Command=CMD_WRITE;
 wmes->message.io_Data=(APTR)speech;
 wmes->message.io_Length=strlen(speech);
 wmes->ch_masks=audChanMasks;
 wmes->nm_masks=sizeof(audChanMasks);


 if(OpenDevice("narrator.device",0,wmes,0)!=0)
   return(ERR);

 wmes->mouths=0;
```

Listing 8-4 cont.

```
wmes->volume=32;
wmes->rate=20;
wmes->sex=MALE;
wmes->pitch=DEFPITCH;

rmes->voice.message.io_Device=wmes->message.io_Device;
rmes->voice.message.io_Unit=wmes->message.io_Unit;
rmes->width=0;
rmes->height=0;
rmes->voice.message.io_Command=CMD_READ;
rmes->voice.message.io_Error=0;


SendIO(wmes);

while (rmes->voice.message.io_Error!=ND_NoWrite)
  DoIO(rmes);

return(SUCCESS);

}
```

Before delving headlong into a discussion of these two listings, we must explore another structure associated with the narrator device:

```
struct mouth_rb {
    struct narrator_rb voice;
    UBYTE  width,
           height,
           shape,
           pad;
};
```

This structure is used to send information back from the Narrator to the calling routine. Specifically, it returns two values, width and height, which can be used to produce an animated picture of a mouth. The narrator device calculates these two variables based on the phoneme it is now speaking. If these values are to be used, the mouth field in the narrator__rb structure must be set to a value other than 0.

Even if you are not interested in associating a screen image with the spoken word issuing from the computer, you can use the mouth__rb structure to set up a monitoring task that allows you to send messages to the Narrator, but not wait for their completion. This is illustrated in Listing 8-4. This program is similar to the earlier Listing 8-2; it accepts a single line as input, converts it to phonemes, and then speaks it. Here, however, we declare two associated structures: a narrator__rb and a mouth structure. To accomodate them, we open two ports: one to write to and one to read from. We open the device with the narrator__rb structure and then copy the message__io.Device and *message__io.Unit* to the mouth__rb structure. This insures that the two are linked during the I/O operations.

Once initialization is complete, we access the Narrator via a *SendIO()* command. This transmits our command message and then continues with the rest of the program. Meanwhile, a *DoIO()* operation is performed using the mouth__rb structure. When the Narrator has finally finished speaking the entire message, it sets the *voice.message.Error* field to *ND__NoWrite*. These I/O operations are performed until this condition is met. Listing 8-5 also uses the *SendIO()* function and the dual structures, but in the context of a continuous loop in the main program.

Listing 8-5. Multitasking format used with the speech synthesis subsystem. An unlimited number of lines can be spoken.

```
*/

#define ERR 1
#define SUCCESS 0
#define REV 0

#include "exec/types.h"
#include "exec/exec.h"
#include "exec/nodes.h"
#include "exec/lists.h"
#include "exec/memory.h"
#include "exec/interrupts.h"
#include "exec/ports.h"
#include "exec/libraries.h"
#include "exec/io.h"
#include "exec/tasks.h"
#include "exec/execbase.h"
#include "libraries/translator.h"
#include "devices/audio.h"
#include "devices/narrator.h"
#include "lattice/stdio.h"

struct Library *TranslatorBase=NULL;
extern struct Library *OpenLibrary();
struct MsgPort *WPort,*RPort;
extern struct IORequest *CreateExtIO();
extern struct Library *OpenLibrary();
struct narrator_rb *wmes;
struct mouth_rb *rmes;

BYTE audChanMasks[]={3,5,10,12};

main()
{

UBYTE in_string[80],out_string[300];

if(set_to_talk()==ERR)
  exit(FALSE);
```

Listing 8-5 cont.

```
for(;;)  {
  printf("enter string ");
  gets(in_string);

  if(!strcmp(in_string,"%%"))
    break;

if(get_phoneme(in_string,strlen(in_string),out_string,300)==ERR)
    exit(FALSE);

  if(talk_to_me(out_string)==ERR)
    exit(FALSE);
  }

CloseDevice(wmes);

}

get_phoneme(in,inlen,out,outlen)
UBYTE *in,*out;
SHORT inlen,outlen;
{

  TranslatorBase=(struct Library *)
                OpenLibrary("translator.library",REV);

  if(TranslatorBase==NULL)
    return(ERR);

  if((Translate(in,inlen,out,outlen))!=0)
    return(ERR);

  CloseLibrary(TranslatorBase);

  return(SUCCESS);

}

talk_to_me(speech)
UBYTE *speech;
{
 wmes->message.io_Data=(APTR)speech;
 wmes->message.io_Length=strlen(speech);
 wmes->ch_masks=audChanMasks;
 wmes->nm_masks=sizeof(audChanMasks);


 wmes->mouths=0;
 wmes->volume=32;
 wmes->rate=20;
 wmes->sex=MALE;
 wmes->pitch=DEFPITCH;
```

Listing 8-5 cont.

```
SendIO(wmes);

while (rmes->voice.message.io_Error!=ND_NoWrite)
  DoIO(rmes);


}
```

```
set_to_talk()
{
 if((WPort=(struct MsgPort *)CreatePort(0,0))==NULL)
   return(ERR);

 if((RPort=(struct MsgPort *)CreatePort(0,0))==NULL)
   return(ERR);

 if((wmes=(struct narrator_rb *)
   CreateExtIO(WPort,sizeof(struct narrator_rb)))==NULL)
   return(ERR);

 if((rmes=(struct mouth_rb *)
   CreateExtIO(RPort,sizeof(struct narrator_rb)))==NULL)
   return(ERR);

 wmes->message.io_Command=CMD_WRITE;

 if(OpenDevice("narrator.device",0,wmes,0)!=0)
   return(ERR);

 rmes->voice.message.io_Device=wmes->message.io_Device;
 rmes->voice.message.io_Unit=wmes->message.io_Unit;
 rmes->width=0;
 rmes->height=0;
 rmes->voice.message.io_Command=CMD_READ;
 rmes->voice.message.io_Error=0;

 return(SUCCESS);
}
```

Experimenting with the Narrator

Now that you understand the basic operation of the speech synthesis subsystem on the Amiga, it is important to also consider the effects of varying the parameters that are sent to this device. Although a great deal can be done with just the basic operation—the speech, as it stands, is clear and easily understandable—slight modifications to the default values can provide even more controlled performance. It is even possible to correct some of the ambiguities that are understandably found in this complicated set of procedures.

Listing 8-6. Use of set__params( ) function to set the parameters of speech.

```
*/

#define ERR 1
#define SUCCESS 0
#define REV 0

#include "exec/types.h"
#include "exec/exec.h"
#include "exec/nodes.h"
#include "exec/lists.h"
#include "exec/memory.h"
#include "exec/interrupts.h"
#include "exec/ports.h"
#include "exec/libraries.h"
#include "exec/io.h"
#include "exec/tasks.h"
#include "exec/execbase.h"
#include "libraries/translator.h"
#include "devices/audio.h"
#include "devices/narrator.h"
#include "lattice/stdio.h"

struct Library *TranslatorBase=NULL;
extern struct Library *OpenLibrary();
struct MsgPort *WPort,*RPort;
extern struct IORequest *CreateExtIO();
extern struct Library *OpenLibrary();
struct narrator_rb *wmes;
struct mouth_rb *rmes;

BYTE audChanMasks[]={3,5,10,12};

main()
{

  UBYTE in_string[80],out_string[300];
  UWORD volume=55,rate=20;

  if(set_to_talk()==ERR)
    exit(FALSE);

  for(;;)  {
    printf("enter string ");
    gets(in_string);

    if(!strcmp(in_string,"%halt"))
      break;

    if(!strcmp(in_string,"%set")) {
```

Listing 8-6 cont.

```
        set_params(&volume,&rate);
        continue;
      }

if(get_phoneme(in_string,strlen(in_string),out_string,300)==ERR)
      exit(FALSE);

    if(talk_to_me(out_string,volume,rate)==ERR)
      exit(FALSE);
  }

 CloseDevice(wmes);

}

get_phoneme(in,inlen,out,outlen)
UBYTE *in,*out;
SHORT inlen,outlen;
{

  TranslatorBase=(struct Library *)
                 OpenLibrary("translator.library",REV);

  if(TranslatorBase==NULL)
     return(ERR);

  if((Translate(in,inlen,out,outlen))!=0)
     return(ERR);

  CloseLibrary(TranslatorBase);

  return(SUCCESS);

}

talk_to_me(speech,vol,rate)
UBYTE *speech;
UWORD vol,rate;
{

  wmes->message.io_Data=(APTR)speech;
  wmes->message.io_Length=strlen(speech);
  wmes->ch_masks=audChanMasks;
  wmes->nm_masks=sizeof(audChanMasks);

  wmes->mouths=0;
  wmes->volume=vol;
  wmes->rate=rate;
  wmes->sex=MALE;
  wmes->pitch=DEFPITCH;

  SendIO(wmes);

  while (rmes->voice.message.io_Error!=ND_NoWrite)
```

Listing 8-6 cont.

```
   DoIO(rmes);
}

set_to_talk()
{
 if((WPort=(struct MsgPort *)CreatePort(0,0))==NULL)
   return(ERR);

 if((RPort=(struct MsgPort *)CreatePort(0,0))==NULL)
   return(ERR);

 if((wmes=(struct narrator_rb *)
   CreateExtIO(WPort,sizeof(struct narrator_rb)))==NULL)
   return(ERR);

 if((rmes=(struct mouth_rb *)
   CreateExtIO(RPort,sizeof(struct narrator_rb)))==NULL)
   return(ERR);

 wmes->message.io_Command=CMD_WRITE;

 if(OpenDevice("narrator.device",0,wmes,0)!=0)
   return(ERR);

 rmes->voice.message.io_Device=wmes->message.io_Device;
 rmes->voice.message.io_Unit=wmes->message.io_Unit;
 rmes->width=0;
 rmes->height=0;
 rmes->voice.message.io_Command=CMD_READ;
 rmes->voice.message.io_Error=0;

 return(SUCCESS);
}
```

```
set_params(vol,rate)
UWORD *vol,*rate;
{
 int x,y;

 printf("volume==>");
 scanf("%d",&x);

 printf("rate  ==>");
 scanf("%d",&y);

 *vol=(UWORD)x;
 *rate=(UWORD)y;

}
```

Listing 8-6 contains a prototype program that allows us to enter values for the volume and rate fields of the narrator__rb structure. It is similar in design to the example in Listing 8-7, but we have added a fourth function, *set_params()*. This new function prompts the user to provide values for these fields, and then passes them back to the main part of the program. *Talk_to_me()* has also been modified to accept these parameters. This is a very simple example. There are no default values for these fields; they must be set by the user before the loop in *main()* begins. *Set_Params()* is the first function call in the program. Note, too, that the assignments to the fields in the narrator_rb structure are done after the *OpenDevice()* call but before any I/O function is accessed. Although we haven't provided code for error checking on entered values, the example illustrates a way to better understand the results of varying the Narrator values.

**Listing 8-7. Addition of pitch, mode and sex values to
set_params() function. This expands the range
of speech parameters.**

```
*/

#define ERR 1
#define SUCCESS 0
#define REV 0

#include "exec/types.h"
#include "exec/exec.h"
#include "exec/nodes.h"
#include "exec/lists.h"
#include "exec/memory.h"
#include "exec/interrupts.h"
#include "exec/ports.h"
#include "exec/libraries.h"
#include "exec/io.h"
#include "exec/tasks.h"
#include "exec/execbase.h"
#include "libraries/translator.h"
#include "devices/audio.h"
#include "devices/narrator.h"
#include "lattice/stdio.h"

struct Library *TranslatorBase=NULL;
extern struct Library *OpenLibrary();
struct MsgPort *WPort,*RPort;
extern struct IORequest *CreateExtIO();
extern struct Library *OpenLibrary();
struct narrator_rb *wmes;
struct mouth_rb *rmes;

BYTE audChanMasks[]={3,5,10,12};

main()
{

  UBYTE in_string[80],out_string[300];
  UWORD volume=55,rate=20,pitch=DEFPITCH,mode=DEFMODE,sex=DEFSEX;
```

Listing 8-7 cont.

```
  if(set_to_talk()==ERR)
    exit(FALSE);

  for(;;)  {
    printf("enter string ");
    gets(in_string);

    if(!strcmp(in_string,"%halt"))
      break;

    if(!strcmp(in_string,"%set")) {
      set_params(&volume,&rate,&pitch,&mode,&sex);
      continue;
      }

if(get_phoneme(in_string,strlen(in_string),out_string,300)==ERR)
      exit(FALSE);

    if(talk_to_me(out_string,volume,rate,pitch,mode,sex)==ERR)
      exit(FALSE);
  }

  CloseDevice(wmes);

}

get_phoneme(in,inlen,out,outlen)
UBYTE *in,*out;
SHORT inlen,outlen;
{

  TranslatorBase=(struct Library *)
                 OpenLibrary("translator.library",REV);

  if(TranslatorBase==NULL)
     return(ERR);

  if((Translate(in,inlen,out,outlen))!=0)
     return(ERR);

  CloseLibrary(TranslatorBase);

  return(SUCCESS);

}

talk_to_me(speech,vol,rate,pitch,mode,sex)
UBYTE *speech;
UWORD vol,rate,pitch,mode,sex;
{

  wmes->message.io_Data=(APTR)speech;
  wmes->message.io_Length=strlen(speech);
```

Listing 8-7 cont.

```
  wmes->ch_masks=audChanMasks;
  wmes->nm_masks=sizeof(audChanMasks);

  wmes->mouths=0;
  wmes->volume=vol;
  wmes->rate=rate;
  wmes->sex=sex;
  wmes->pitch=pitch;
  wmes->mode=mode;

  SendIO(wmes);

  while (rmes->voice.message.io_Error!=ND_NoWrite)
    DoIO(rmes);
}

set_to_talk()
{
  if((WPort=(struct MsgPort *)CreatePort(0,0))==NULL)
    return(ERR);

  if((RPort=(struct MsgPort *)CreatePort(0,0))==NULL)
    return(ERR);

  if((wmes=(struct narrator_rb *)
    CreateExtIO(WPort,sizeof(struct narrator_rb)))==NULL)
    return(ERR);

  if((rmes=(struct mouth_rb *)
    CreateExtIO(RPort,sizeof(struct narrator_rb)))==NULL)
    return(ERR);

  wmes->message.io_Command=CMD_WRITE;

  if(OpenDevice("narrator.device",0,wmes,0)!=0)
    return(ERR);

  rmes->voice.message.io_Device=wmes->message.io_Device;
  rmes->voice.message.io_Unit=wmes->message.io_Unit;
  rmes->width=0;
  rmes->height=0;
  rmes->voice.message.io_Command=CMD_READ;
  rmes->voice.message.io_Error=0;

  return(SUCCESS);
}

set_params(vol,rate,pitch,mode,sex)
UWORD *vol,*rate,*pitch,*mode,*sex;
{
  int x,y,z;
  char ch[80];

  printf("volume==>");
```

Listing 8-7 cont.

```
scanf("%d",&x);

printf("rate   ==>");
scanf("%d",&y);

*vol=(UWORD)x;
*rate=(UWORD)(MINRATE+y);

printf("pitch ==>");
scanf("%d",&z);

*pitch=z;

printf("mode   ==>");
scanf("%s",ch);

if(!strcmp(ch,"inflected"))
   *mode=NATURALFO;
if(!strcmp(ch,"monotone"))
   *mode=ROBOTICFO;

printf("sex     ==>");
scanf("%s",ch);

if(!strcmp(ch,"male"))
   *sex=MALE;

if(!strcmp(ch,"female"))
   *sex=FEMALE;

}
```

In Listing 8-7, we have a program almost identical to 8-6. Here, however, we have added the *pitch*, *mode*, and *sex* values to both the *set_params()* and *talk_to_me()* functions. This gives a greater range of parameters with which to experiment when producing speech. The example described in Listing 8-8 adds more complexity. In this program we also enter the sampling frequency, *sampfreq*, in the narrator_rb structure. Additional features include:

- A logical structure that allows us to call the *set_params()* function at any time
- Support for default values. It is no longer necessary to enter values for each parameter if we want to vary just one.

This is a more complete example, which can be used directly to play with the speech synthesizer values or as inspiration for embedded functions that bring the capability of speech to other kinds of programs.

Listing 8-8. Expanded use of set__params( ) function. Sampling frequency is included and default values are supported.

```
*/

#define ERR 1
#define SUCCESS 0
#define REV 0

#include "exec/types.h"
#include "exec/exec.h"
#include "exec/nodes.h"
#include "exec/lists.h"
#include "exec/memory.h"
#include "exec/interrupts.h"
#include "exec/ports.h"
#include "exec/libraries.h"
#include "exec/io.h"
#include "exec/tasks.h"
#include "exec/execbase.h"
#include "libraries/translator.h"
#include "devices/audio.h"
#include "devices/narrator.h"
#include "lattice/stdio.h"

struct Library *TranslatorBase=NULL;
extern struct Library *OpenLibrary();
struct MsgPort *WPort,*RPort;
extern struct IORequest *CreateExtIO();
extern struct Library *OpenLibrary();
struct narrator_rb *wmes;
struct mouth_rb *rmes;

BYTE audChanMasks[]={3,5,10,12};

main()
{

  UBYTE in_string[80],out_string[300];
  UWORD volume=55,rate=20,pitch=DEFPITCH,mode=DEFMODE,
      sex=DEFSEX,freq=DEFFREQ;

  if(set_to_talk()==ERR)
    exit(FALSE);

  for(;;) {
    printf("enter string ");
    gets(in_string);

    if(!strcmp(in_string,"%halt"))
      break;

    if(!strcmp(in_string,"%set")) {
      set_params(&volume,&rate,&pitch,&mode,&sex,&freq);
      continue;
```

Listing 8-8 cont.

```
    }

if(get_phoneme(in_string,strlen(in_string),out_string,300)==ERR)
     exit(FALSE);


if(talk_to_me(out_string,volume,rate,pitch,mode,sex,freq)==ERR)
      exit(FALSE);
  }

 CloseDevice(wmes);

}

get_phoneme(in,inlen,out,outlen)
UBYTE *in,*out;
SHORT inlen,outlen;
{

 TranslatorBase=(struct Library *)
               OpenLibrary("translator.library",REV);

 if(TranslatorBase==NULL)
    return(ERR);

 if((Translate(in,inlen,out,outlen))!=0)
    return(ERR);

 CloseLibrary(TranslatorBase);

 return(SUCCESS);

}

talk_to_me(speech,vol,rate,pitch,mode,sex,freq)
UBYTE *speech;
UWORD vol,rate,pitch,mode,sex,freq;
{

 wmes->message.io_Data=(APTR)speech;
 wmes->message.io_Length=strlen(speech);
 wmes->ch_masks=audChanMasks;
 wmes->nm_masks=sizeof(audChanMasks);

 wmes->mouths=0;
 wmes->volume=vol;
 wmes->rate=rate;
 wmes->sex=sex;
 wmes->pitch=pitch;
 wmes->mode=mode;
 wmes->sampfreq=freq;

 SendIO(wmes);
```

Listing 8-8 cont.

```
 while (rmes->voice.message.io_Error!=ND_NoWrite)
   DoIO(rmes);
}

set_to_talk()
{
 if((WPort=(struct MsgPort *)CreatePort(0,0))==NULL)
   return(ERR);

 if((RPort=(struct MsgPort *)CreatePort(0,0))==NULL)
   return(ERR);

 if((wmes=(struct narrator_rb *)
   CreateExtIO(WPort,sizeof(struct narrator_rb)))==NULL)
   return(ERR);

 if((rmes=(struct mouth_rb *)
   CreateExtIO(RPort,sizeof(struct narrator_rb)))==NULL)
   return(ERR);

 wmes->message.io_Command=CMD_WRITE;

 if(OpenDevice("narrator.device",0,wmes,0)!=0)
   return(ERR);

 rmes->voice.message.io_Device=wmes->message.io_Device;
 rmes->voice.message.io_Unit=wmes->message.io_Unit;
 rmes->width=0;
 rmes->height=0;
 rmes->voice.message.io_Command=CMD_READ;
 rmes->voice.message.io_Error=0;

 return(SUCCESS);
}

set_params(vol,rate,pitch,mode,sex,freq)
UWORD *vol,*rate,*pitch,*mode,*sex,*freq;
{
 int x;
 char ch[80];

 printf("volume==>");
 gets(ch);
 if(ch[0]=='\0')
  ;
 else {
  x=atoi(ch);
  *vol=x;
 }

 printf("rate  ==>");
 gets(ch);
 if(ch[0]=='\0')
  ;
```

Listing 8-8 cont.

```
else {
 x=atoi(ch);
 *rate=x;
}

printf("pitch ==>");
gets(ch);
if(ch[0]=='\0')
 ;
else {
 x=atoi(ch);
 *pitch=x;
}

printf("mode  ==>");
gets(ch);
if(ch[0]=='\0')
 ;
 else if(!strcmp(ch,"inflected"))
      *mode=NATURALFO;
else if(!strcmp(ch,"monotone"))
      *mode=ROBOTICFO;

printf("sex    ==>");
gets(ch);
if(ch[0]=='\0')
 ;
else if(!strcmp(ch,"male"))
       *sex=MALE;
else if(!strcmp(ch,"female"))
       *sex=FEMALE;

printf("sample freq==>");
gets(ch);

if(ch[0]=='\0')
 ;
else {
   x=atoi(ch);
   *freq=x;
 }
}
```

As mentioned earlier, it is possible to do without the services of the translator library altogether and enter a string of phonetic characters directly. This capability is added to Listing 8-6 in Listing 8-9. Creating your own phoneme streams allows a more accurate representation of the sound of certain words, particularly uncommon ones. In addition, it allows you to manipulate the stress and intonation of individual words and sentences.

```
*/

#define ERR 1
#define SUCCESS 0
#define REV 0

#include "exec/types.h"
#include "exec/exec.h"
#include "exec/nodes.h"
#include "exec/lists.h"
#include "exec/memory.h"
#include "exec/interrupts.h"
#include "exec/ports.h"
#include "exec/libraries.h"
#include "exec/io.h"
#include "exec/tasks.h"
#include "exec/execbase.h"
#include "libraries/translator.h"
#include "devices/audio.h"
#include "devices/narrator.h"
#include "lattice/stdio.h"

struct Library *TranslatorBase=NULL;
extern struct Library *OpenLibrary();
struct MsgPort *WPort,*RPort;
extern struct IORequest *CreateExtIO();
extern struct Library *OpenLibrary();
struct narrator_rb *wmes;
struct mouth_rb *rmes;

BYTE audChanMasks[]={3,5,10,12};

main()
{

  UBYTE in_string[80],out_string[300];
  UWORD volume=55,rate=20,pitch=DEFPITCH,mode=DEFMODE,
        sex=DEFSEX,freq=DEFFREQ;

  if(set_to_talk()==ERR)
    exit(FALSE);

  for(;;)  {
    printf("enter string ");
    gets(in_string);

    if(!strcmp(in_string,"%halt"))
      break;

    if(!strcmp(in_string,"%set")) {
      set_params(&volume,&rate,&pitch,&mode,&sex,&freq);
      continue;
```

Listing 8-9 cont.

```
    }

    if(!strcmp(in_string,"%direct"))  {
      printf(">>");
      gets(out_string);
      }
    else
if(get_phoneme(in_string,strlen(in_string),out_string,300)==ERR)
        exit(FALSE);

if(talk_to_me(out_string,volume,rate,pitch,mode,sex,freq)==ERR)
      exit(FALSE);
  }

 CloseDevice(wmes);

}

get_phoneme(in,inlen,out,outlen)
UBYTE *in,*out;
SHORT inlen,outlen;
{

  TranslatorBase=(struct Library *)
                 OpenLibrary("translator.library",REV);

  if(TranslatorBase==NULL)
     return(ERR);

  if((Translate(in,inlen,out,outlen))!=0)
     return(ERR);

  CloseLibrary(TranslatorBase);

  return(SUCCESS);

}

talk_to_me(speech,vol,rate,pitch,mode,sex,freq)
UBYTE *speech;
UWORD vol,rate,pitch,mode,sex,freq;
{

 wmes->message.io_Data=(APTR)speech;
 wmes->message.io_Length=strlen(speech);
 wmes->ch_masks=audChanMasks;
 wmes->nm_masks=sizeof(audChanMasks);

 wmes->mouths=0;
 wmes->volume=vol;
 wmes->rate=rate;
 wmes->sex=sex;
 wmes->pitch=pitch;
```

Listing 8-9 cont.

```
 wmes->mode=mode;
 wmes->sampfreq=freq;

 SendIO(wmes);

 while (rmes->voice.message.io_Error!=ND_NoWrite)
    DoIO(rmes);
}

set_to_talk()
{
 if((WPort=(struct MsgPort *)CreatePort(0,0))==NULL)
    return(ERR);

 if((RPort=(struct MsgPort *)CreatePort(0,0))==NULL)
    return(ERR);

 if((wmes=(struct narrator_rb *)
    CreateExtIO(WPort,sizeof(struct narrator_rb)))==NULL)
    return(ERR);

 if((rmes=(struct mouth_rb *)
    CreateExtIO(RPort,sizeof(struct narrator_rb)))==NULL)
    return(ERR);

 wmes->message.io_Command=CMD_WRITE;

 if(OpenDevice("narrator.device",0,wmes,0)!=0)
    return(ERR);

 rmes->voice.message.io_Device=wmes->message.io_Device;
 rmes->voice.message.io_Unit=wmes->message.io_Unit;
 rmes->width=0;
 rmes->height=0;
 rmes->voice.message.io_Command=CMD_READ;
 rmes->voice.message.io_Error=0;

 return(SUCCESS);
}

set_params(vol,rate,pitch,mode,sex,freq)
UWORD *vol,*rate,*pitch,*mode,*sex,*freq;
{
 int x;
 char ch[80];

 printf("volume==>");
 gets(ch);
 if(ch[0]=='\0')
  ;
 else {
  x=atoi(ch);
  *vol=x;
 }
```

Listing 8-9 cont.

```
printf("rate   ==>");
gets(ch);
if(ch[0]=='\0')
 ;
else {
 x=atoi(ch);
 *rate=x;
}

printf("pitch ==>");
gets(ch);
if(ch[0]=='\0')
 ;
else {
 x=atoi(ch);
 *pitch=x;
}

printf("mode   ==>");
gets(ch);
if(ch[0]=='\0')
 ;
 else if(!strcmp(ch,"inflected"))
      *mode=NATURALFO;
else if(!strcmp(ch,"monotone"))
      *mode=ROBOTICFO;

printf("sex     ==>");
gets(ch);
if(ch[0]=='\0')
 ;
else if(!strcmp(ch,"male"))
      *sex=MALE;
else if(!strcmp(ch,"female"))
      *sex=FEMALE;

printf("sample freq==>");
gets(ch);

if(ch[0]=='\0')
 ;
else {
   x=atoi(ch);
   *freq=x;
 }
}
```

In order to specify a phoneme stream, it is necessary to understand the rules that apply to the narrator device. First, you must become familiar with the phonetic alphabet used in the representation. This alphabet is listed in Table 8-1; it is a modification of the standard phonetic alphabet used through-

Table 8-1.   Some common Arpabet symbols.

Sound	Symbol	Example
A	AE	HAT
	AO	BALK
	EY	PAID
B	B	BACK
C	K	CARL
	CH	CHOICE
D	D	DIG
E	IY	MEET
	EH	PET
F	F	FORT
G	G	GOOD
H	/H	HOLY
I	ER	DIRTY
	IH	HIT
	AY	PIE
J	J	JOIN
K	K	KEEP
L	L	LOW
M	M	MICE
N	N	NICE
	NX	PING
O	AA	POT
	UH	LOOK
	OH	HORDE
	AX	TOUT
	IX	SOLID
	OY	TOIL
	OW	KNOW
	AW	TOWER
P	P	PET
Q	K	QUIET
R	R	READ
S	S	SIT
	SH	SHOOT
T	T	TIE
	TH	THING
	DH	THE
U	AH	BUNDLE
	UW	POOL
V	V	VOTE
W	W	WASH
X	/C	YECCH
Y	Y	YELP
Z	Z	ZEAL
	ZH	MEASURE

out the world. This particular implementation allows the specification of any sound with two or more standard alphabetic characters. It is known as *Arpabet* from its origins with the Advanced Research Projects Agency. In translating directly into this phonetic language, you must choose symbols that indicate the various sounds that go to make up the word. This is not necessarily the same as the English spelling.

Vowels have two qualities that can also be specified in the phonetic alphabet: *stress* and *intonation*. In any given English word, some syllables are stressed; others are not. You indicate this stress to the Narrator by placing a digit between 1 and 9 immediately after a vowel in the stressed syllable. The digit serves a dual purpose; it also specifies the intonation of that vowel. There are basically three kinds of intonation available: *rising, flat,* and *falling*. The ten digits available give us varying degrees of these three. Intonation values are shown in Figure 8-1. Finally, the narrator device recognizes several common punctuation marks. These punctuation marks also indicate intonation values or pauses, of various length, between individual utterances. The recognizable punctuation marks and their values are summarized in Figure 8-2.

Figure 8-1. Some intonation values

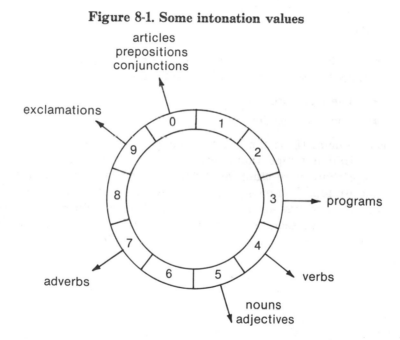

Directly passing phonetic strings to the narrator device opens up new areas for speech experimentation:

1. You can try to improve the pronounciation of special words peculiar to your application.
2. You can save the overhead of the translator library, if you just have a few words to say.
3. You can even experiment with foreign languages.

However, keep in mind that for general purpose speech synthesis, it is still more efficient to use the translator library and the narrator device together.

Figure 8-2. Uses of common punctuation marks

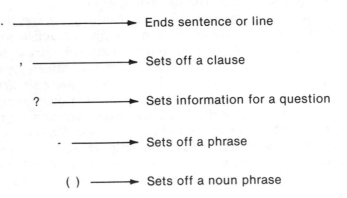

. ⟶ Ends sentence or line

, ⟶ Sets off a clause

? ⟶ Sets information for a question

- ⟶ Sets off a phrase

( ) ⟶ Sets off a noun phrase

Summary

In this chapter we have explored the Amiga's speech synthesis capability. We have seen how this capability is split across two separate subsystems:

- The translator library
- The narrator device

Each one of these can function independently of the other.

In many important respects, the speech synthesis subsystem is no more exotic than more traditional devices, such as printers and display screens, that are found on most computers. Access on the Amiga is obtained through the message system that connects all devices defined on the Amiga. Furthermore, this message system allows you to run the narrator device in a multitasking mode; this makes it even easier to integrate with the Amiga's other features.

Programming with Disk Files

Chapter 9

I n this chapter, we will explore the Amiga file system. Topics covered include:

- The directory system
- Traditional file read and write problems
- Access to the file system

We will also discuss those problems peculiar to a multiprocessing environment where processes share files.

The File Management System

Files, their creation and manipulation, are the responsibility of AmigaDOS. Both Intuition and the executive kernel depend upon this coexistent operating system to handle the details of directories and file names. It is true that the executive kernel handles a device called the TrackDisk device, which interfaces the main computer to the floppy disk drive; however, the TrackDisk is interested only in this transfer and its parameters—buffer size, location etc.

A file system is more than a mere mechanism for transferring data back and forth; it must create some structure on the disk so that data can be easily recovered. This structure includes the notion of a file as a basic storage unit, a directory that reports the contents of a disk area, and important parameters such as size, date, and access rights. Also needed are high level routines that allow you to read and write data to a file.

The file management system actually does much more than this behind the scenes. For example, it is easy to think of the directory as a display list on the screen; but in addition to giving us this inventory, it also:

- Keeps track of the locations of each file on the disk, so that a file can be found when you need to access it

- Notes the size of the file and the location of its extensions
- Recognizes the type of file, and distinguishes between files and directories

Most of this information is available through one of the specialized AmigaDOS system calls.

The standard TTY-style interface is also maintained by the file management system. The display screen, the keyboard and the printer are all treated as disk files even though the executive kernel recognizes them as different devices. Additionally, the serial and parallel ports are also represented as file types. AmigaDOS has a number of functions that support input and output from devices. Figure 9-1 lists the device files configured in a typical Amiga system.

Figure 9-1. Device file identifiers

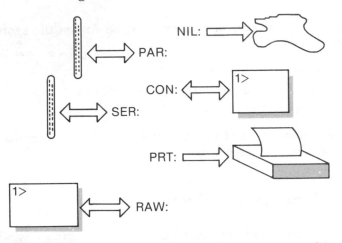

The system functions that we will be dealing with in this chapter are part of AmigaDOS. Just as with the multiprocessing examples in Chapter 4, these have been compiled using the initalization file *AStartUp.obj* and the library *amiga.lib*, rather than the more common *LStartUp.obj* and *lc.lib*. This is necessary because the standard C library—found in *lc.lib*—contains functions that have the same name as the AmigaDOS system calls; this library will take precedence if it is linked first. A complete explanation for this is found in Chapter 2. The necessary declarations are found in *libraries/dos.h* and *libraries/dosextens.h*.

The Notion of a File

Most programmers have a rough idea of what constitutes a file. At its minimum, it can be defined as a named location on an external storage medium—usually some kind of disk—where values can be placed and later retrieved. You can distinguish between a variable in memory and a disk file in a number of ways, not the least of which is the ephermeral nature of the first and the

long-lasting qualities of the second. Variables retain their values only as long
as a program maintains them. Files keep their values even after a machine is
turned off; these values remain until something removes them. Another dis-
tinguishing point is that a file can be shared among many applications, but a
variable is usually restricted to a single program.

You use the notion of a file every time you access a computer. You use an
editor to create a text file. You use the compiler and linker to create a binary
object file. You may even have a database manager that creates database files.
Programs that you load and run are files; you can see that this is a central
notion to the programming environment.

Within AmigaDOS a file is represented by two entities. The most important of these is the *file handle*. Within an executing process that reads or
writes data to a file, that file is represented by a file handle. This object is
defined by the FileHandle structure. This structure is:

```
struct FileHandle {
    struct Msg          *fh_Link;
    struct MsgPort      *fh_Port;
    struct MsgPort      *fh_Type;
    LONG                fh_Buf,
                        fh_Pos,
                        fh_End,
                        fh_Funcs,
                        fh_Func2,
                        fh_Func3,
                        fh_Args,
                        fh_Arg2;
};
```

where

fh_Link, fh_Port, fh_Type link the structure to the executive kernel.

fh_Buf, fh_Pos, fh_End support internal buffering.

fh_Funcs, fh_Func2, fh_Func3 point to handler processes.

fh_Args, fh_Arg2 are arguments specific file types.

None of the fields in this structure are altered by user applications. This is
not a variable whose values are set by the executing process; it is used to
interact with the various system functions.

Almost as important is the *file lock*; this allows you to effectively share
a file among competing and simultaneously executing processes. Like the file
handle, the lock is defined by a structure variable and is manipulated primarily by system functions. The FileLock structure is as follows:

```
struct FileLock {
    BPTR                fl_Link;
    LONG                fl_Key,
                        fl_Access;
    struct MsgPort      *fl_Task;
    BPTR                fl_Volume;
};
```

where

> **fl__Link** points to the next file lock on the linked list.
>
> **fl__Key** is the number of the disk block.
>
> **fl__Access** contains the access mode.
>
> **fl__Task** indicates the port of the handler task.
>
> **fl__Volume** points to the device list.

Practical File I/O

Reading and writing from a file is the most basic operation that you can perform. Every complete operating system must supply this capability. Many programmers, however, never use the system functions built in to the operating system environment, but are content with whatever facility is offered in the language that they have chosen to implement their application. In some contexts this can be a mistake. Nothing works as well as a direct request to the system. In addition, a system call is often straightforward, while the statements offered by a programming language may be awkward, with a large overhead and strange syntax.

The C programming language provides a good illustration of the need to dip below the level of programming language to the underlying software environment. The standard file in C is defined in terms of a complex structure data type called FILE. This structure contains information about the file, information about the position of the pointer in the file, and a buffer to hold data from the file. The C functions that manipulate a file work through this data type; however, most of this buffering—indeed most of the information held in the FILE variable—is redundant. It is already available as part of the directory listing or the file header itself. Using FILE adds an unnecessary layer of overhead to the program (Figure 9-2). This redundancy may not adversely affect many non-critical programs, but an equal number will suffer from the overhead.

Figure 9-2. The redundancy of the C FILE structure

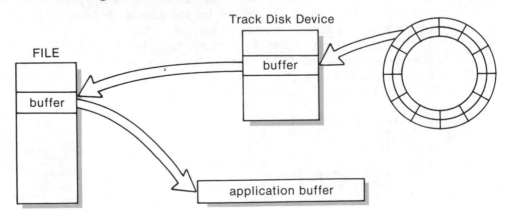

To be fair, most implementations of C—and Lattice C is no exception—offer more basic file I/O functions as part of their standard libraries. Thus, you will find functions for unbuffered file I/O, in which you supply the memory location to store data that is either coming in or going out. In many operating system environments, these functions are themselves system calls, but on most, they are not. Lattice C offers two levels of input/output statements:

1. Buffered I/O, whether formatted or not
2. A set of low-level, stream-oriented statements

The latter set views a file as a stream of bytes with no inherent structure. Even with this dual level, for many applications AmigaDOS is an attractive alternative.

Before you can do anything to a file, you must negotiate with the operating system and convince it to give you access to it. This is accomplished by the *Open()* command. This function has the format:

```
file_handle=Open(file_name,mode);
```

where

file_handle is a variable of type struct FileHandle. This identifies the file in subsequent commands; 0 indicates a failure to open the file.

file_name is a character string that contains the file name as it appears in the directory.

mode is the access mode being requested.

Mode may be one of two values:

MODE_OLDFILE opens an existing file.

MODE_NEWFILE specifies a new file.

In both cases, the file is open for reading and writing.

The *Open()* system call can be used to open certain devices as well as disk files; specifically, CON:, NIL:, and RAW: can be accessed through this command. In place of the *file_name*, put one of these device names with the format that it expects. For example:

```
f_handle=Open("CON:0/0/200/150/Window",MODE_OLDFILE)
```

This opens a new console window with the specified parameters.

Once you have finished using the file, it is necessary to relinquish control over it. This is easily accomplished by calling:

```
Close(file_handle);
```

Here, *file_handle* is a variable of type struct FileHandle, initialized by a previous call to *Open()*. AmigaDOS is not civilized enough to clean up after you. There is no mechanism for automatically closing files; you must do it explicitly or risk running out of resources. This is a particularly important

Programming with Disk Files

matter with a multiprocessing system, where a resource that you forget to close becomes unavailable to a simultaneously executing process. This can even lead to a deadlock situation, where both processes come to a halt because of contention over resources.

Finally, we come to the statement that enables transfer of data from disk into memory. Recall that AmigaDOS treats a file as a stream of bytes—almost as an infinitely long character string. This architecture is reflected in the input function call:

```
byte_count=Read(file_handle,buffer,buf_size)
```

where

byte_count is the number of bytes actually transferred.

file_handle is the file identifier.

buffer is a pointer to a hunk of contiguous characters.

buf_size is the number of locations in the buffer.

Both *byte_count* and *buf_size* are integer values, but remember that for AmigaDOS this means thirty-two bits. When executed, *Read()* attempts to transfer the next *buf_size* bytes in the buffer array. If it succeeds, *byte_count* is equal to *buf_size*. If there are fewer bytes left then have been requested, these are transferred and *byte_count* is set accordingly. A value of 0 in this variable indicates that the end of the file has been reached. A value of −1 shows an error condition.

The output function is complementary to the input:

```
byte_count=Write(file_handle,buffer,buf_size)
```

Here, the parameters are the same as those for the *Read()* function. You must fill the buffer with the characters or bytes that you want transferred to the file. The parameter *buf_size* indicates how many of these are to be sent over. *Write()* returns the number of bytes actually placed on the file; in most situations, *byte_count* and *buf_size* should be equal. A −1 value in this variable indicates an error condition.

These four system calls are illustrated in Listing 9-1. This program copies the contents of a file to a window on the display screen. First we access the file name through the command line arguments. Once we have this name, a call to *Open()* with a mode of MODE_OLDFILE prepares this file for reading. If the file cannot be opened, we unceremoniously stop execution with an *Exit()* call. We perform a similar service for the new window that will be our display medium.

Once we have our two files open, we prepare a buffer. Instead of the simpler process of declaring a large array of characters, we use *AllocMem()* to dynamically allocate this space. This has the felicitous property of allocating this buffer on 32-bit boundaries—something that AmigaDOS likes a great deal. A simple "do" loop empties the file into the buffer, and the buffer into the window. This loop continues until the variable *len* indicates that the end of the "form" file has been reached.

Listing 9-1. Use of Open( ), Close( ), Read( ), and Write( ). Program accepts a file, opens a window, and displays the contents of the file in that window.

```
*/

#include "exec/types.h"
#include "exec/nodes.h"
#include "exec/lists.h"
#include "exec/libraries.h"
#include "exec/ports.h"
#include "exec/interrupts.h"
#include "exec/io.h"
#include "exec/memory.h"
#include "libraries/dos.h"
#include "libraries/dosextens.h"

#define BUFF_SIZE 256

extern struct FileHandle *Open();

main(argc,argv)
int argc;
char *argv[];
{
 struct FileHandle *fp,*sp;
 char *buffer;
 int len;

 if((fp=Open(argv[1],MODE_OLDFILE))==0)
   Exit();

 if((sp=Open("CON:10/10/500/180/Window",MODE_OLDFILE))==0)
   Exit();

 buffer=(char *)AllocMem(BUFF_SIZE,MEMF_CHIP|MEMF_CLEAR);

 do  {
     len=Read(fp,buffer,BUFF_SIZE);
     Write(sp,buffer,len);
  }
 while(len!=0);

 FreeMem(buffer,BUFF_SIZE);

 Close(sp);
 Close(fp);
}

/*********************END OF FILE*********************/
```

The first priority of clean-up requires de-allocation of memory via a call to *FreeMem( )*. We close both files with two separate calls to *Close( )*; this only acts on a single file, thus we need one call for each open file. We do use one undiscussed system call in this program—*Exit()*—but its operaton is straightforward and obvious.

AmigaDOS supplies one additional system function related to file input and output:

```
old=Seek(file_handle,new,from_mode)
```

This moves the file cursor to a position specified by the parameters. *Old* and *new* are both integers. *Old* marks the current position of the file cursor. *New* specifies the new position as an offset from one of three positions:

1. The beginning of the file
2. The current position of the cursor
3. The end of the file

The active position is a function of the value found in the *from_mode* parameter: OFFSET_BEGINNING, OFFSET_CURRENT, or OFFSET_END. This system function can be used in conjunction with *Read()* and *Write()* to update a file.

File Maintenance Functions

Reading and writing are not the only things you do to a file; you may need to manipulate it in other ways. AmigaDOS offers system services to support a variety of those needs.

The *Rename()* function allows you to change the name of an existing file; it has the general form:

```
boolean=Rename(old,new)
```

where

boolean is the return value—either 1 (true) or 0 (false).

old is a character string containing the current name of the file.

new is also a character string, this one with the new name.

If the name mentioned in *new* is of an existing file, the call will fail. Both *old* and *new* can be fully qualified file names; it is possible to move a file from one directory to another by taking advantage of this capability. It is not, however, possible to move a file from one volume to another.

Listing 9-2. Use of Rename(). Program accepts two file names and changes the name of the file from the first to the second.

```
*/

#include "exec/types.h"
#include "exec/nodes.h"
```

Listing 9-2 cont.

```
#include "exec/lists.h"
#include "exec/libraries.h"
#include "exec/ports.h"
#include "exec/interrupts.h"
#include "exec/io.h"
#include "exec/memory.h"
#include "libraries/dos.h"
#include "libraries/dosextens.h"


extern struct FileHandle *Open();

main(argc,argv)
int argc;
char *argv[];
{
 struct FileHandle *sp;

 if((sp=Open("CON:10/10/300/150/Window",MODE_OLDFILE))==0)
   Exit();

 Write(sp,"Renaming Files.....",20);

 if((Rename(argv[1],argv[2]))==0)  {
   Write(sp,"Files Not Renamed",20);
   Close(sp);
   Exit();
  }

 Close(sp);
}
```

Listing 9-2 displays a simple but typical use of *Rename()*. Here we accept two file names through the command line arguments—an old file name and a proposed new one. We also open a new window to display a little message that the renaming is taking place. If *Rename()* fails we report this fact and exit the program.

Another important—if drastic—task is to remove a file from the disk. You do this with a system call:

```
boolean=DeleteFile(file_name)
```

Here, *boolean* is a return value indicating the success of the action and *file_name* is a character string containing the name of the file to be removed. This system function removes either an ordinary file or a directory. The directory must be empty before it can be removed. Listing 9-3 illustrates the action of this function. Again, we display a message while the deletion is taking place; if it fails, we exit the program with an error message.

Listing 9-3. Use of DeleteFile(). Program accepts a file name from the command line and removes it from the disk.

```
*/

#include "exec/types.h"
#include "exec/nodes.h"
#include "exec/lists.h"
#include "exec/libraries.h"
#include "exec/ports.h"
#include "exec/interrupts.h"
#include "exec/io.h"
#include "exec/memory.h"
#include "libraries/dos.h"
#include "libraries/dosextens.h"


extern struct FileHandle *Open();

main(argc,argv)
int argc;
char *argv[];
{
  struct FileHandle *sp;

  if((sp=Open("CON:10/10/300/150/Window",MODE_OLDFILE))==0)
    Exit();

  Write(sp,"Deleting.......",15);

  if((DeleteFile(argv[1]))==0)  {
    Write(sp,"File Not Deleted",20);
    Close(sp);
    Exit();
  }

  Close(sp);
}
```

Files and Multiprocessing

One new problem faced by Amiga programmers arises from the interaction of many concurrent processes and files. On a single tasking system, only one program runs at a time. Any file that is open for reading or writing is the exclusive property of that program. On the Amiga, you can have many processes running simultaneously, and more than one process can access the same file. Under certain circumstances, this can cause problems.

One of the most common problem areas concerns files that are accessed and updated by two processes. Consider process A: it opens file *FileA* to do an update operation. Some value in the file is to be read, changed, and then written back to the same location. At the same time process B also opens

FileA, also to do an update on the same data value. What can happen? One disasterous possibility is that process A will get the file and read the value; then, before it can change and write the value back to the file, process B will read the old data. Meanwhile A will write back its new version of the data item followed by B's value. Whatever change process A meant to do to the file has been lost. This confusing situation—known as the "Lost Update" problem—is illustrated in Figure 9-3.

Figure 9-3. The Lost Update problem

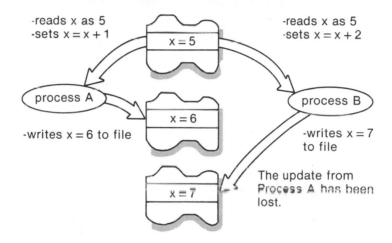

The Lost Update is even more of a problem than most software failures. It does not happen at every file access, but depends upon a set of circumstances that is difficult to predict. Whenever more than one process is running in memory, doing different actions, it is impossible to know the order in which each process will execute. The solution to the Lost Update problem and other similar scheduling difficulties is to guarantee the order in which two processes will access the same file. You can do this by allowing one process to stake out a claim for exclusive access to the file; this is accomplished with the *file lock*.

A file lock is a simple notion. A particular process requests and is granted some level of exclusive access to the file. On a large multi-user system, the notion of a lock is a complex concept with many levels or combinations of access possible. Often a process can lock a portion of a file. AmigaDOS supports a simpler mechanism. A process can request a shared access to a given file—in this case any other process can simultaneously access it—or it can ask for exclusive access rights, barring all other processes. The mechanism for this is the system call:

```
lock_value=Lock(file_name,mode)
```

where

lock_value is the identifier for this particular file system lock.

file_name is a character string that contains the name of the file as it appears in the directory.

mode indicates the access mode for the lock: ACCESS_READ creates a shared lock; ACCESS_WRITE grants exclusive access.

A *lock_value* of 0 indicates that the *Lock()* call failed. This does not necessarily indicate a problem. A failure here might indicate that some other process has put a lock on that file.

The Lost Update problem is solved by the use of file locks. Now Process A puts an exclusive lock on *FileA* until its update operation is complete. Process B has to wait to do its update, and that will be done not to the original value but to the value as altered by Process A. Figure 9-4 diagrams this situation.

Figure 9-4. The Lost Update problem solved

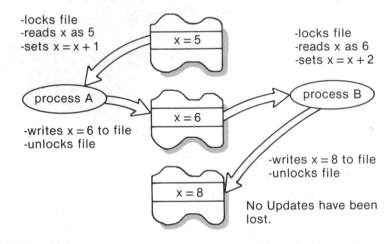

There is a complementary function to *Lock()* that releases a file to general use:

```
UnLock(lock_value)
```

Here *lock_value* is an identifier from a previously executed *Lock()* function. This function does not return a value.

Disk Update Functions

One kind of update we might wish to perform on a file is to write into its comment field. This field may be filled with any desired text and is meant to serve as additional information about the file. This comment field can be displayed by the *List* command. Access to this part of the file is through an AmigaDOS function:

```
boolean=SetComment(file_name,comment_field)
```

where

> **boolean** indicates the success or failure of the call.
>
> **file_name** is a character string containing the name of a file as it appears in a directory.
>
> **comment_field** is a pointer to a character string that contains the text of the comment.

This comment field may be up to eighty characters long.

Listing 9-4. use of SetComment() to attach a comment to a file.

```
*/

#include "exec/types.h"
#include "exec/nodes.h"
#include "exec/lists.h"
#include "exec/libraries.h"
#include "exec/ports.h"
#include "exec/interrupts.h"
#include "exec/io.h"
#include "exec/memory.h"
#include "libraries/dos.h"
#include "libraries/dosextens.h"


main(argc,argv)
int argc;
char *argv[];
{
 struct FileLock *lock,*Lock();
 struct FileHandle *sp,*Input();
 char buffer[80],fname[70];

 sp=Input();

 if((lock=Lock(argv[1],ACCESS_WRITE))==0)  {
   printf("\nCan't open file\n");
   UnLock(lock);
   Exit();
  }


 printf("Comment: ");
 get_string(sp,buffer,80);


 if((SetComment(argv[1],buffer))==0)
    switch(IoErr())  {
       case ERROR_COMMENT_TOO_BIG:     printf("Use a shorter comment\n");
                                       break;
       case ERROR_DEVICE_NOT_MOUNTED: printf("Device not mounted\n");
```

Listing 9-4 cont.

```
                                     break;
     case ERROR_WRITE_PROTECTED:
          printf("Diskette is write protected\n");
                                     break;
     case ERROR_NO_DISK:            printf("No diskette in the drive\n");
                                     break;
     }

  UnLock(lock);

}

get_string(fp,buffer,maxlen)
struct FileHandle *fp;
char *buffer;
int maxlen;
{
 int len;

 len=Read(fp,buffer,maxlen);
 buffer+=len+1;
 *buffer='\0';
}
```

Listing 9-4 contains a program that allows the user to set the comment field in a specific file. The file name is entered through the command line arguments. The first thing we do with this file is try to put a lock on it; if the lock fails, we exit with an error message. If we are successful in locking the file, we prompt the user for the comment string; this is then used in a call to *SetComment()*. If the call fails we invoke a new system function *IoErr()* for a more specific error message. Finally we call *UnLock()* to release the file. It is necessary to use the home grown input routine *get_string()*, because we are using the *amiga.lib* library and not *lc.lib*. Common amenities like *scanf()* are not available.

IoErr() takes no parameters but returns an integer value that represents a global error message. This numeric value is associated with a particular error message. No global error message array—such as you find in the C standard library—is available. It is the responsibility of the application to create such an error message. Each error number is associated with a condition, using a *#define* statement. These statements are found in *libraries/dos.h*. In our example program, we use a *switch* statement to perform this error reporting function.

Before you do anything to a disk by way of reading, writing, or updating, it is important that you have some way of judging that disk's key parameters. Things like the size of the disk, its format, and other operational parameters are necessary for certain kinds of access. This information is stored in a special variable of type struct InfoData. The form of this structure is:

```
        struct InfoData {
            LONG        id_NumSoftErrors,
                        id_UnitNumber,
                        id_DiskState,
                        id_NumBlocks,
                        id_NumBlocksUsed,
                        id_BytesPerBlock,
                        id_DiskType;
            BSTR        id_VolumeNode;
            LONG        id_InUse;
        };
```

where

> **id_NumSoftErrors** indicates the number of errors found on the disk.
>
> **id_UnitNumber** indicates the unit of the disk.
>
> **id_DiskState** indicates the current condition of the disk.
>
> **id_NumBlocks** counts the number of blocks on the disk.
>
> **id_NumBlocksUsed** is the number of blocks currently in use.
>
> **id_BytesPerBlock** shows the number of bytes contained in a block.
>
> **id_DiskType** contains the type code.
>
> **id_VolumeNode** points to a BCPL string containing the volume name.
>
> **id_InUse** is a flag value.

The variable itself is filled by a call to:

```
boolean=Info(lock_value,info_variable)
```

where

> **boolean** indicates the success or failure of the call.
>
> **lock_value** is a lock identifier from a call to Lock().
>
> **info_variable** is a pointer to a variable of type struct InfoData.

This system function returns information on the disk as a whole and not on specific files or directories in that disk. The variable *lock_value* can refer to a disk or any file on that disk. The information is returned through the InfoData structure.

> **Listing 9-5. Use of Lock() and Info() to accept the name of a disk volume and return interesting parameters relating to it.**

```
*/

#include "exec/types.h"
#include "exec/nodes.h"
#include "exec/lists.h"
#include "exec/libraries.h"
#include "exec/ports.h"
```

Listing 9-5 cont.

```
#include "exec/interrupts.h"
#include "exec/io.h"
#include "exec/memory.h"
#include "libraries/dos.h"
#include "libraries/dosextens.h"



main(argc,argv)
int argc;
char *argv[];
{
 struct FileLock *lock,*Lock();

 struct InfoData *i_data;
 if((lock=(struct FileLock *)
   AllocMem(sizeof(struct FileLock),MEMF_CHIP|MEMF_CLEAR))==0)
   Exit();

 if((i_data=(struct InfoData *)
   AllocMem(sizeof(struct InfoData),MEMF_CHIP|MEMF_CLEAR))==0)
   Exit();

 if((lock=Lock(argv[1],ACCESS_READ))==0)
   Exit();

 if((Info(lock,i_data))==0)
   Exit();

 printf("Soft errors===>%ld\n",i_data->id_NumSoftErrors);
 printf("Unit number===>%ld\n",i_data->id_UnitNumber);
 printf("Total blocks==>%ld\n",i_data->id_NumBlocks);
 printf("Blocks in use=>%ld\n",i_data->id_NumBlocksUsed);
 printf("Blocks
free===>%ld\n",i_data->id_NumBlocks-i_data->id_NumBlocksUsed);

 UnLock(lock);

}
```

Listing 9-5 illustrates a program that accesses information about a specific disk. We accept a name through the command line arguments. This can be either a file, a directory, or simply a disk identifier—either *dfnn* or a volume label. The program creates a lock pointer variable by a call to *AllocMem()*. This is desirable because AmigaDOS requires variables that are aligned with 32-bit values and using this function guarantees this alignment. Similarly, we create the variable *i_data*. Then an attempt is made to create a lock using the entered file name. If the attempt succeeds, we call *Info()*, passing it *lock* and *i_data*. If this, in turn, succeeds, we print out some interesting information about the disk. In operation, this program is similar to the CLI command *Info.Cleanup* and exit requires a call to *UnLock()*.

Directory Maintenance

Disk directories play a large role in maintaining the file system. They report the contents of individual disks, tell important things about the individual files on the disk, and even report idiosyncratic information through the file comment field. AmigaDOS offers a variety of system calls to deal with this very important software object.

A vital element in accessing a directory is the FileInfoBlock structure. The directory functions pass information back about files and directories through variables of this type. The structure contains a field for every important parameter:

```
struct FileInfoBlock {
    LONG    fib_Diskey,
            fib_DirEntryType;
    BYTE    fib_FileName[108];
    LONG    fib_EntryType,
            fib_Size,
            fib_NumBlocks;
    struct DateStamp    fib_Date;
    char                fib_Comment[116];
};
```

where

fib_DirEntryType indicates the type of entry:
—a value < 0 indicates a file;
—a value > 0, a directory.

fib_FileName is a character string containing the name of a file or directory.

fib_Protection contains the protection code.

fib_Size contains the number of bytes in the file.

fib_NumBlocks reports on the number of blocks in the file.

fib_Date is the date last changed.

fib_Comment is the comment field.

fib_Diskey and **fib_EntryType** are not for user applications.

Variables of this type are passed to the directory and file functions, which in turn fill the fields with current data.

To gather information about a file or directory, you can call:

```
boolean=Examine(lock_value,fblock_ptr)
```

where

boolean indicates the success or failure of the call.

lock_value is a lock identifier from a previous call to Lock( ).

fblock_ptr is a pointer to a variable of type FileInfoBlock.

This fills the specified *FileInfoBlock* variable with the current values for the file, or the directory associated with the *lock* value. Listing 9-6 indicates how this function can be used to make a report. The program accepts the name of the disk object through the command line arguments, a lock variable and a *FileInfoBlock* variable. *AllocMem* is used to ensure the proper memory word alignment. An attempt is made to create a lock for this object—ACCESS_ READ is acceptable because we are not doing an update, only getting information. A call to *Examine()* fills the variable and then displays some interesting values on the screen. *UnLock()* completes the program.

Listing 9-6. Use of Lock( ) and Examine( ) to accept the name of a file or directory and display interesting information about it.

```
*/

#include "exec/types.h"
#include "exec/nodes.h"
#include "exec/lists.h"
#include "exec/libraries.h"
#include "exec/ports.h"
#include "exec/interrupts.h"
#include "exec/io.h"
#include "exec/memory.h"
#include "libraries/dos.h"
#include "libraries/dosextens.h"


main(argc,argv)
int argc;
char *argv[];
{
 struct FileLock *lock,*Lock();
 struct FileInfoBlock *f_info;

 if((lock=(struct FileLock *)
   AllocMem(sizeof(struct FileLock),MEMF_CHIP|MEMF_CLEAR))==0)
   Exit();

 if((f_info=(struct FileInfoBlock *)
   AllocMem(sizeof(struct FileInfoBlock),MEMF_CHIP|MEMF_CLEAR))==0)
   Exit();

 if((lock=Lock(argv[1],ACCESS_READ))==0)
   Exit();

 if((Examine(lock,f_info))==0)
   Exit();
```

Listing 9-6 cont.

```
if(f_info->fib_DirEntryType<0)
   printf("Type====>File\n");
else
   printf("Type====>Directory\n");
printf("Name====>%s\n",f_info->fib_FileName);
printf("Size====>%ld\n",f_info->fib_Size);
printf("Blocks==>%ld\n",f_info->fib_NumBlocks);
printf("Note====>%s\n",f_info->fib_Comment);

UnLock(lock);

}
```

Examine() releases information on a single file or a directory; however, we also want to go to a particular directory and display information for all the files in that directory. We cannot do this with *Examine()* alone, but also need to use:

```
boolean=ExNext(lock_value,fblock_ptr)
```

The parameters here take on the same values as *Examine()*. This system function returns information on the next file in the directory. *ExNext()* is used in conjunction with *Examine()* to read through a directory. The following set of procedures yields this directory listing:

1. Use *Examine()* to gather information about the directory.
2. Use repeated calls to *ExNext()* to get data on the subsequent files in the directory.

It is necessary to create a loop to repeatedly execute *ExNext*, until it finally returns an error condition. Once this has occurred, a call to *IoErr()* verifies that the current condition signals the end of the directory and not a true error. This algorithm is illustrated in Listing 9-7. This program is similar to Program 9-6, except that here we have a *while* loop that continues until *ExNext()* returns 0. The display function has been imported to a function to make the program flow more structured.

Listing 9-7. Use of Lock(), Examine(), ExNext(), IoErr(), and UnLock(). The program accepts the name of a directory and displays information about the file it contains.

```
*/

#include "exec/types.h"
#include "exec/nodes.h"
#include "exec/lists.h"
#include "exec/libraries.h"
#include "exec/ports.h"
```

Listing 9-7 cont.

```
#include "exec/interrupts.h"
#include "exec/io.h"
#include "exec/memory.h"
#include "libraries/dos.h"
#include "libraries/dosextens.h"



main(argc,argv)
int argc;
char *argv[];
{
 struct FileLock *lock,*Lock();
 struct FileInfoBlock *f_info;

 if((lock=(struct FileLock *)
   AllocMem(sizeof(struct FileLock),MEMF_CHIP|MEMF_CLEAR))==0)
   Exit();

 if((f_info=(struct FileInfoBlock *)
   AllocMem(sizeof(struct FileInfoBlock),MEMF_CHIP|MEMF_CLEAR))==0)
   Exit();

 if((lock=Lock(argv[1],ACCESS_READ))==0)
   Exit();

 if((Examine(lock,f_info))==0)
   Exit();

 spill_the_beans(f_info);

 while ((ExNext(lock,f_info))!=0)
   spill_the_beans(f_info);

 if(IoErr()==ERROR_NO_MORE_ENTRIES)
   printf("\nEnd of directory===================\n");
 else
   printf("\nError reading directory===========\n");

 UnLock(lock);

}
spill_the_beans(info)
struct FileInfoBlock *info;
{
 printf("\n\nName====>%s\n",info->fib_FileName);
 printf("Size====>%ld\n",info->fib_Size);
 printf("Blocks==>%ld\n",info->fib_NumBlocks);
 printf("Note====>%s\n",info->fib_Comment);
}
```

AmigaDOS offers some important capabilities in addition to those already discussed—for example:

```
lock_value=CreateDir(direct_name)
```

This takes the name of a new directory and creates that directory on the disk. A lock is automatically opened and returned by this function. A 0 is returned if the proposed name is the same as an existing directory.

Listing 9-8. Use of CreateDir() to create a new directory.

```
*/

#include "exec/types.h"
#include "exec/nodes.h"
#include "exec/lists.h"
#include "exec/libraries.h"
#include "exec/ports.h"
#include "exec/interrupts.h"
#include "exec/io.h"
#include "exec/memory.h"
#include "libraries/dos.h"
#include "libraries/dosextens.h"


main(argc,argv)
int argc;
char *argv[];
{
 struct FileLock *lock,*CreateDir();

 if((lock=CreateDir(argv[1]))==0)
    Exit();

 UnLock(lock);

}
```

Listing 9-8 contains a simple example. Listing 9-9 illustrates another system call:

```
old=CurrentDir(new)
```

Here *old* and *new* are lock values. This function changes the current working directory to the directory associated with *new*; it returns the current directory value before the change is made.

AmigaDOS offers one last directory function:

```
boolean=SetProtection(file_name,mask_value)
```

**Listing 9-9. Use of CreateDir( ) and CurrentDir( ) to create a
new directory and make it the current directory.**

```
*/

#include "exec/types.h"
#include "exec/nodes.h"
#include "exec/lists.h"
#include "exec/libraries.h"
#include "exec/ports.h"
#include "exec/interrupts.h"
#include "exec/io.h"
#include "exec/memory.h"
#include "libraries/dos.h"
#include "libraries/dosextens.h"


main(argc,argv)
int argc;
char *argv[];
{
 struct FileLock *lock,*last,*CreateDir(),*CurrentDir();

 if((lock=CreateDir(argv[1]))==0)
    Exit();

 if((last=CurrentDir(lock))==0)
    Exit();

 UnLock(lock);
 UnLock(last);


}
```

Crashes with dir/cd combination afterwards

This function sets the protection attributes of the file. Here *file_name* is a character string containing the file name, and *Mask_value* is a bit mask containing the protection code. Figure 9-5 indicates values for this mask. *Read*, *write*, *execute*, and *delete* modes are all set by this function.

Device File Functions

Our final example program deals not with disk files, but with device files—input/output peripherals treated as if they were files. It is economical and productive to have a common interface to the outside world; this is the motivation for using the file metaphor so widely in the Amiga and most other computer systems. However, there are activities that are peculiar to devices, particularly interactive devices such as the keyboard and display screen.

Figure 9-5. SetProtection( ) bit mask values

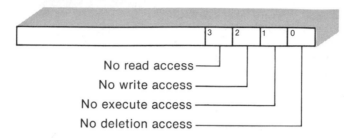

Fortunately, AmigaDOS recognizes these peculiarities and supplies functions that address them.

The first set of device file functions is a pair of system calls that lets you get a handle on the standard input and output that is automatically attached to a process when it starts executing.

```
file_handle_in=Input()
```

returns the file handle of *stdin*.

```
file_handle_out=OutPut()
```

does the same for *stdout*. These functions allow you to use these devices with the other file manipulation system functions, to create reasonable output displays and to take in values in a straightforward manner.

The last function we will discuss is also very useful in creating reasonable input routines.

```
boolean=WaitForChar(file_handle,timer)
```

puts a time limit on input from the keyboard or any other interactive device. It returns true (-1) if a character is entered before the time specified in *timer* is used up; otherwise, a value of false is returned. The parameter timer is measured in microseconds.

Listing 9-10 illustrates the use of *Input( )* and *WaitForChar( )*. We declare *sp*, a pointer to a FileHandle structure and a *buffer*, a pointer to a character. Using *AllocMem( )* we allocate the buffer space; using *Input( )*, we set *sp* equal to our standard input file. A call to *WaitForChar( )* sets up our measurement and a subsequent call to *Read( )* puts the characters into our buffer. If we wait too long and use up our time, a message is printed and the program is exited; otherwise we print out the character string that we entered.

**Listing 9-10. Use of Input( ), WaitForChar( ), and Read( ) to wait
for a character, then read from the keyboard.**

```
*/

#include "exec/types.h"
```

Listing 9-10 cont.

```
#include "exec/nodes.h"
#include "exec/lists.h"
#include "exec/libraries.h"
#include "exec/ports.h"
#include "exec/interrupts.h"
#include "exec/io.h"
#include "exec/memory.h"
#include "libraries/dos.h"
#include "libraries/dosextens.h"

#define SEC 1000000

main()
{
 struct FileHandle *sp,*Input();
 int len,result;
 char *buffer,*AllocMem();

 if((buffer=AllocMem(128,MEMF_CLEAR))==0)  {
   printf("Not enough memory for a buffer\n");
   Exit();
  }

 sp=Input();


 result=WaitForChar(sp,SEC);

 if(result==0)  {
     printf("\nTimeout\n");
     Exit();
    }

 len=Read(sp,buffer,128);
 *(buffer+(len+1))='\0';

 printf("==>%s\n",buffer);

}
```

Summary

In this chapter we have covered the AmigaDOS file management system. We have seen how files are defined and accessed. We have dealt with the notion of file locks and how they help manipulate files in a multiprocessing environment.

We have discussed directories and the functions that report on their status and list their files. AmigaDOS also supplies functions that create new directories and change the current working directory.

Finally, we have dealt with the difference between disk files and device files. We have seen how to get access to the standard input and output devices and use them in programs to create interesting input and output screens. We have explored the uses of the *WaitForChar()* function and how it can be used to time input requests.

Index

A

AddGadget( ) function, 120
Alerts, 148–49
ALINK linker utility, the, 15
    how it works, 24–26
    libraries and, 67–68
    MAP parameter of, 26–46, 67
    purpose of, 24
    WIDTH parameter of, 26, 67
    XREF parameter of, 26, 46–67
AmigaDOS, 5, 6, 12
    calling, 178–79
    CLI and, 179–82
    console device, 157–61
    description of, 13, 176–78
    executive kernel compared to, 176–77
    file management system of, 395–419
    Intuition compared to, 73, 176
    libraries and, 67–68
Audio device, the
    accessing, 320–43
    BeginIO( ) function and, 317, 324, 326, 335, 347
    CheckIO( ) function and, 317
    CloseDevice( ) function and, 317, 324
    commands for, 322–24
    controlling, 324–43
    DoIO( ) function and, 317
    listing for playing note first on left channel, on both, then on right channel, 347–50
    listing for playing note first on left channel, then on right, 344–46
    listing for simple use of, 323
        sending explicit finish command to stop tone, 325–26
        with square wave, 327–28
        with triangular wave, 328–30
    listing for starting note and varying its loudness via messages sent to, 336–38

Audio device—cont
    listing for starting note and varying its period via messages sent to, 333–35
    listing for using all four channels of, 350–53
    listing for using single channel of, 331–32
    listings for varying loudness of note, 336–38, 338–41
    listings for varying period of note, 333–35, 341–43
    message structure of, 317–18
    multichannel sound and, 343–53
    OpenDevice( ) function and, 317, 320–322, 330
    purpose of, 317–18
    sound data representation with, 318–20
    WaitIO( ) function and, 317, 324, 326, 335, 347
AutoRequest( ) function, 144–45

B

BeginIO( ) function, 317, 324, 326, 335, 347
Blitter, the, 4, 11, 237

C

CheckIO( ) function, 317
ClearMenuStrip( ) function, 129–30, 132, 139
CLI (command interpreter), processes and, 179–82
CloseDevice( ) function
    audio device and the, 317, 324
    narrator device and the, 366
Close( ) function
    console device and the, 157
    file management system and the, 401–2
CloseLibrary( ) function, 359
Color registers, 4
Console device, the
    Close( ) function and, 157

X

MORE
FROM
SAMS

☐ **Commodore 128® Reference Guide for Programmers**   *David L. Heiserman*
This is *the* authoritative guide for programmers: from the beginner who wants to know about the C128's power to the advanced programmer who requires specific information about the Commodore 128. Learn BASIC as well as assembly language, 40- and 80-column text and graphics programming, and the intricacies of the operating system.
ISBN: 0-672-22479-8, $19.95

☐ **The Official Book for the Commodore 128® Personal Computer**
Mitch Waite, Robert Lafore, and Jerry Volpe, The Waite Group
Learn to create detailed graphics and animation and to run thousands of existing Commodore 64 programs. Find out how to program in three-voice sound and how to use spreadsheets, word processing, the database, and much more.
ISBN: 0-672-22456-9, $12.95

☐ **Commodore 64®/128® Assembly Language Programming**   *Mark Andrews*
This step-by-step guide to programming the Commodore 64, Merlin 64™ and Panther C64™ shows you how to design your own character set, write action games, draw high-resolution graphics, create animated sprite graphics, convert numbers, mix BASIC and machine language, and program music and sound.
ISBN: 0-672-22444-5, $15.95

☐ **Commodore 64® & 128® Programs for Amateur Radio & Electronics**   *Joseph J. Carr*
The electronics hobbyist, programmer, engineer, and technician will enjoy the 23 task-oriented programs for amateur radio and 19 electronics programs in this book.

It contains two general categories of programs—amateur radio technology and general electronics—that will save time and simplify programming tasks when incorporated into the custom-designed software programs provided.
ISBN: 0-672-22516-6, $14.95

☐ **Modem Connections Bible**
Carolyn Curtis and Daniel L. Majhor, The Waite Group
Describes modems, how they work, and how to hook 10 well-known modems to 9 name-brand microcomputers. A handy Jump Table shows where to find the connection diagram you need and applies the illustrations to 11 more computers and 7 additional modems. Also features an overview of communications software, a glossary of communications terms, an explanation of the RS-232C interface, and a section on troubleshooting.
ISBN: 0-672-22446-1, $16.95

☐ **Printer Connections Bible**
Kim G. House and Jeff Marble, The Waite Group
At last, a book that includes extensive diagrams specifying exact wiring, DIP-switch settings and external printer details; a Jump Table of assorted printer/computer combinations; instructions on how to make your own cables; and reviews of various printers and how they function.
ISBN: 0-672-22406-2, $16.95

☐ **Computer Connection Mysteries Solved**
Graham Wideman
This book provides the how's and why's of connecting a personal computer to its peripherals for anyone with a computer system. It provides an introduction to the machinery available: printers, MIDI, musical interface, Centronics, video hookups, and the RS-232. This quick and easy troubleshooting guide with case studies will assist users who deal with a variety of system configurations.
ISBN: 0-672-22526-3, $18.95

MORE
FROM
SAMS

☐ **Experiments in Artificial Intelligence for Microcomputers (2nd Edition)** *John Krutch*
Duplicate such human functions as reasoning, creativity, problem solving, verbal communication, and game planning. Sample programs furnished.
ISBN: 0-672-22501-8, $14.95

☐ **Commodore 64® Programmer's Reference Guide** *Commodore Computer*
Includes a complete dictionary of all Commodore BASIC commands, statements, and functions. BASIC program samples then show you how each item works. Mix machine language with BASIC and use hi-res effectively with this easy-to-use guide.
ISBN: 0-672-22056-3, $19.95

☐ **Commodore 64® Troubleshooting & Repair Guide** *Robert C. Brenner*
Repair your Commodore 64 yourself, simply and inexpensively. Troubleshooting flowcharts let you diagnose and remedy the probable cause of failure. A chapter on advanced troubleshooting shows the more adventuresome how to perform complex repairs. Some knowledge of electronics is required.
ISBN: 0-672-22363-5, $19.95

☐ **Commodore 1541 Troubleshooting & Repair Guide** *Mike Peltier*
This guide presents the theory and general operation of the disk drive and points out some of the common problems that you might encounter.
ISBN: 0-672-22470-4, $19.95

☐ **Computer Dictionary (4th Edition)**
Charles J. Sippl
This dictionary of basic computer terms and handbook of computer-related topics includes fiber optics, sensors and vision systems, computer-aided design, engineering, and manufacturing. Clarifies micro, mini, and mainframe terminology. The 1,000 new entries in this edition focus on the RAF classifications: robotics, artificial intelligence, and factory automation. A must for every library.
ISBN: 0-672-22205-1, $24.95

☐ **CP/M® Primer (2nd Edition)**
Mitchell Waite and Stephen Murtha, The Waite Group
This tutorial companion to the *CP/M Bible* includes the details of CP/M terminology, operation, capabilities, and internal structure, plus a convenient tear-out reference card with CP/M commands. This revised edition allows you to begin using new or old CP/M versions immediately in any application.
ISBN: 0-672-22170-5, $16.95

☐ **Soul of CP/M®: How to Use the Hidden Power of Your CP/M System**
Mitchell Waite and Robert Lafore, The Waite Group
Recommended for those who have read the *CP/M Primer* or who are otherwise familiar with CP/M's outer layer utilities. This companion volume teaches you how to use and modify CP/M's internal features, including how to modify BIOS and use CP/M system calls in your own programs.
ISBN: 0-672-22030-X, $19.95

MORE
FROM
SAMS

☐ **CP/M® Bible: The Authoritative Reference Guide to CP/M**
Mitchell Waite and John Angermeyer, The Waite Group
Already a classic, this highly detailed reference manual puts CP/M's commands and syntax at your fingertips. Instant one-stop access to all CP/M keywords, commands, utilities, and conventions are found in this easy-to-use format.
ISBN: 0-672-22015-6, $19.95

☐ **Commodore 64® Graphics and Sounds**
Timothy Orr Knight
Learn to exploit the powerful graphic and sound capabilities of the Commodore 64. Create your own spectacular routines utilizing graphics and sounds instantly. Loaded with sample programs, detailed illustrations, and thorough explanations covering bit-mapped graphics, three-voice music, sprites, sound effects, and multiple graphics combinations.
ISBN: 0-672-22278-7, $8.95

☐ **Commodore 64® Starter Book**
Jonathan A. Titus and Christopher A. Titus
An ideal desktop companion intended to get every Commodore 64 owner and user up and running with a minimum of fuss. Each chapter is packed with experiments which you can perform immediately. Sample programs which load and run are perfect tools to help the first-time user get acquainted with the Commodore 64.
ISBN: 0-672-22293-0, $17.95

☐ **Learn BASIC Programming in 14 Days on Your Commodore 64®** *Gil Schechter*
A chapter a day, and you're on your way! Fourteen clearly written and illustrated chapters will show you how to program your Commodore 64. Each lesson contains sample programs to build your programming skills and knowledge. Designed for those who want to learn to program quickly and painlessly!
ISBN: 0-672-22279-5, $12.95

Look for these Sams Books at your local bookstore.

To order direct, call 800-428-SAMS or fill out the form below.

Please send me the books whose titles and numbers I have listed below.

_____

_____

_____

_____

_____

Name *(please print)* _____

Address _____

City _____

State/Zip _____

Signature _____
(required for credit card purchases)

Enclosed is a check or money order for $ _____
Include $2.50 postage and handling.
AR, CA, FL, IN, NC, NY, OH, TN, WV residents add local sales tax.

Charge my: ☐ VISA ☐ MC ☐ AE

Account No. _____ Expiration Date _____

☐☐☐☐ ☐☐☐☐ ☐☐☐☐ ☐☐☐☐

Mail to: Howard W. Sams & Co.
Dept. DM
4300 West 62nd Street
Indianapolis, IN 46268

DC070

SAMS ™

More Books from Sams and The Waite Group